O N E

The seasons are passing at a ferocious pace!

—ONE

Manga creator ONE began *One-Punch Man* as a webcomic, which quickly went viral, garnering over 10 million hits. In addition to *One-Punch Man*, ONE writes and draws the series *Mob Psycho 100* and *Makai no Ossan*.

Y U S U K E M U R A T A

I believe I can solve 90 percent of my problems through sheer force of will.

—Yusuke Murata

A highly decorated and skilled artist best known for his work on *Eyeshield 21*, Yusuke Murata won the 122nd Hop Step Award (1995) for *Partner* and placed second in the 51st Akatsuka Award (1998) for *Samui Hanashi*.

ONE-PUNCH MAN | 28

ONE + YUSUKE MURATA

☆THE STORIES, CHARACTERS, AND INCIDENTS

MENTIONED IN THIS PUBLICATION
ARE ENTIRELY FICTIONAL.

STORY BY ONE ART BY YUSUKE MURATA

ONE-PUNCH MAN

28

INTO THE ABYSS

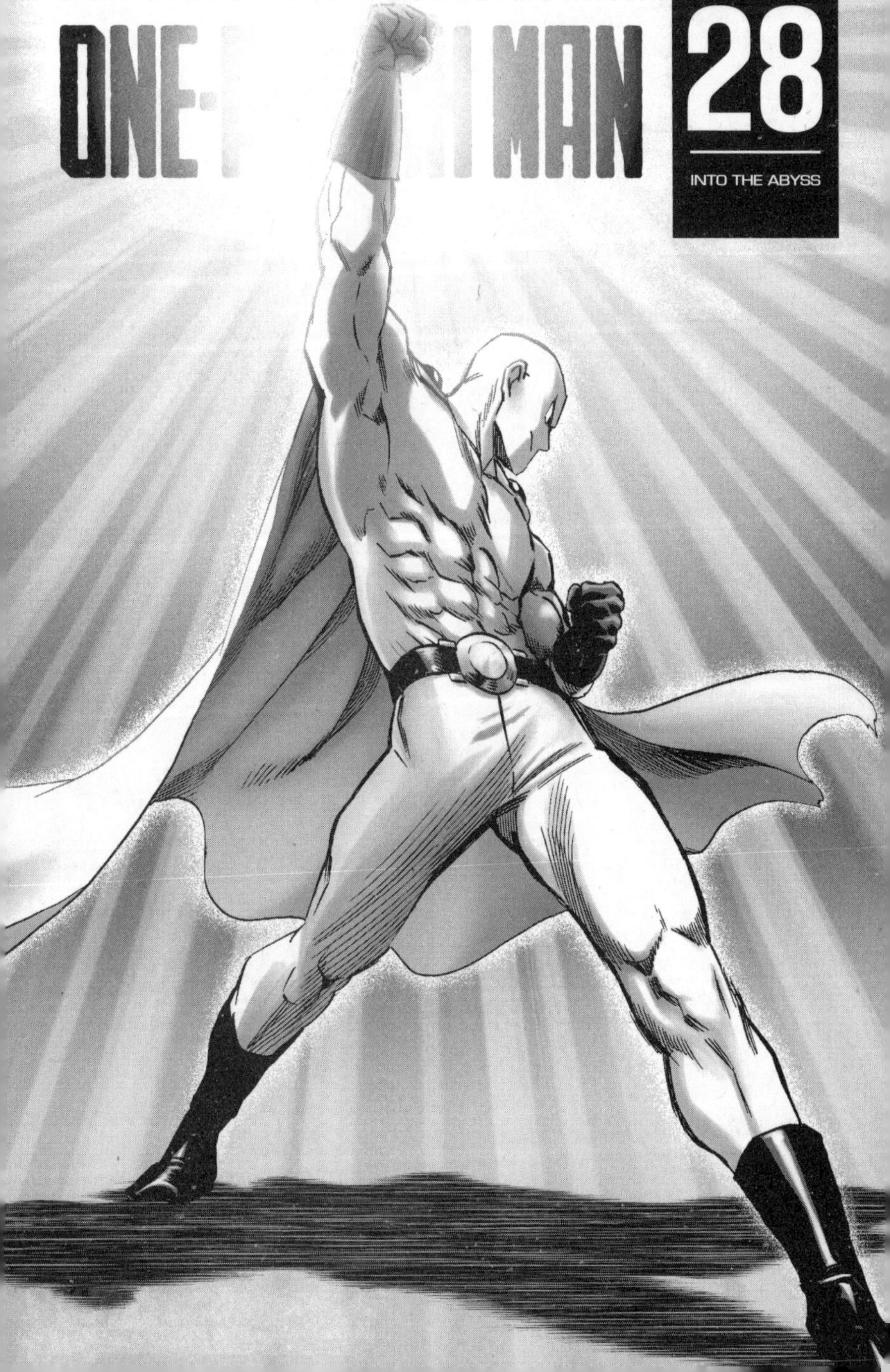

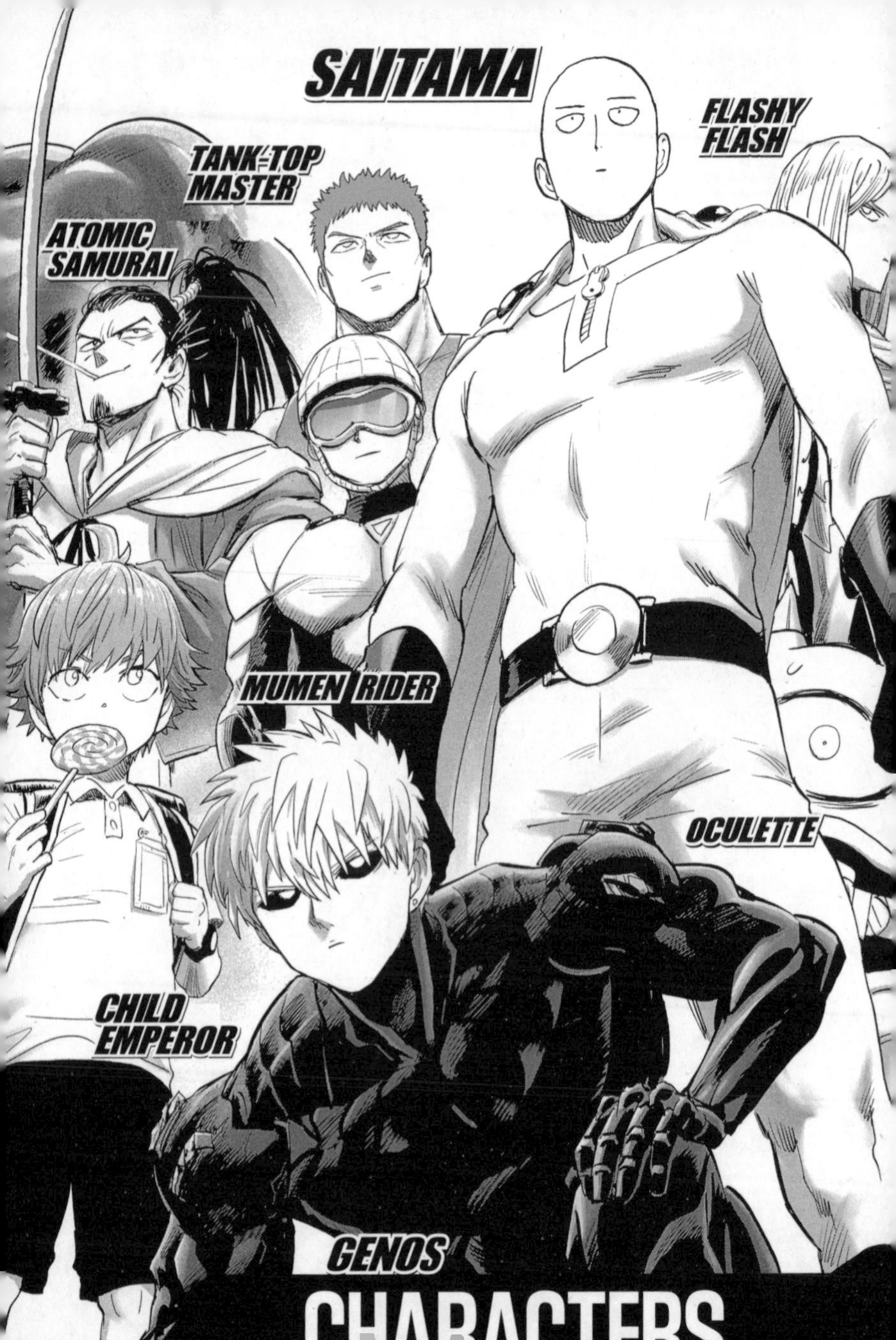
SAITAMA
FLASHY FLASH
TANK-TOP MASTER
ATOMIC SAMURAI
MUMEN RIDER
OCULETTE
CHILD EMPEROR
GENOS

CHARACTERS

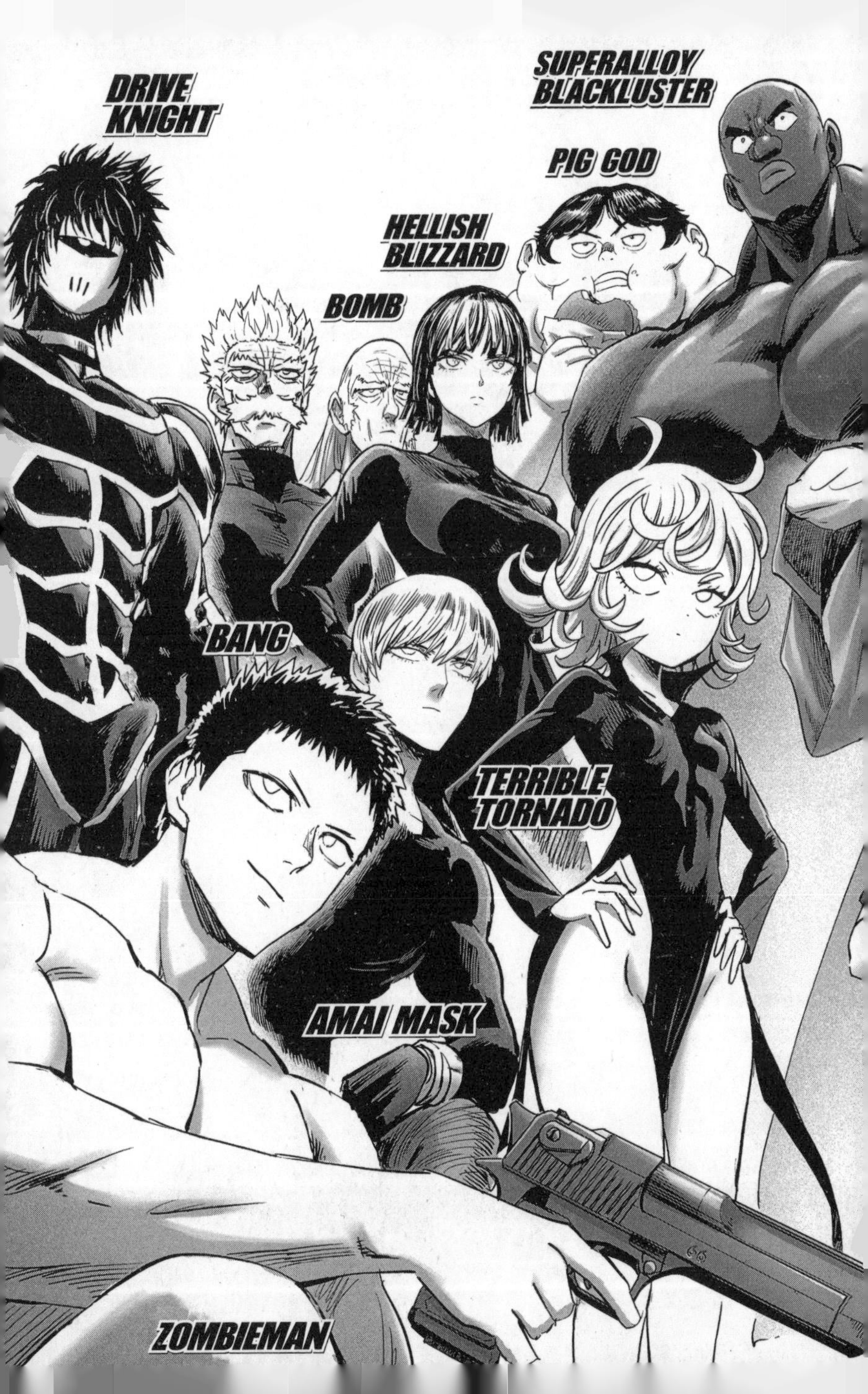
SUPERALLOY BLACKLUSTER
DRIVE KNIGHT
PIG GOD
HELLISH BLIZZARD
BOMB
BANG
TERRIBLE TORNADO
AMAI MASK
ZOMBIEMAN

CONTENTS

ONE-PUNCH MAN VOL.28

STORY

Gyoro-Gyoro, the supposed brains of the Monster Association, is revealed to be a decoy for the psychic Psychos, the true mastermind. Finding herself on the losing end of a fierce battle against Tornado, Psychos fuses with the Monster King Orochi and accesses unbelievable power. A frightful battle between psychics ensues. Seeing an opening, Psychos delivers a grievous wound to Tornado.

However, Genos arrives to assist Tornado, thereby earning Psychos's wrath. Meanwhile, Saitama is digging out Flashy Flash from a mound of rubble in the underground labyrinth...

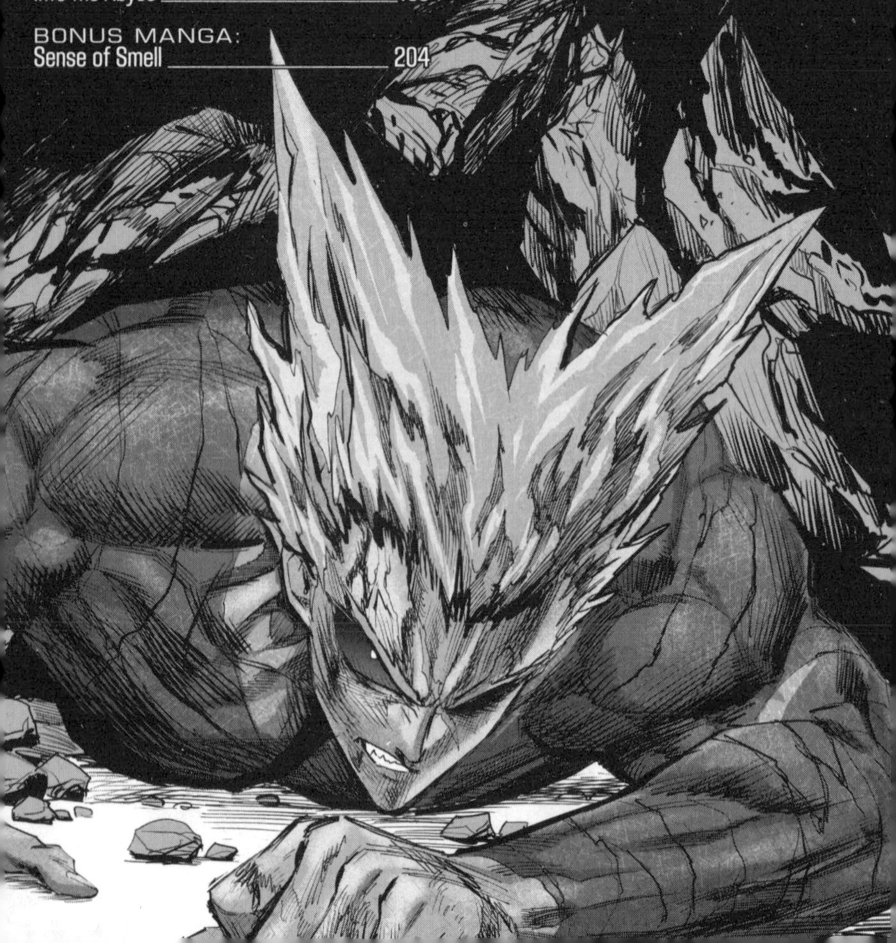

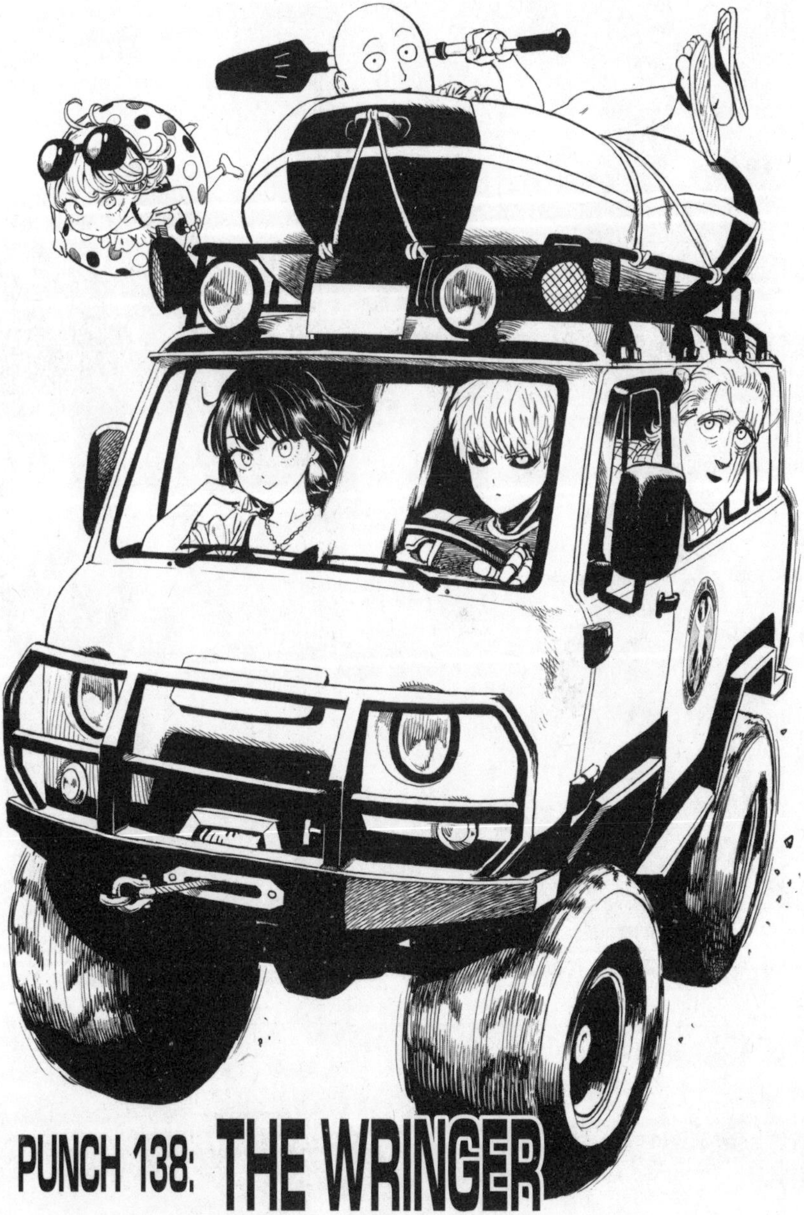

PUNCH 138: THE WRINGER

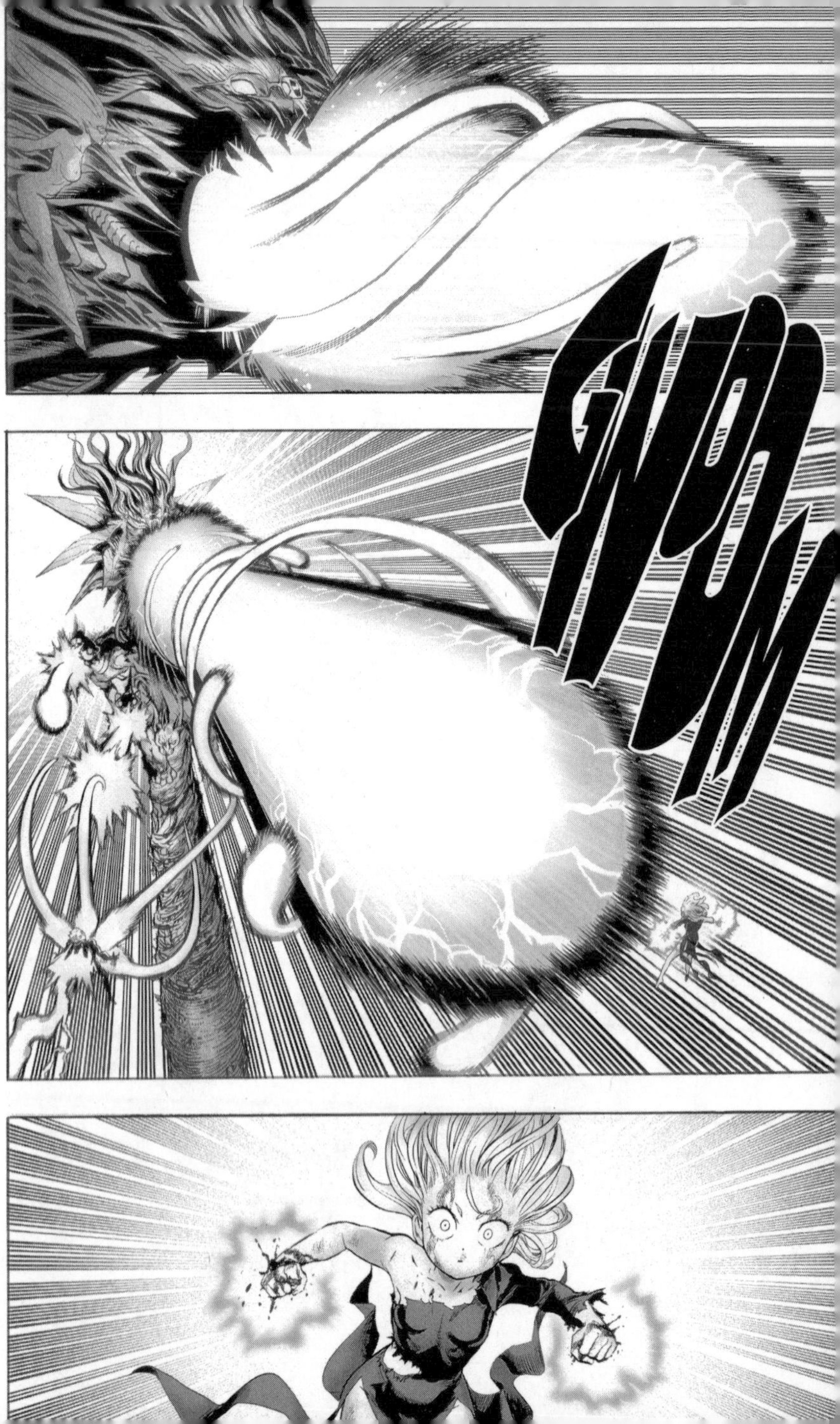
GWOOM

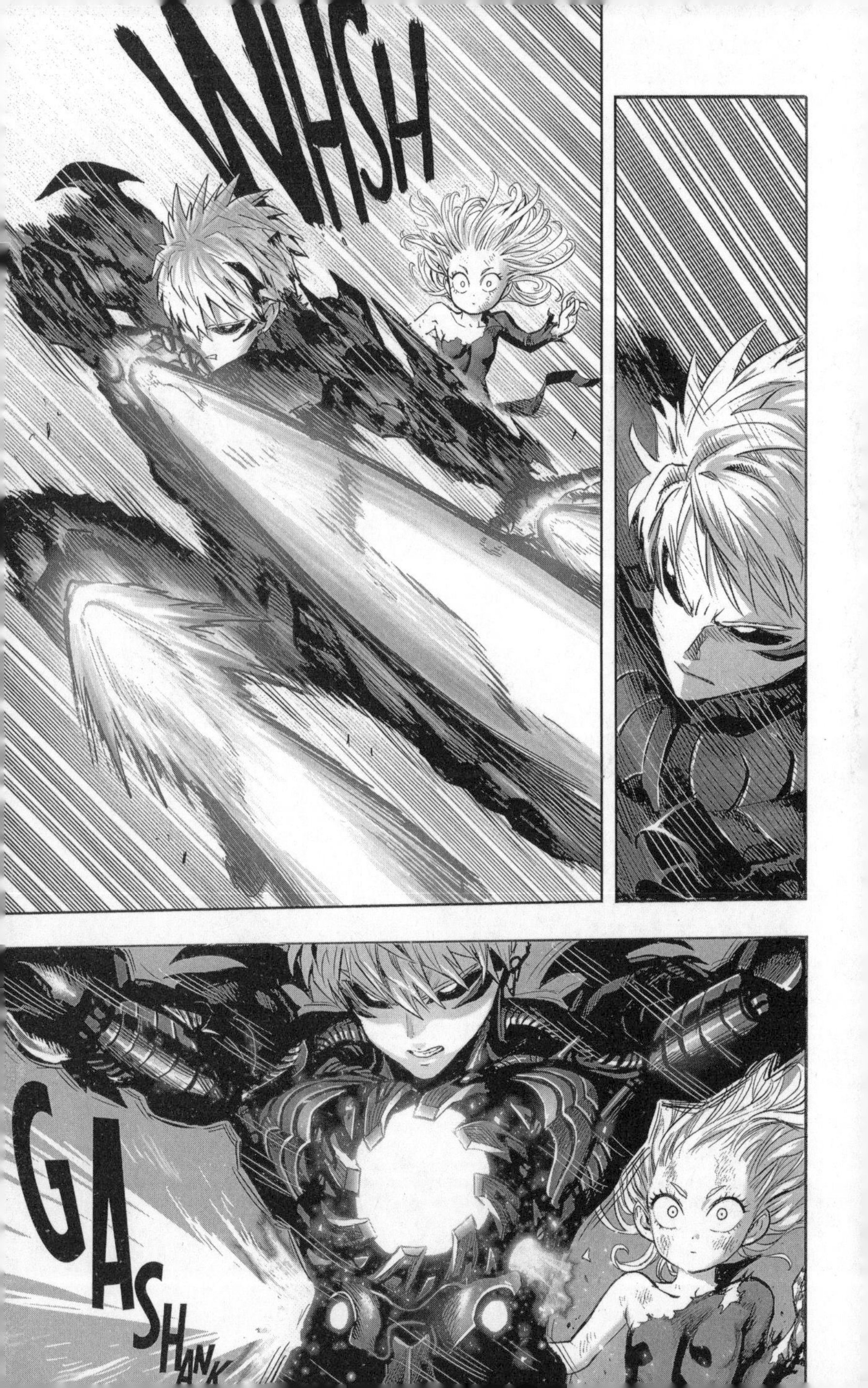
WHSH
GASHANK

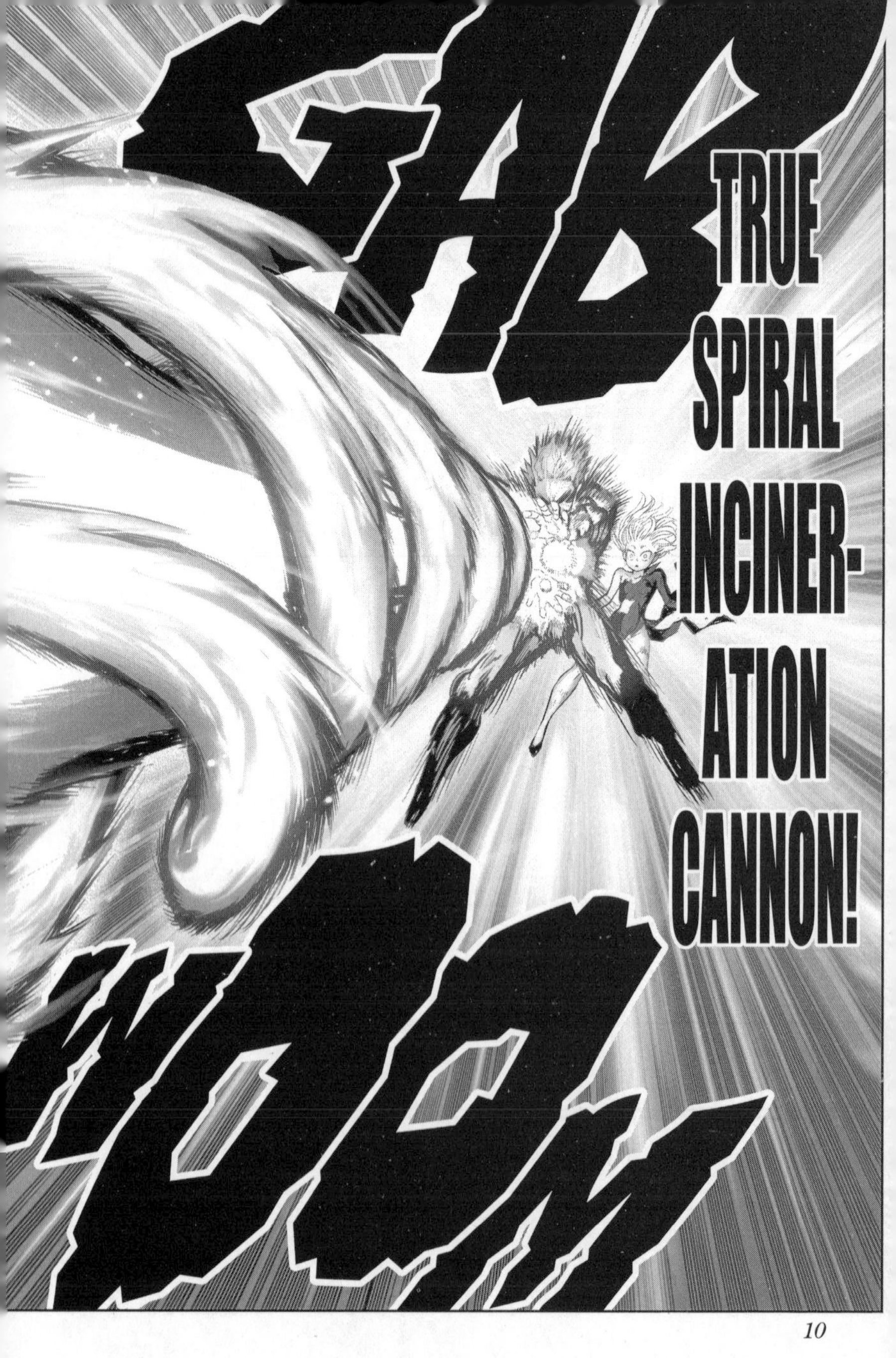
TRUE SPIRAL INCINER-ATION CANNON!

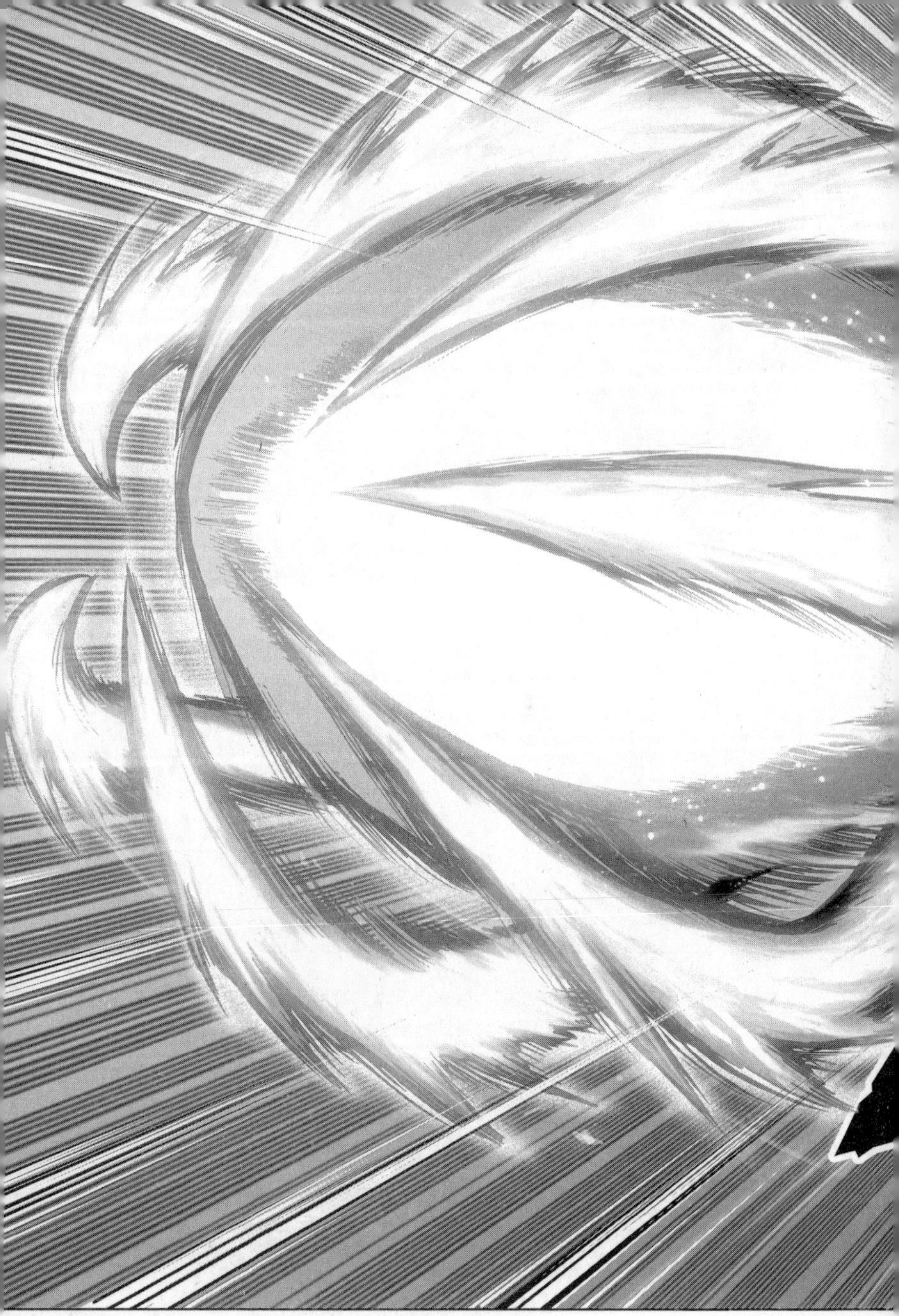

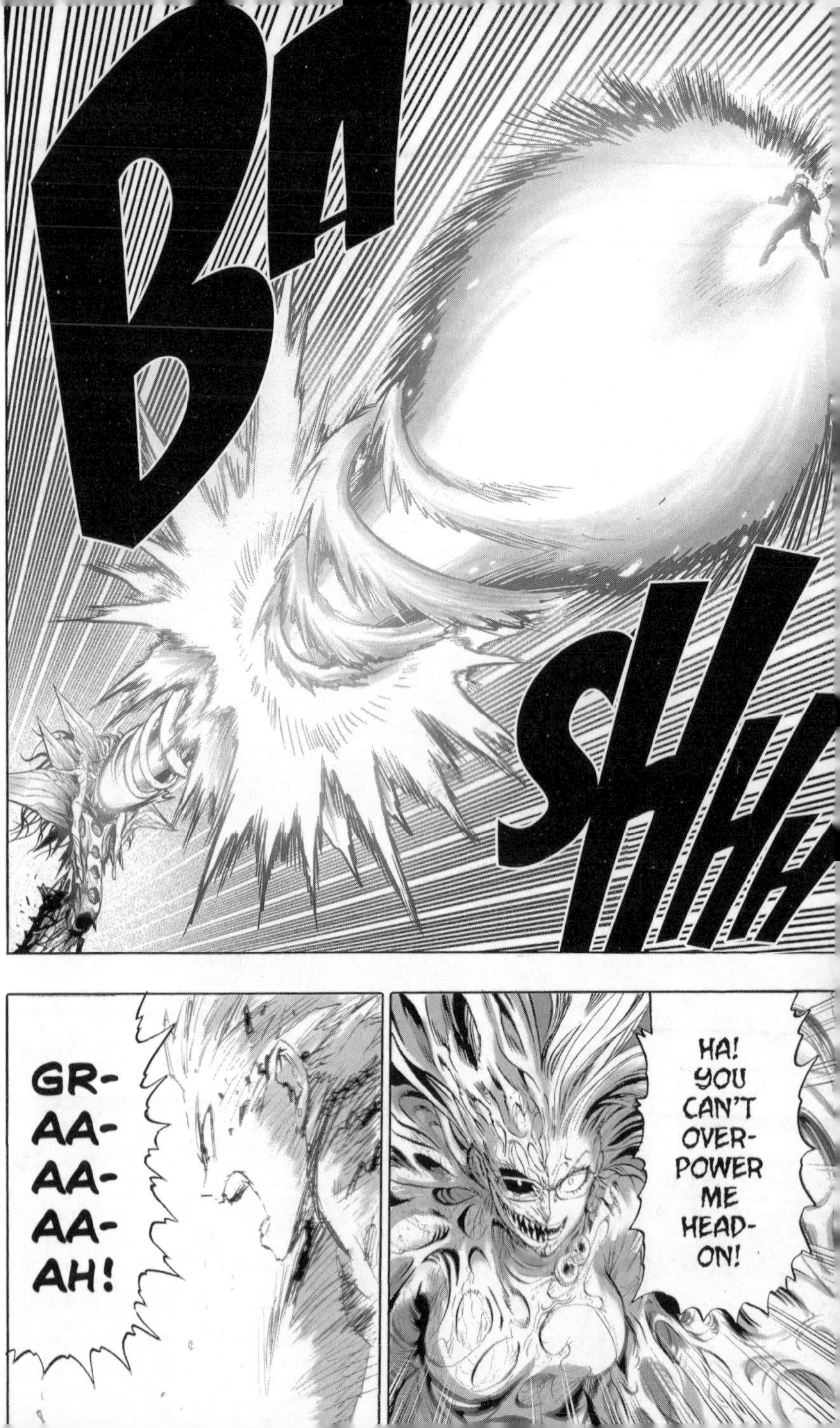
BA
SHHH
HA! YOU CAN'T OVER-POWER ME HEAD-ON!
GR-AA-AA-AA-AH!

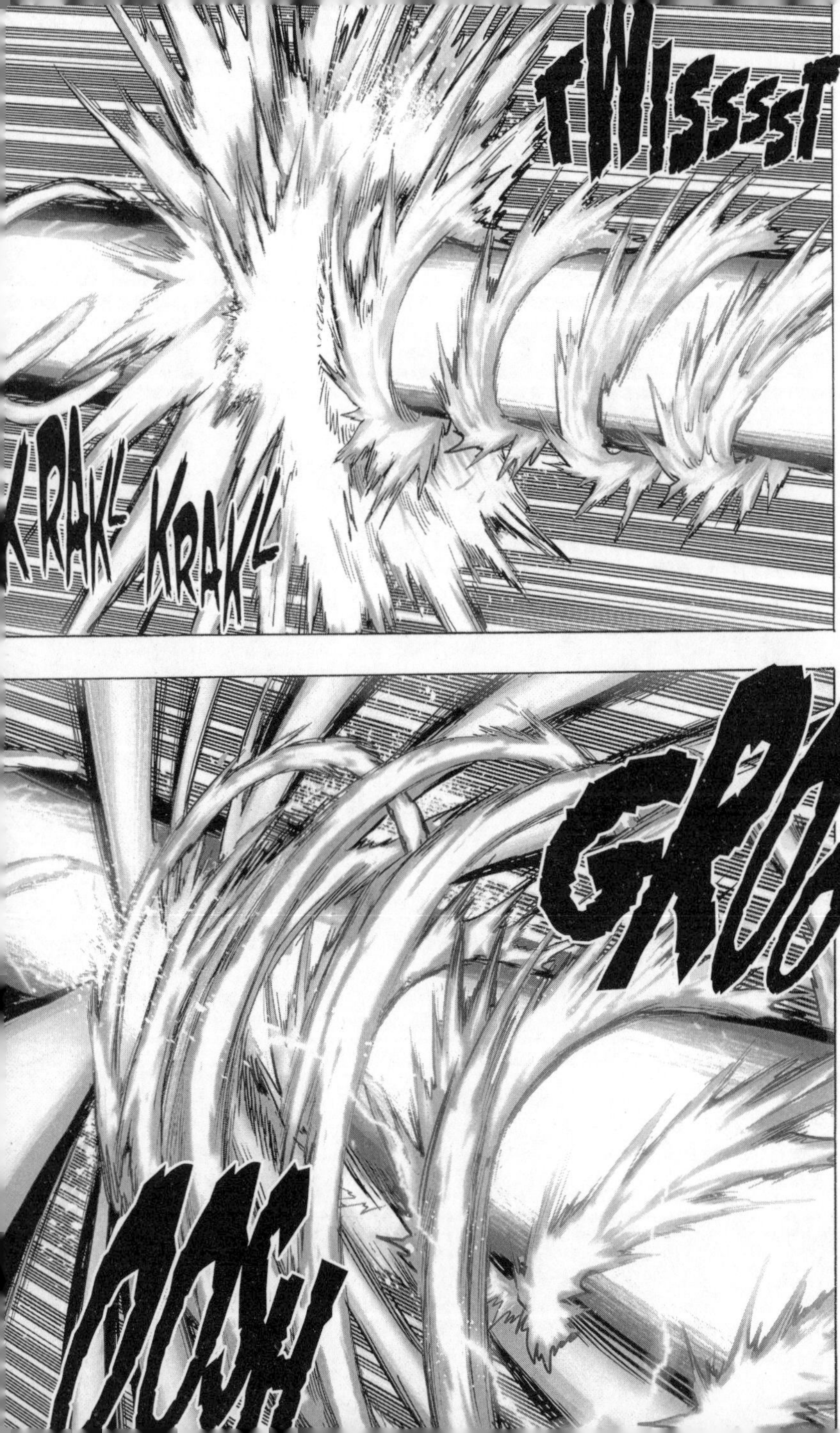
TWISSST
KRAK'L KRAK'L
GROO

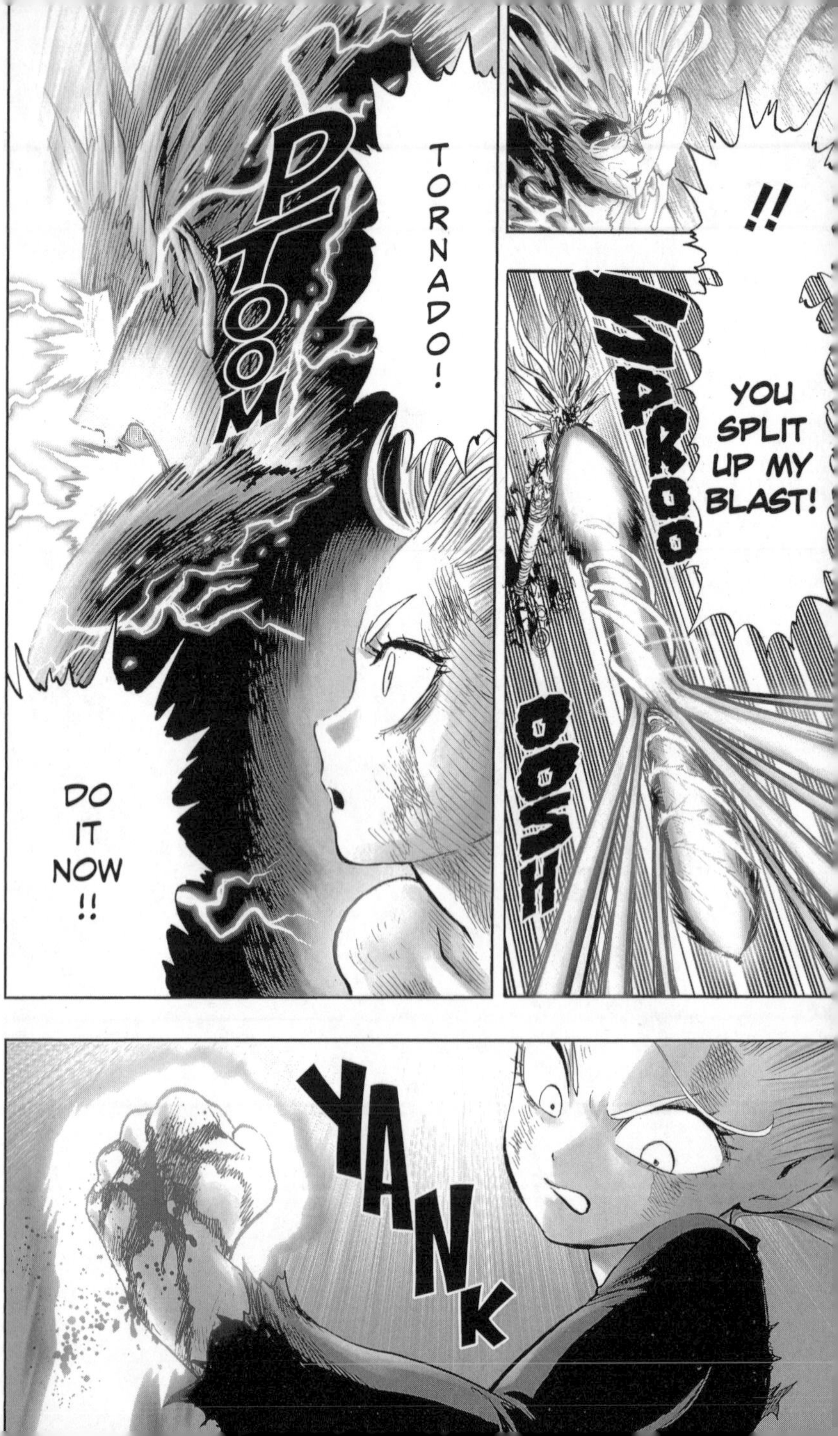
!!
SPROO
OOSH
YOU SPLIT UP MY BLAST!
TORNADO!
DTOOM
DO IT NOW!!
YANK

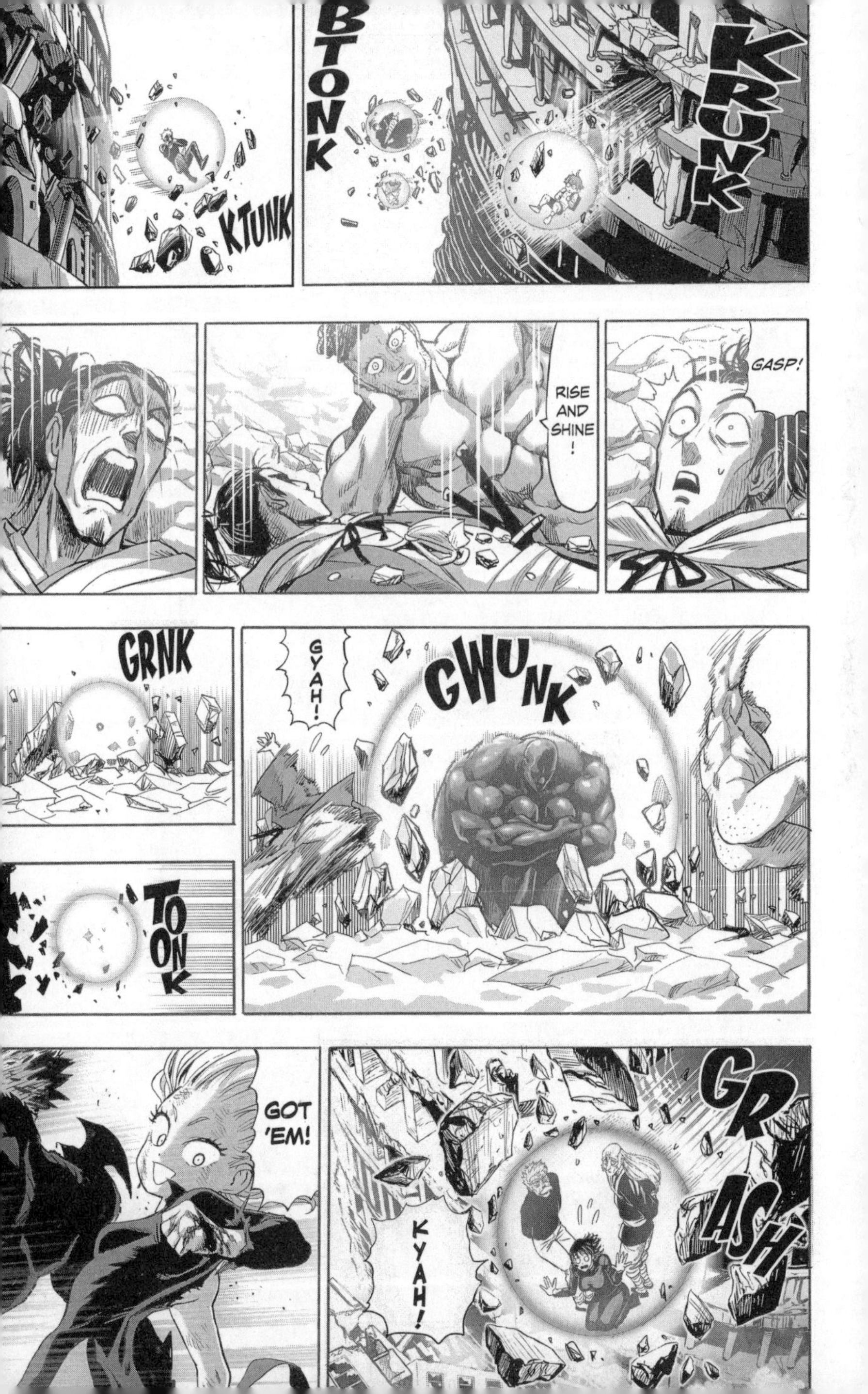
KRUNK
BTONK
KTUNK
GASP!
RISE AND SHINE!
GWUNK
GYAH!
GRNK
TOONK
GRASH
KYAH!
GOT 'EM!

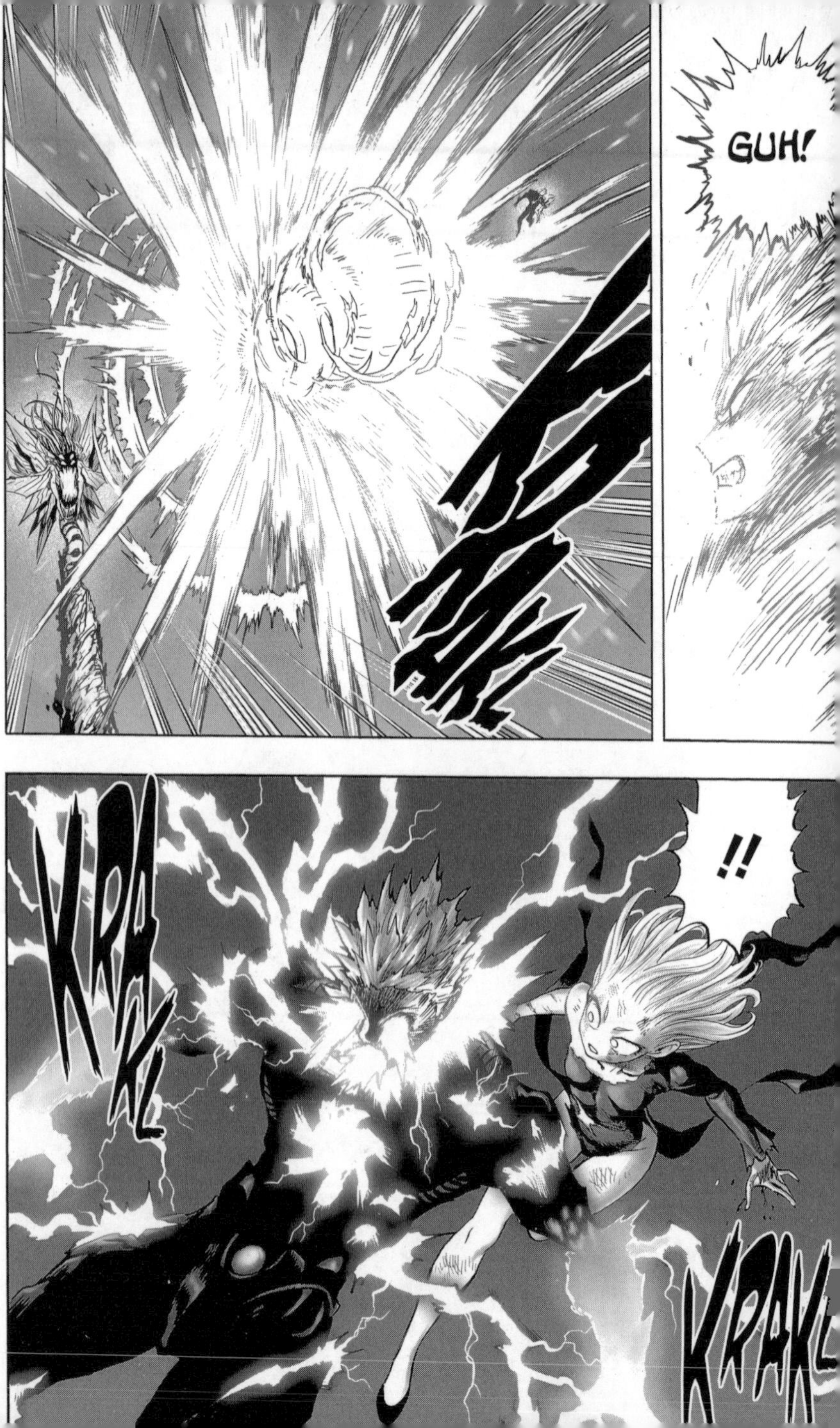
GUH!
!!
KRAKL
KRAKL

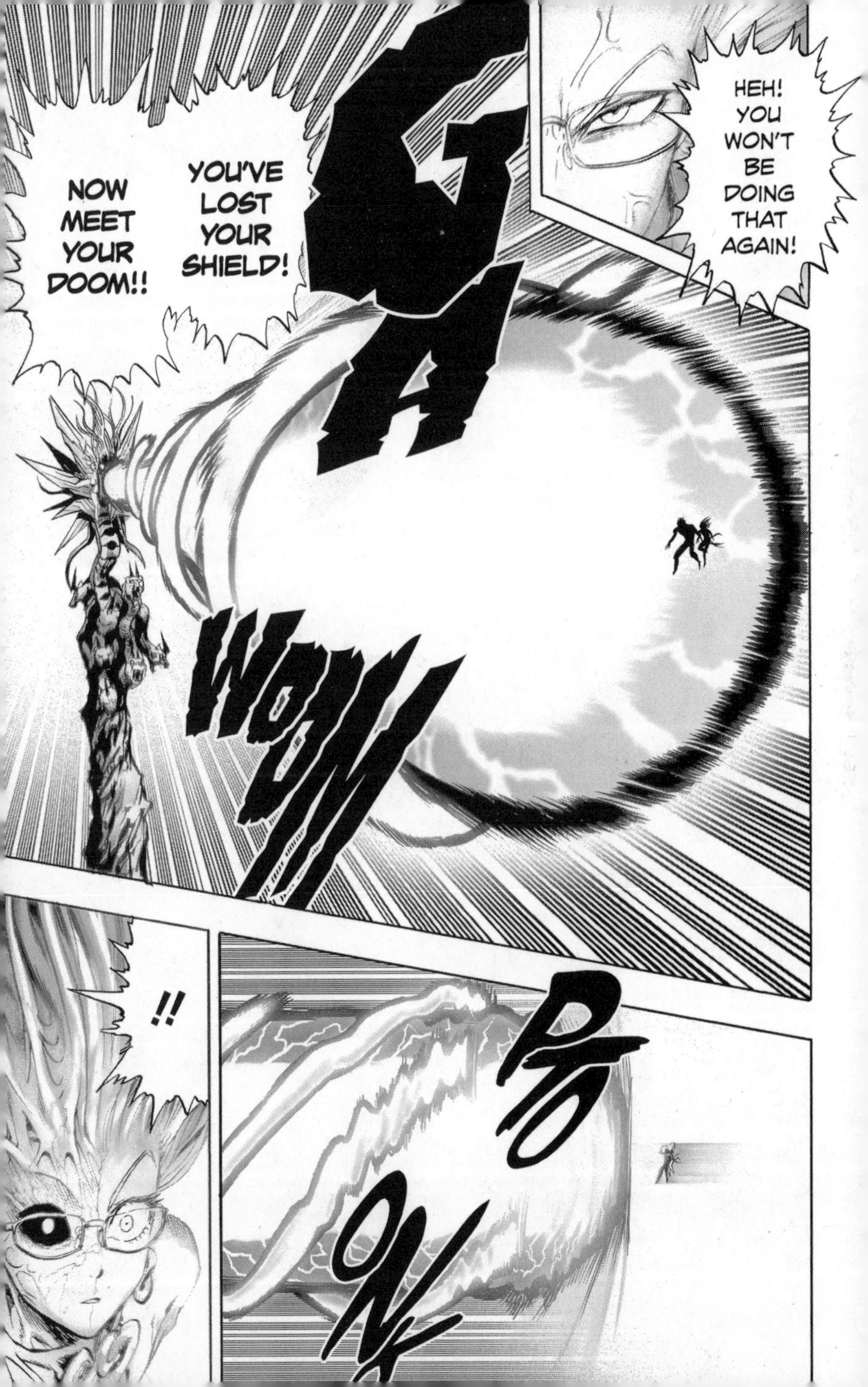
HEH! YOU WON'T BE DOING THAT AGAIN!
YOU'VE LOST YOUR SHIELD!
NOW MEET YOUR DOOM!!
!!

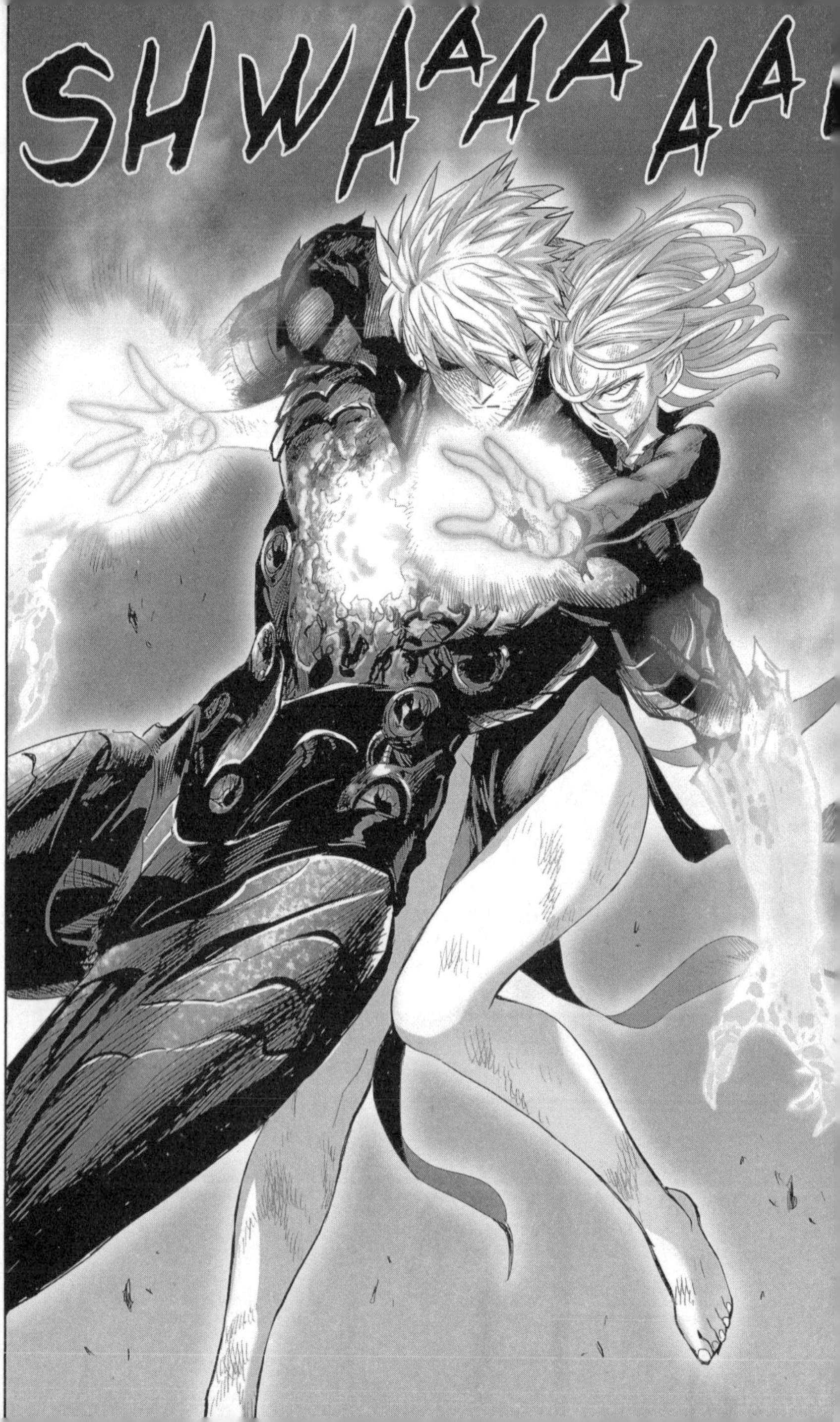
SHWAAAAAA

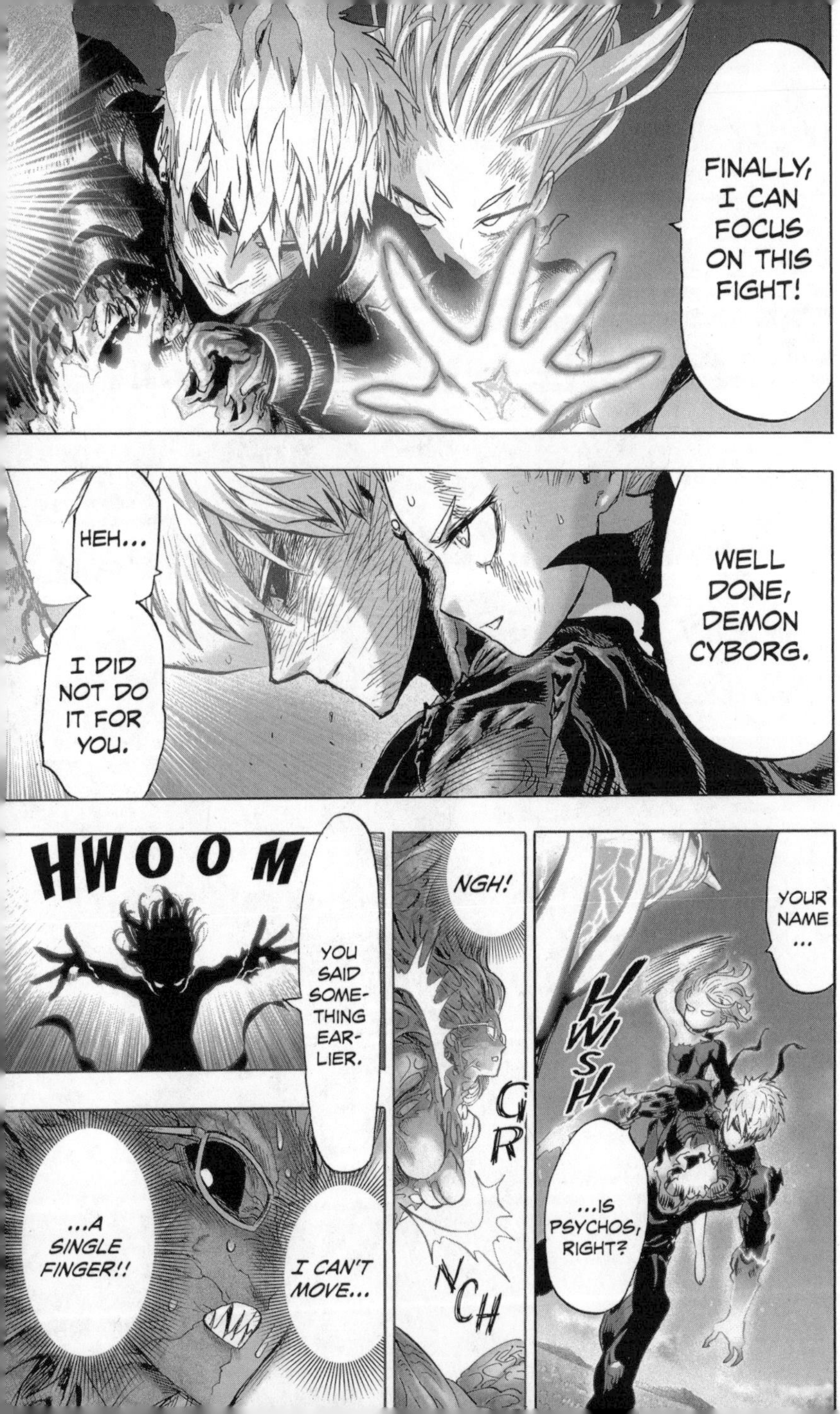
FINALLY, I CAN FOCUS ON THIS FIGHT!
WELL DONE, DEMON CYBORG.
HEH...
I DID NOT DO IT FOR YOU.
YOUR NAME...
HWISH
...IS PSYCHOS, RIGHT?
NGH!
GR
NCH
HWOOM
YOU SAID SOME-THING EAR-LIER.
I CAN'T MOVE...
...A SINGLE FINGER!!

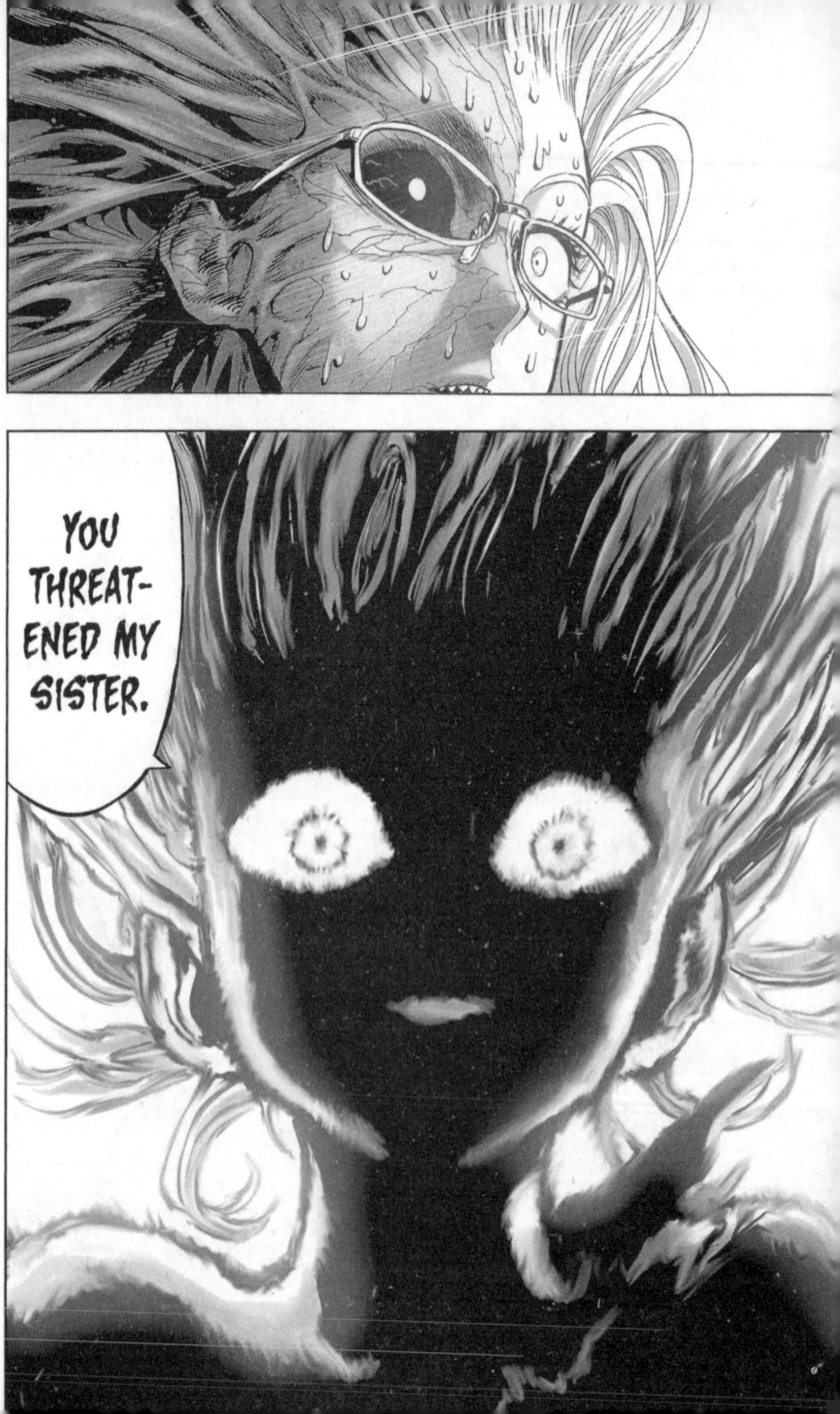
YOU THREAT-ENED MY SISTER.

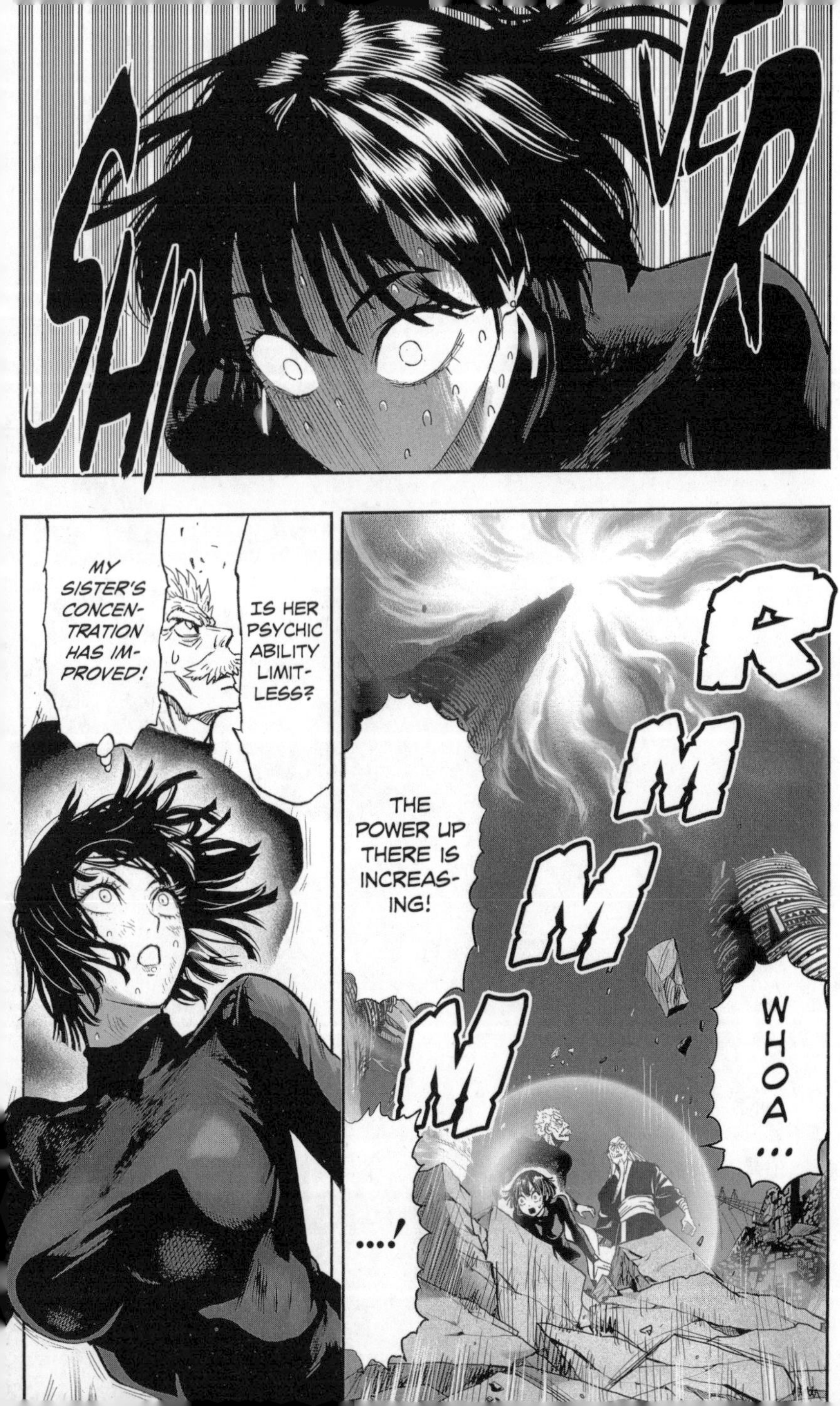
SHIVER
RMMM
THE POWER UP THERE IS INCREAS-ING!
WHOA...
...!
IS HER PSYCHIC ABILITY LIMIT-LESS?
MY SISTER'S CONCEN-TRATION HAS IM-PROVED!

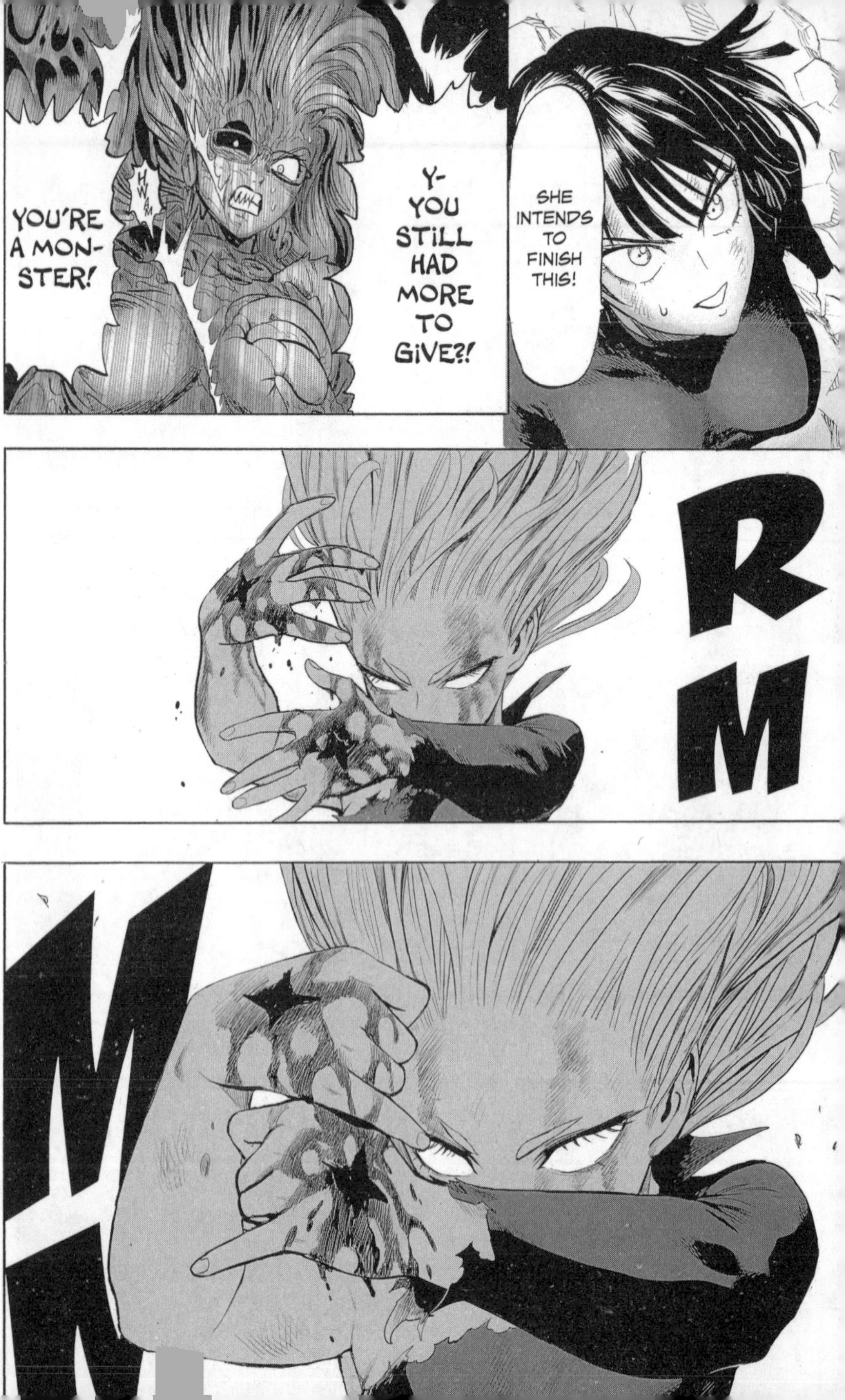
SHE INTENDS TO FINISH THIS!
Y- YOU STILL HAD MORE TO GIVE?!
HWAM
YOU'RE A MONSTER!
RM
M

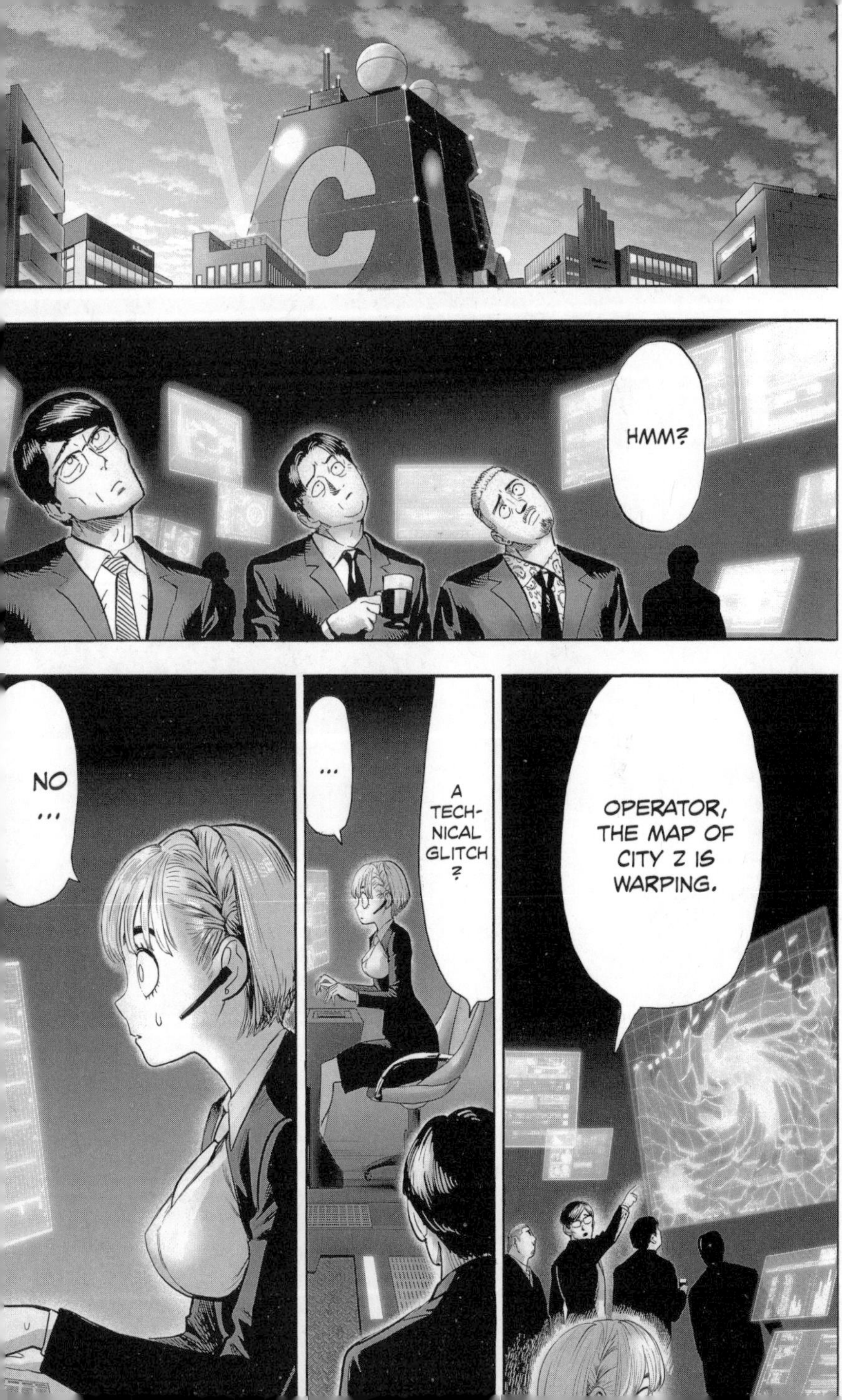
HMM?
OPERATOR, THE MAP OF CITY Z IS WARPING.
A TECH-NICAL GLITCH?
...
NO ...

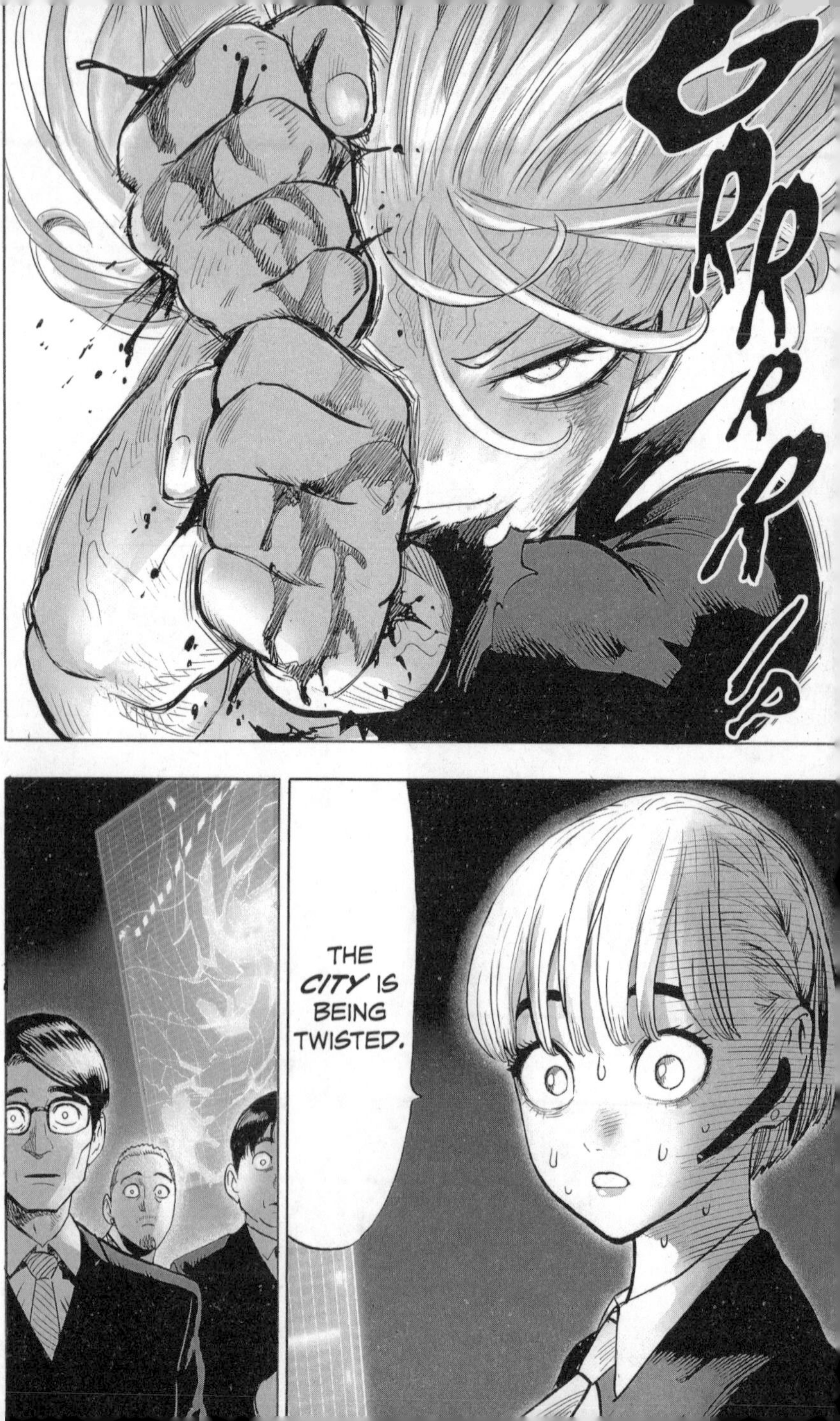
GRRRRRIP
THE CITY IS BEING TWISTED.

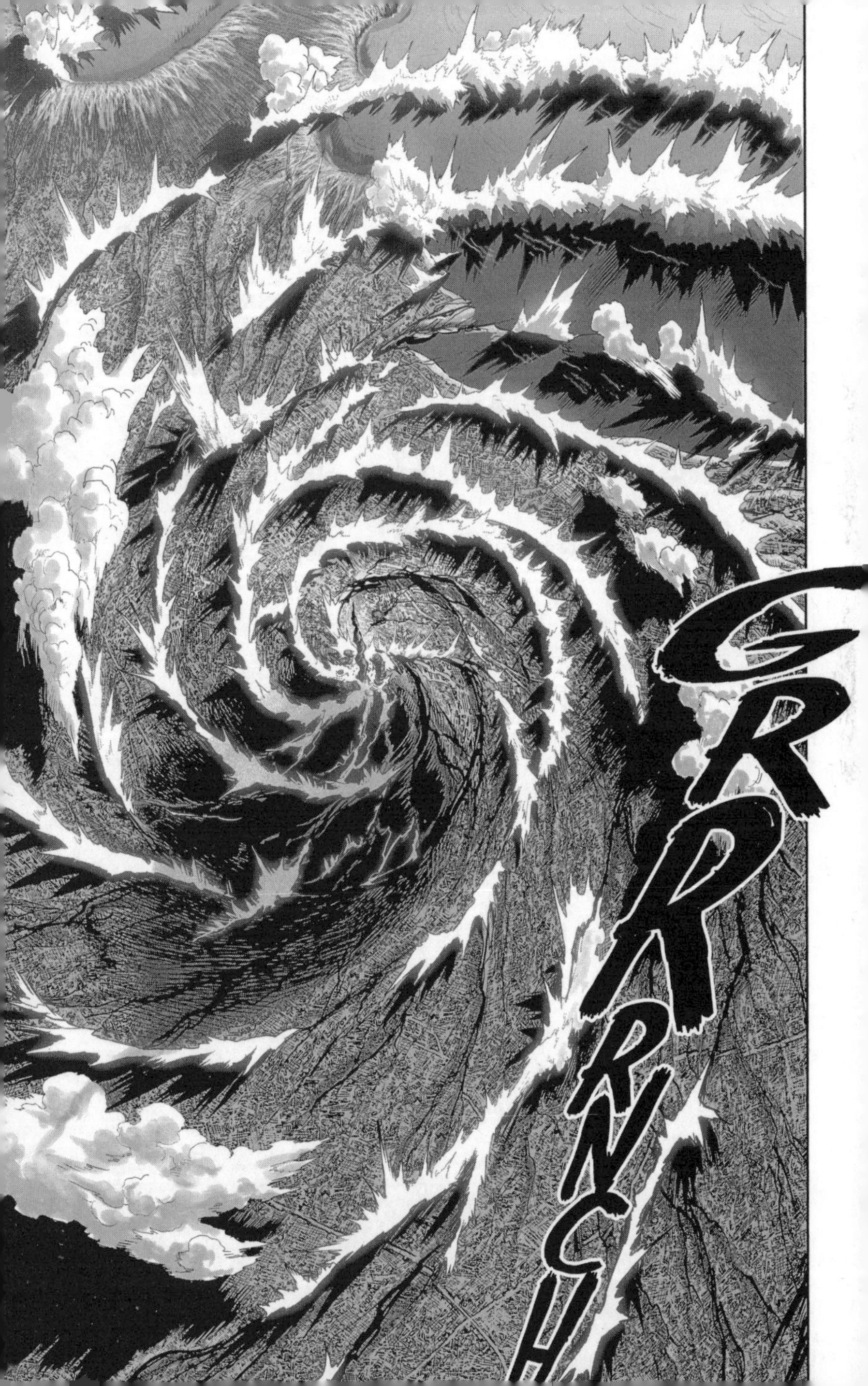
GRRRNCH

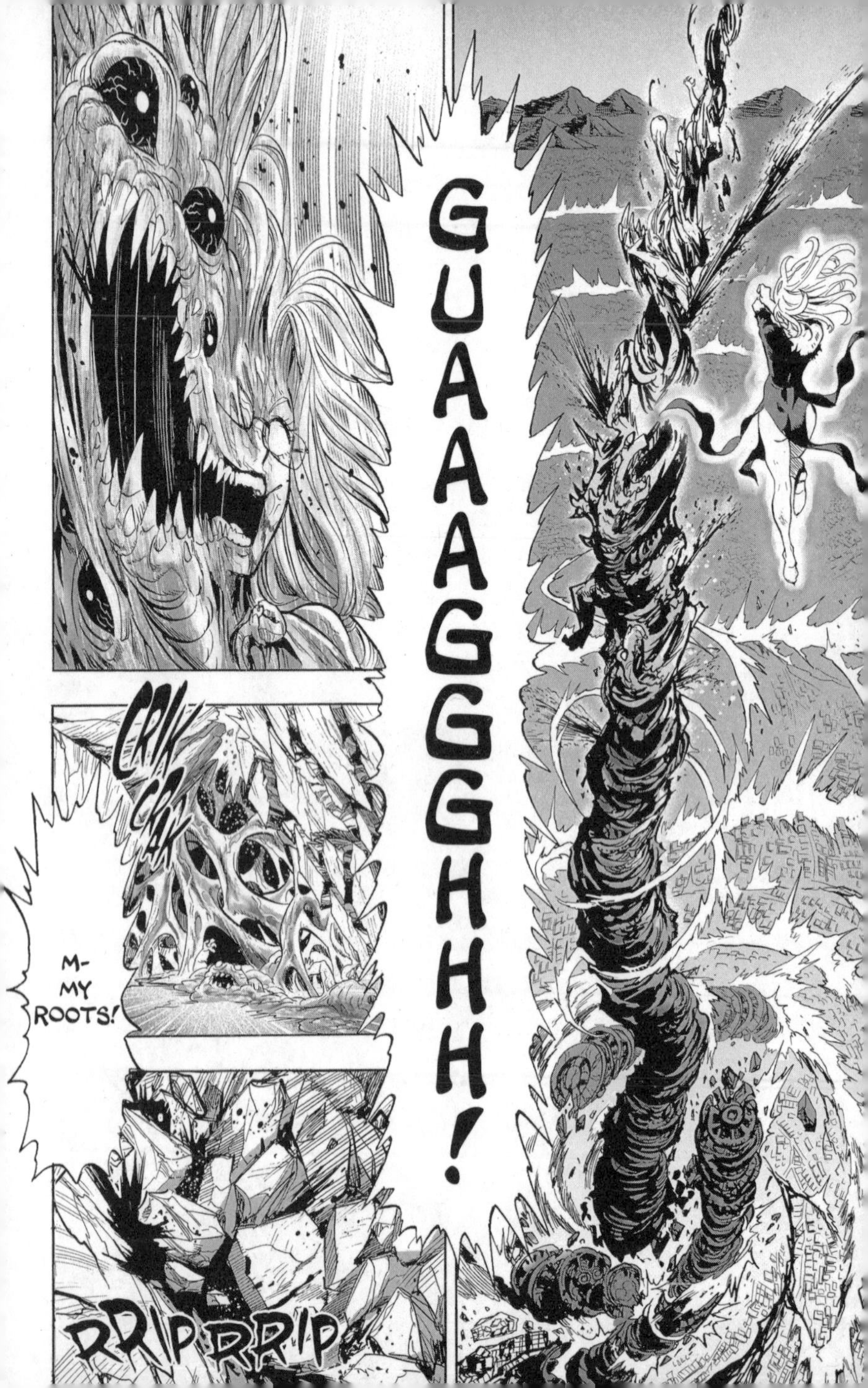
GUAAAGGGHHH!
CRIK CRAK
M- MY ROOTS!
RRIP RRIP

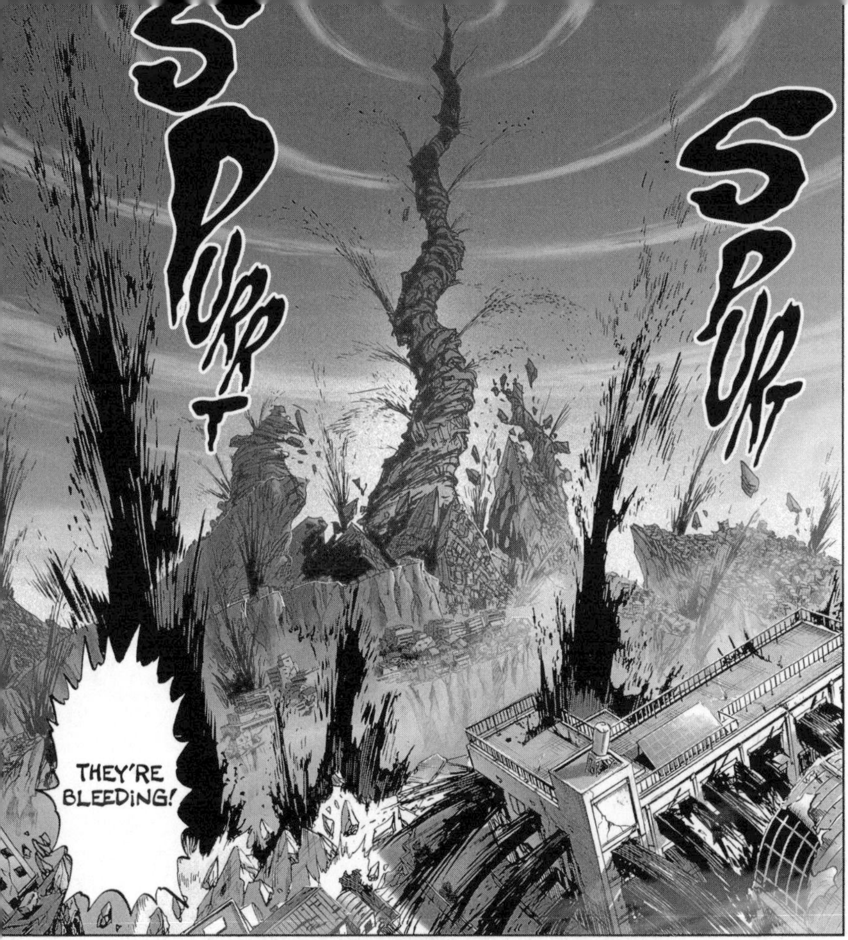
SPURT
SPURRT
THEY'RE BLEEDING!

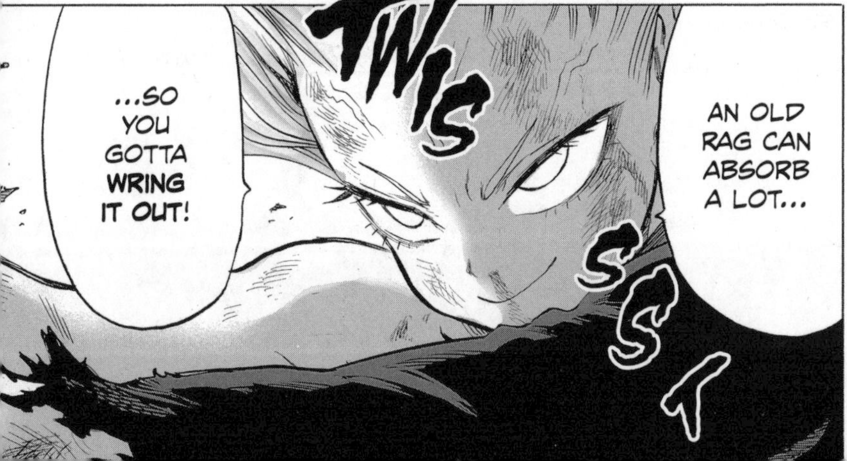
AN OLD RAG CAN ABSORB A LOT...
TWISSST
...SO YOU GOTTA WRING IT OUT!

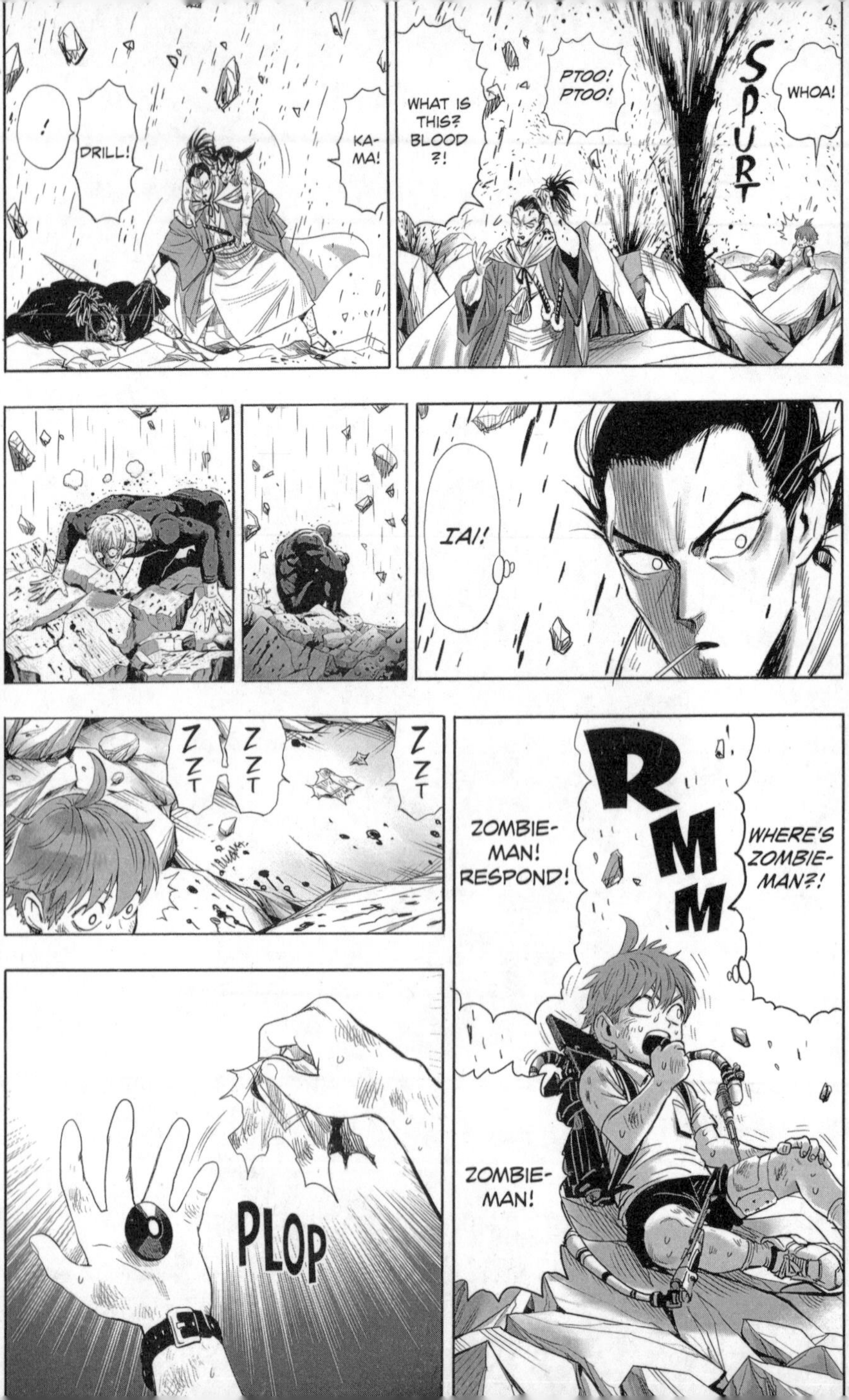
WHOA!
SPURT
PTOO! PTOO!
WHAT IS THIS? BLOOD?!
KA-MA!
DRILL!
!
IAI!
WHERE'S ZOMBIE-MAN?!
RMM
ZOMBIE-MAN! RESPOND!
ZOMBIE-MAN!
ZZZT
ZZZT
ZZZT
PLOP

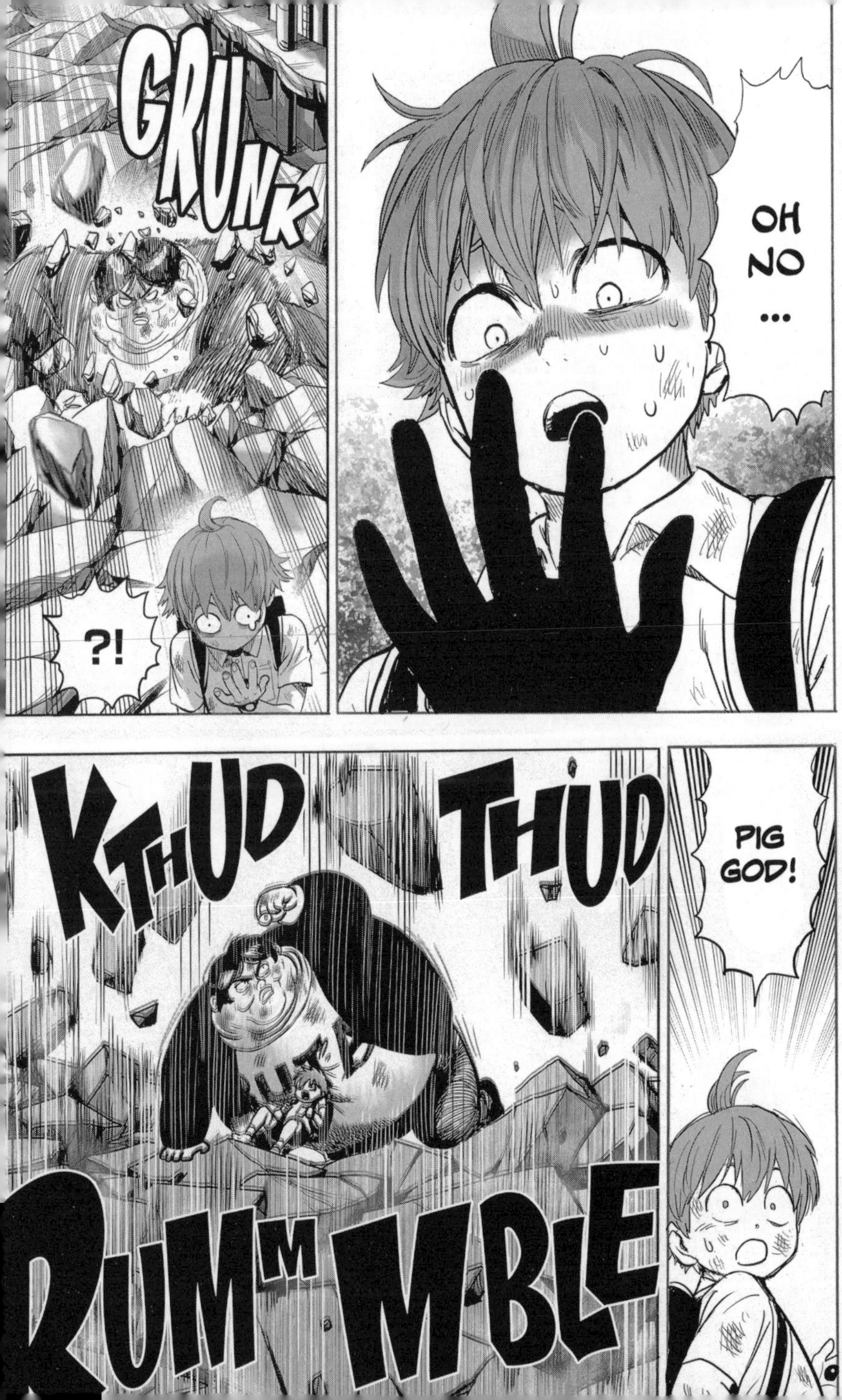
OH NO ...
GRUNK
?!
PIG GOD!
KTHUD
THUD
RUMMMBLE

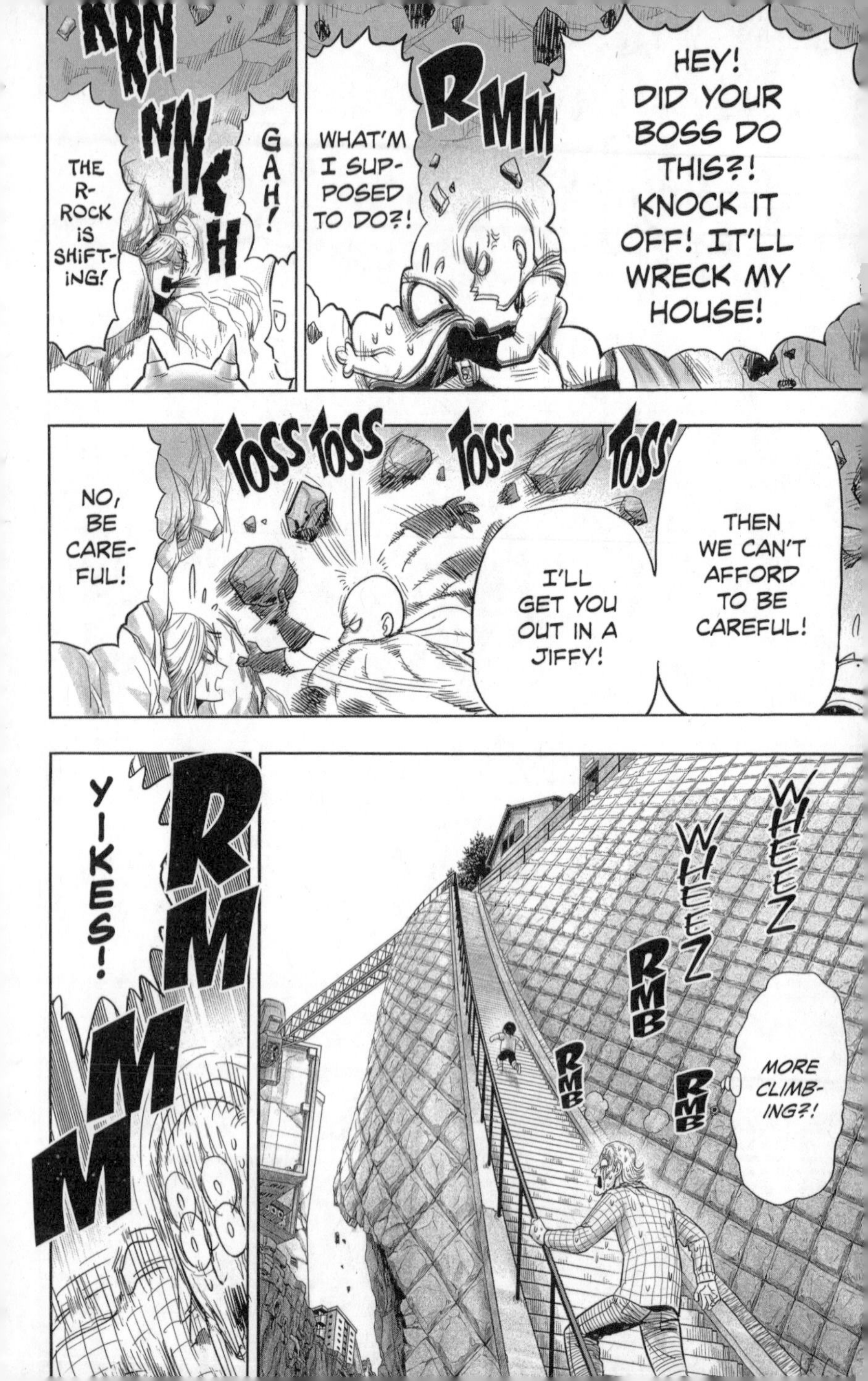
HEY! DID YOUR BOSS DO THIS?! KNOCK IT OFF! IT'LL WRECK MY HOUSE!
RMM
WHAT'M I SUP-POSED TO DO?!
KRNNNKH
GAH!
THE R-ROCK IS SHIFT-ING!
THEN WE CAN'T AFFORD TO BE CAREFUL!
I'LL GET YOU OUT IN A JIFFY!
TOSS TOSS TOSS TOSS
NO, BE CARE-FUL!
WHEEZ
WHEEZ
RMB RMB RMB RMB
MORE CLIMB-ING?!
RMMM
YIKES!

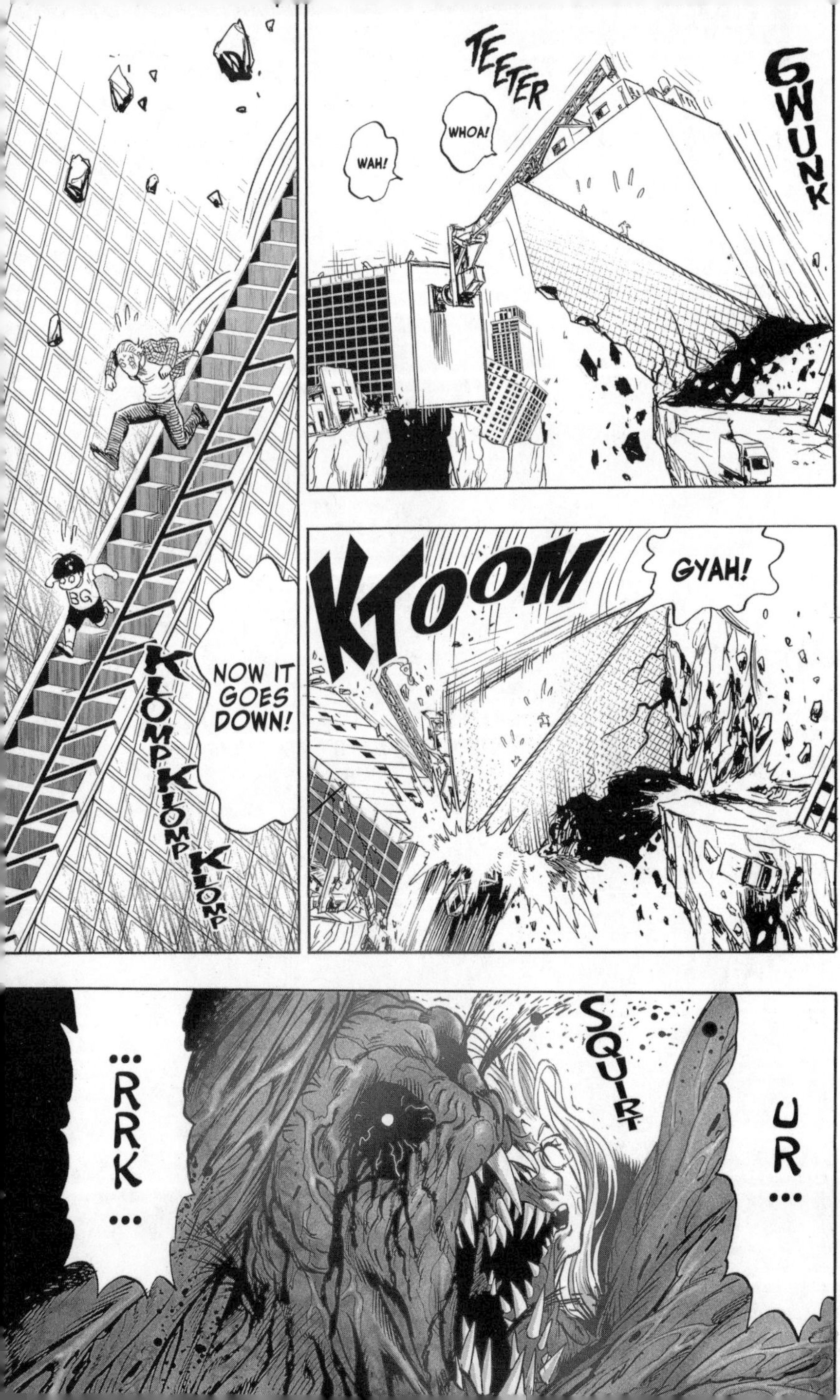
GWUNK
TEETER
WHOA!
WAH!
GYAH!
KTOOM
NOW IT GOES DOWN!
KLOMP KLOMP KLOMP KLOMP
UR...
SQUIRT
...RRK...

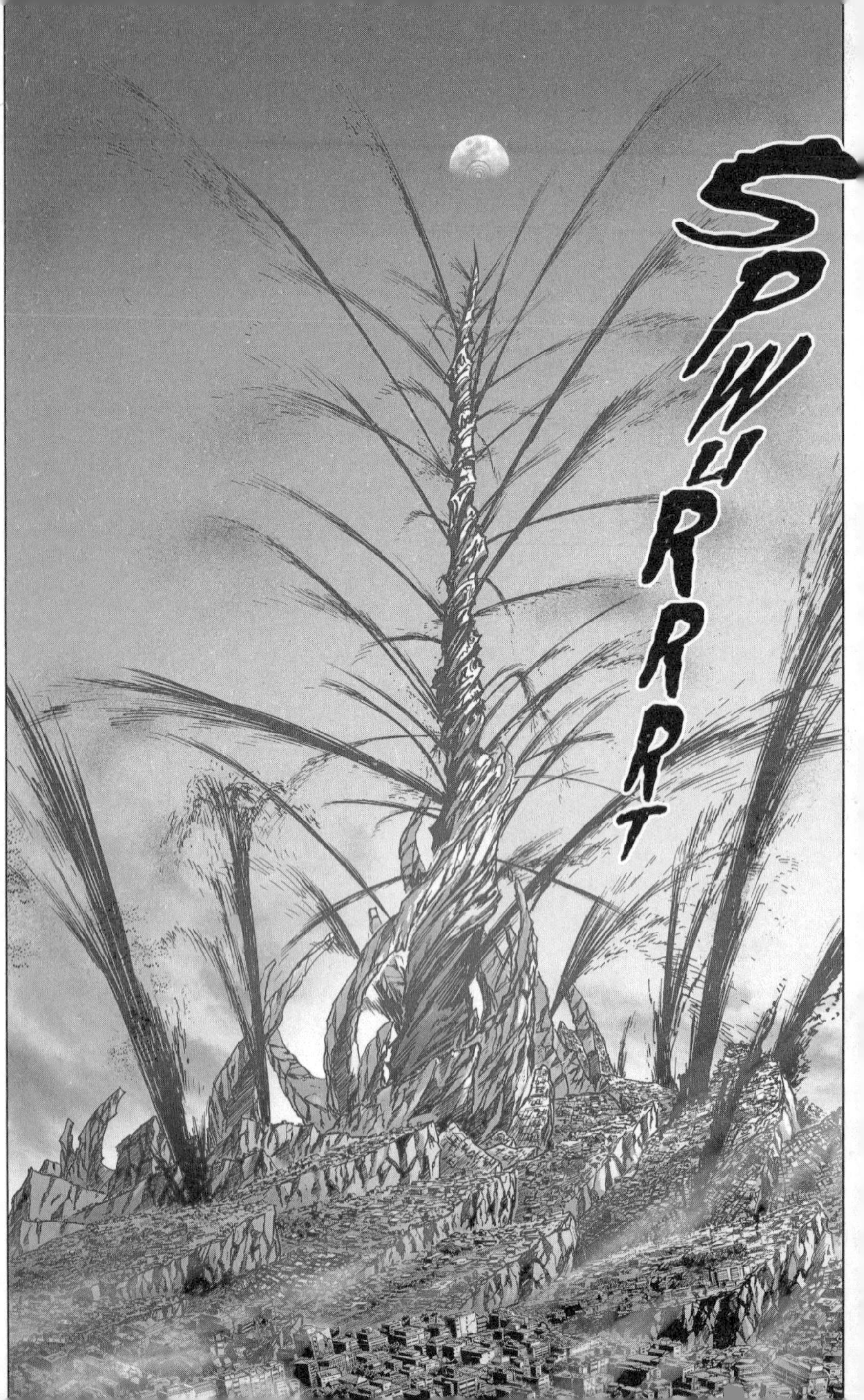
SPWURRRRT

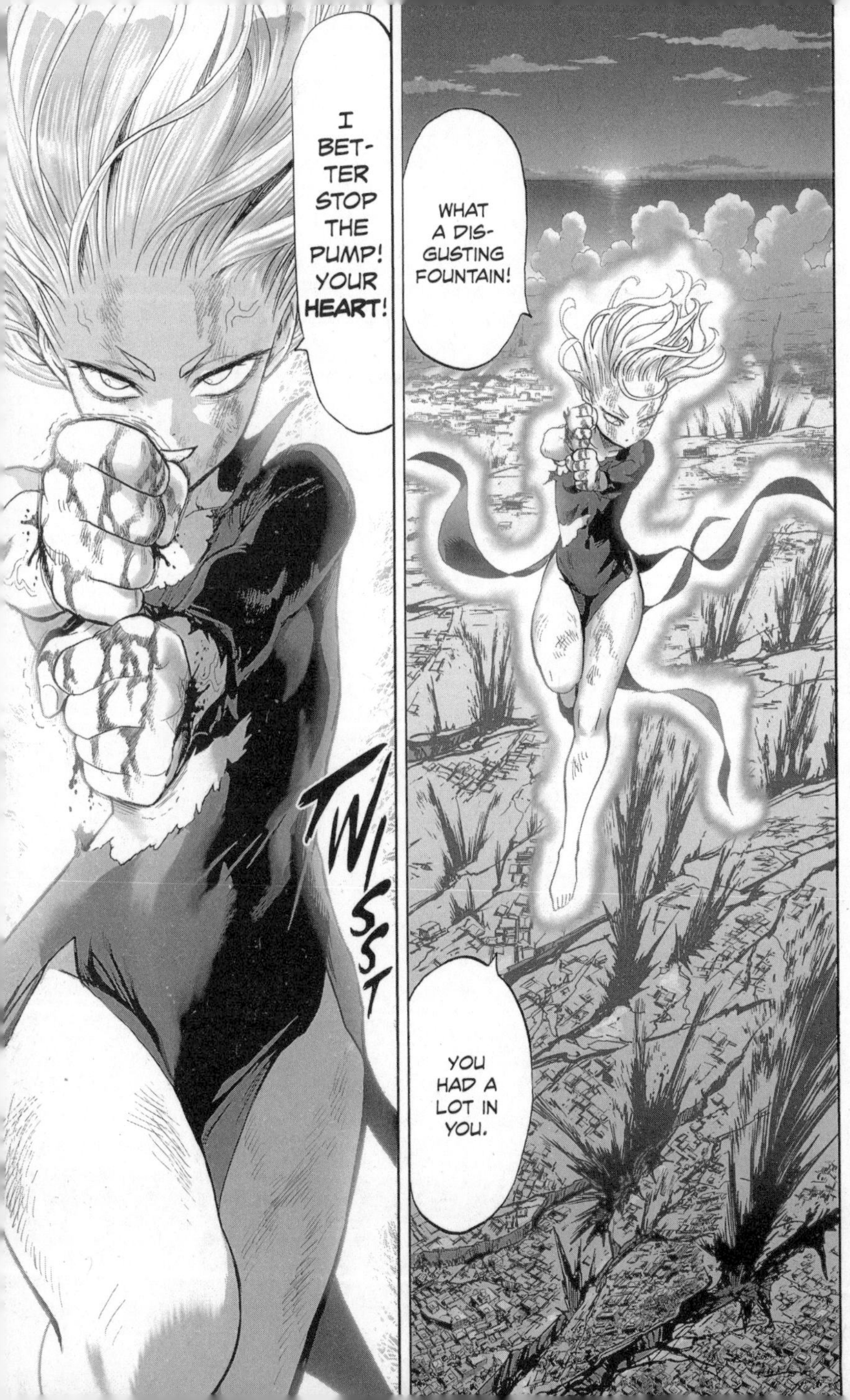
WHAT A DIS-GUSTING FOUNTAIN!
YOU HAD A LOT IN YOU.
I BET-TER STOP THE PUMP! YOUR **HEART**!
TWISSST

PUNCH 139: GIANT BARRIER

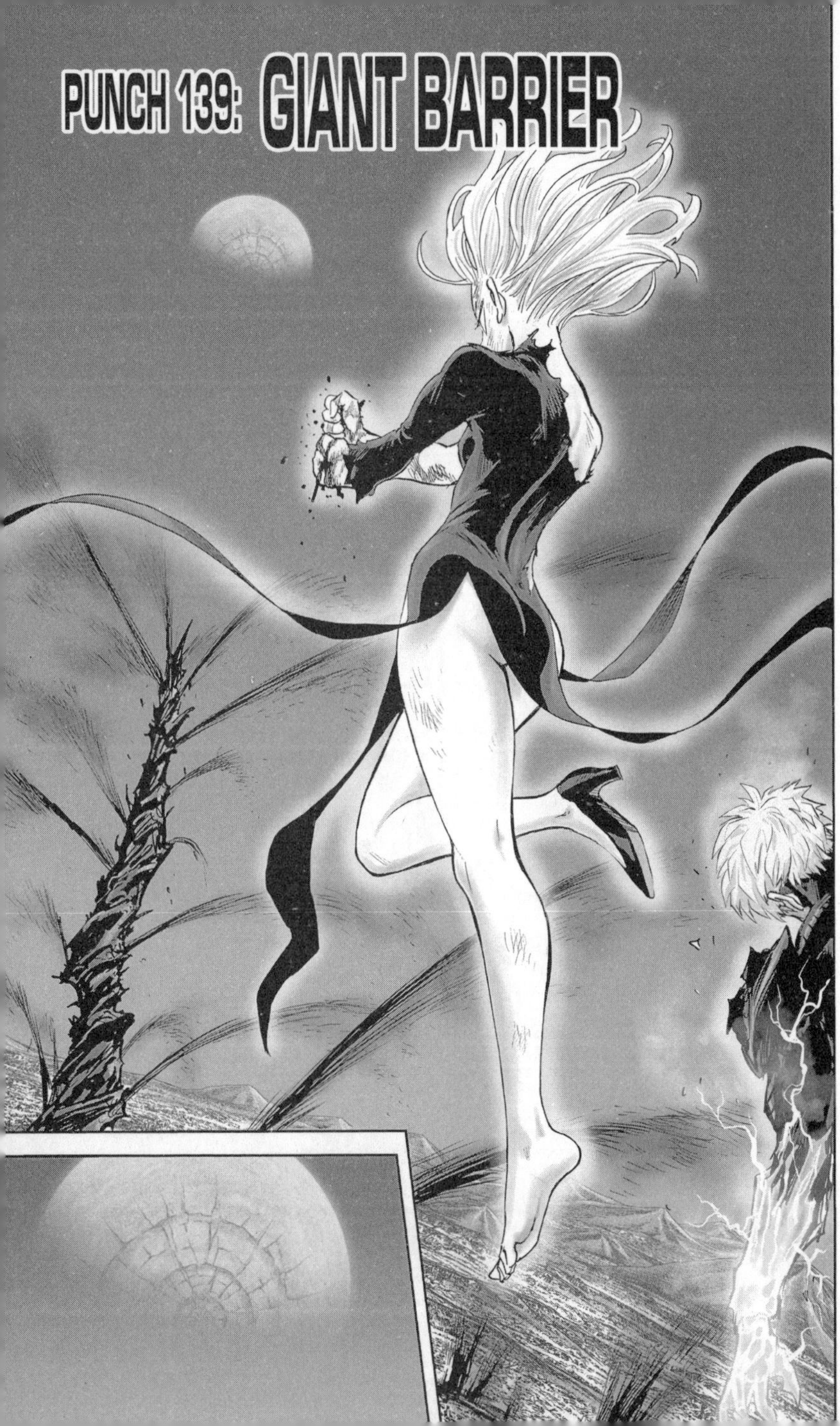

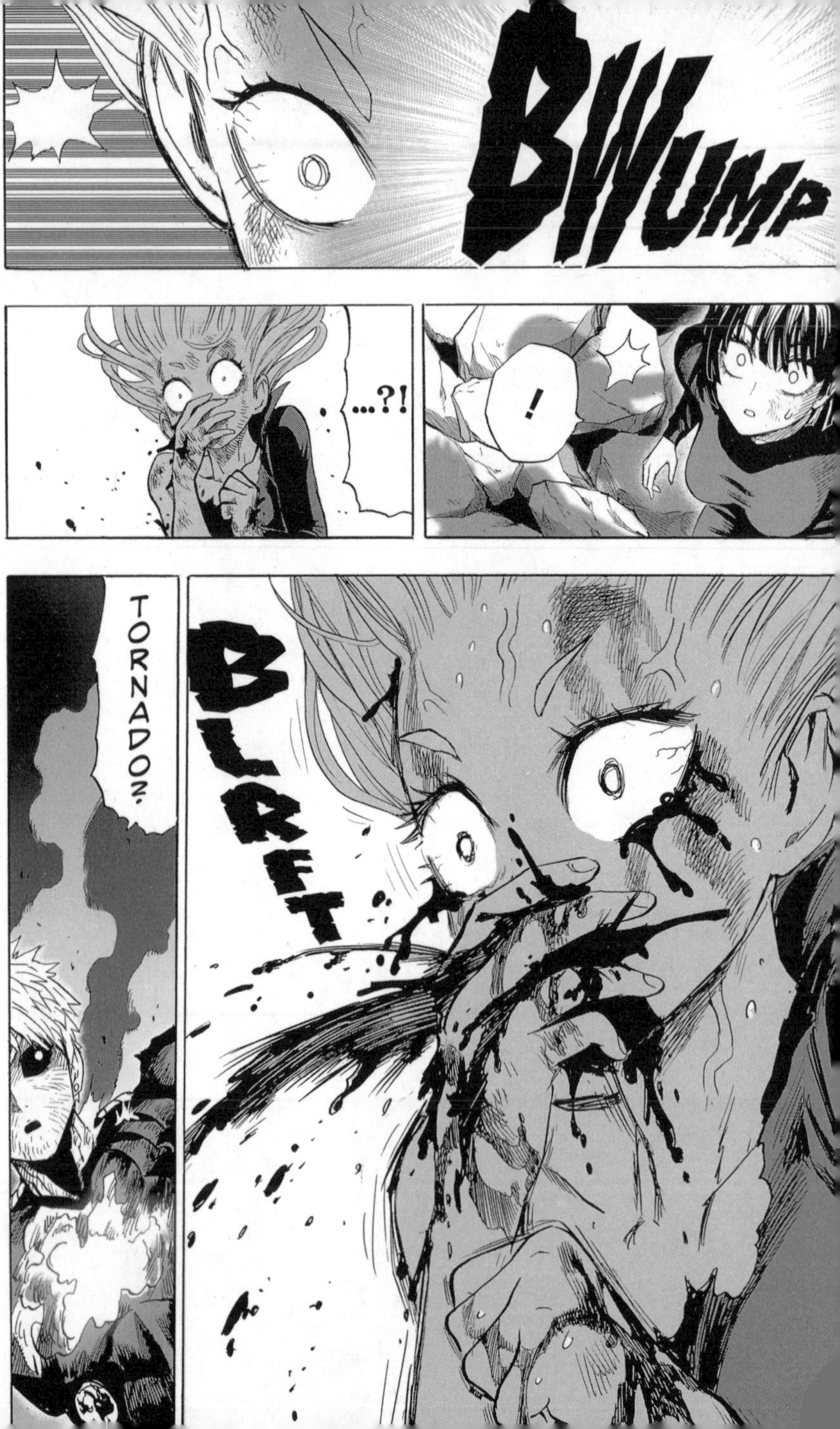
BWUMP
!
...?!
BLRFT
TORNADO?

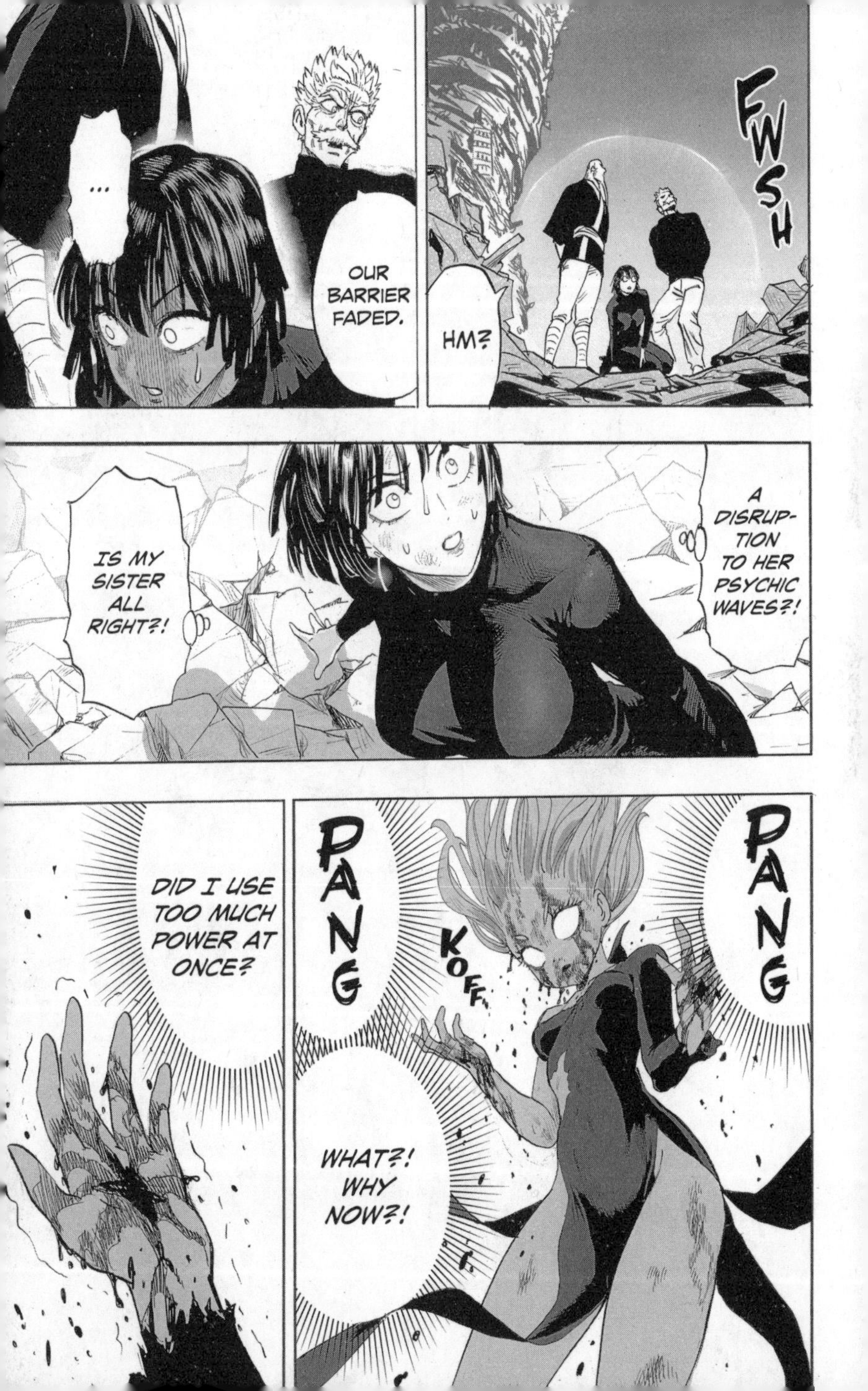
FWSH
HM?
OUR BARRIER FADED.
...
A DISRUP-TION TO HER PSYCHIC WAVES?!
IS MY SISTER ALL RIGHT?!
PANG
PANG
KOFF
WHAT?! WHY NOW?!
DID I USE TOO MUCH POWER AT ONCE?

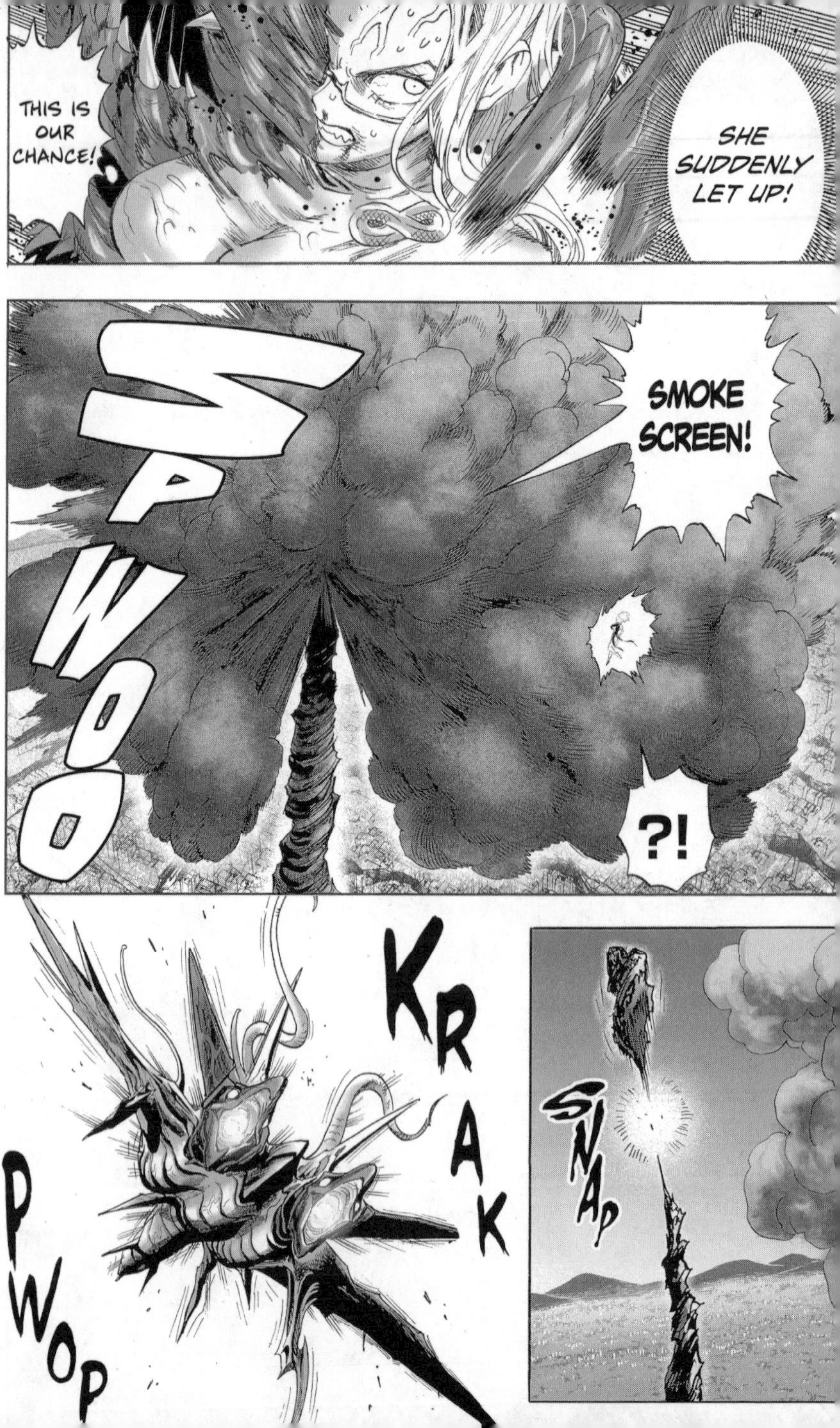
SHE SUDDENLY LET UP!
THIS IS OUR CHANCE!
SMOKE SCREEN!
SPWOOO
?!
SNAP
KRAK
PWOP

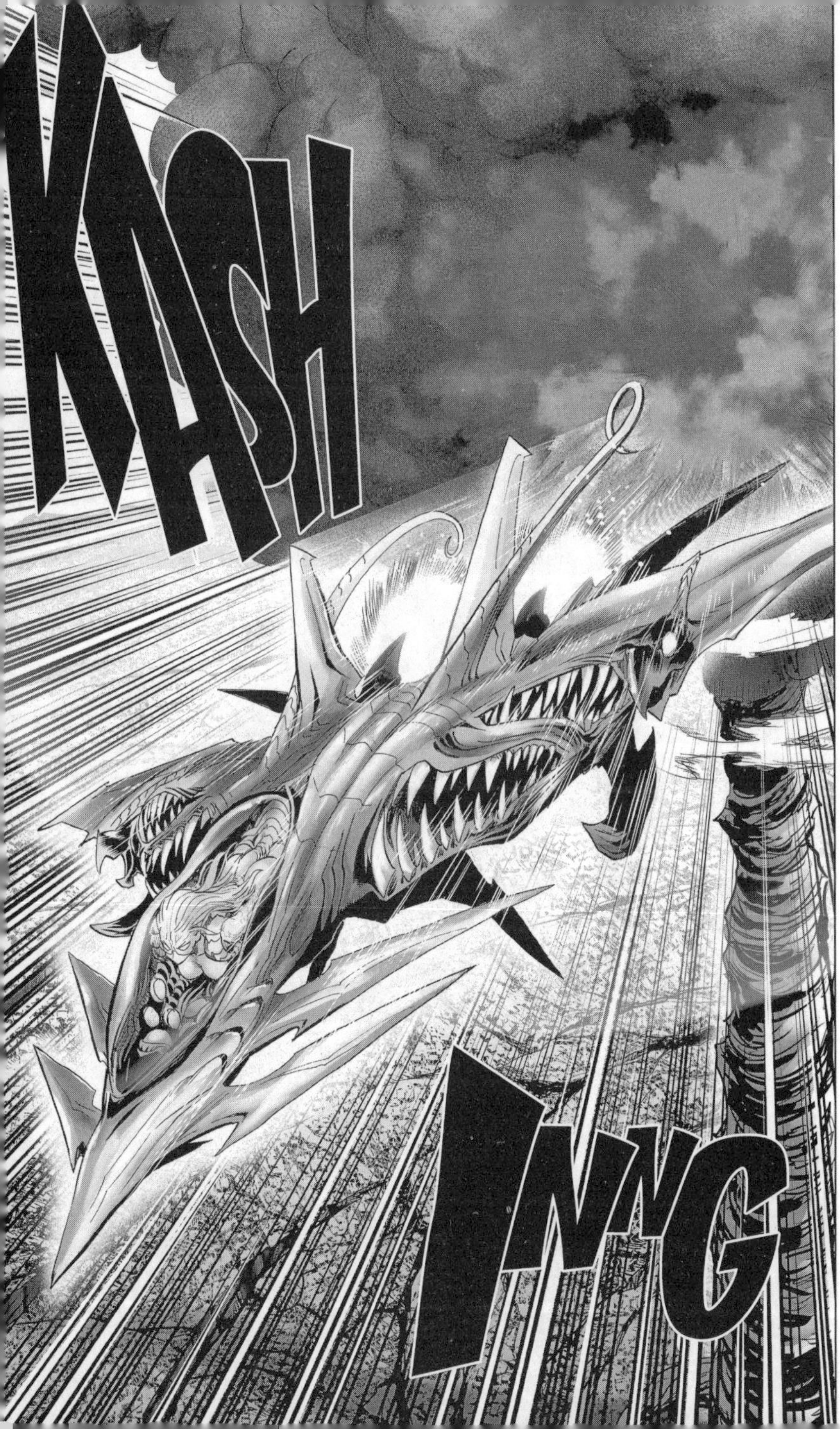
KASH
INNG

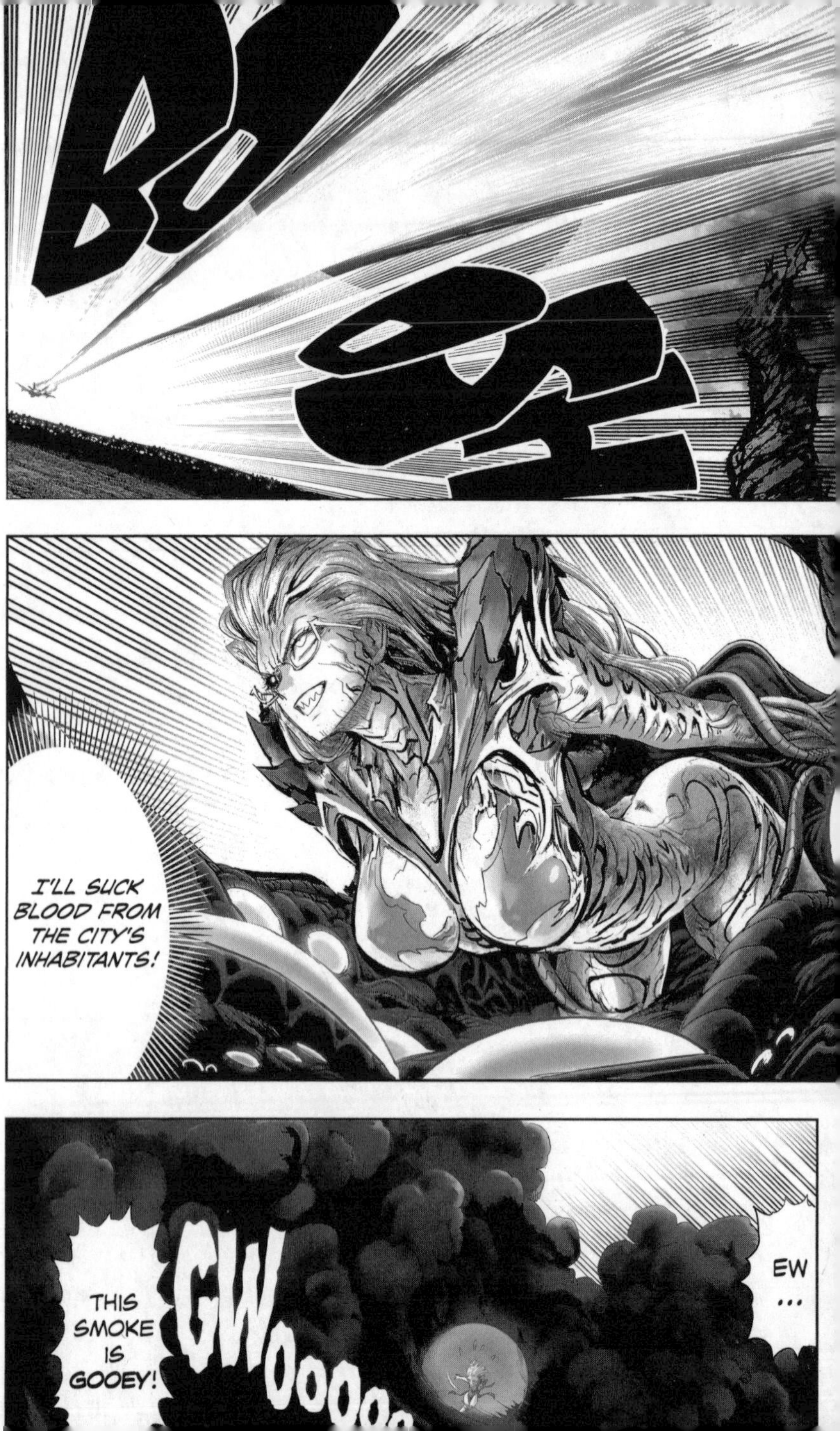
I'LL SUCK BLOOD FROM THE CITY'S INHABITANTS!
EW ...
GWOOOO
THIS SMOKE IS GOOEY!

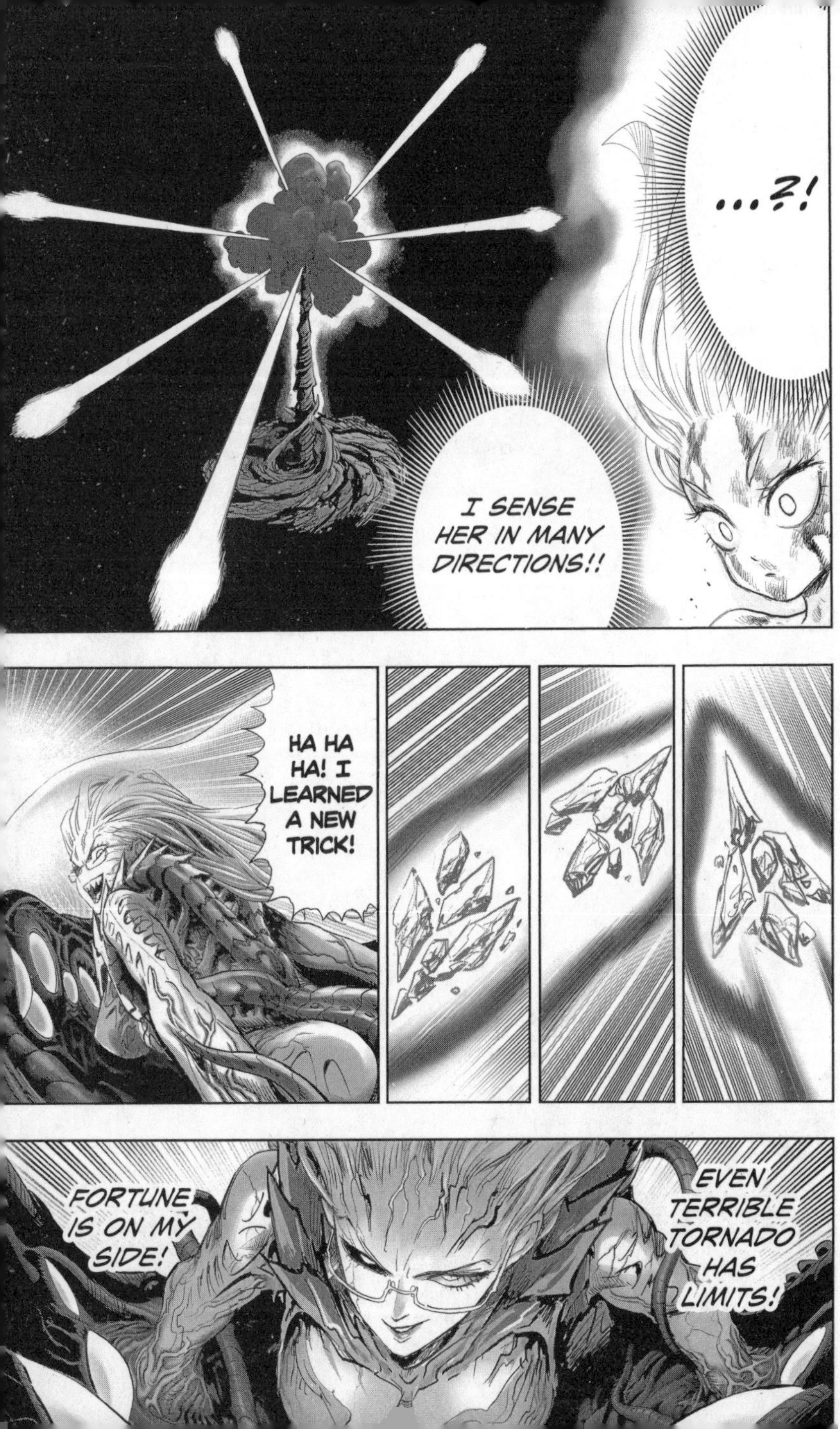
...?!
I SENSE HER IN MANY DIRECTIONS!!
HA HA HA! I LEARNED A NEW TRICK!
EVEN TERRIBLE TORNADO HAS LIMITS!
FORTUNE IS ON MY SIDE!

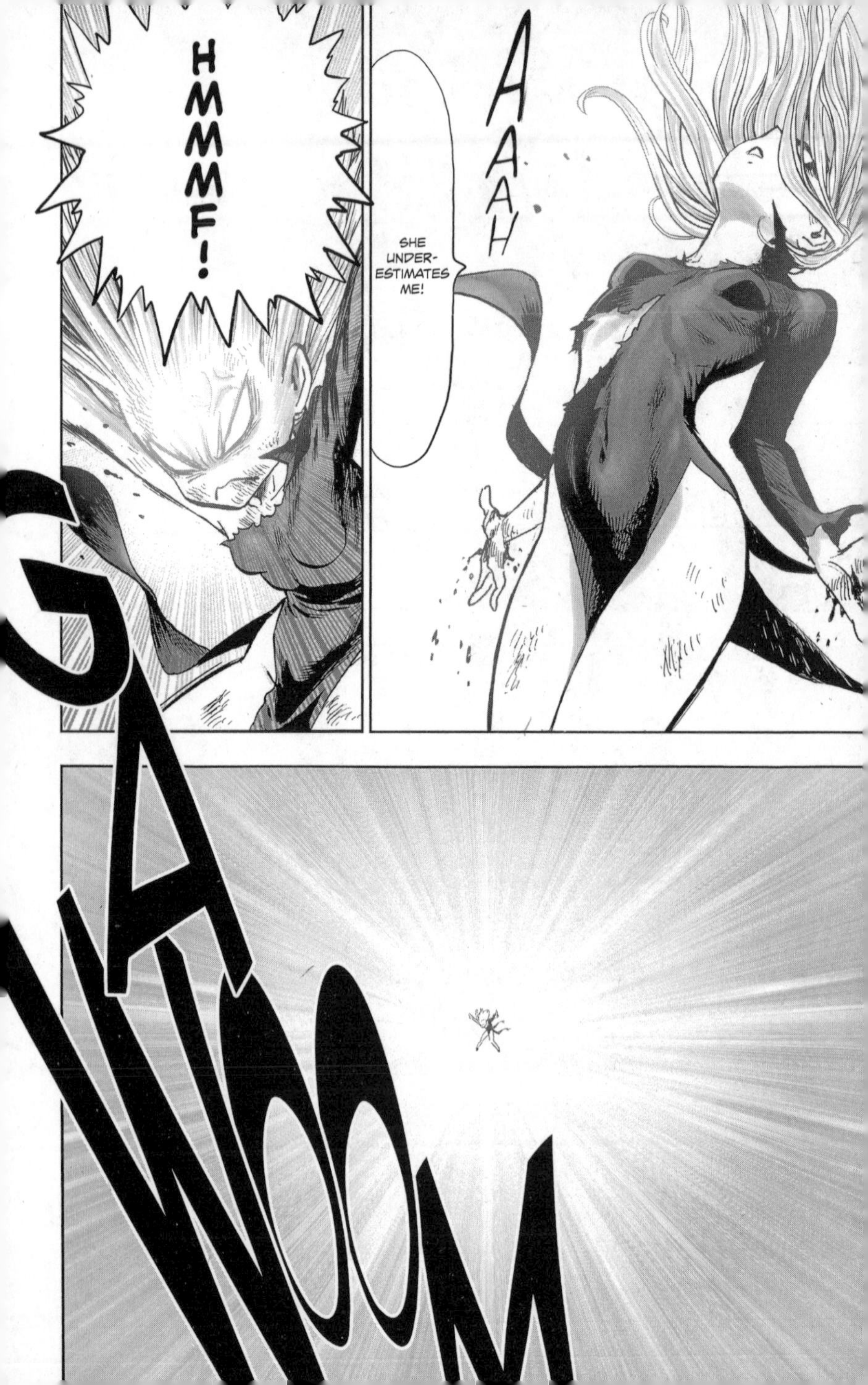
AAAH
SHE UNDER-ESTIMATES ME!
HMMMF!
GAWOOM

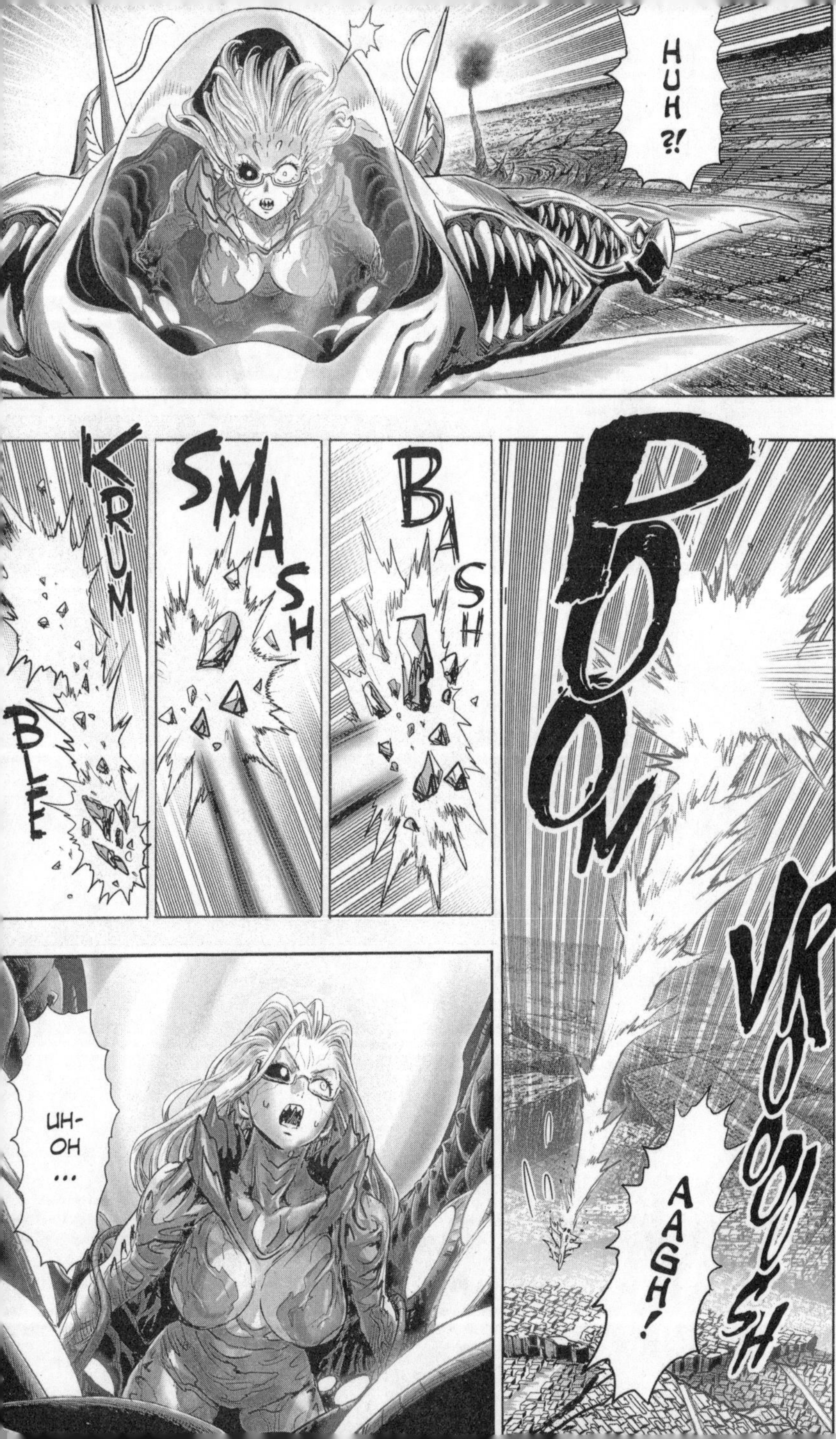
HUH ?!
DOOM
VROOOOSH
AAGH!
BASH
SMASH
KRUMBLE
UH-OH ...

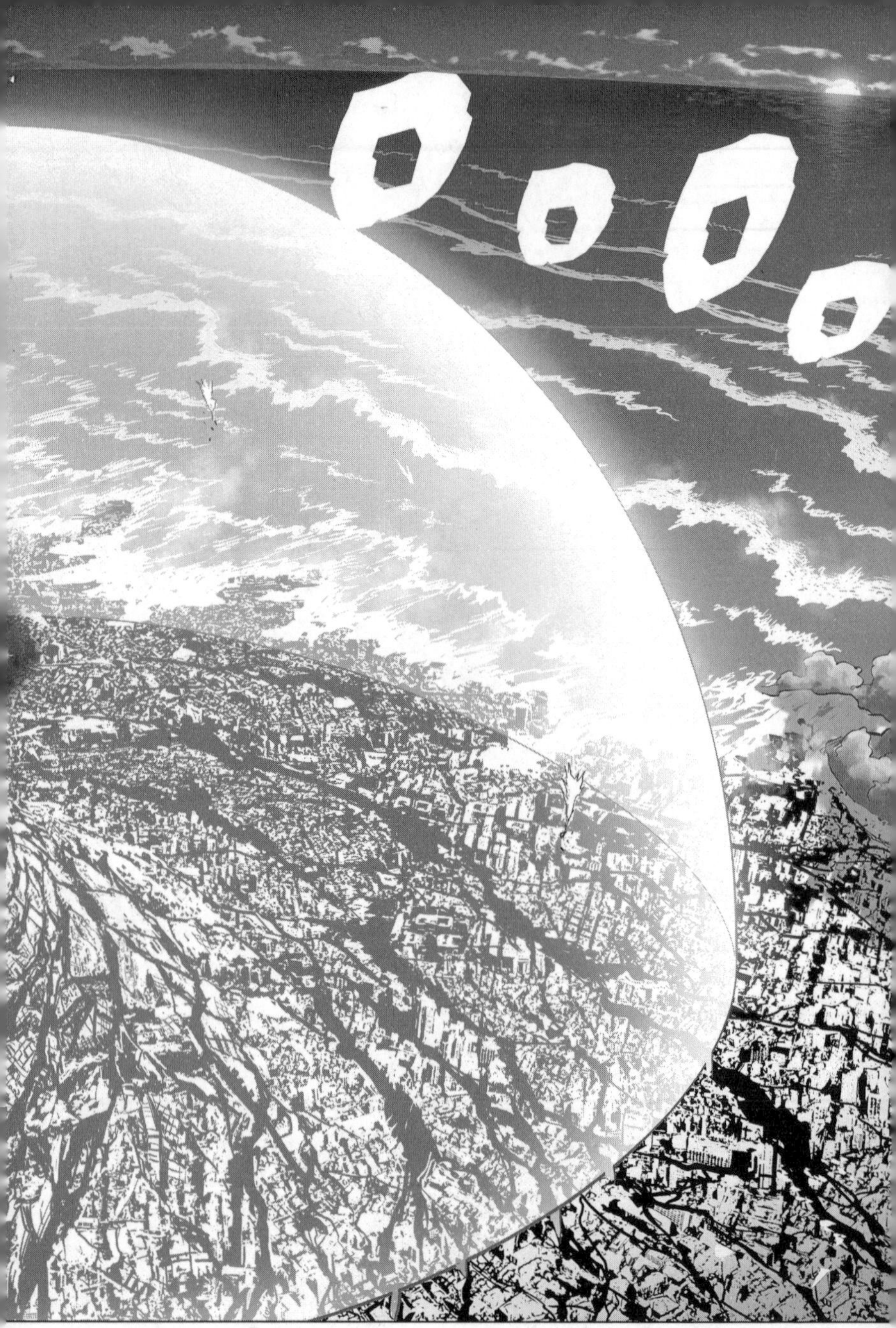
OOOO

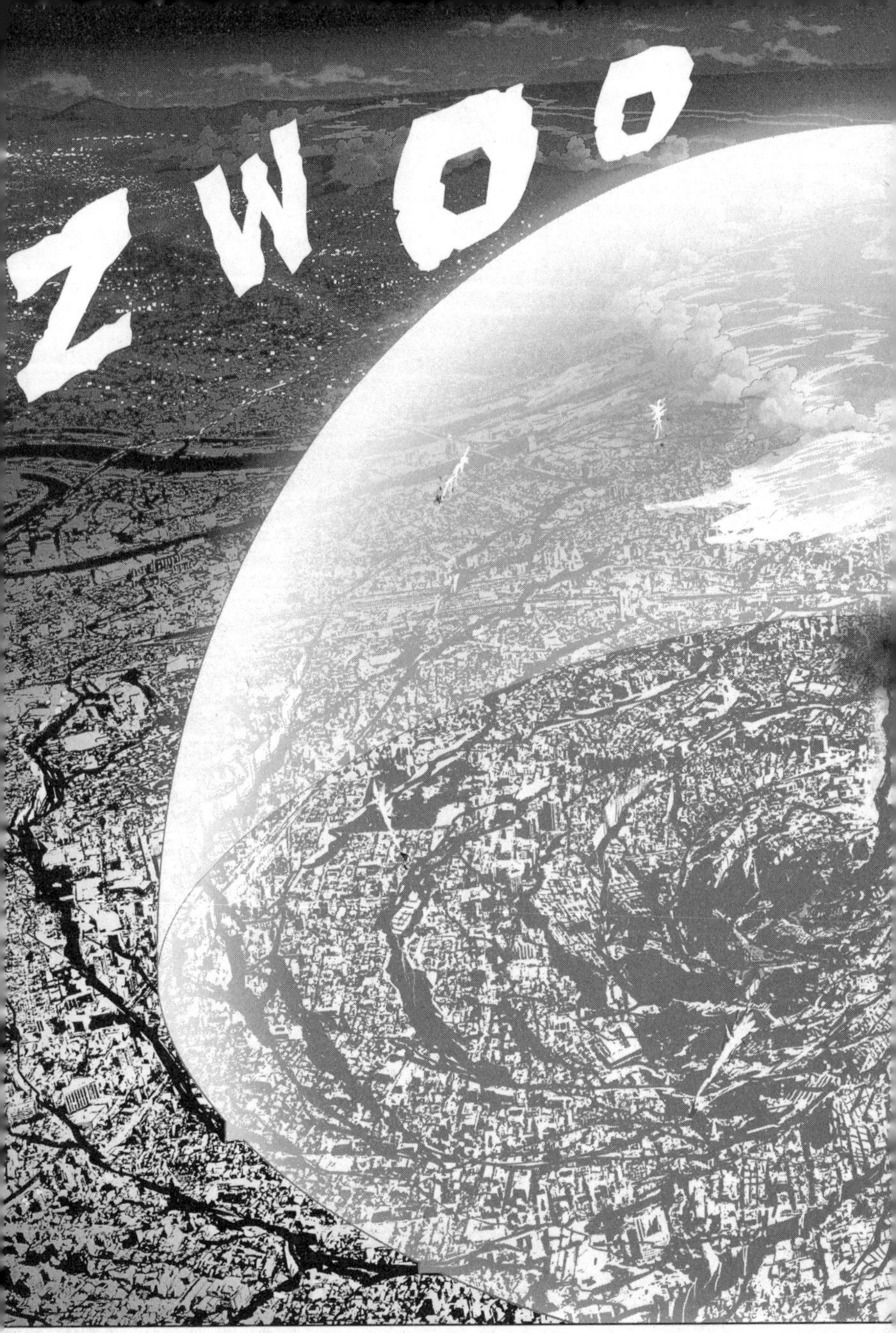
ZWOOO

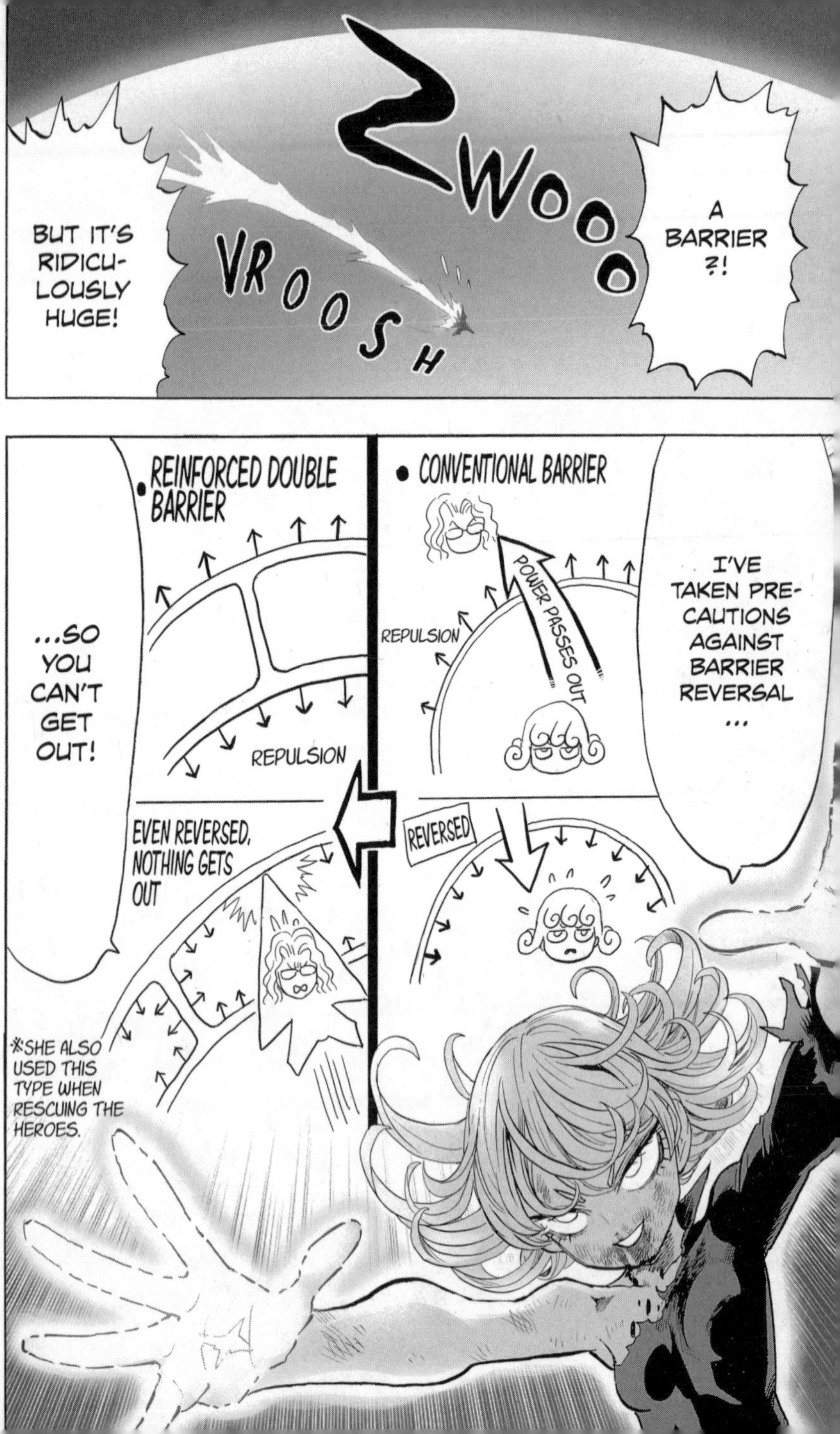
A BARRIER ?!
ZWOOO
VROOSH
BUT IT'S RIDICU-LOUSLY HUGE!
I'VE TAKEN PRE-CAUTIONS AGAINST BARRIER REVERSAL ...
• CONVENTIONAL BARRIER
POWER PASSES OUT
REPULSION
REVERSED
• REINFORCED DOUBLE BARRIER
REPULSION
EVEN REVERSED, NOTHING GETS OUT
...SO YOU CAN'T GET OUT!
※SHE ALSO USED THIS TYPE WHEN RESCUING THE HEROES.

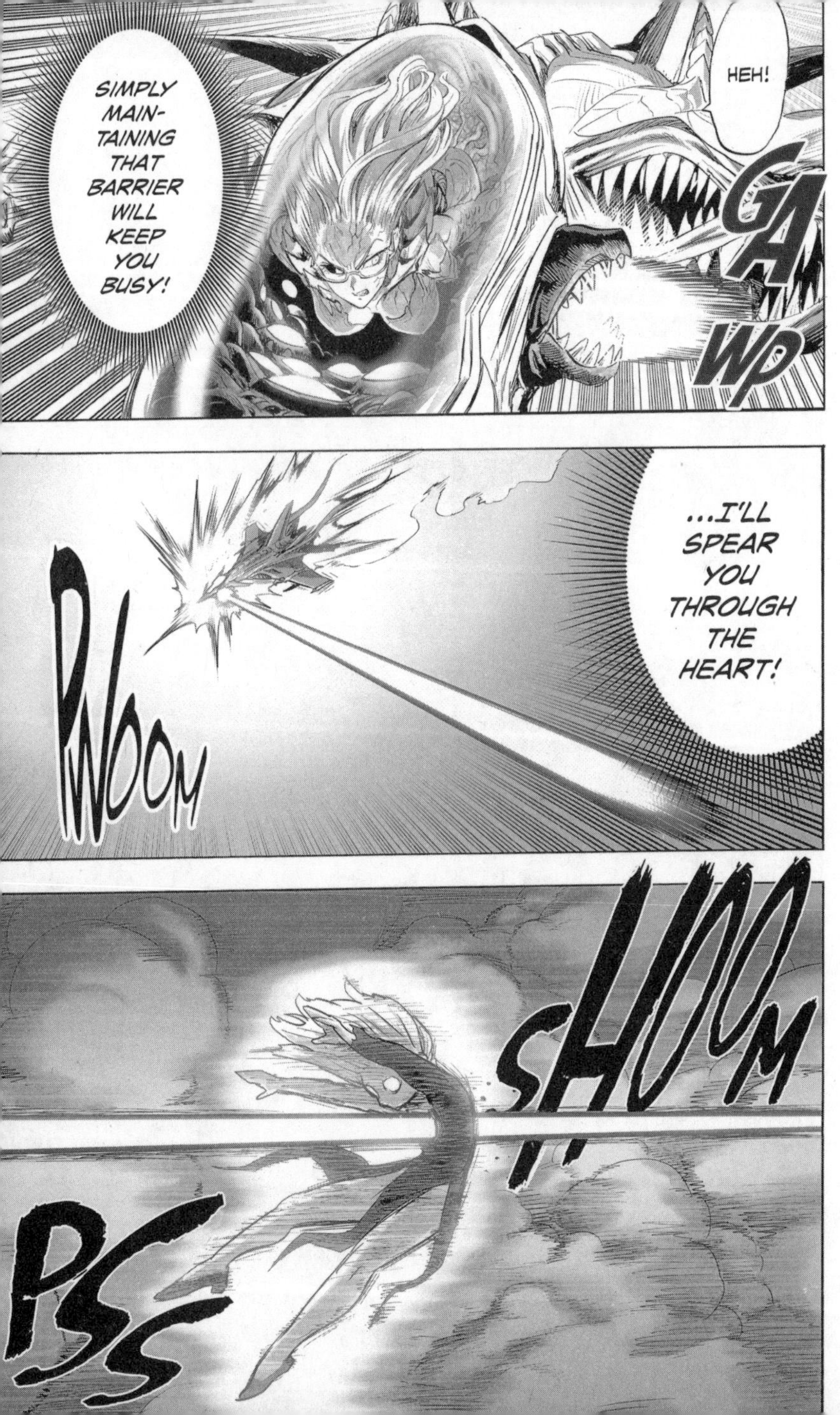
HEH!
GAWP
SIMPLY MAIN-TAINING THAT BARRIER WILL KEEP YOU BUSY!
...I'LL SPEAR YOU THROUGH THE HEART!
PWOOM
SHOOM
PSS

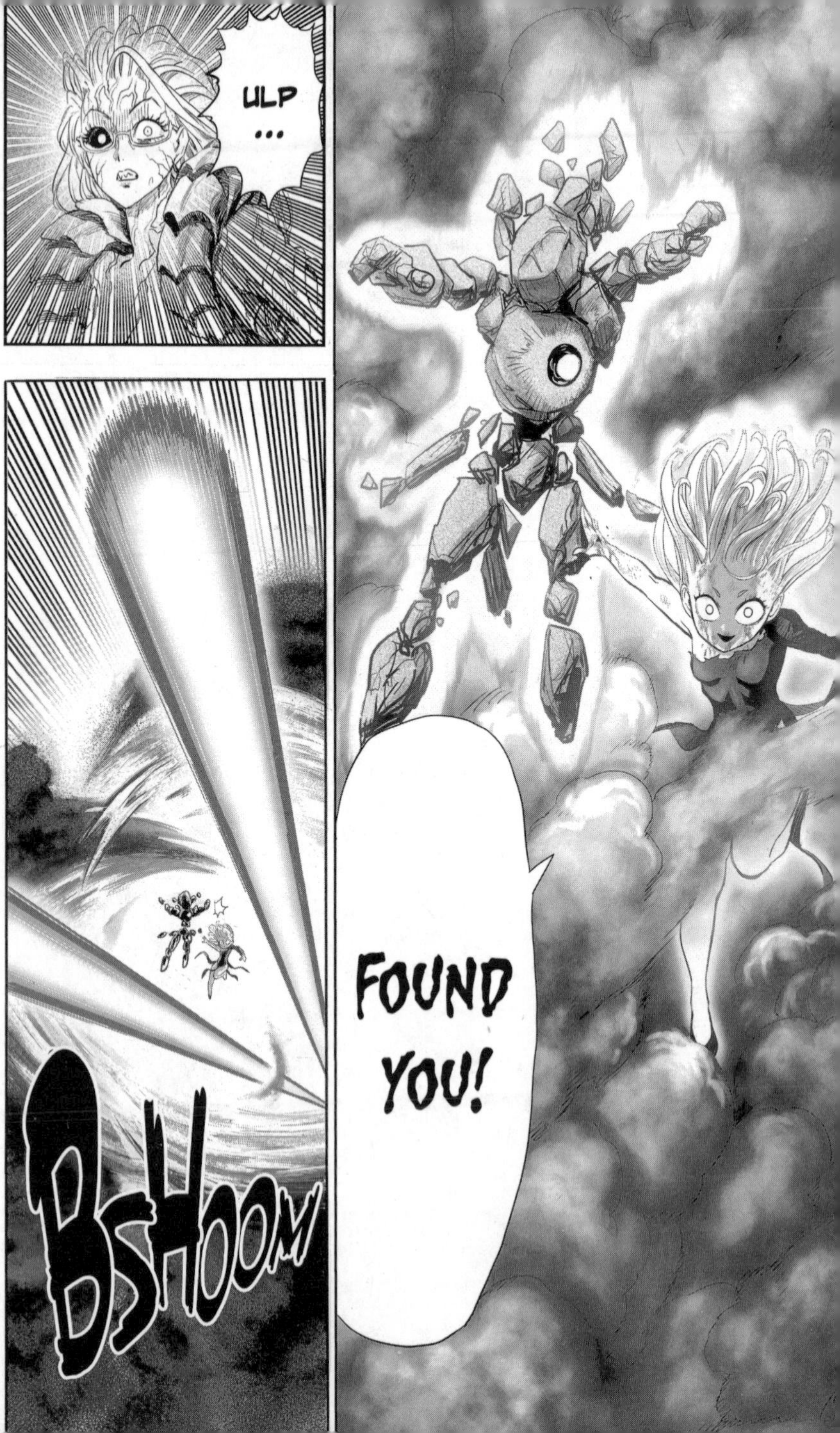
FOUND YOU!
ULP ...
BSHOOM

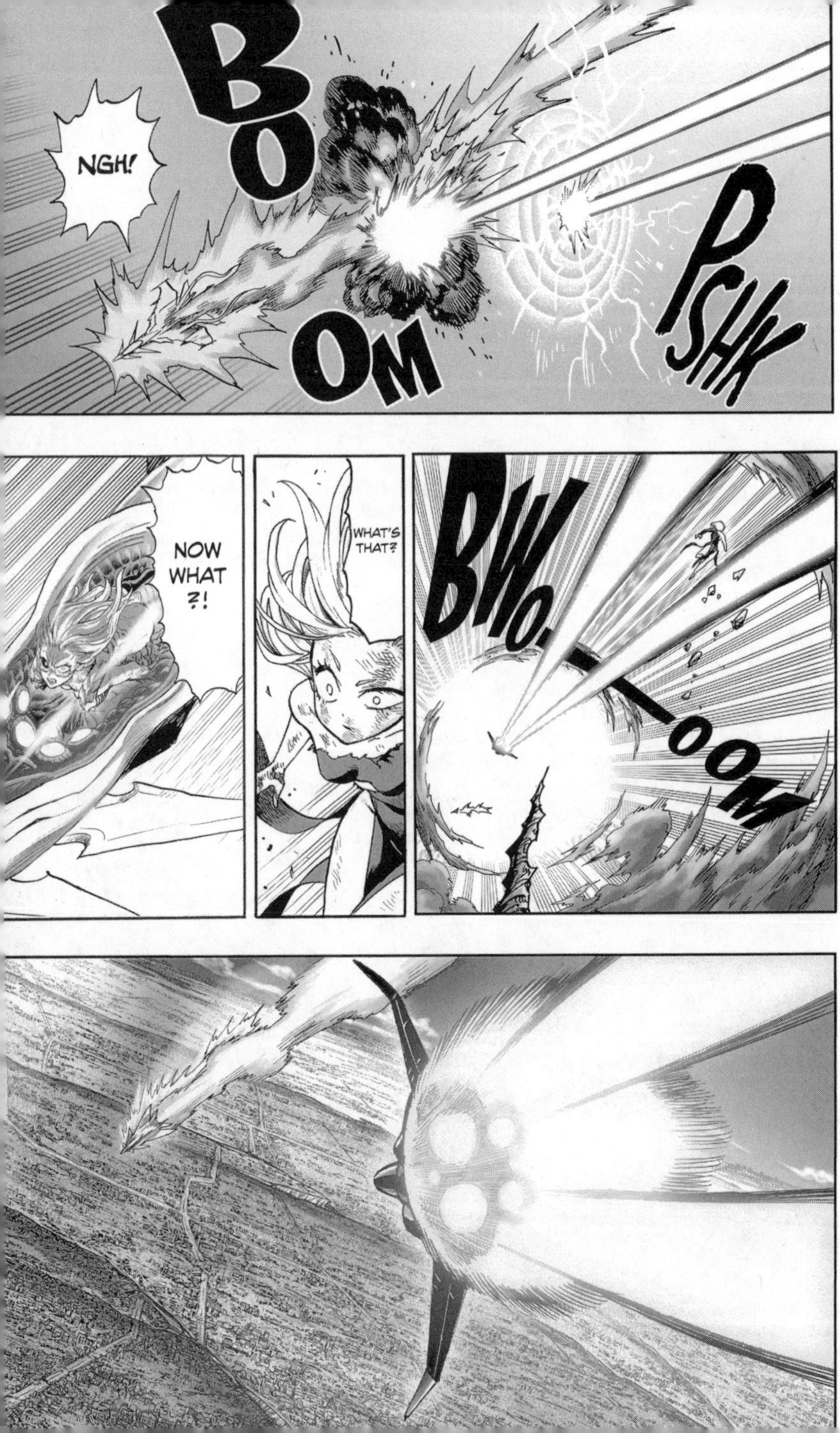
PSHK
BOOM
NGH!
BWOOOM
WHAT'S THAT?
NOW WHAT?!

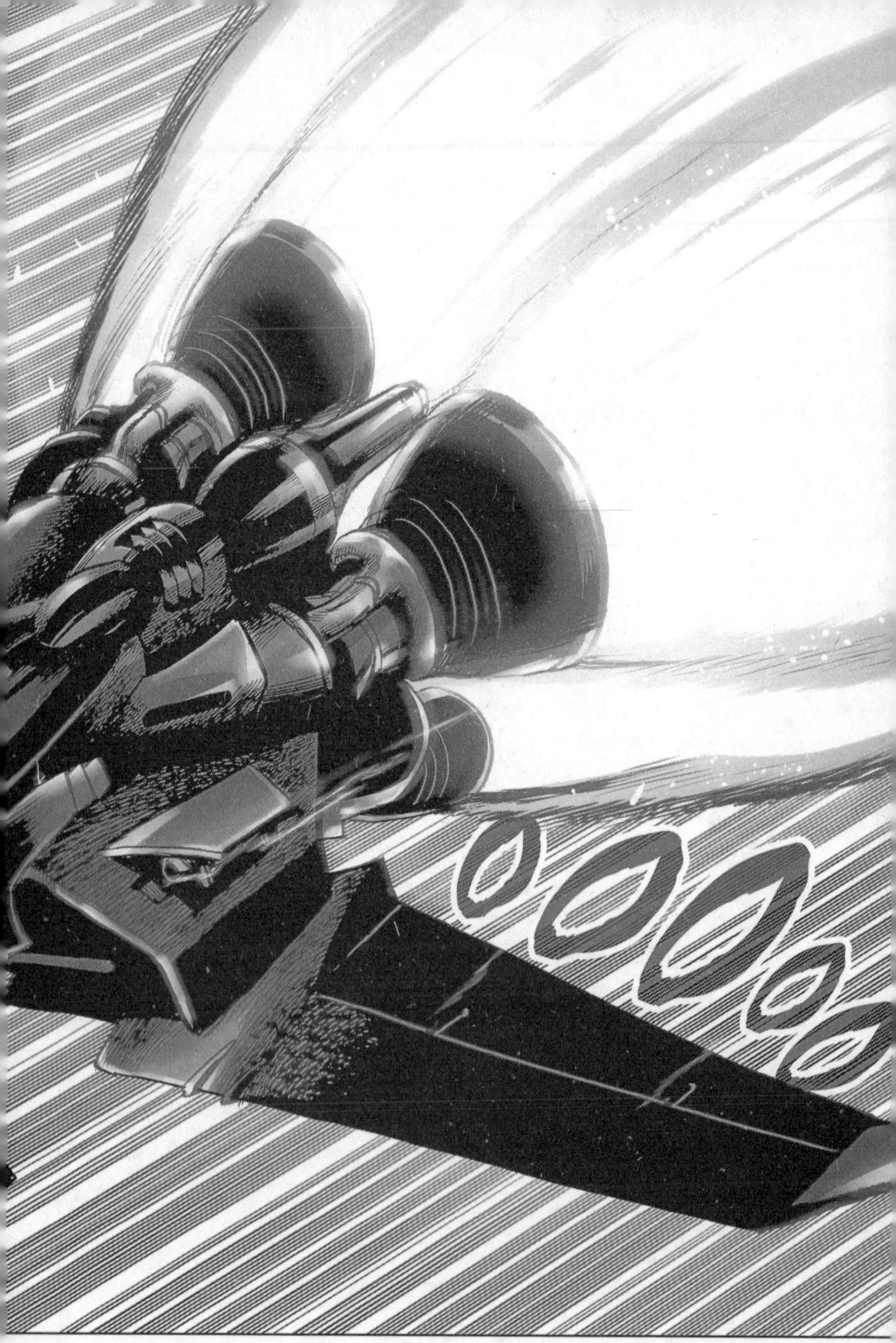

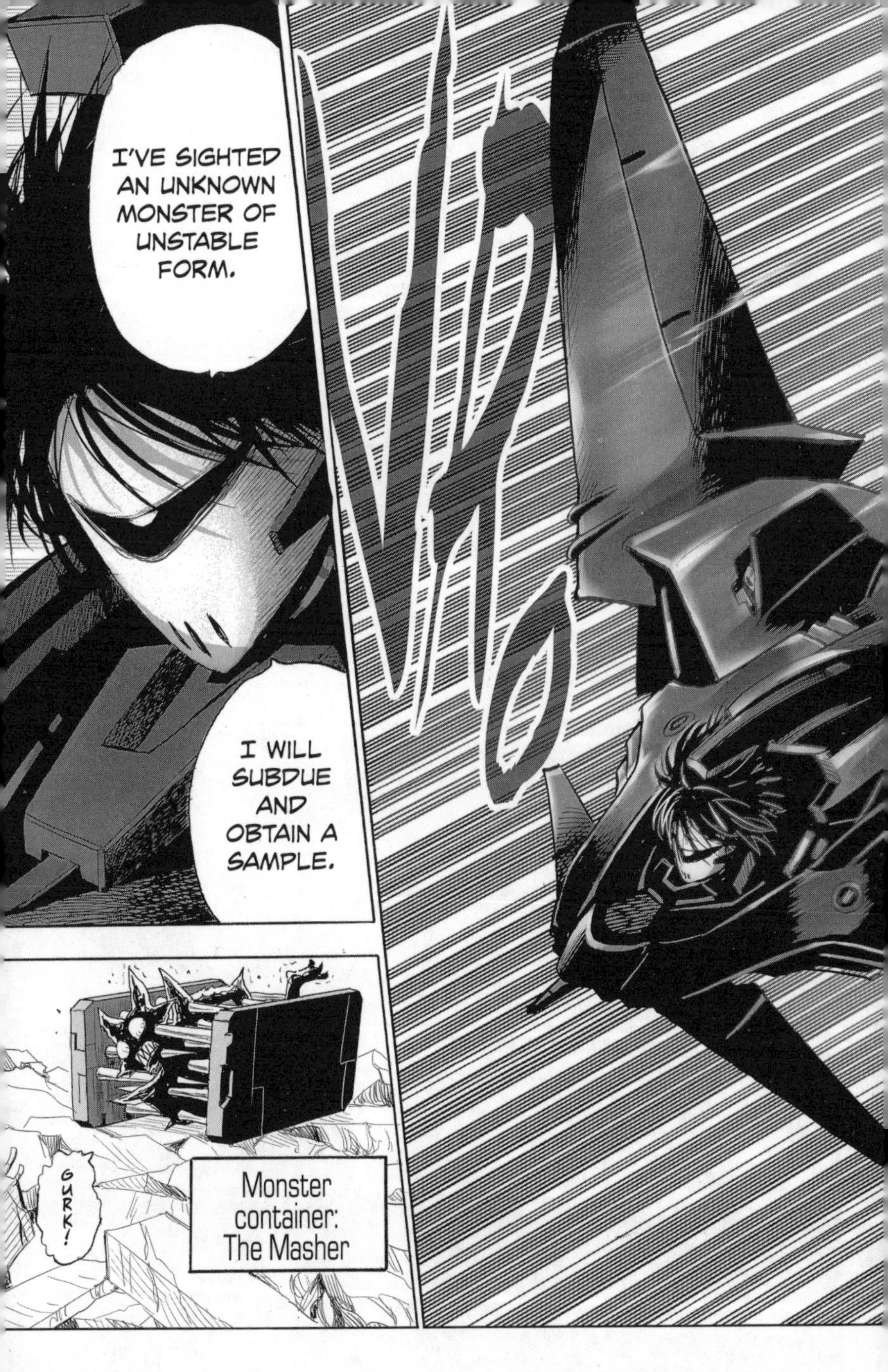
I'VE SIGHTED AN UNKNOWN MONSTER OF UNSTABLE FORM.
I WILL SUBDUE AND OBTAIN A SAMPLE.
Monster container: The Masher
GURK!

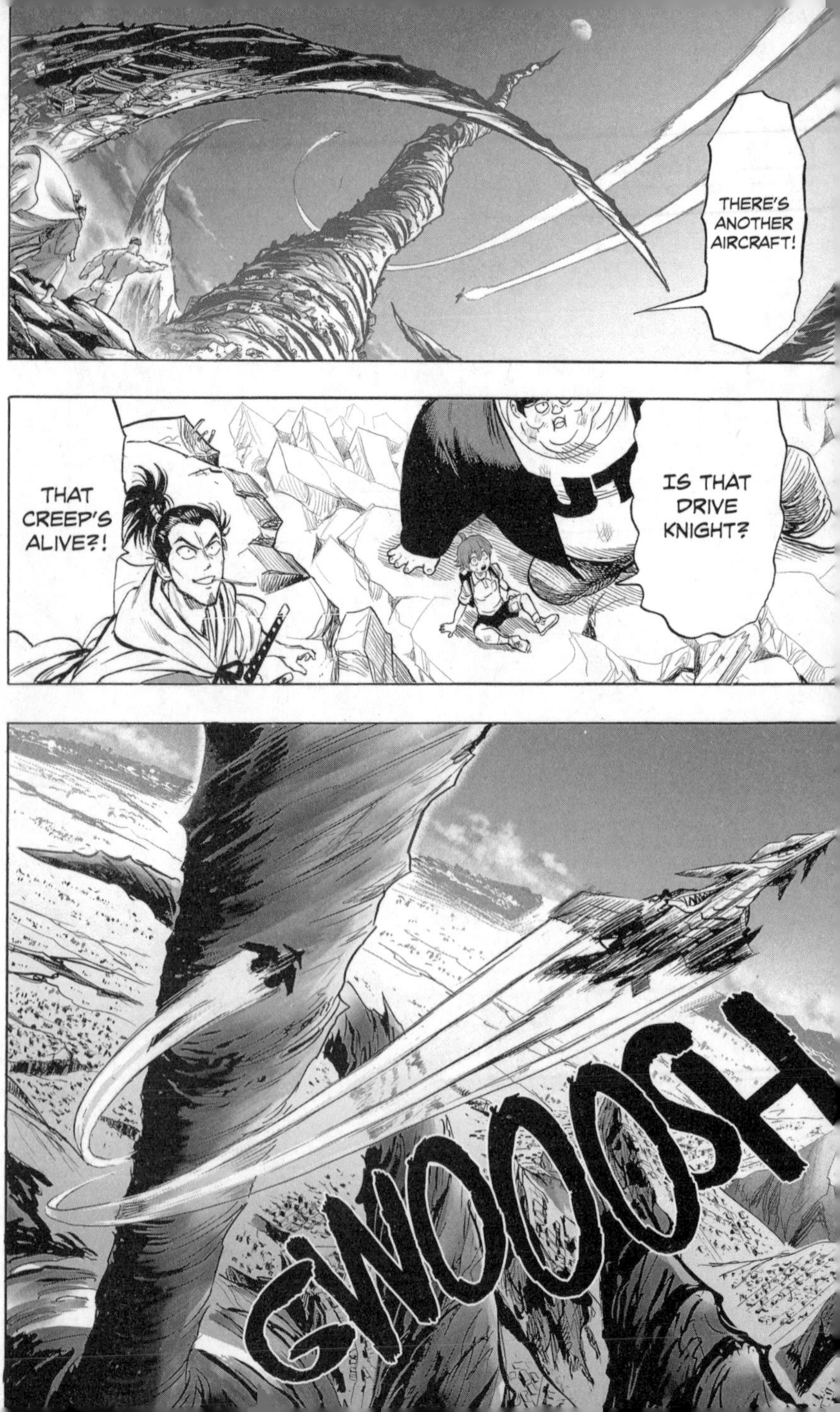
THERE'S ANOTHER AIRCRAFT!
IS THAT DRIVE KNIGHT?
THAT CREEP'S ALIVE?!
GWOOOSH

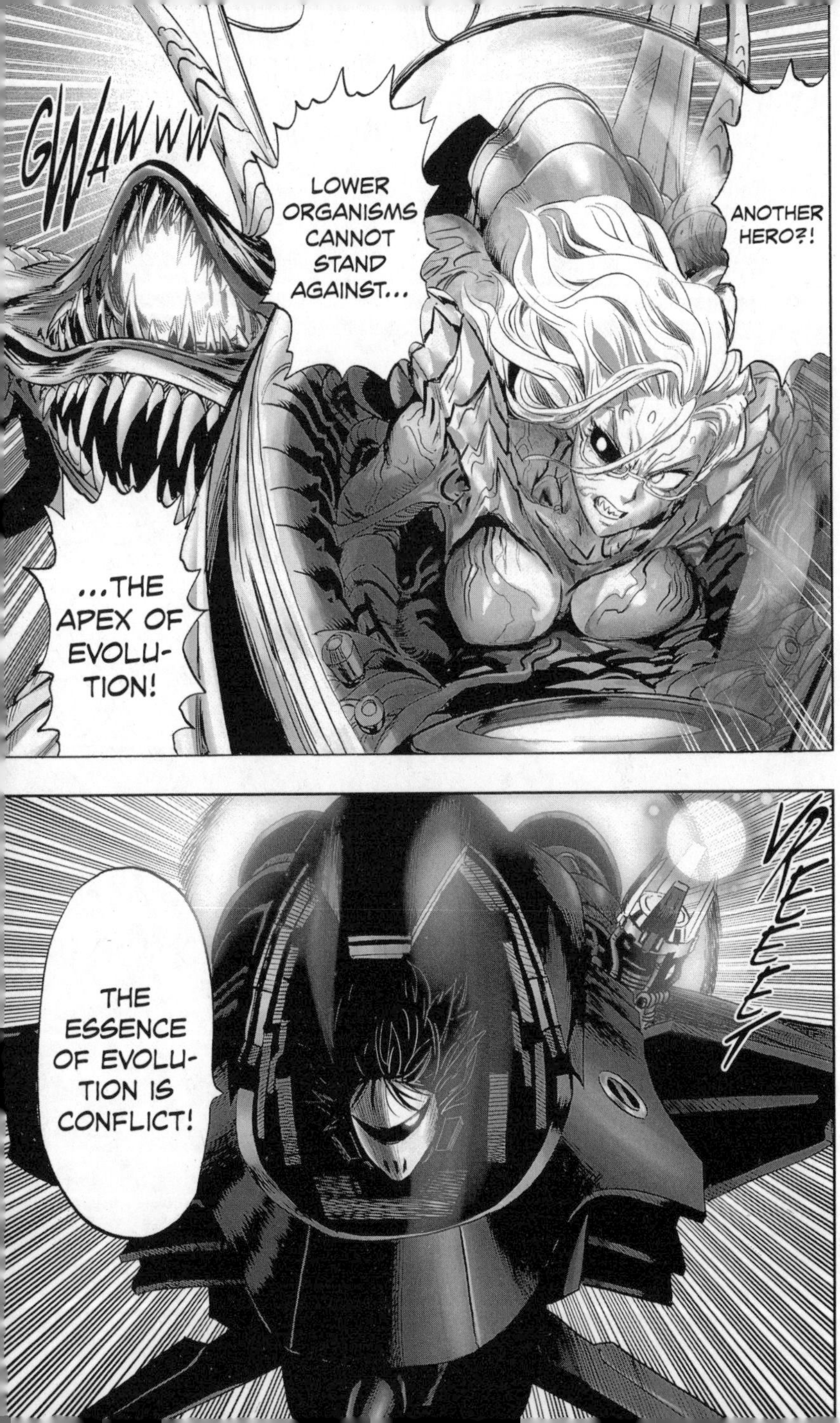
ANOTHER HERO?!
LOWER ORGANISMS CANNOT STAND AGAINST...
GWAWWW
...THE APEX OF EVOLU-TION!
THE ESSENCE OF EVOLU-TION IS CONFLICT!

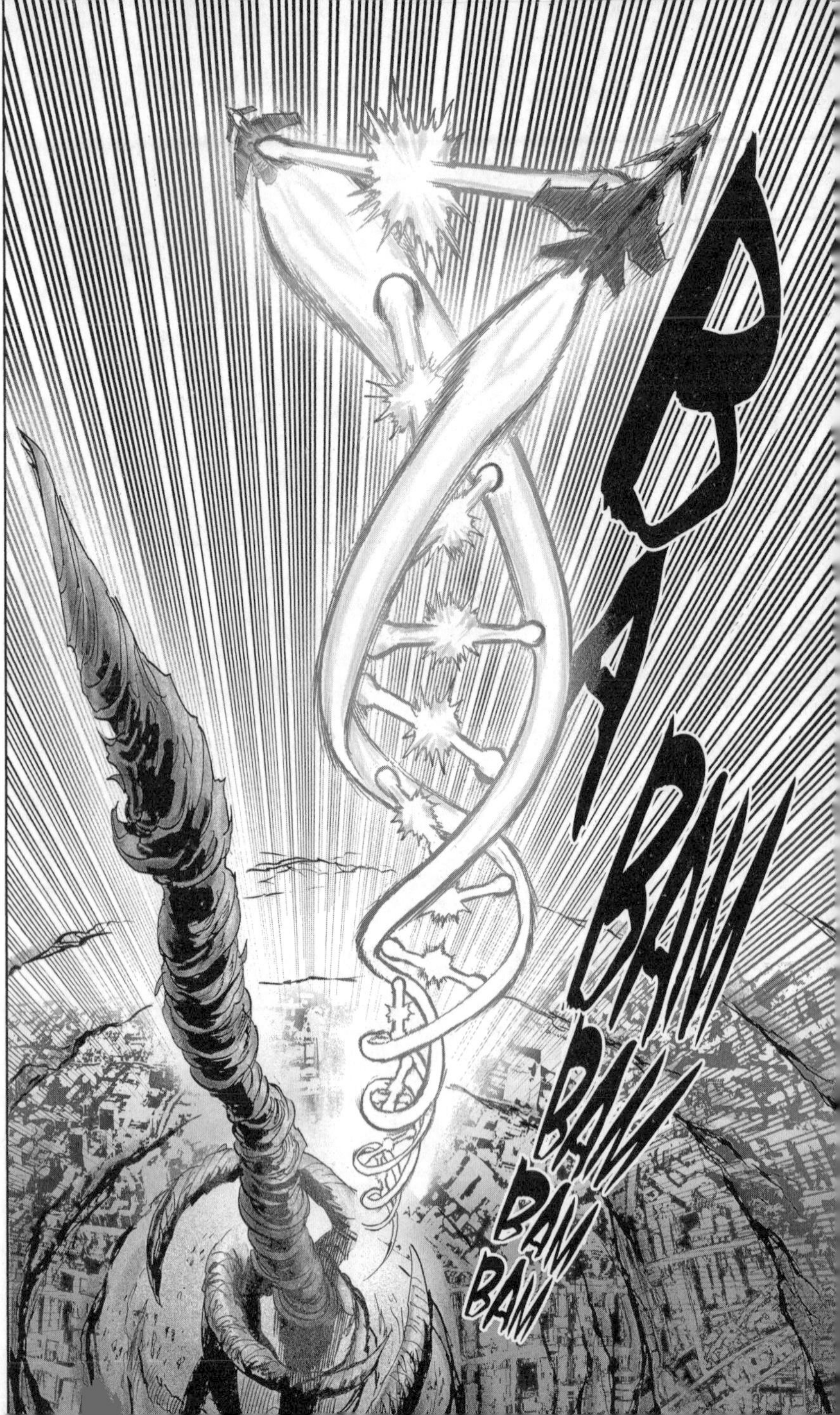
BABAM
BAM
BAM
BAM
BAM

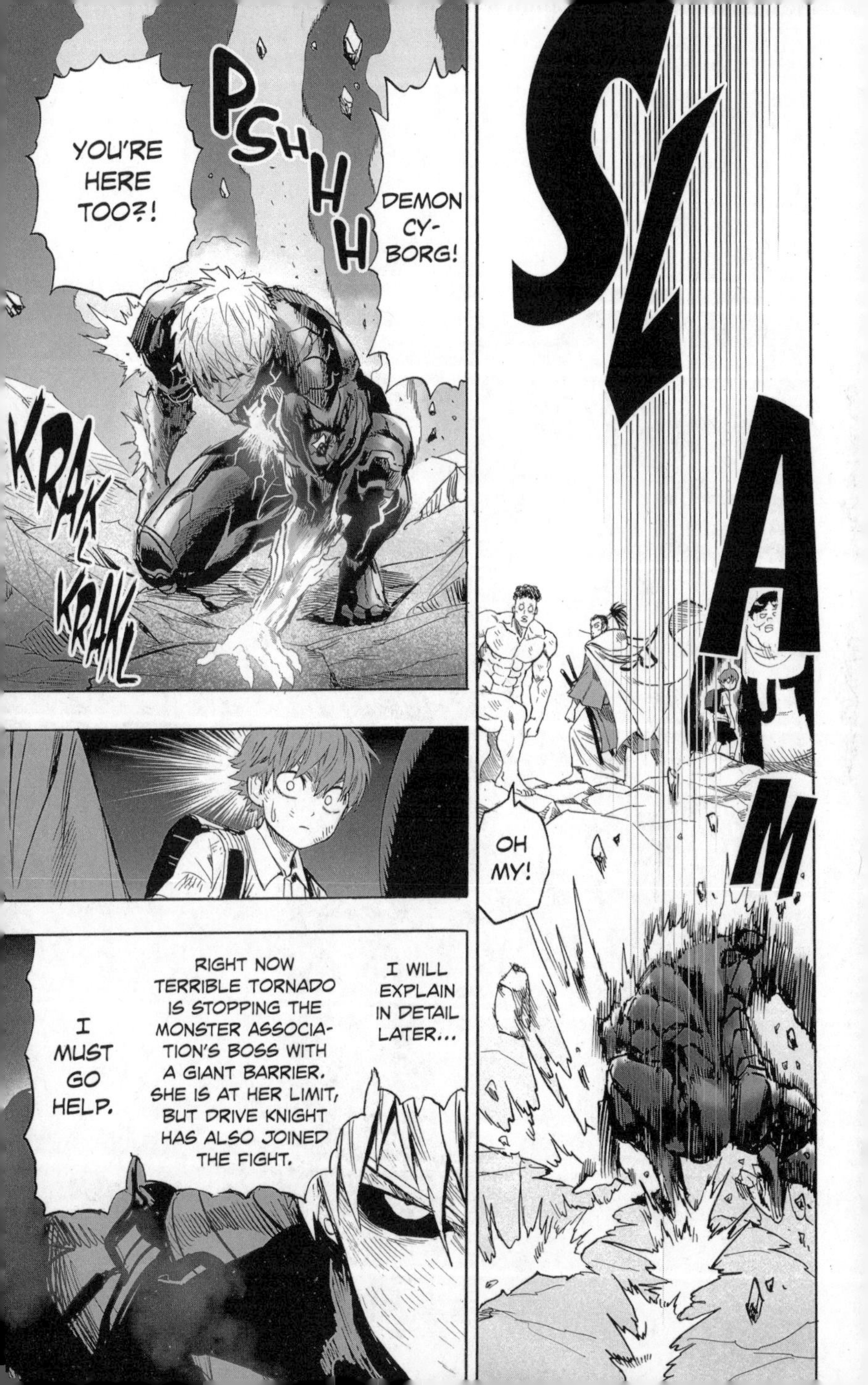
SLAM
OH MY!
DEMON CY-BORG!
PSHHH
YOU'RE HERE TOO?!
KRAKL
KRAKL
I WILL EXPLAIN IN DETAIL LATER...
RIGHT NOW TERRIBLE TORNADO IS STOPPING THE MONSTER ASSOCIA-TION'S BOSS WITH A GIANT BARRIER. SHE IS AT HER LIMIT, BUT DRIVE KNIGHT HAS ALSO JOINED THE FIGHT.
I MUST GO HELP.

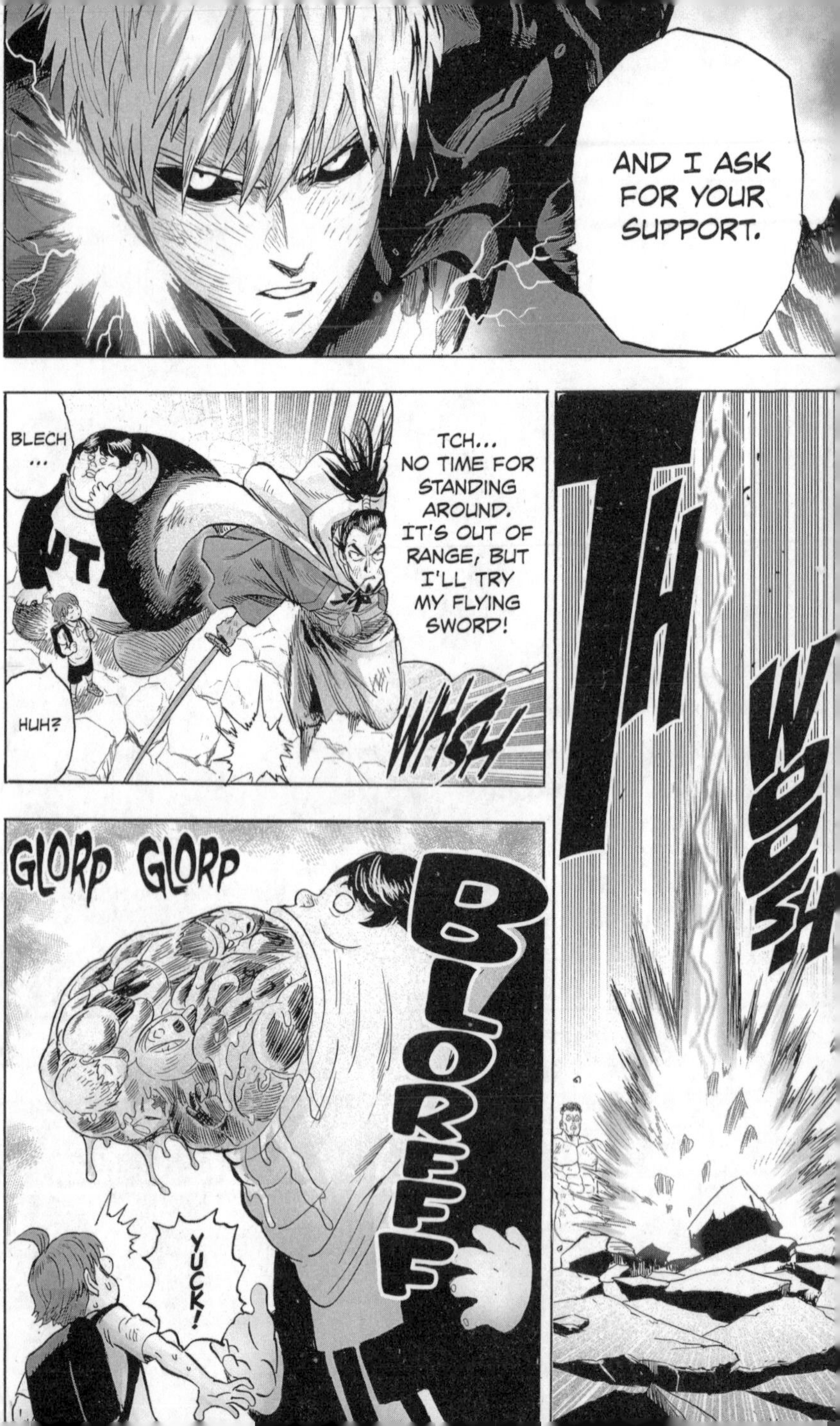
AND I ASK FOR YOUR SUPPORT.
WHOOSH
TCH... NO TIME FOR STANDING AROUND. IT'S OUT OF RANGE, BUT I'LL TRY MY FLYING SWORD!
BLECH ...
WHSH
HUH?
GLORP GLORP
BLORFFF
YUCK!

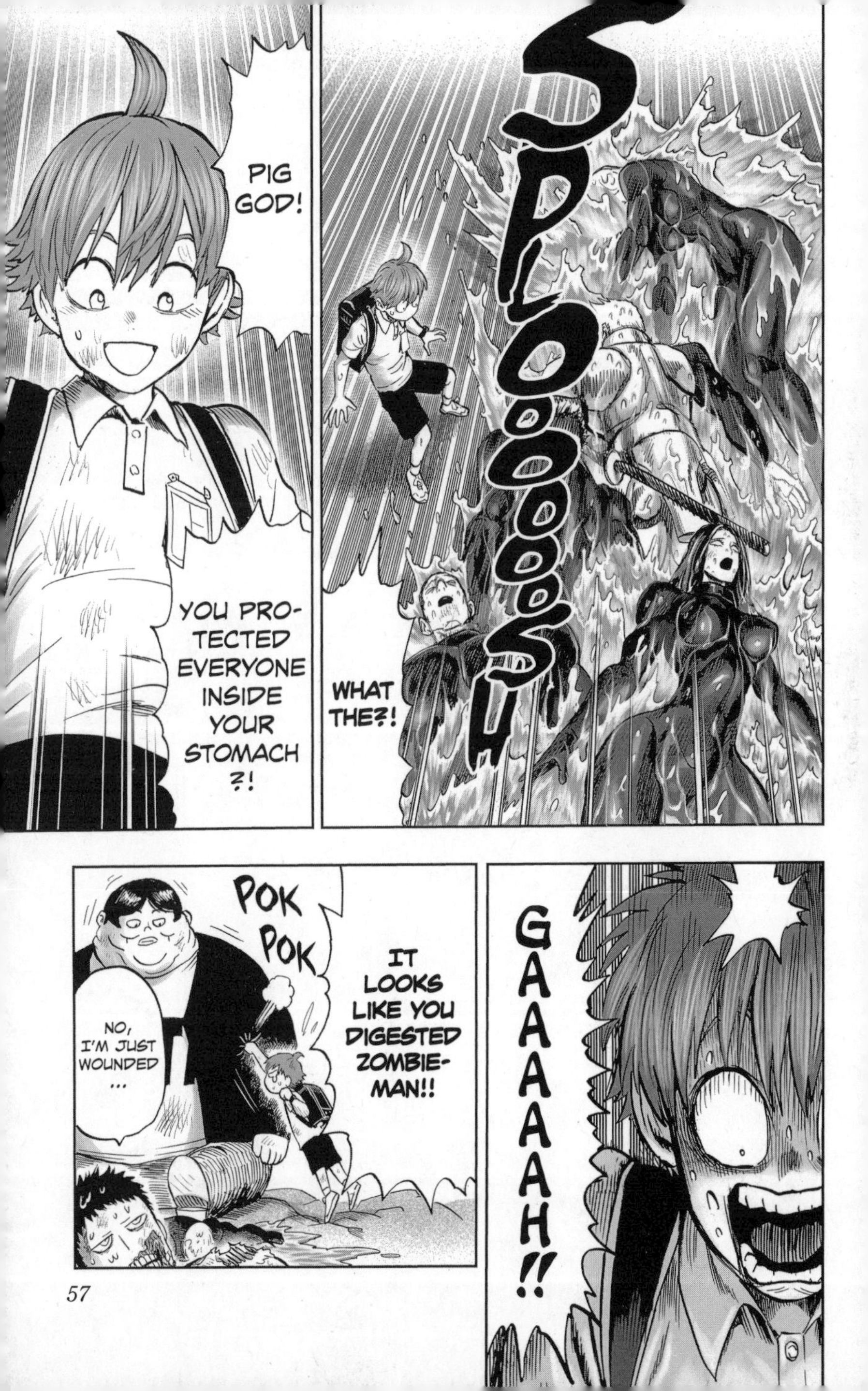
SPLOOOOOOSH
WHAT THE?!
PIG GOD!
YOU PROTECTED EVERYONE INSIDE YOUR STOMACH?!
GAAAAAAH!!
POK POK
IT LOOKS LIKE YOU DIGESTED ZOMBIE-MAN!!
NO, I'M JUST WOUNDED...

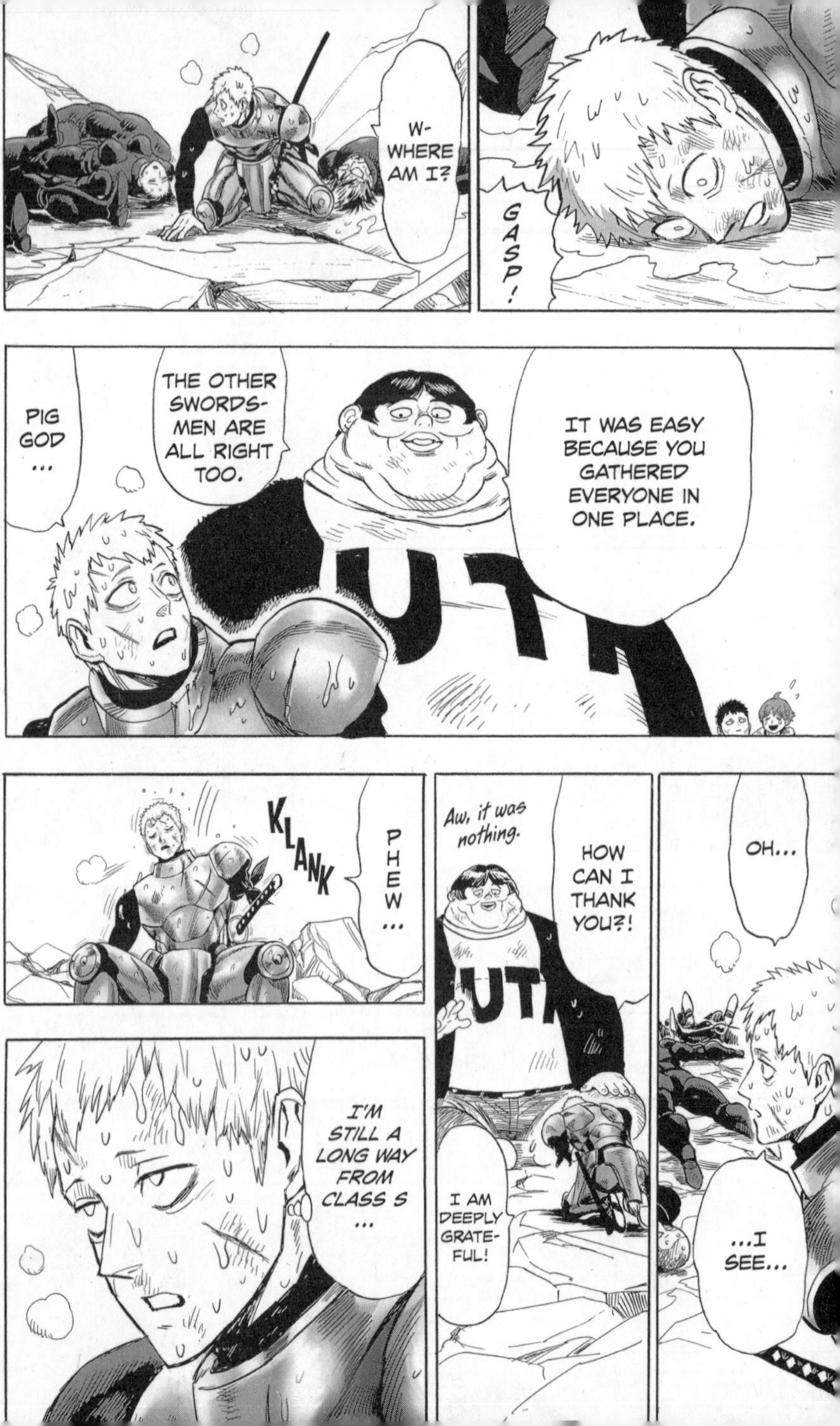
GASP!
W- WHERE AM I?
IT WAS EASY BECAUSE YOU GATHERED EVERYONE IN ONE PLACE.
THE OTHER SWORDS- MEN ARE ALL RIGHT TOO.
PIG GOD ...
OH...
...I SEE...
HOW CAN I THANK YOU?!
Aw, it was nothing.
I AM DEEPLY GRATE- FUL!
PHEW ...
KLANK
I'M STILL A LONG WAY FROM CLASS S ...

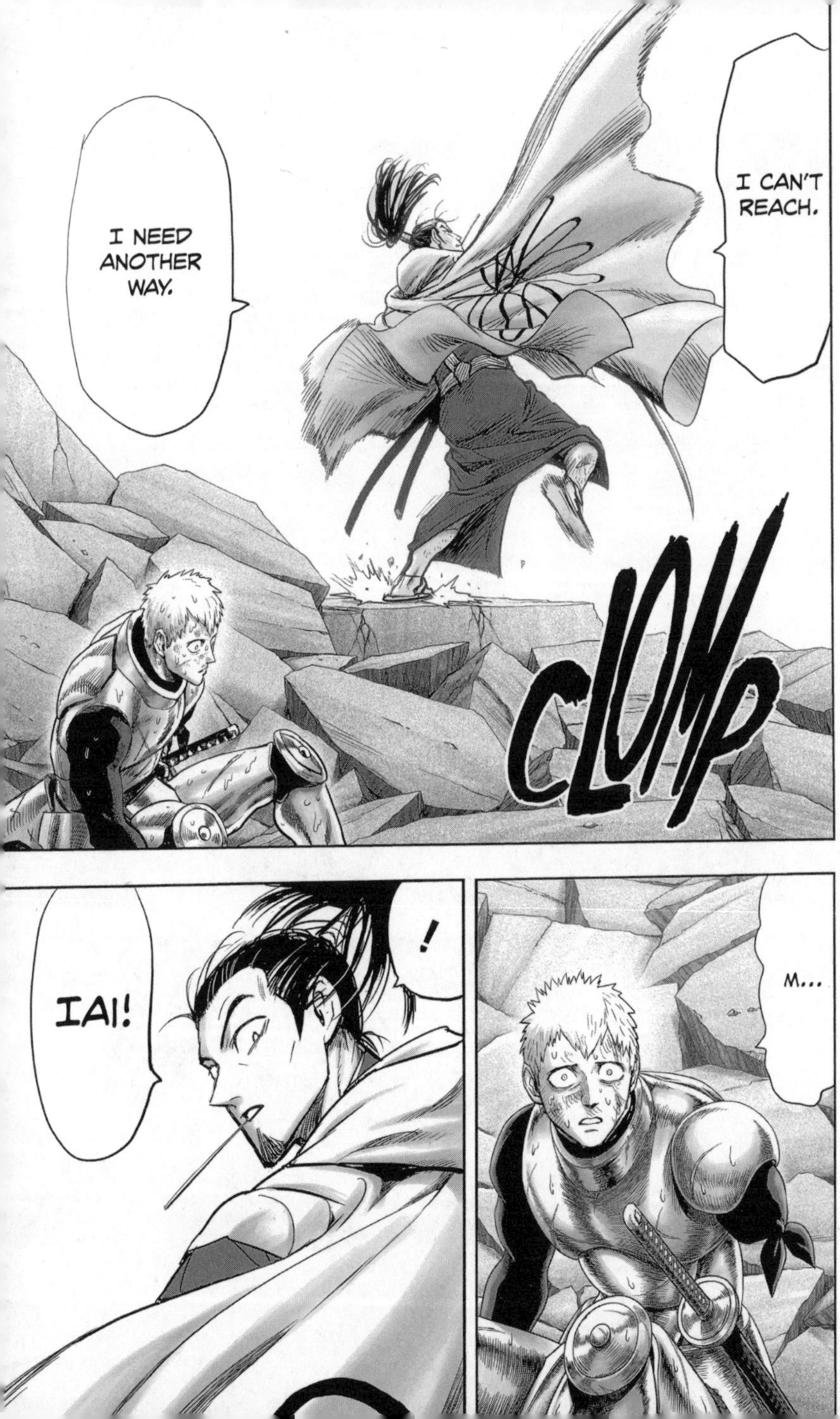
I CAN'T REACH.
I NEED ANOTHER WAY.
CLUMP
M...
!
IAI!

MASTER!

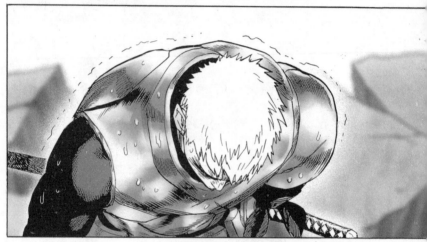

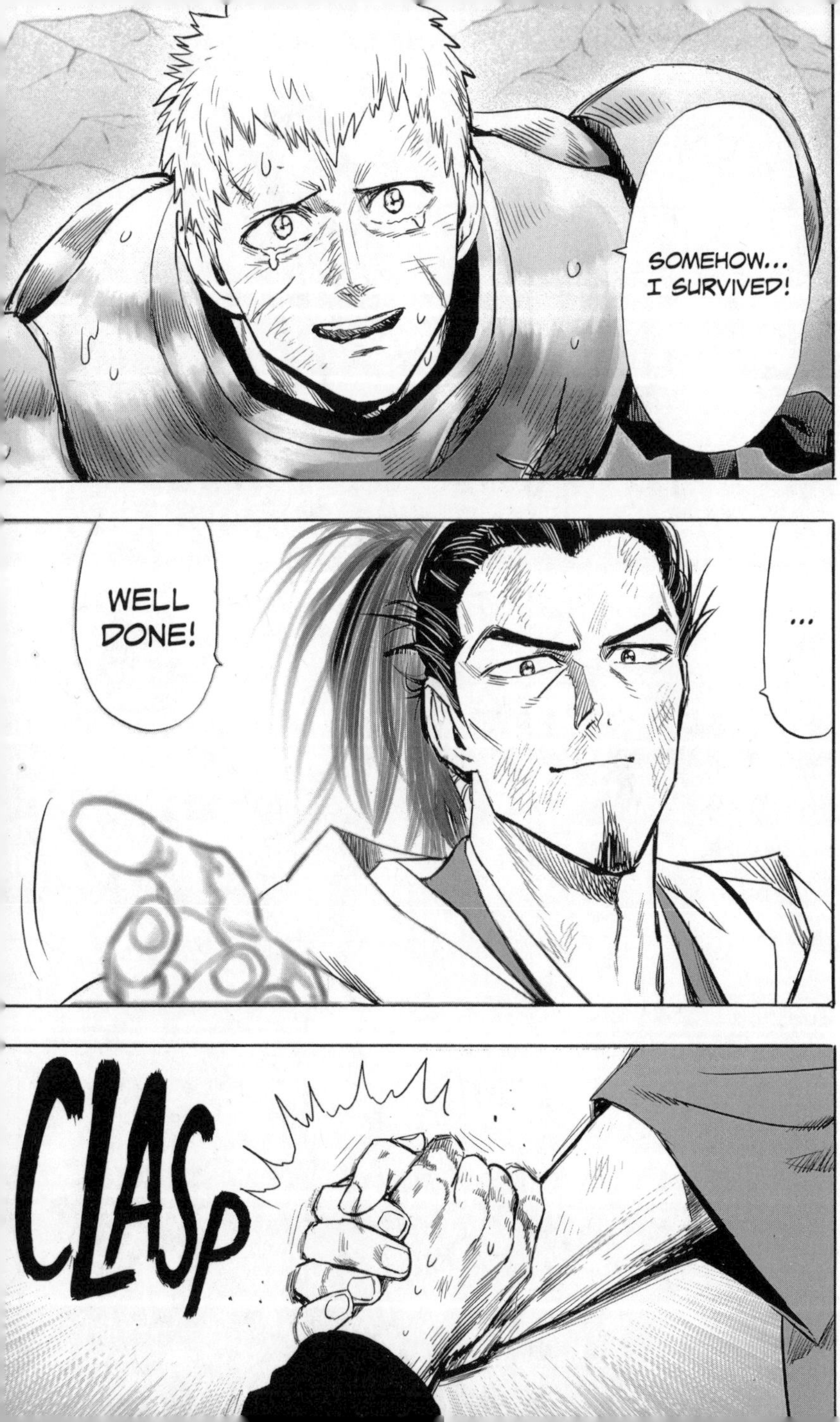
SOMEHOW... I SURVIVED!
...
WELL DONE!
CLASP

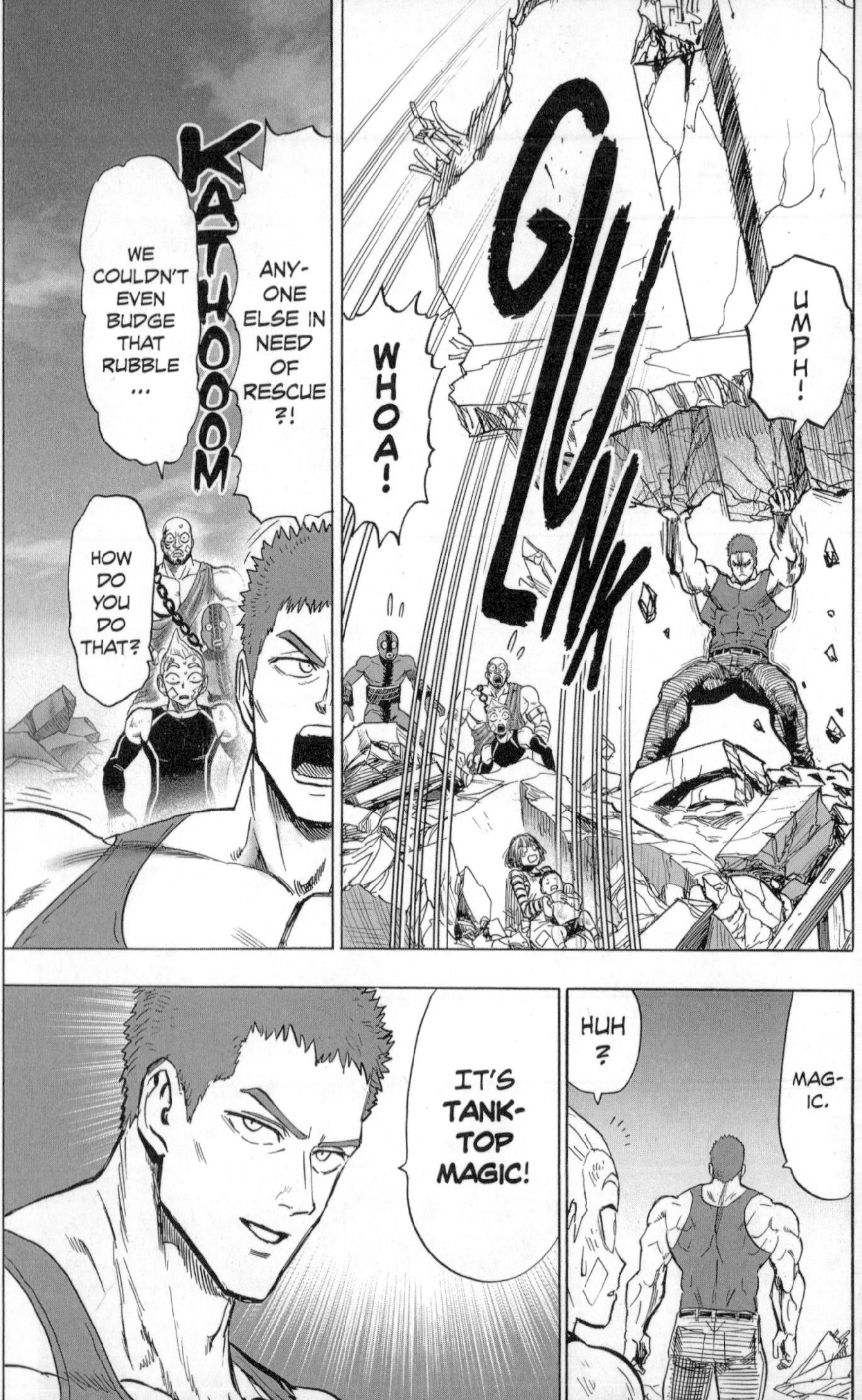
UMPH!
GUNK
WHOA!
ANY-ONE ELSE IN NEED OF RESCUE?!
KATHOOOM
WE COULDN'T EVEN BUDGE THAT RUBBLE...
HOW DO YOU DO THAT?
MAG-IC.
HUH?
IT'S TANK-TOP MAGIC!

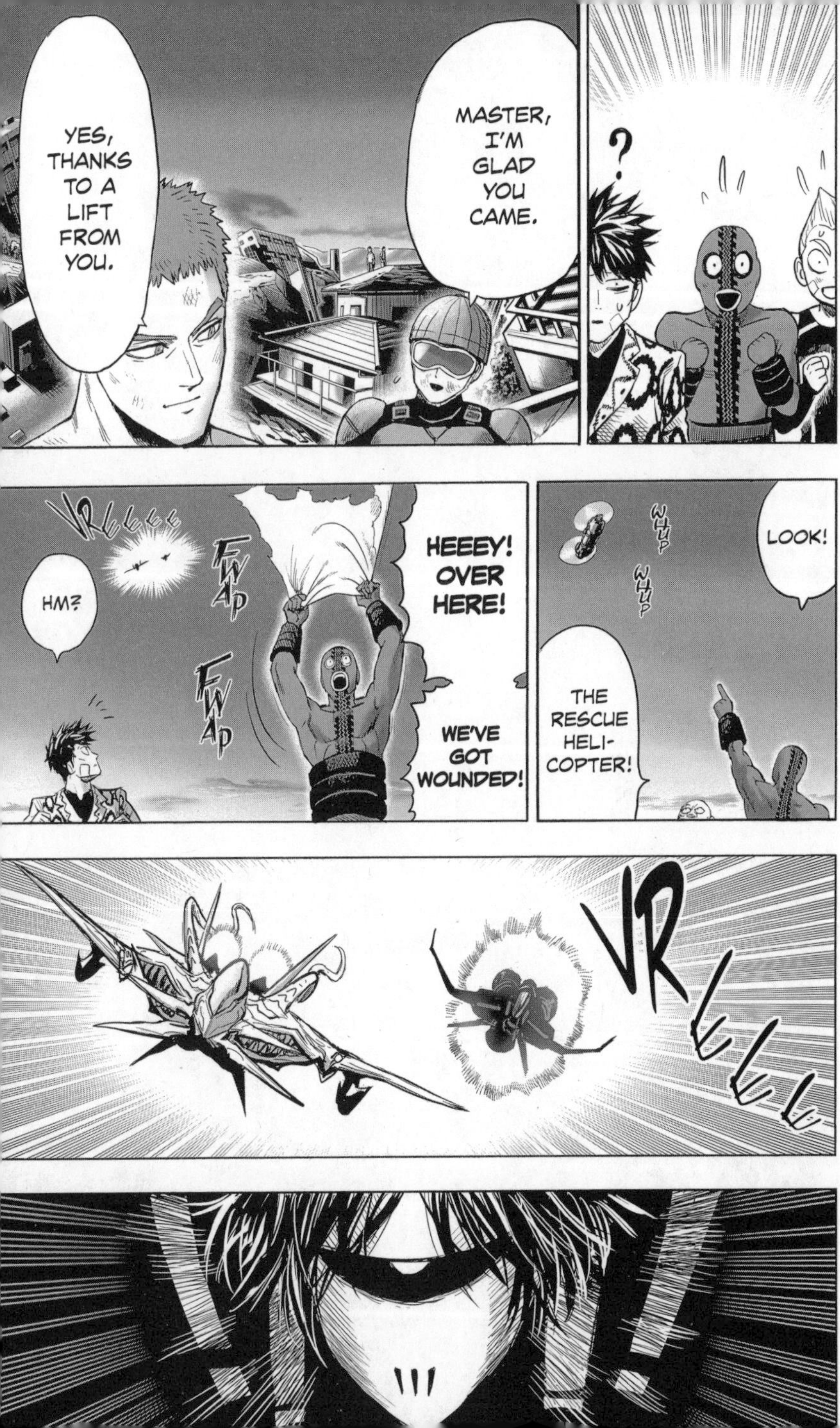
?
MASTER, I'M GLAD YOU CAME.
YES, THANKS TO A LIFT FROM YOU.
LOOK!
WHUP
WHUP
THE RESCUE HELI-COPTER!
HEEEY! OVER HERE!
WE'VE GOT WOUNDED!
FWAP
FWAP
VREEEE
HM?
VREEEE

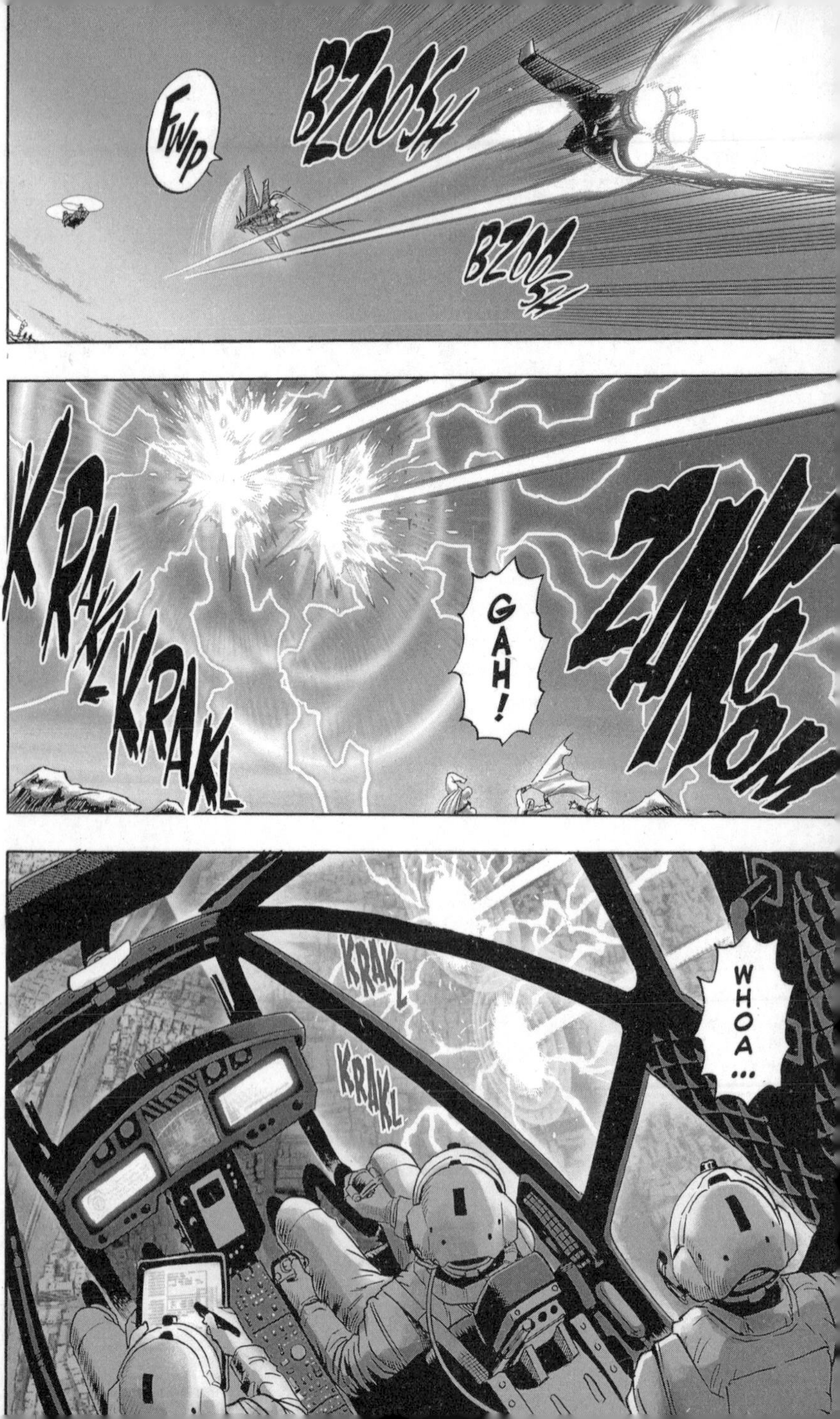
BZOOSH
FWIP
BZOOSH
ZAKOOM
GAH!
KRAKL
KRAKL
WHOA...
KRAKL
KRAKL

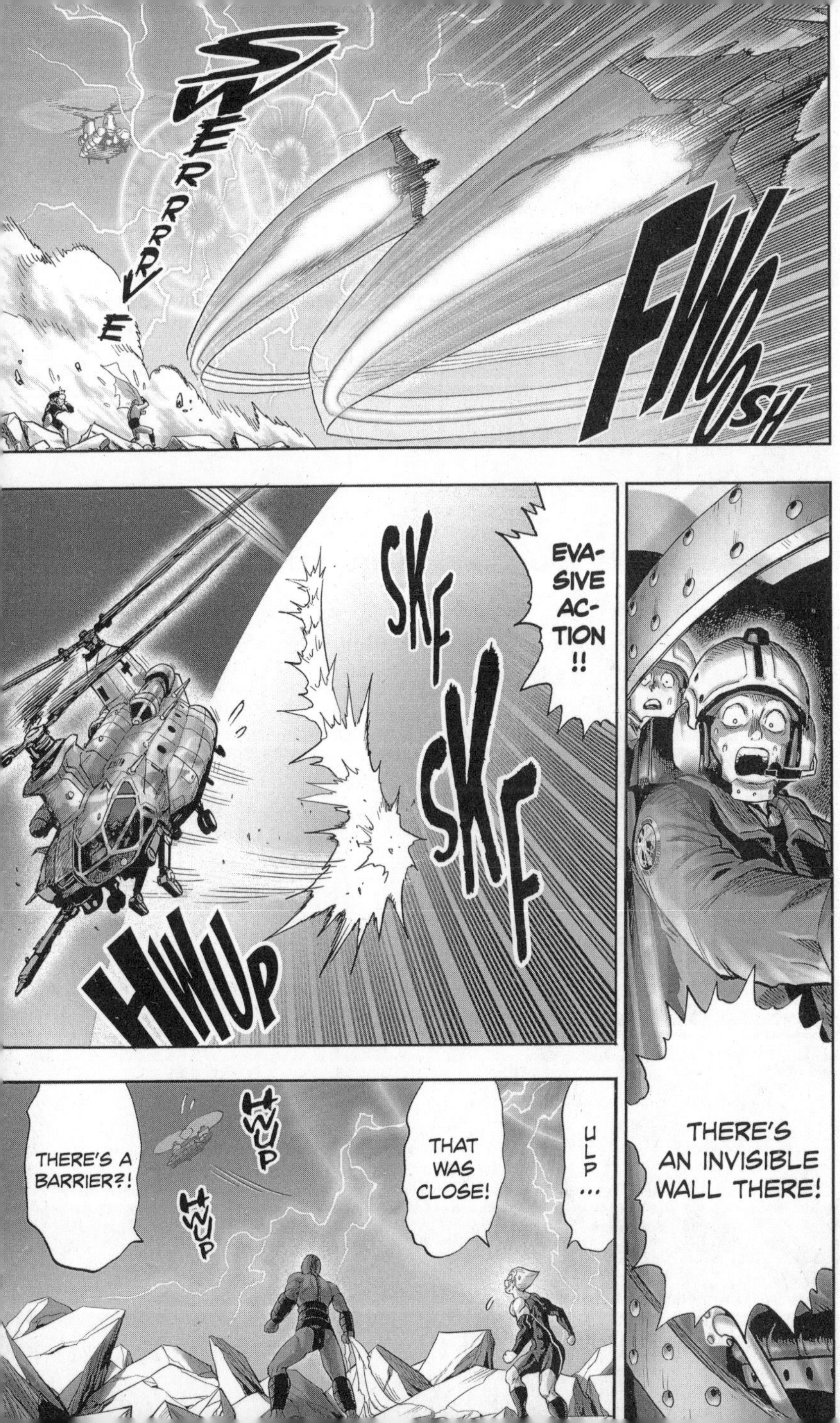
SWERRRRVE
FWOOSH
THERE'S AN INVISIBLE WALL THERE!
EVA-SIVE AC-TION!!
SKF
SKF
HWUP
ULP...
THAT WAS CLOSE!
HWUP
HWUP
THERE'S A BARRIER?!

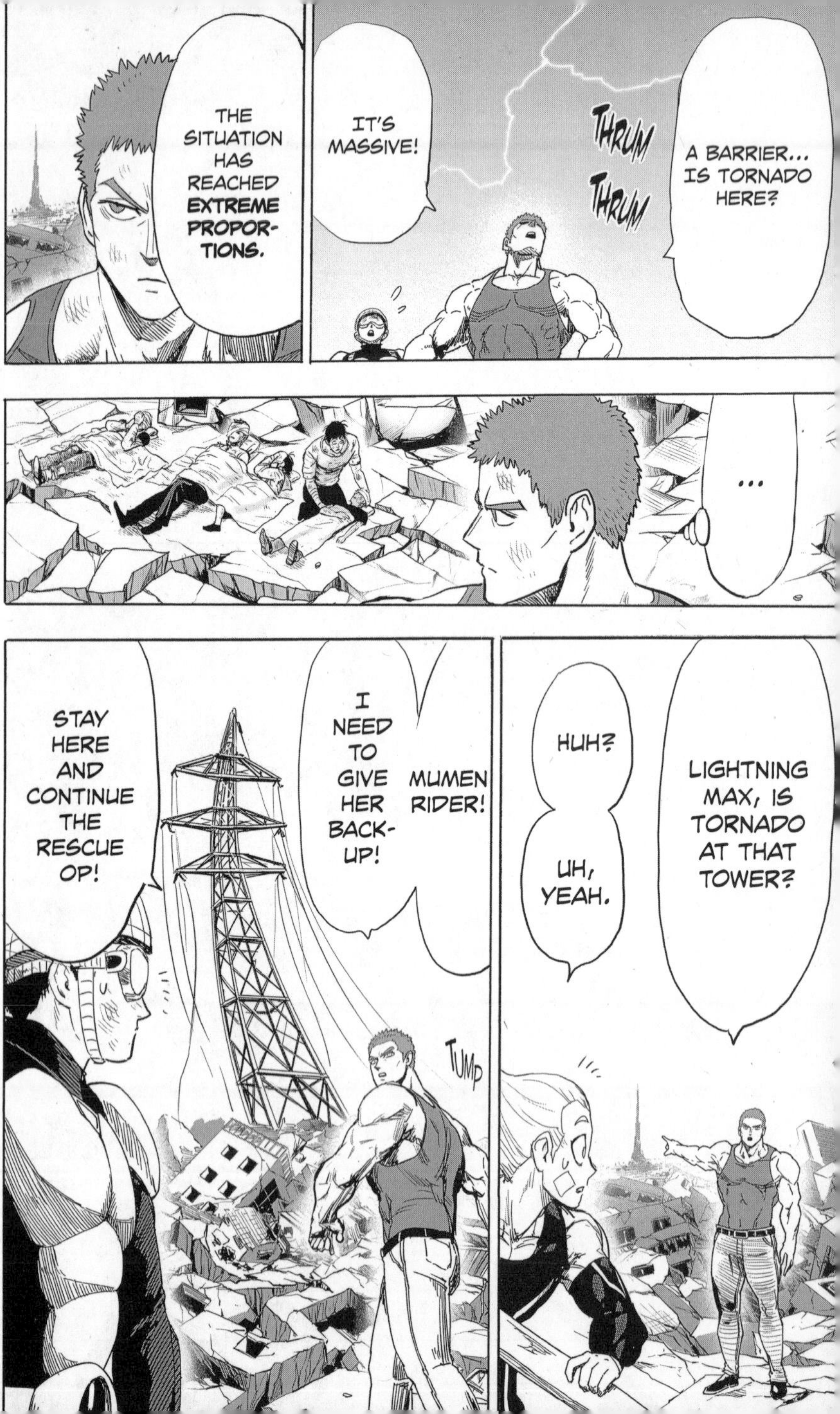
A BARRIER... IS TORNADO HERE?
THRUM THRUM
IT'S MASSIVE!
THE SITUATION HAS REACHED **EXTREME PROPORTIONS.**
...
LIGHTNING MAX, IS TORNADO AT THAT TOWER?
HUH?
UH, YEAH.
MUMEN RIDER!
I NEED TO GIVE HER BACK-UP!
STAY HERE AND CONTINUE THE RESCUE OP!
TUMP

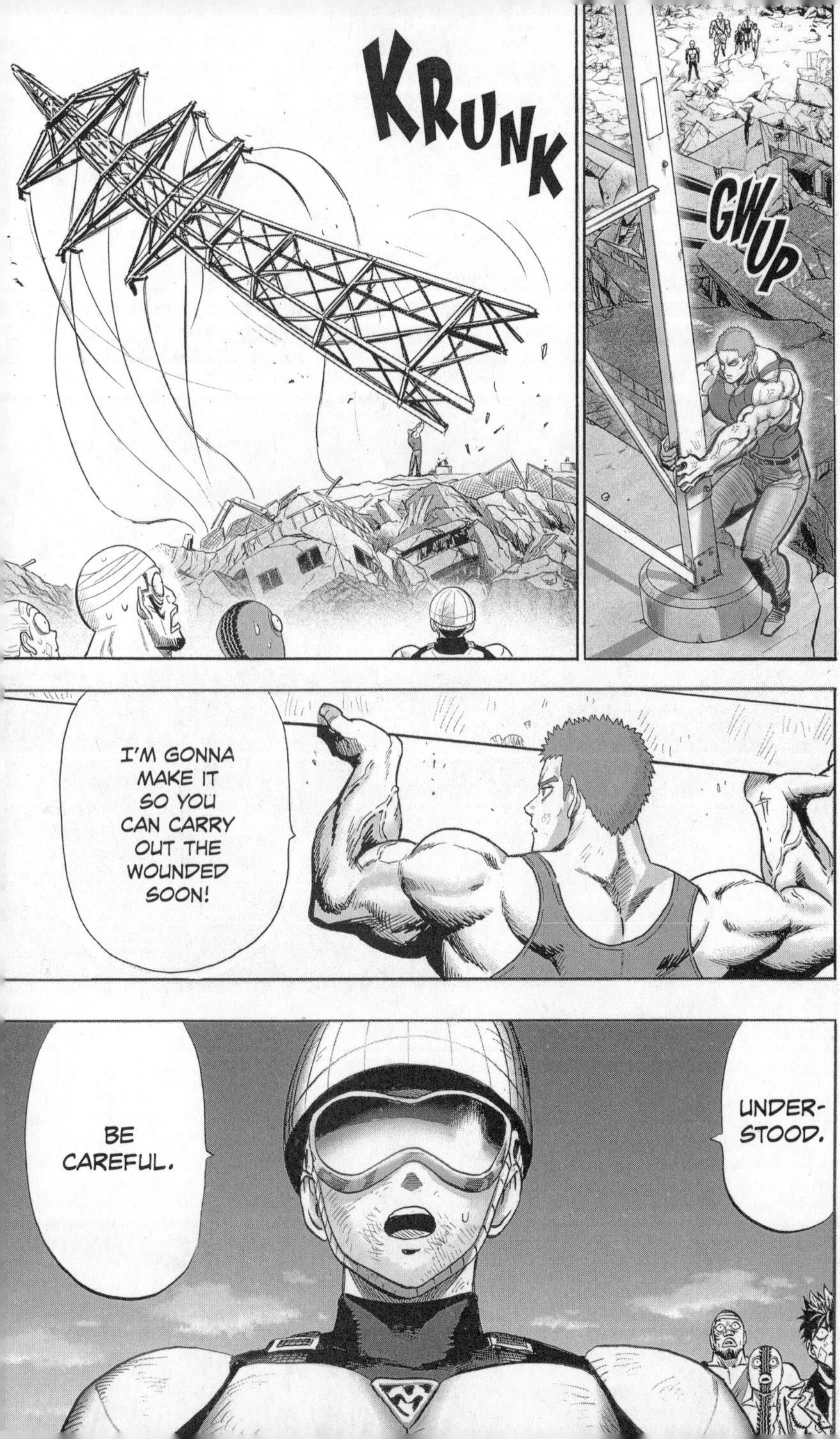
GWUP
KRUNK
I'M GONNA MAKE IT SO YOU CAN CARRY OUT THE WOUNDED SOON!
UNDER-STOOD.
BE CAREFUL.

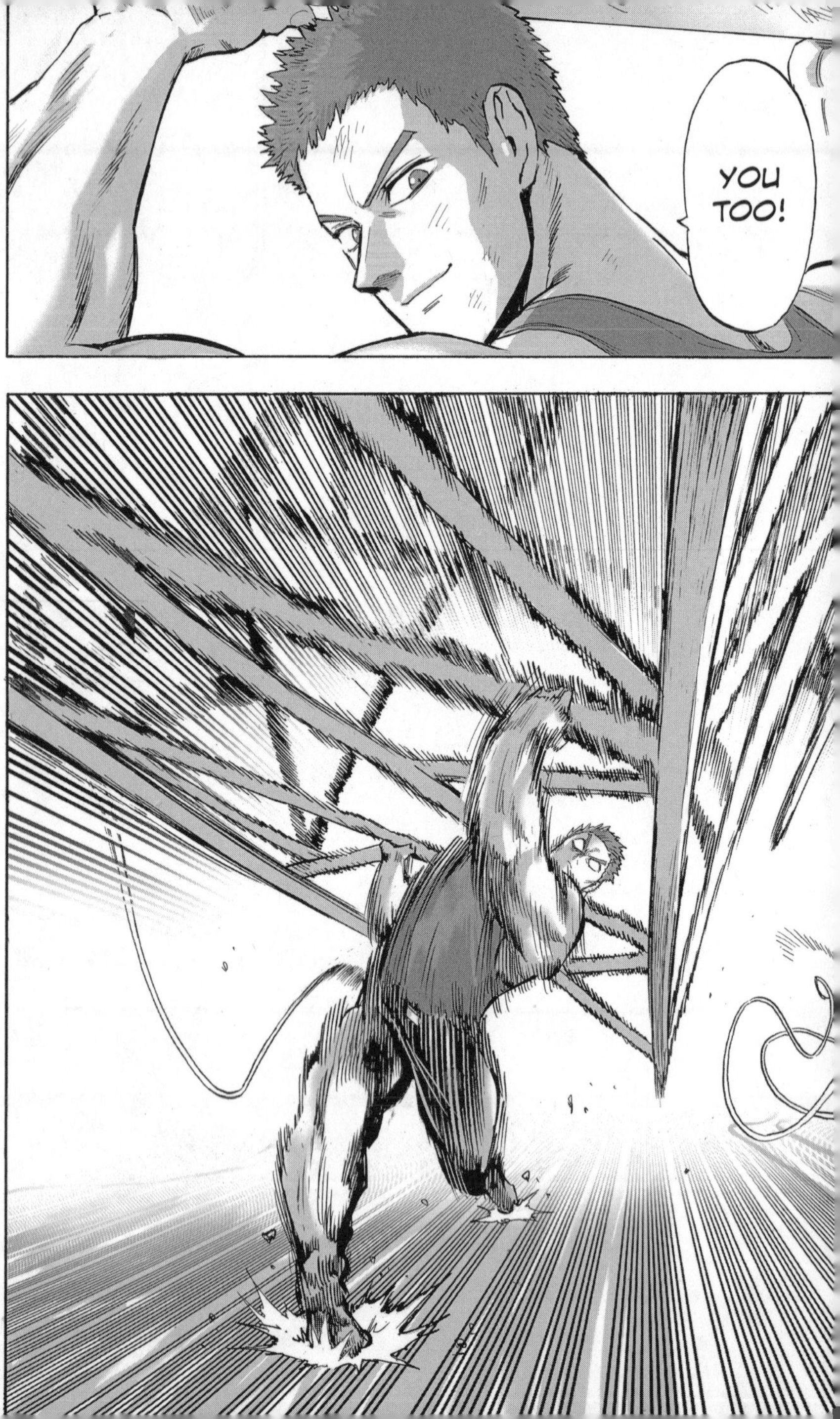
YOU TOO!

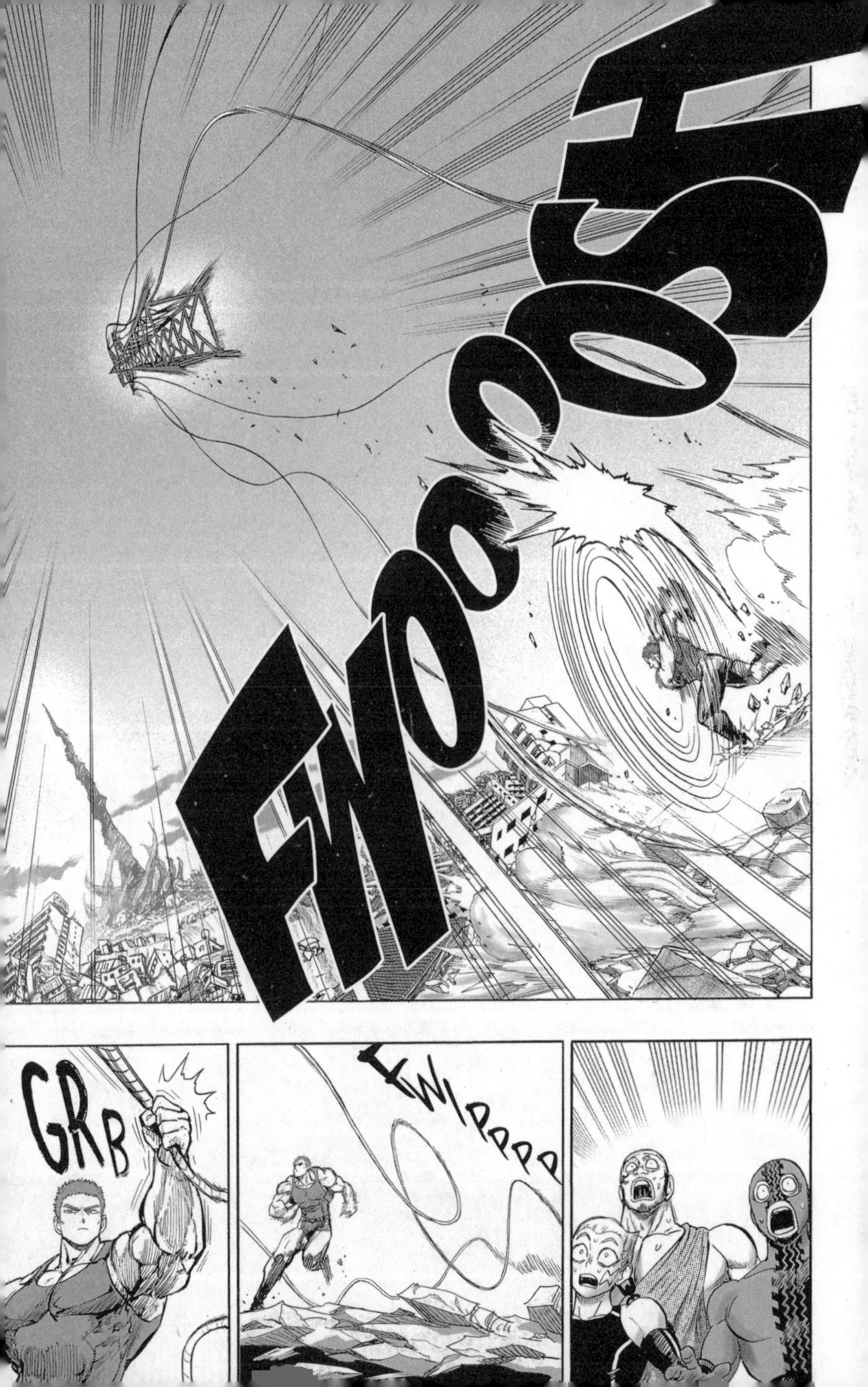
FWOOOOOSH
HWIPPPPP
GRB

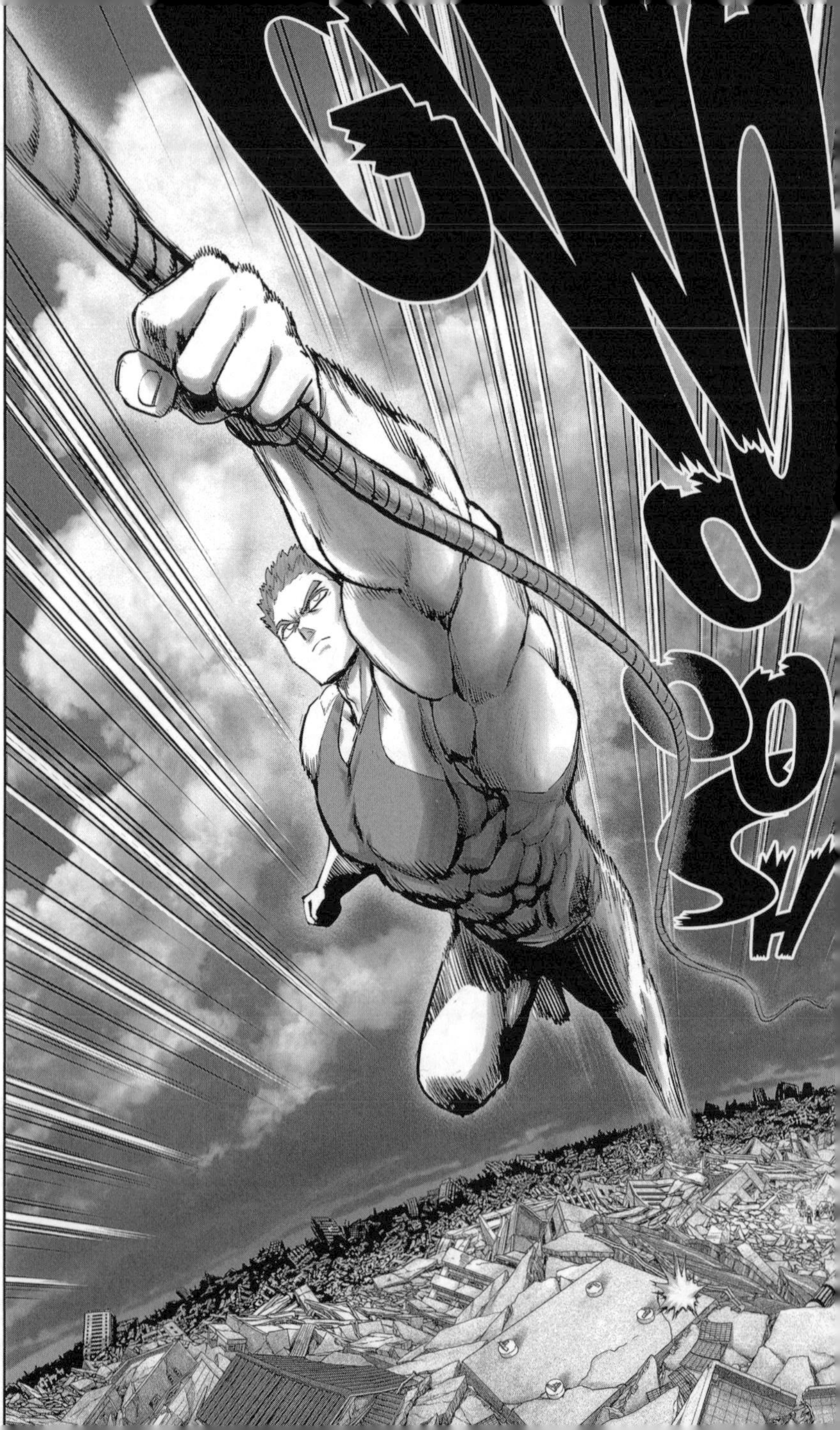
GWOOSH

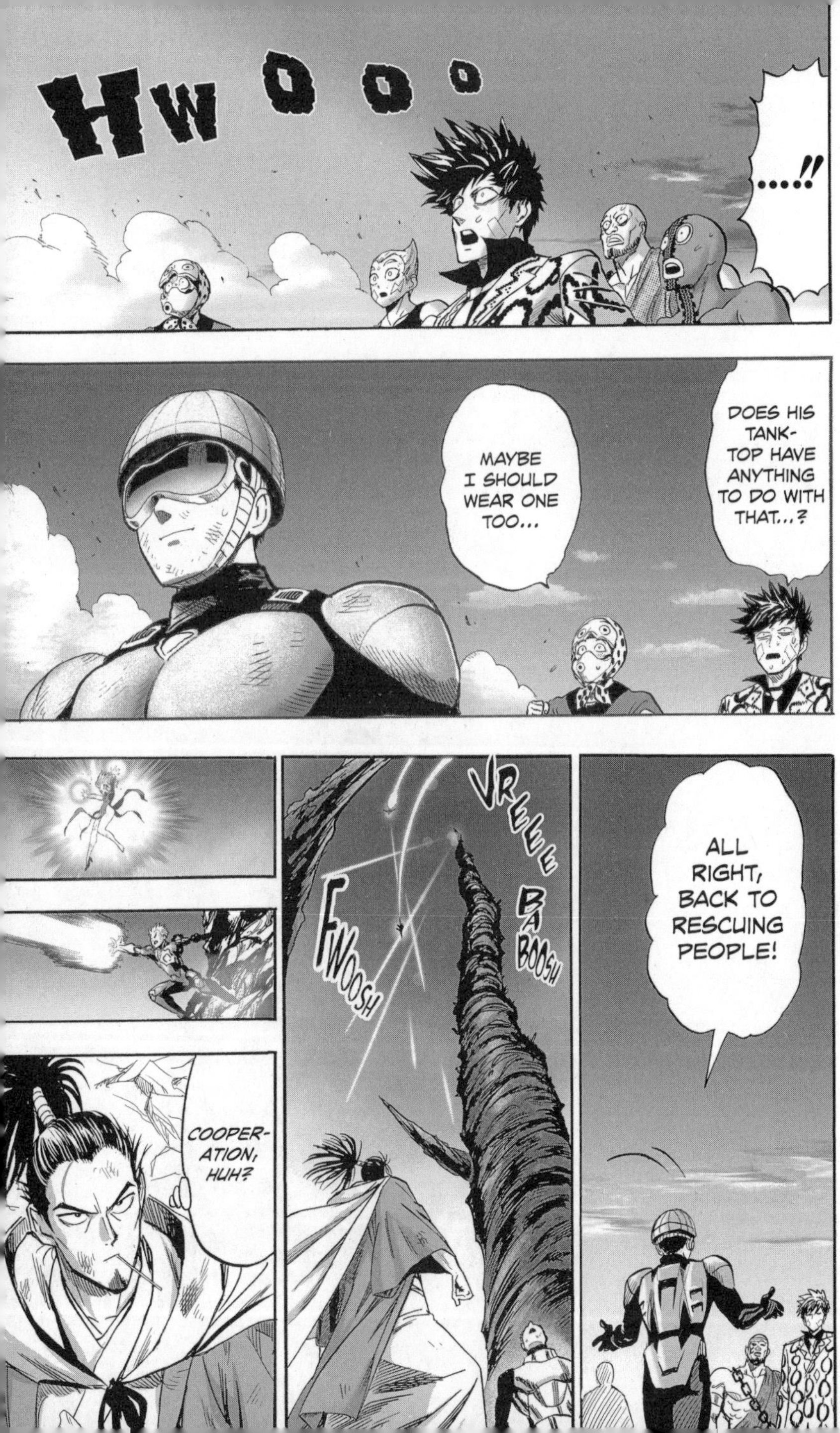
....!!
HW O O O
DOES HIS TANK-TOP HAVE ANYTHING TO DO WITH THAT...?
MAYBE I SHOULD WEAR ONE TOO...
ALL RIGHT, BACK TO RESCUING PEOPLE!
VREEE
BA BOOSH
FWOOSH
COOPER-ATION, HUH?

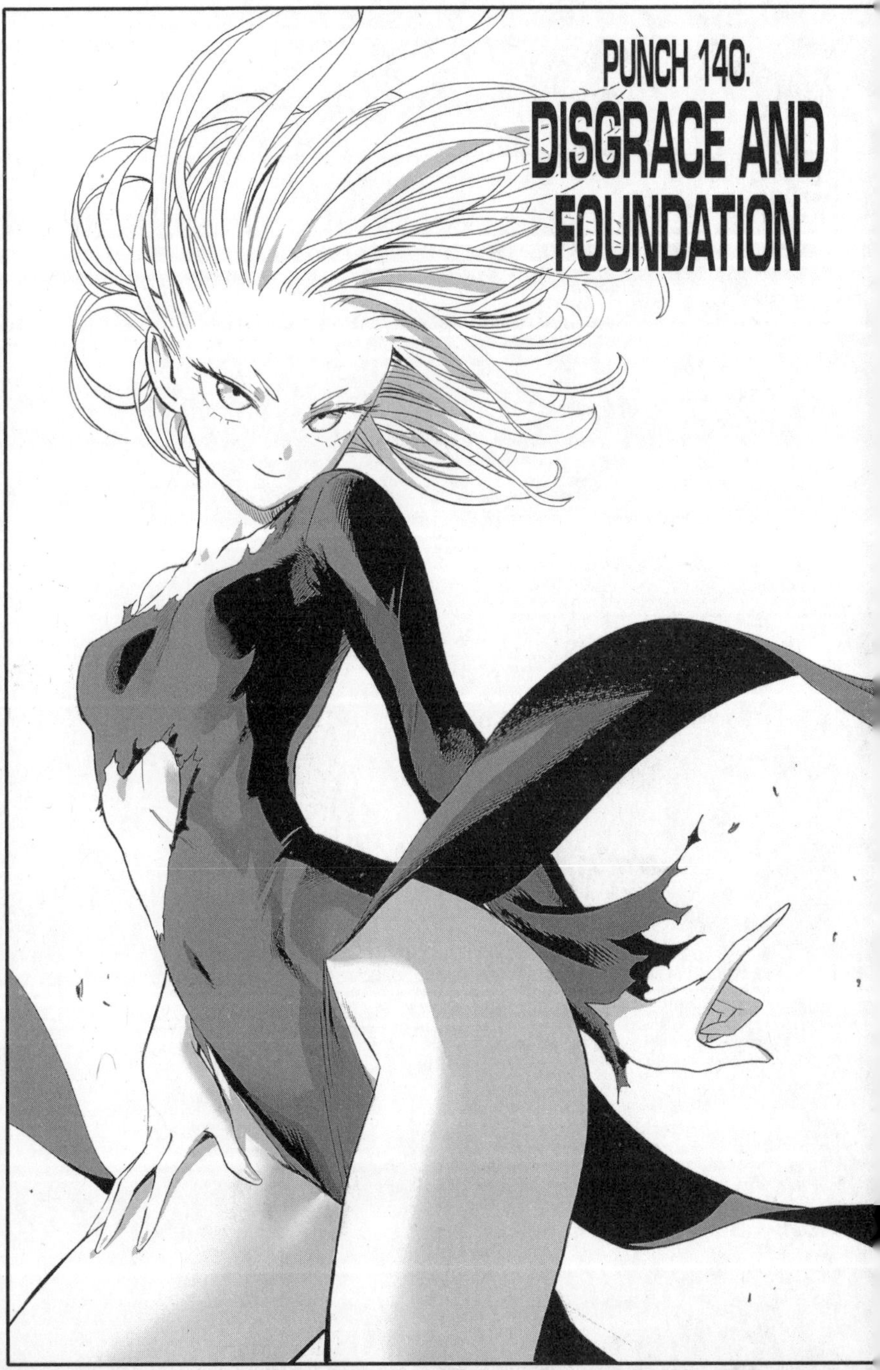
PUNCH 140:
DISGRACE AND FOUNDATION

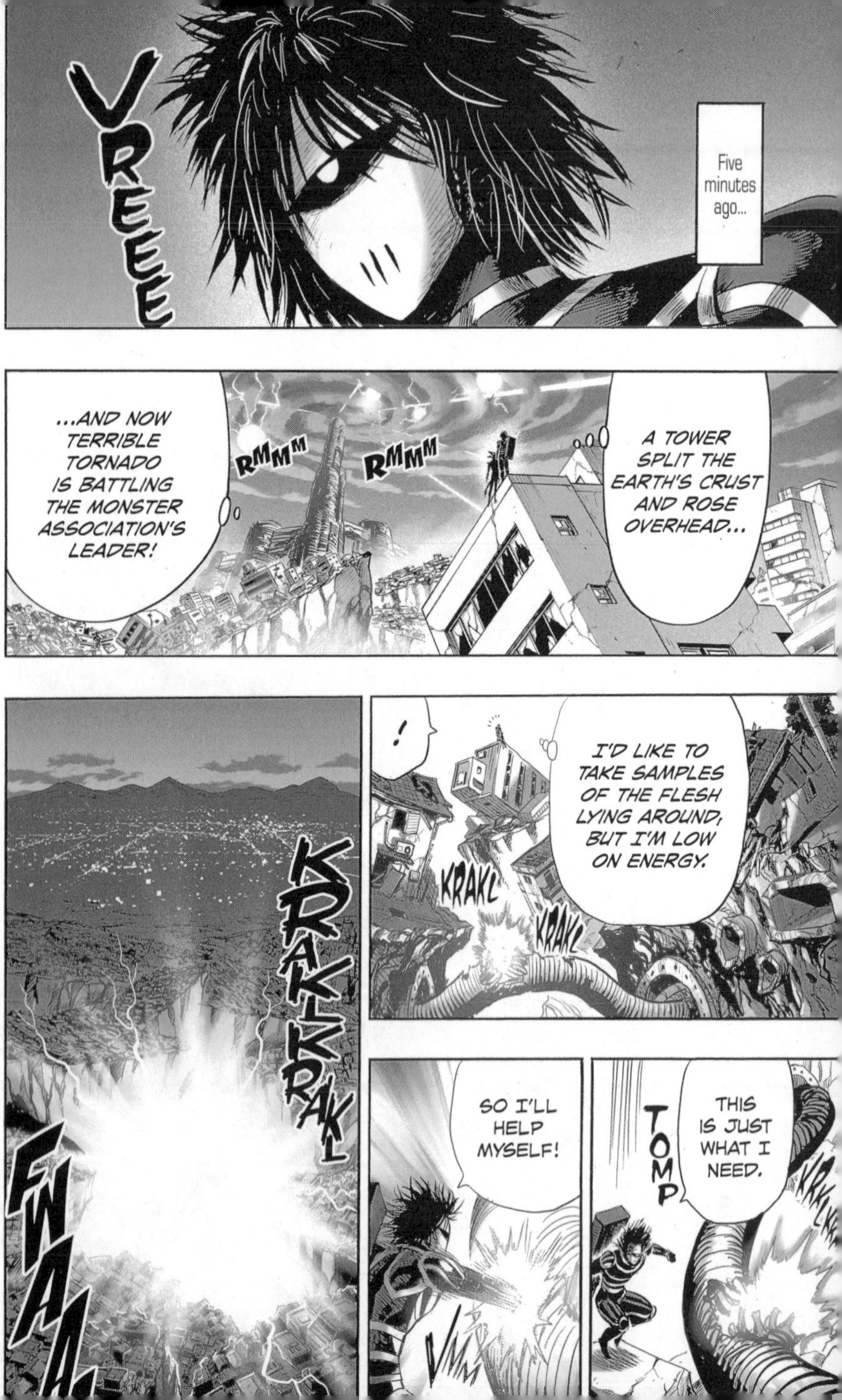
Five minutes ago...
VREEEE
A TOWER SPLIT THE EARTH'S CRUST AND ROSE OVERHEAD...
RMMM
RMMM
...AND NOW TERRIBLE TORNADO IS BATTLING THE MONSTER ASSOCIATION'S LEADER!
I'D LIKE TO TAKE SAMPLES OF THE FLESH LYING AROUND, BUT I'M LOW ON ENERGY.
!
KRAKL
KRAKL
KRAKL
THIS IS JUST WHAT I NEED.
TOMP
SO I'LL HELP MYSELF!
KRAKLRAKL
FWAA

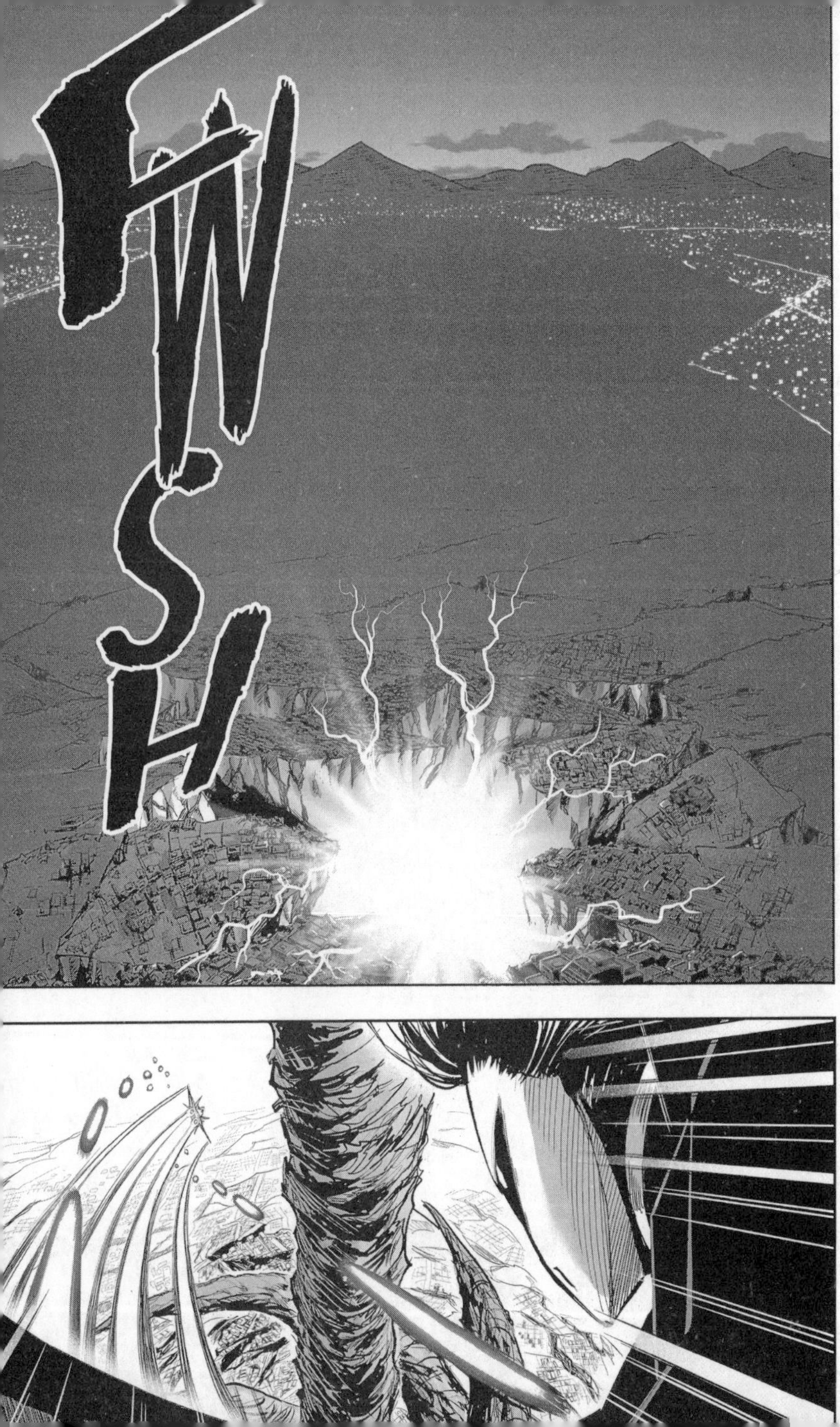
FWSSH

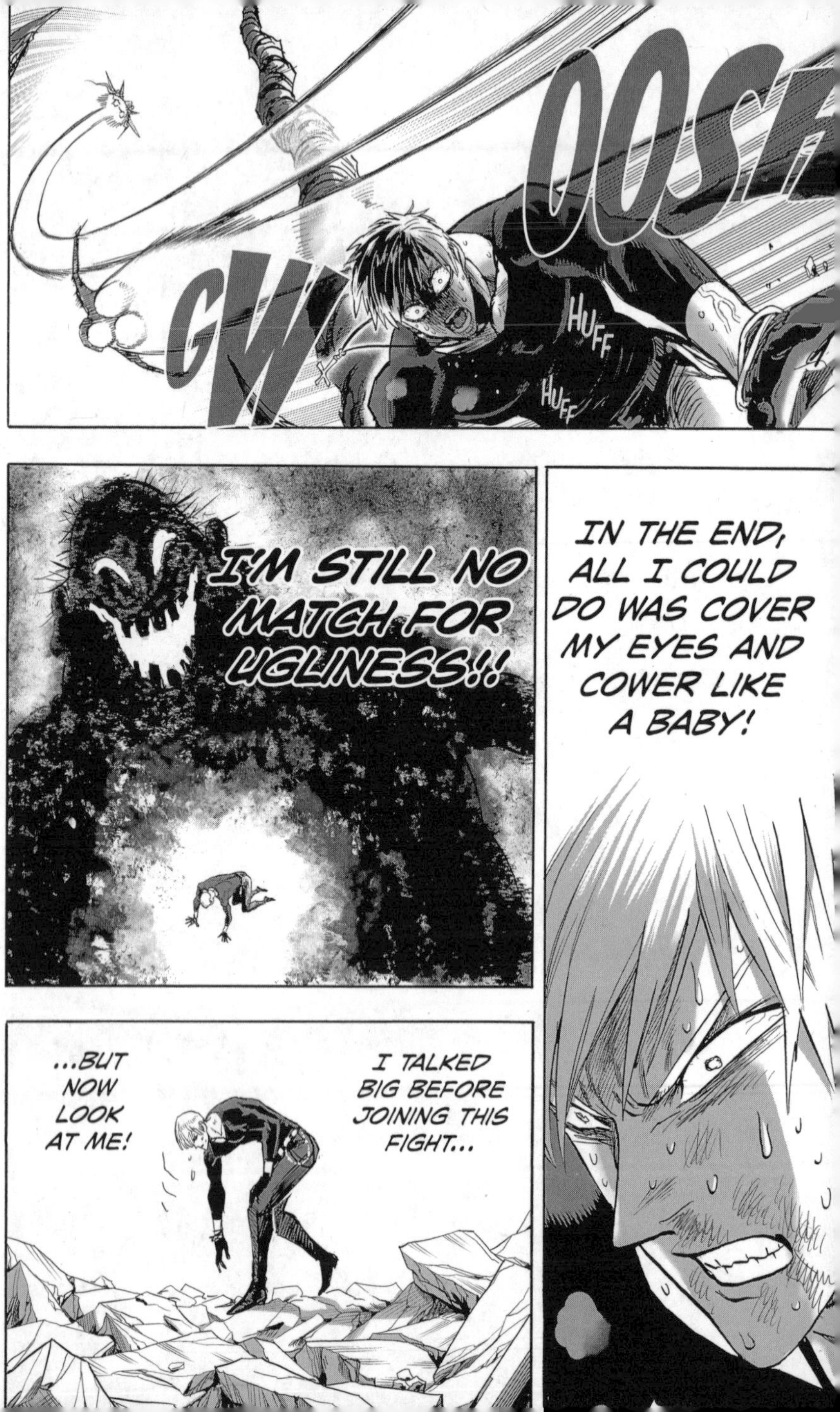
GWOOSH
HUFF
HUFF
IN THE END, ALL I COULD DO WAS COVER MY EYES AND COWER LIKE A BABY!
I'M STILL NO MATCH FOR UGLINESS!!
I TALKED BIG BEFORE JOINING THIS FIGHT...
...BUT NOW LOOK AT ME!

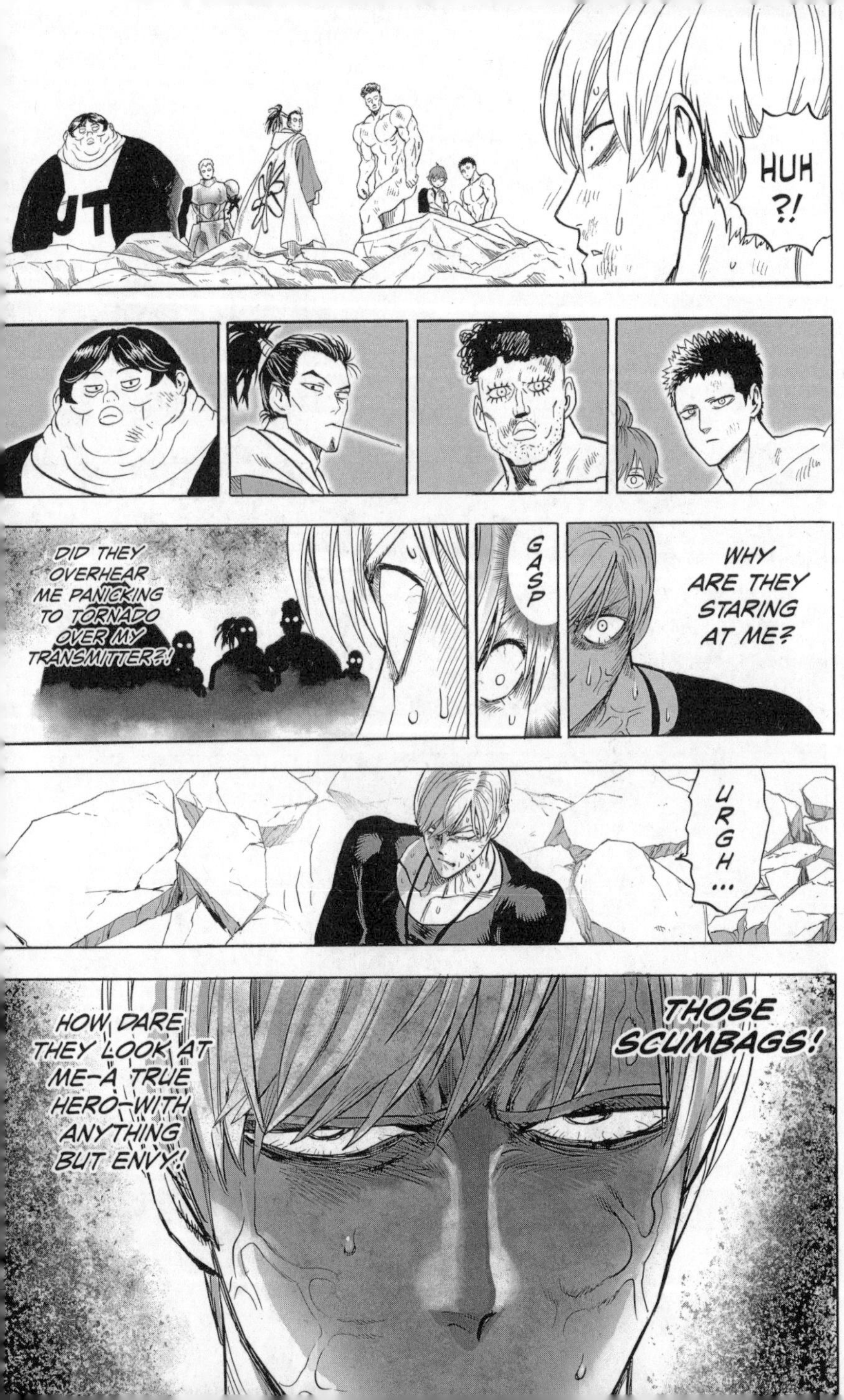
HUH ?!
WHY ARE THEY STARING AT ME?
GASP
DID THEY OVERHEAR ME PANICKING TO TORNADO OVER MY TRANSMITTER?!
URGH...
THOSE SCUMBAGS!
HOW DARE THEY LOOK AT ME—A TRUE HERO—WITH ANYTHING BUT ENVY!

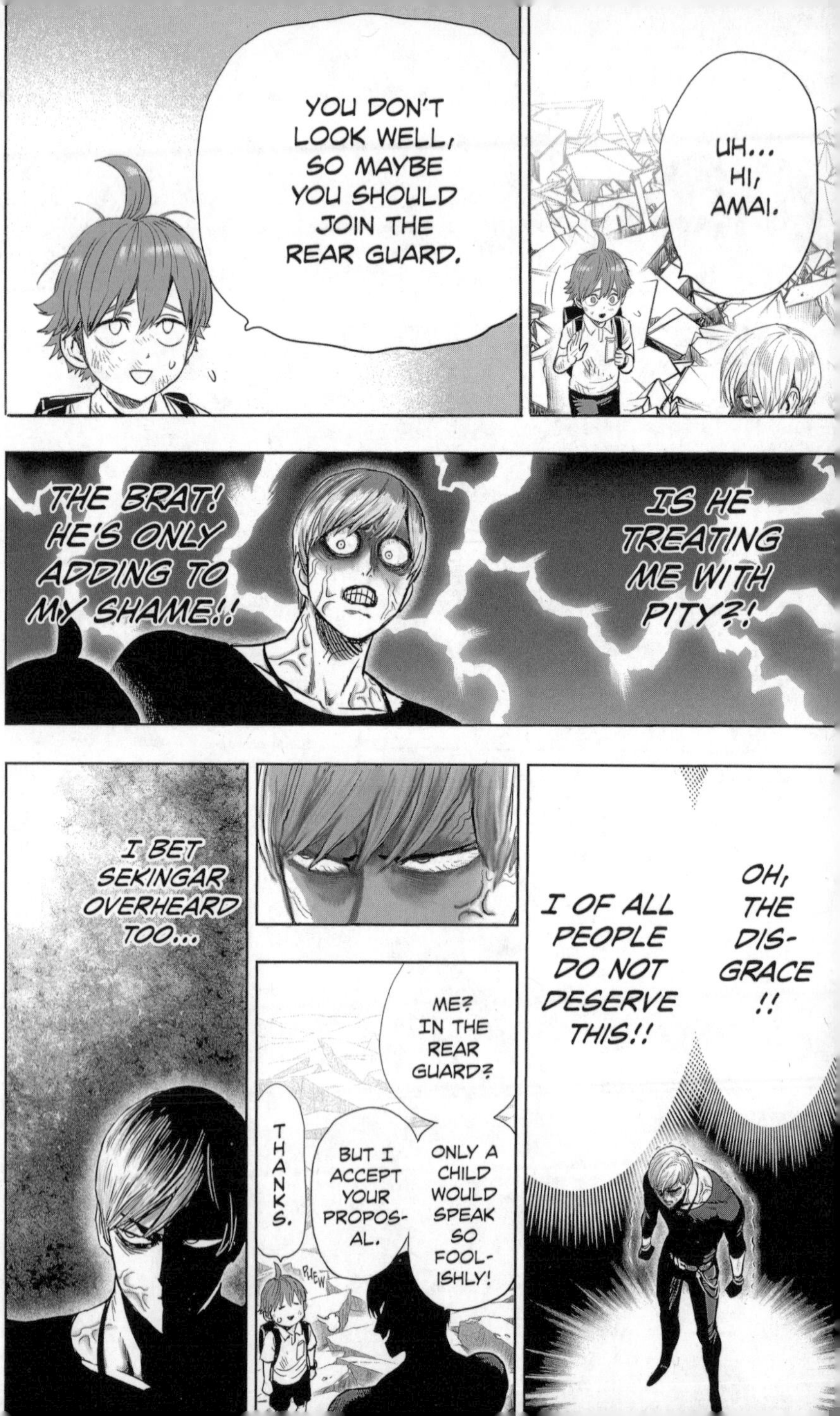
UH... HI, AMAI.
YOU DON'T LOOK WELL, SO MAYBE YOU SHOULD JOIN THE REAR GUARD.
IS HE TREATING ME WITH PITY?!
THE BRAT! HE'S ONLY ADDING TO MY SHAME!!
OH, THE DIS-GRACE!!
I OF ALL PEOPLE DO NOT DESERVE THIS!!
ME? IN THE REAR GUARD?
ONLY A CHILD WOULD SPEAK SO FOOL-ISHLY!
BUT I ACCEPT YOUR PROPOS-AL.
THANKS.
PHEW
I BET SEKINGAR OVERHEARD TOO...

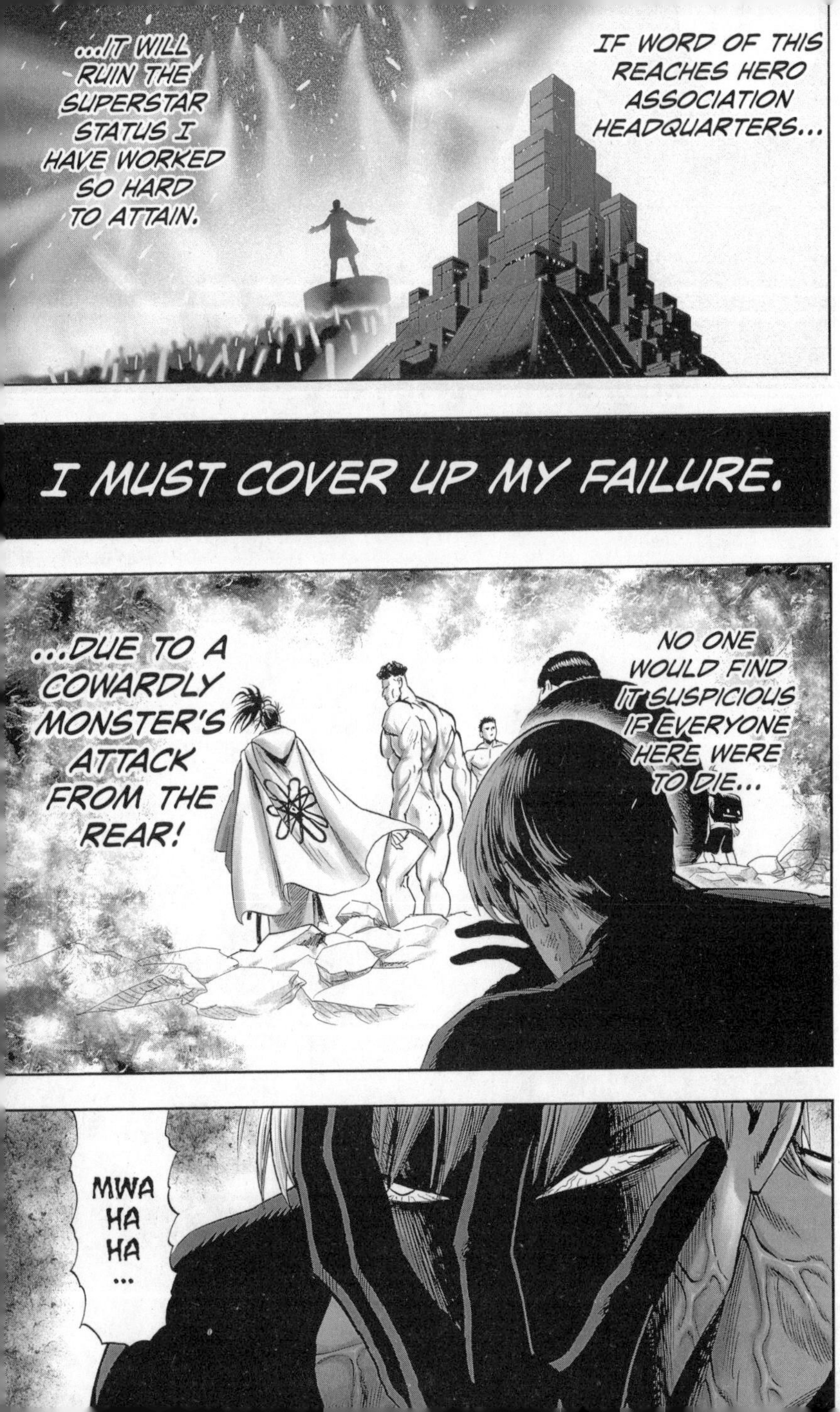
IF WORD OF THIS REACHES HERO ASSOCIATION HEADQUARTERS...
...IT WILL RUIN THE SUPERSTAR STATUS I HAVE WORKED SO HARD TO ATTAIN.
I MUST COVER UP MY FAILURE.
NO ONE WOULD FIND IT SUSPICIOUS IF EVERYONE HERE WERE TO DIE...
...DUE TO A COWARDLY MONSTER'S ATTACK FROM THE REAR!
MWA HA HA ...

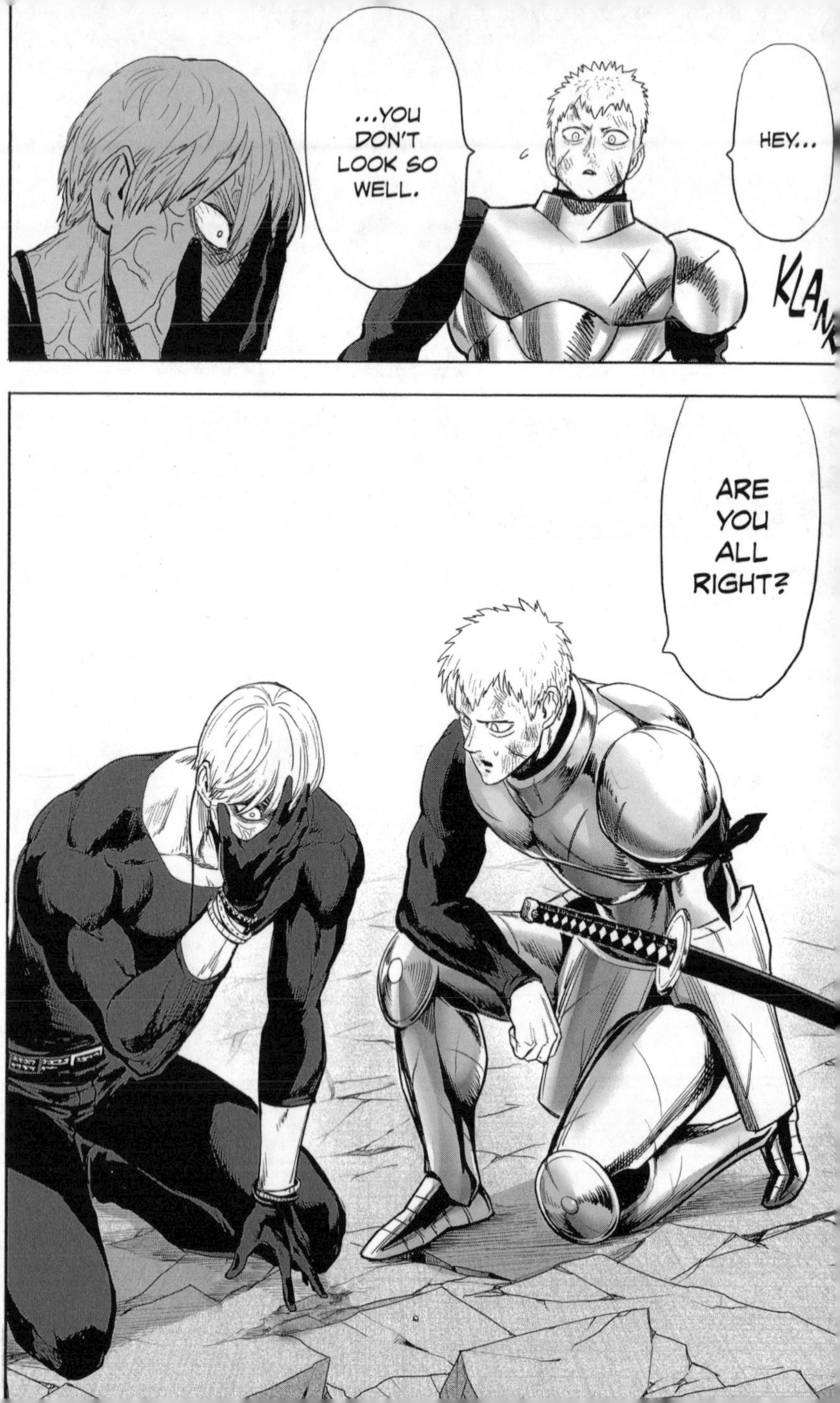
HEY...
KLANK
...YOU DON'T LOOK SO WELL.
ARE YOU ALL RIGHT?

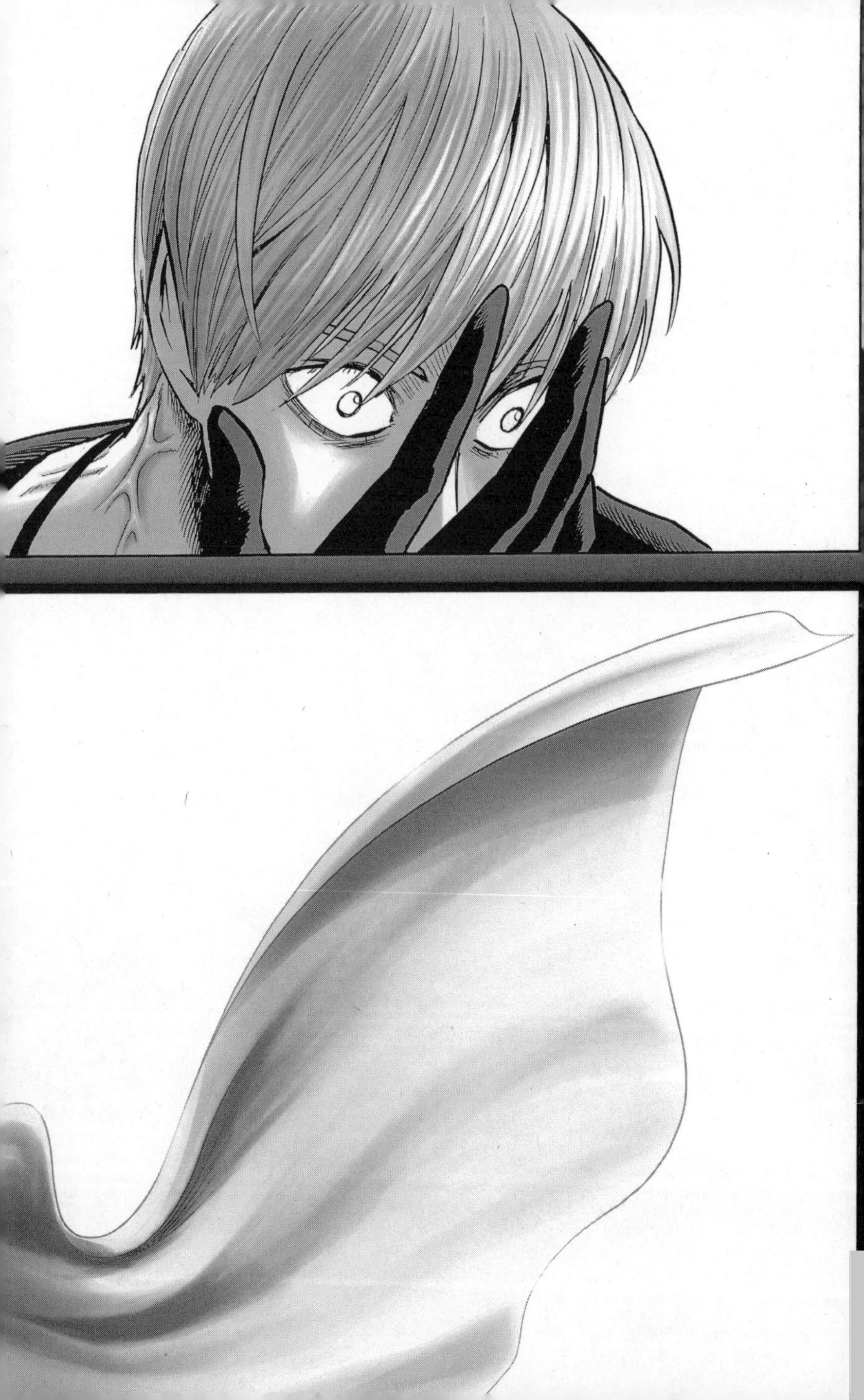

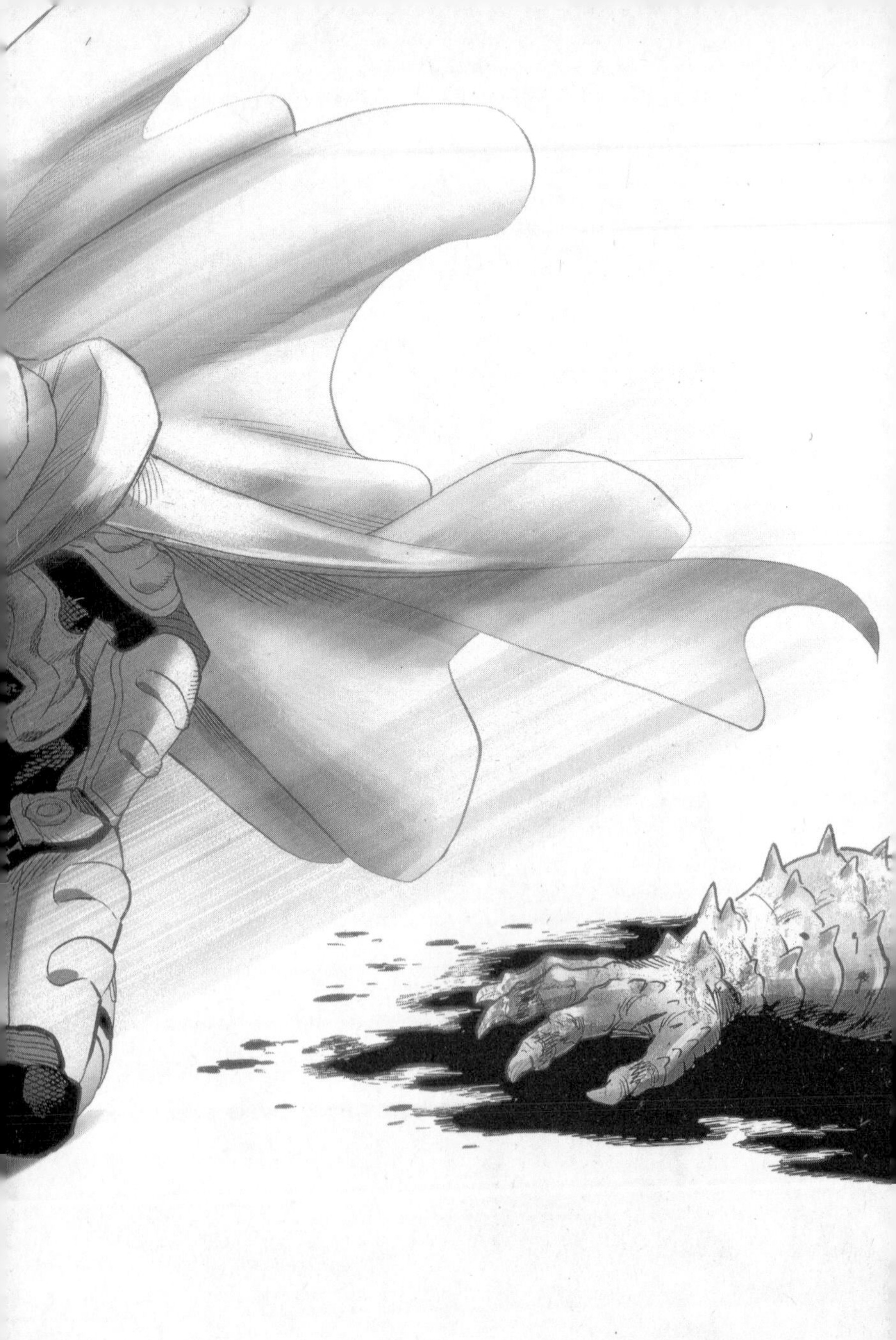

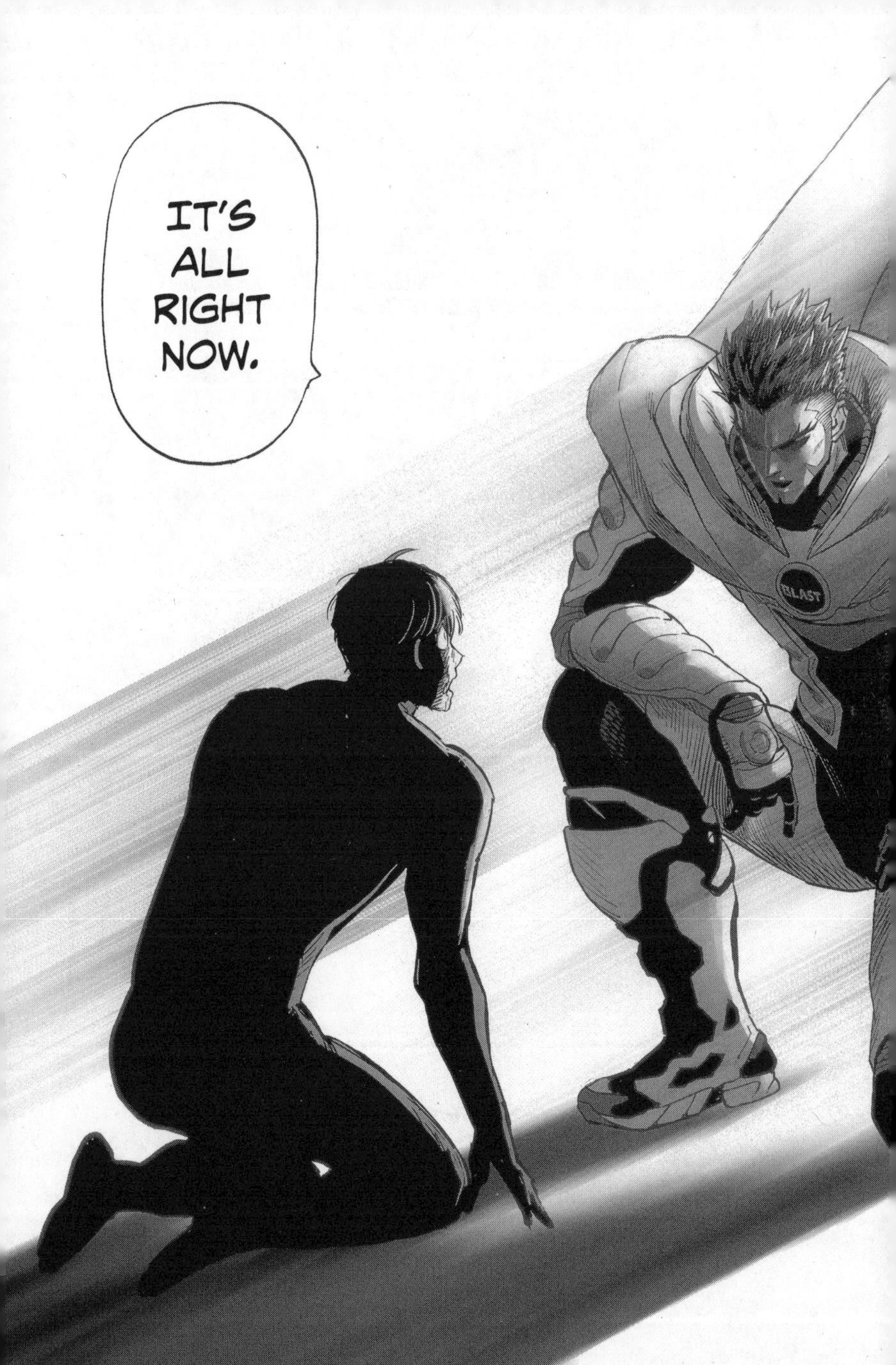
IT'S ALL RIGHT NOW.
BLAST

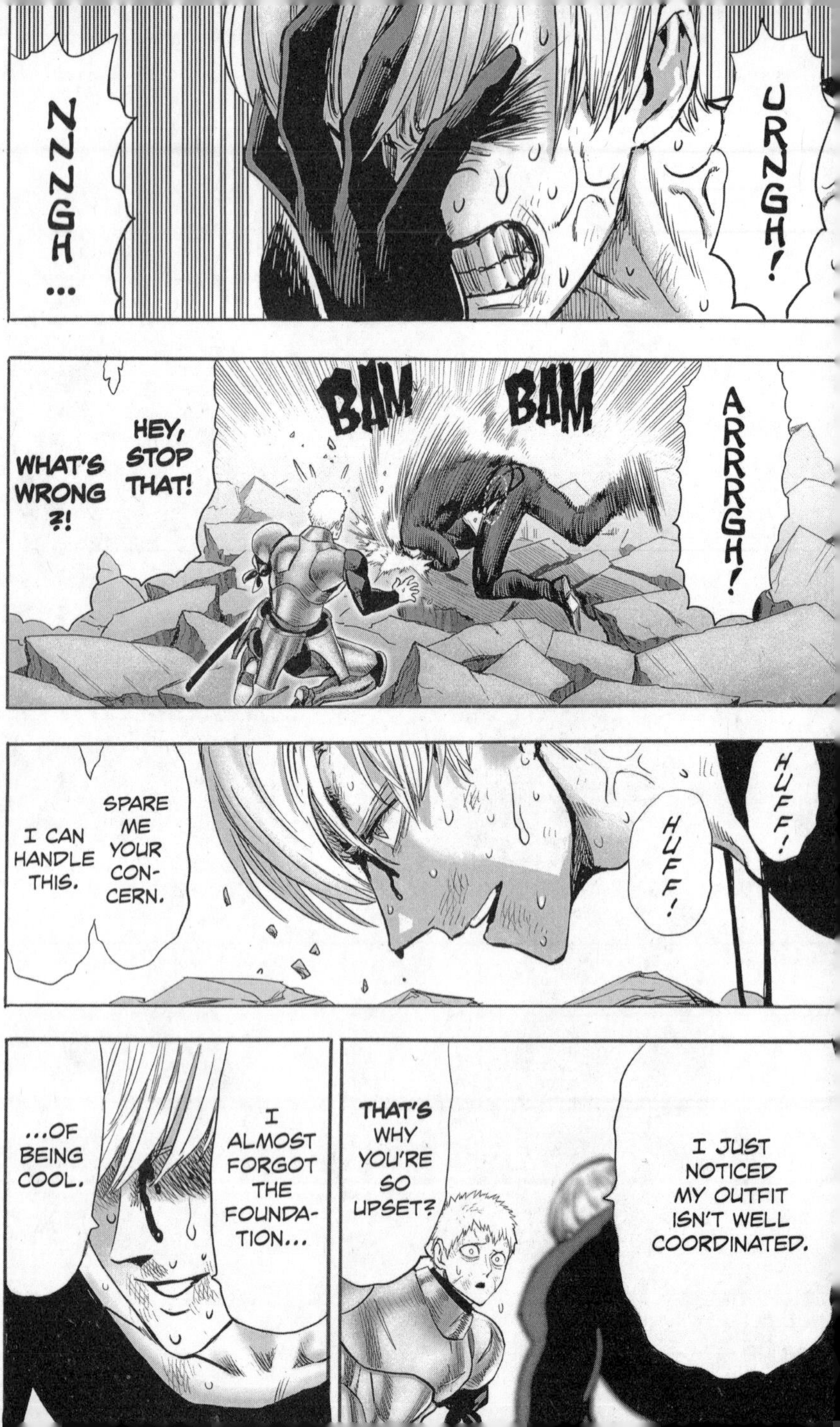
URNGH!
NNNGH...
ARRRGH!
BAM
BAM
HEY, STOP THAT!
WHAT'S WRONG?!
HUFF!
HUFF!
SPARE ME YOUR CONCERN.
I CAN HANDLE THIS.
I JUST NOTICED MY OUTFIT ISN'T WELL COORDINATED.
THAT'S WHY YOU'RE SO UPSET?
I ALMOST FORGOT THE FOUNDATION...
...OF BEING COOL.

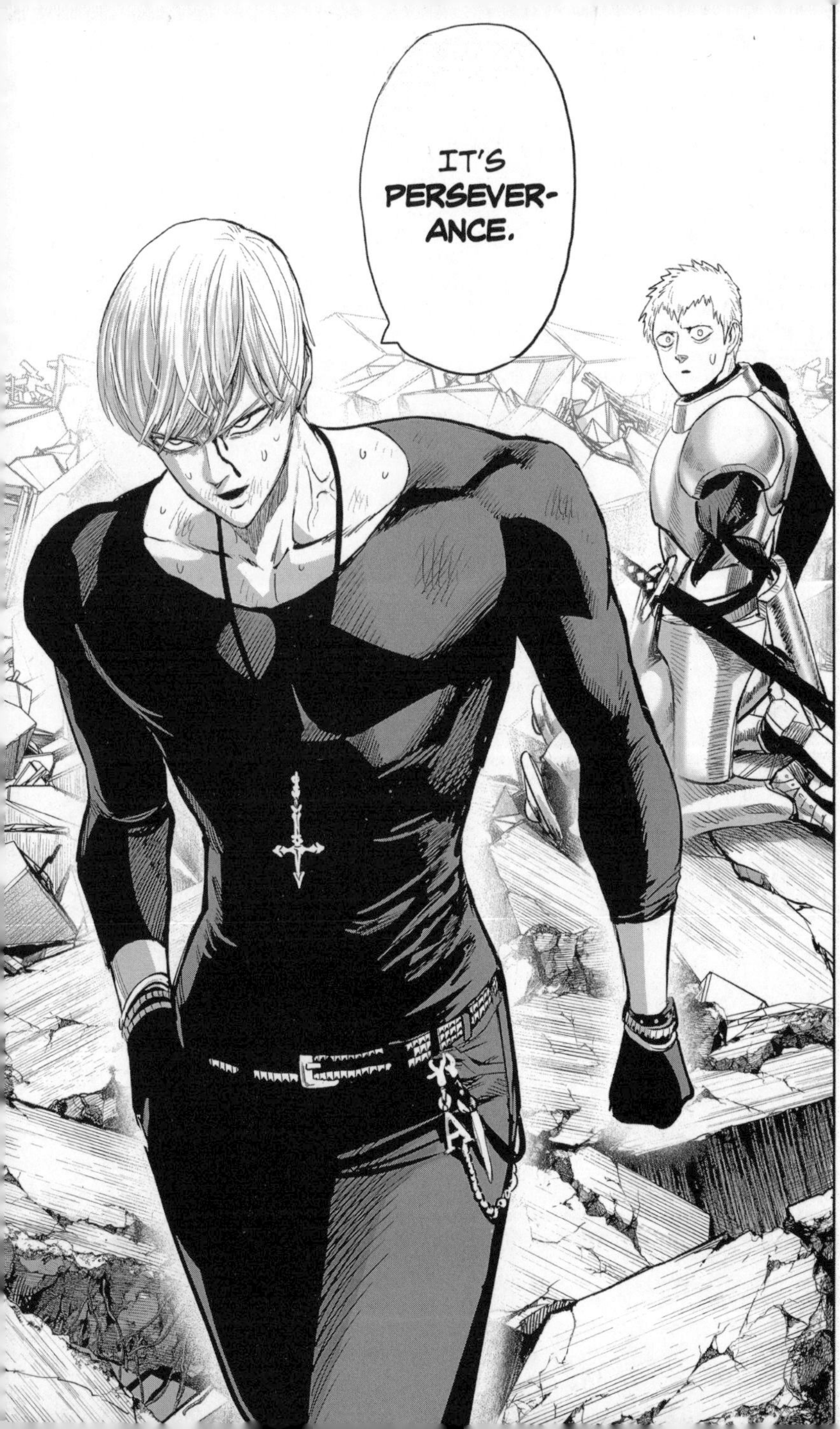
IT'S PERSEVER-ANCE.

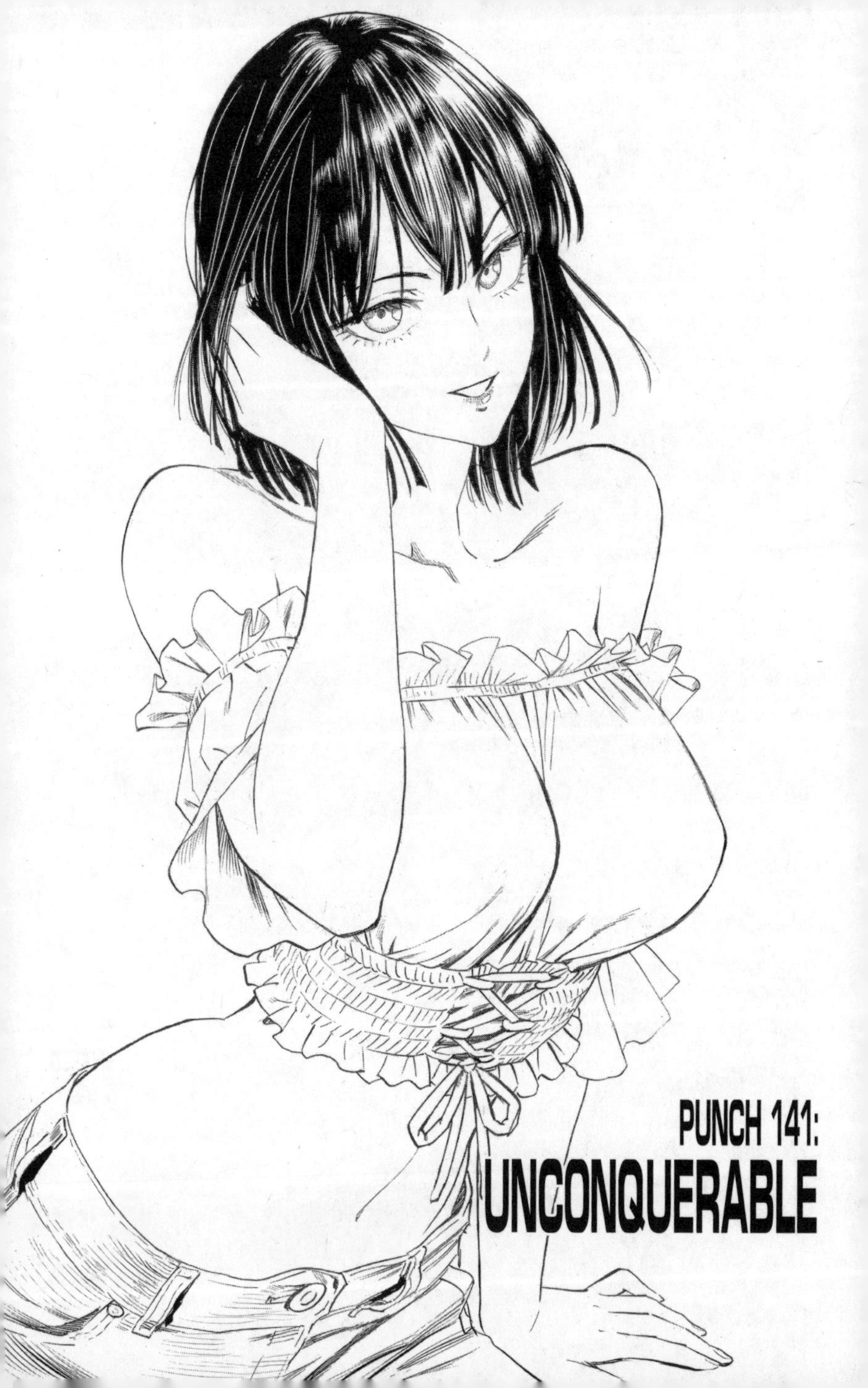
PUNCH 141:
UNCONQUERABLE

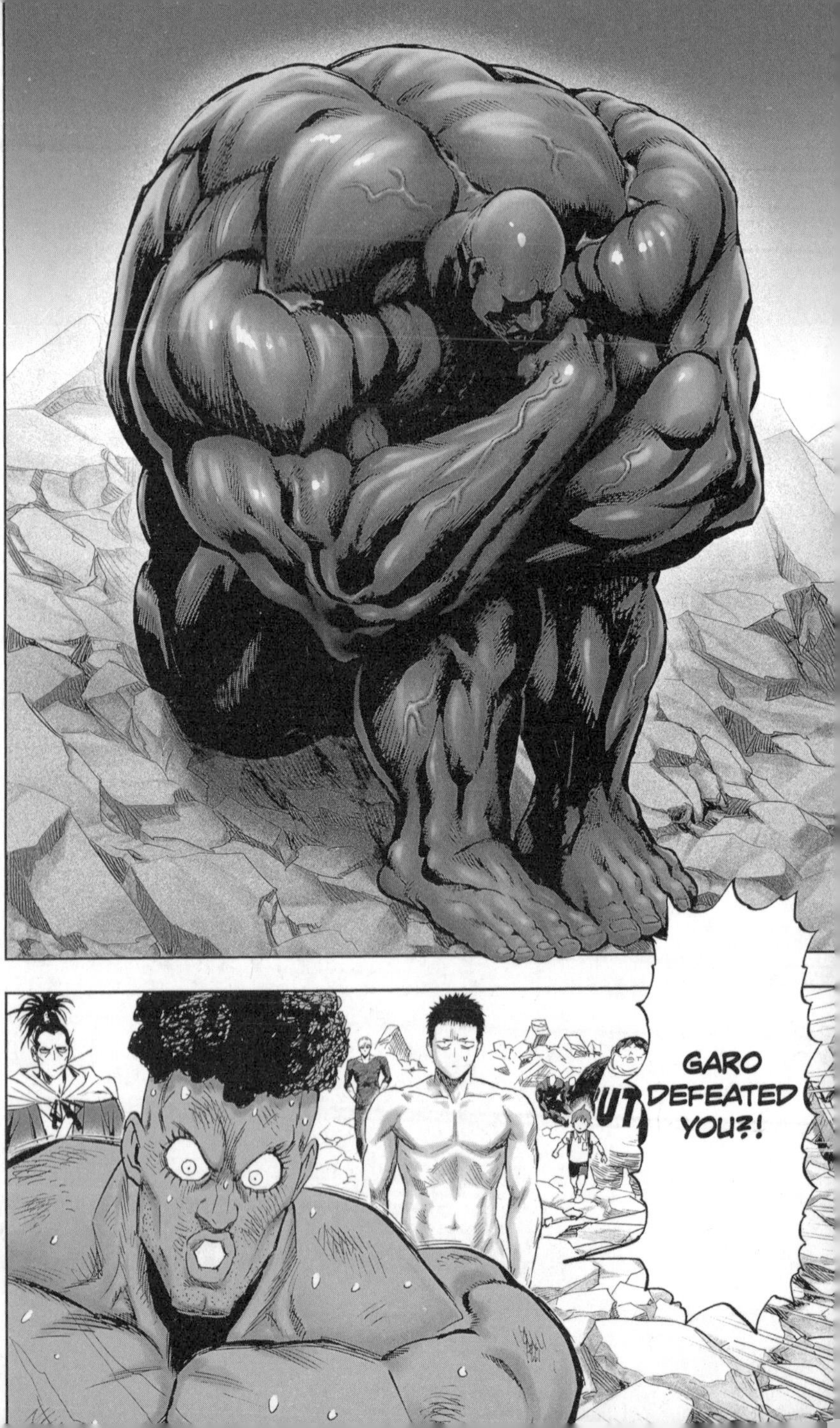
GARO DEFEATED YOU?!

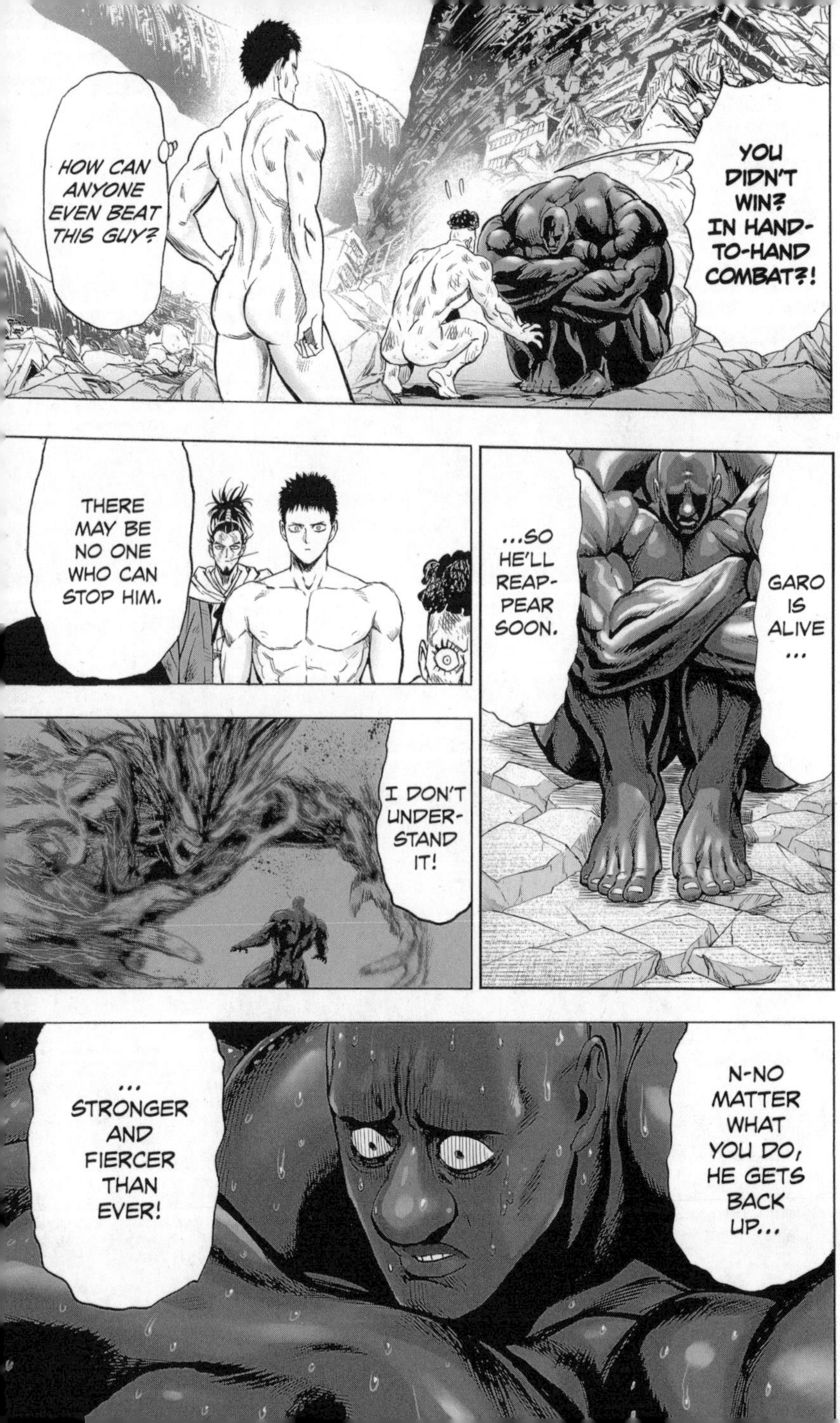
YOU DIDN'T WIN? IN HAND-TO-HAND COMBAT?!
HOW CAN ANYONE EVEN BEAT THIS GUY?
GARO IS ALIVE...
...SO HE'LL REAP-PEAR SOON.
THERE MAY BE NO ONE WHO CAN STOP HIM.
I DON'T UNDER-STAND IT!
N-NO MATTER WHAT YOU DO, HE GETS BACK UP...
...STRONGER AND FIERCER THAN EVER!

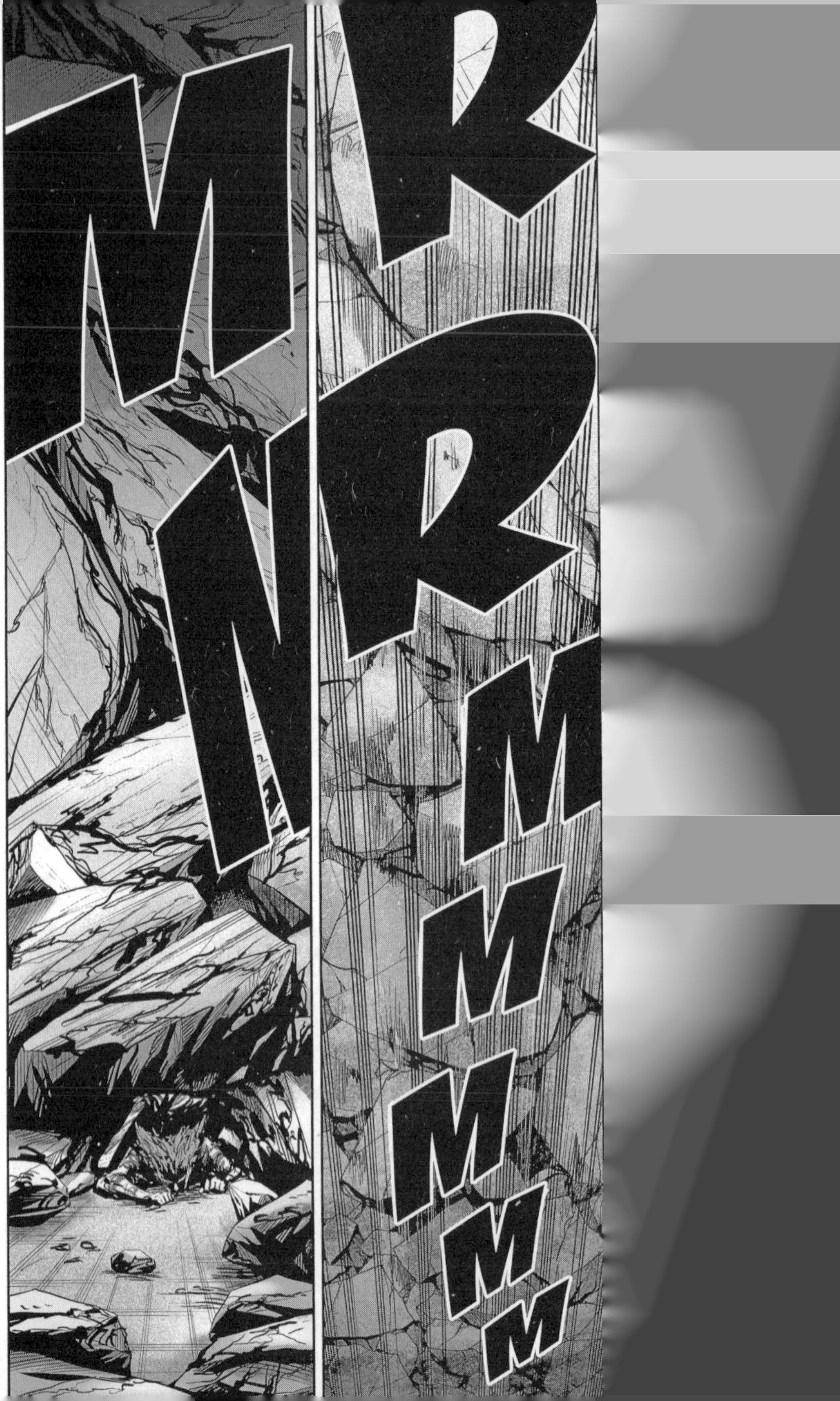
RRMMMMM
M

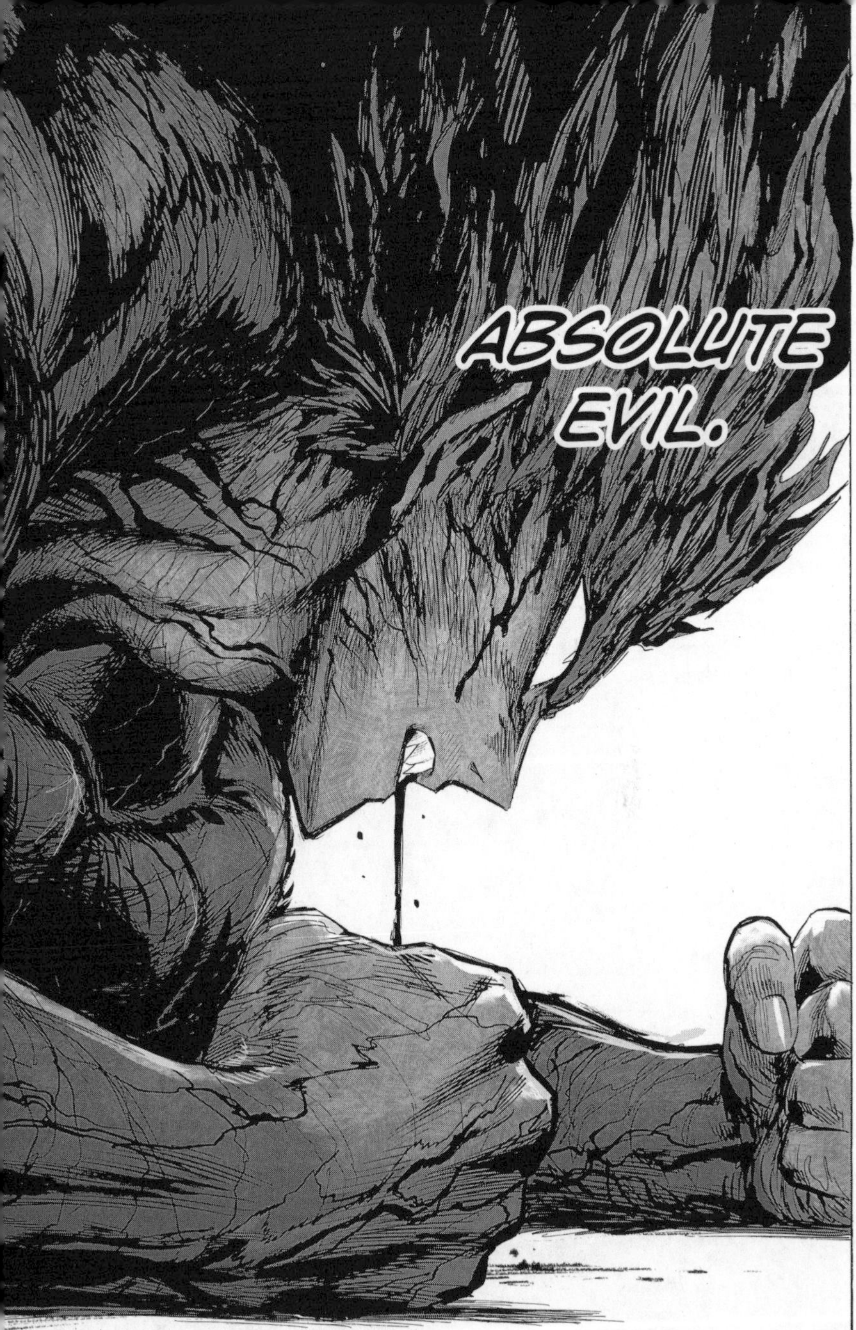
ABSOLUTE EVIL.

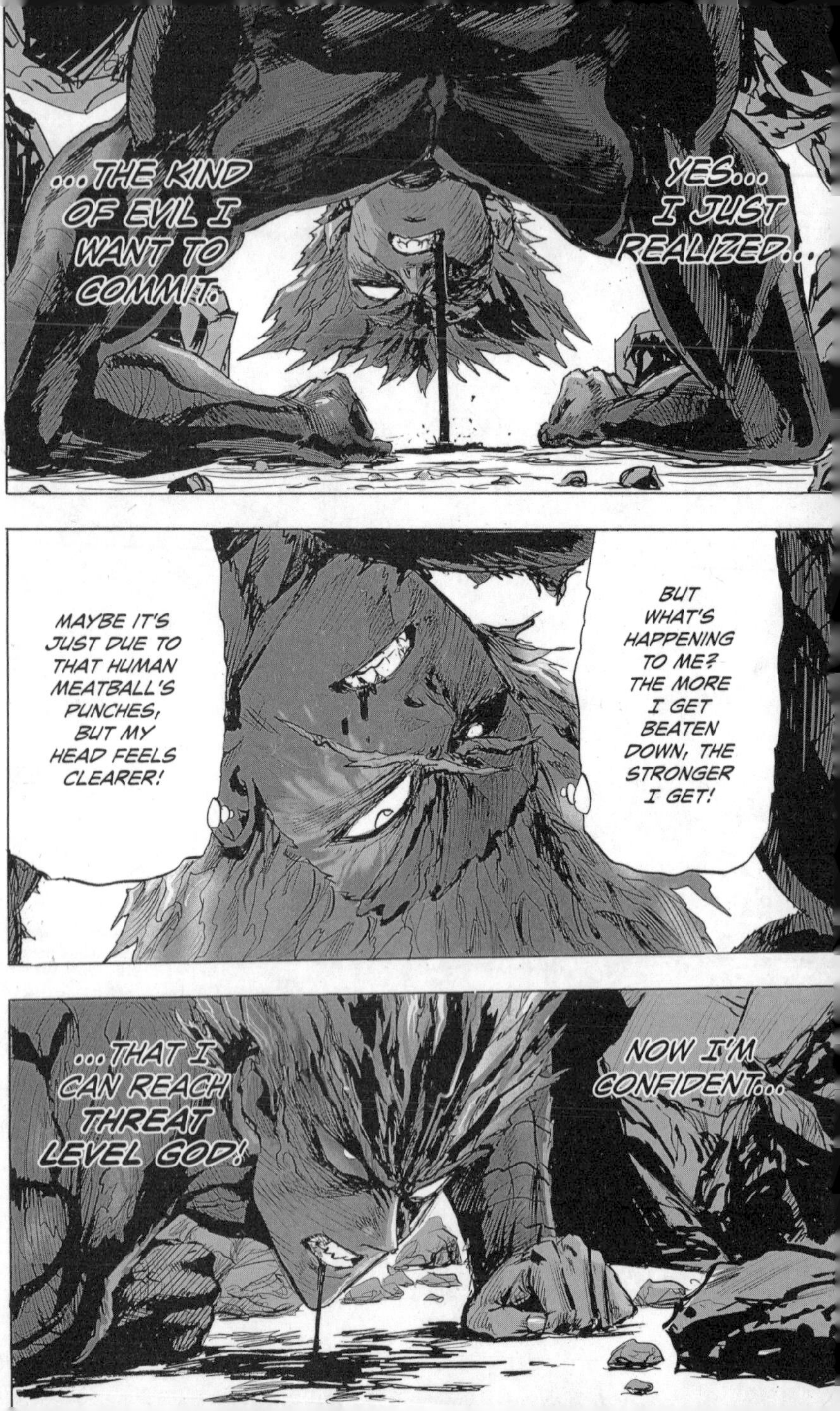
YES... I JUST REALIZED...
...THE KIND OF EVIL I WANT TO COMMIT.
BUT WHAT'S HAPPENING TO ME? THE MORE I GET BEATEN DOWN, THE STRONGER I GET!
MAYBE IT'S JUST DUE TO THAT HUMAN MEATBALL'S PUNCHES, BUT MY HEAD FEELS CLEARER!
NOW I'M CONFIDENT...
...THAT I CAN REACH THREAT LEVEL GOD!

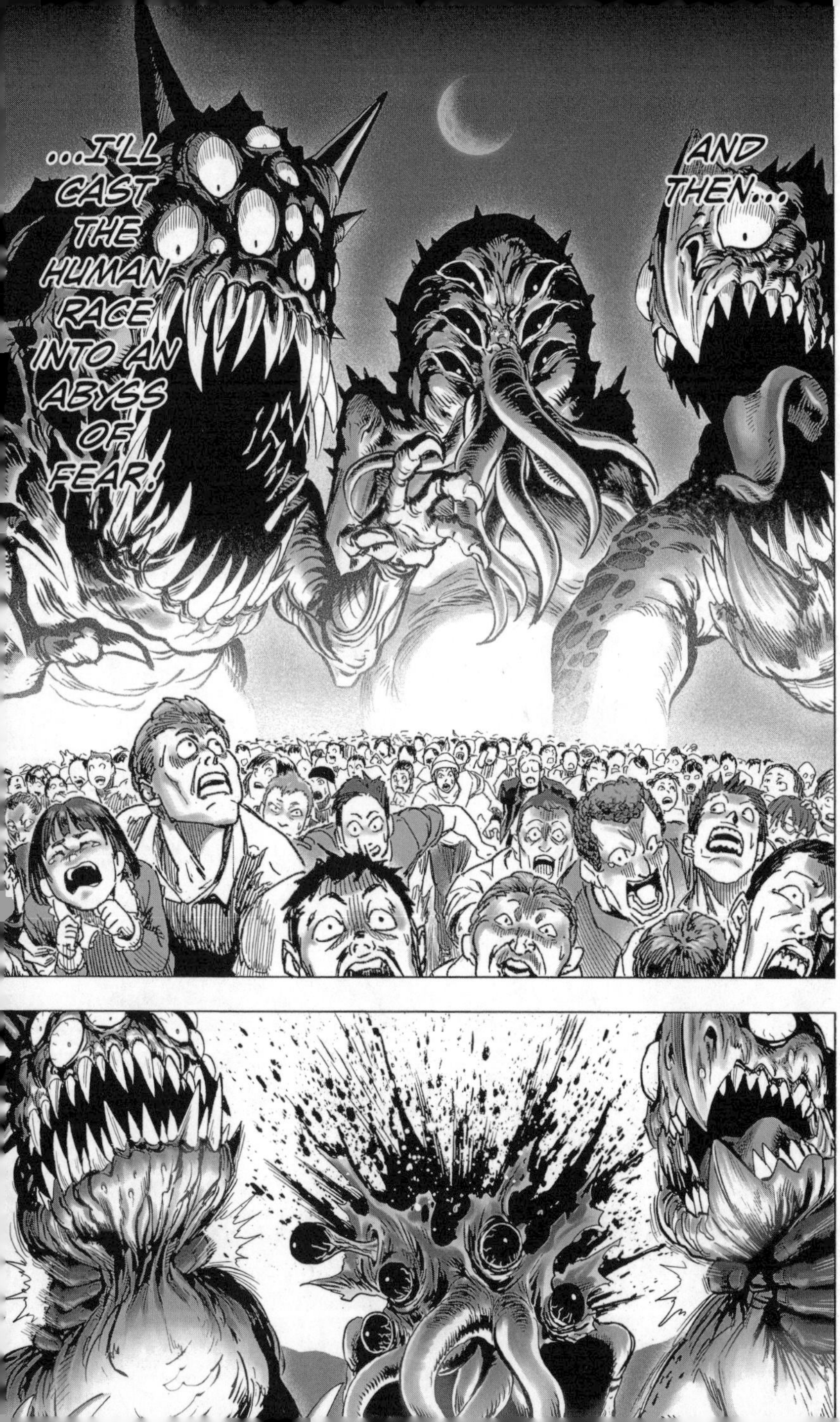
AND THEN...
...I'LL CAST THE HUMAN RACE INTO AN ABYSS OF FEAR!

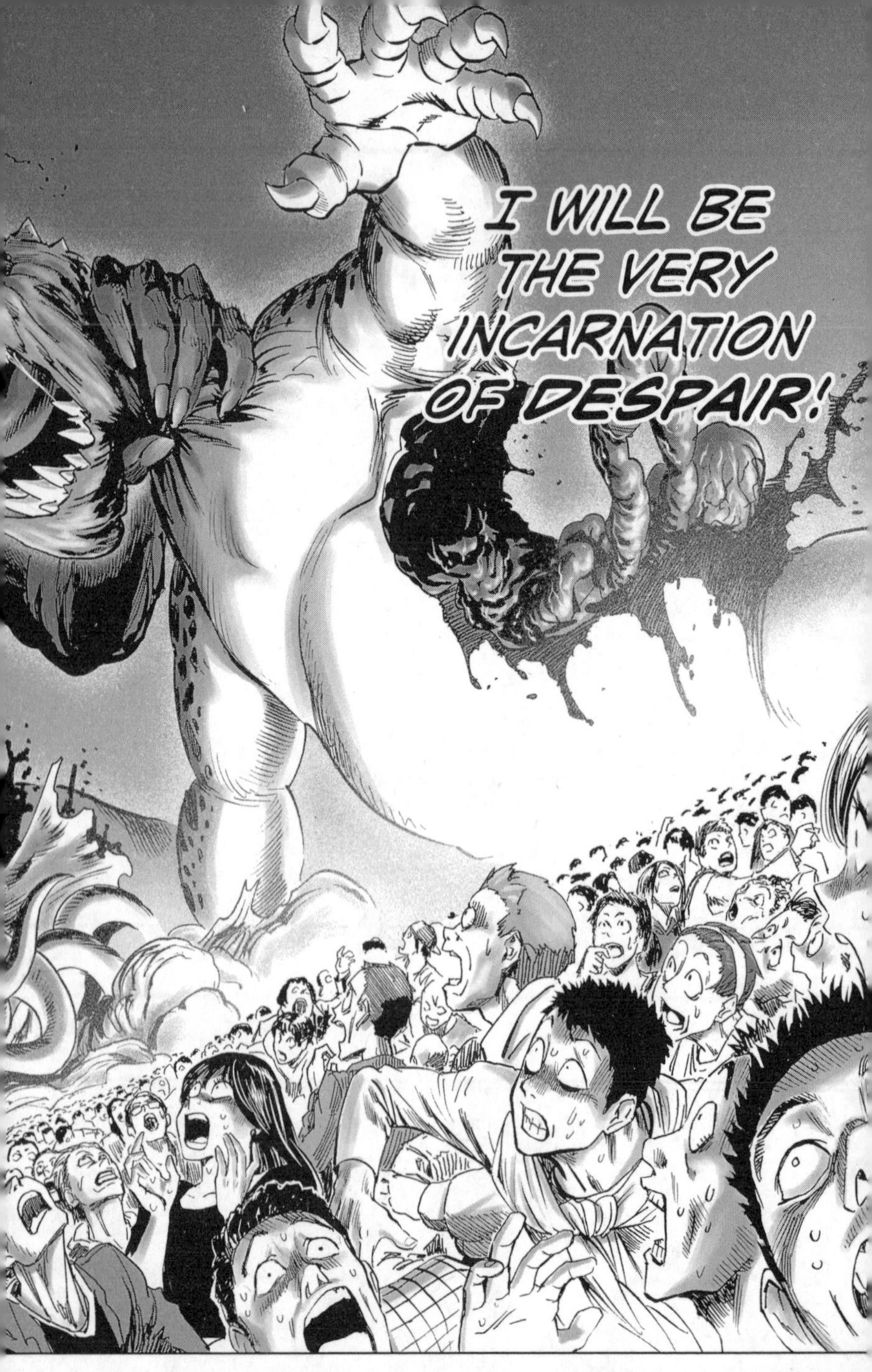
I WILL BE THE VERY INCARNATION OF DESPAIR!

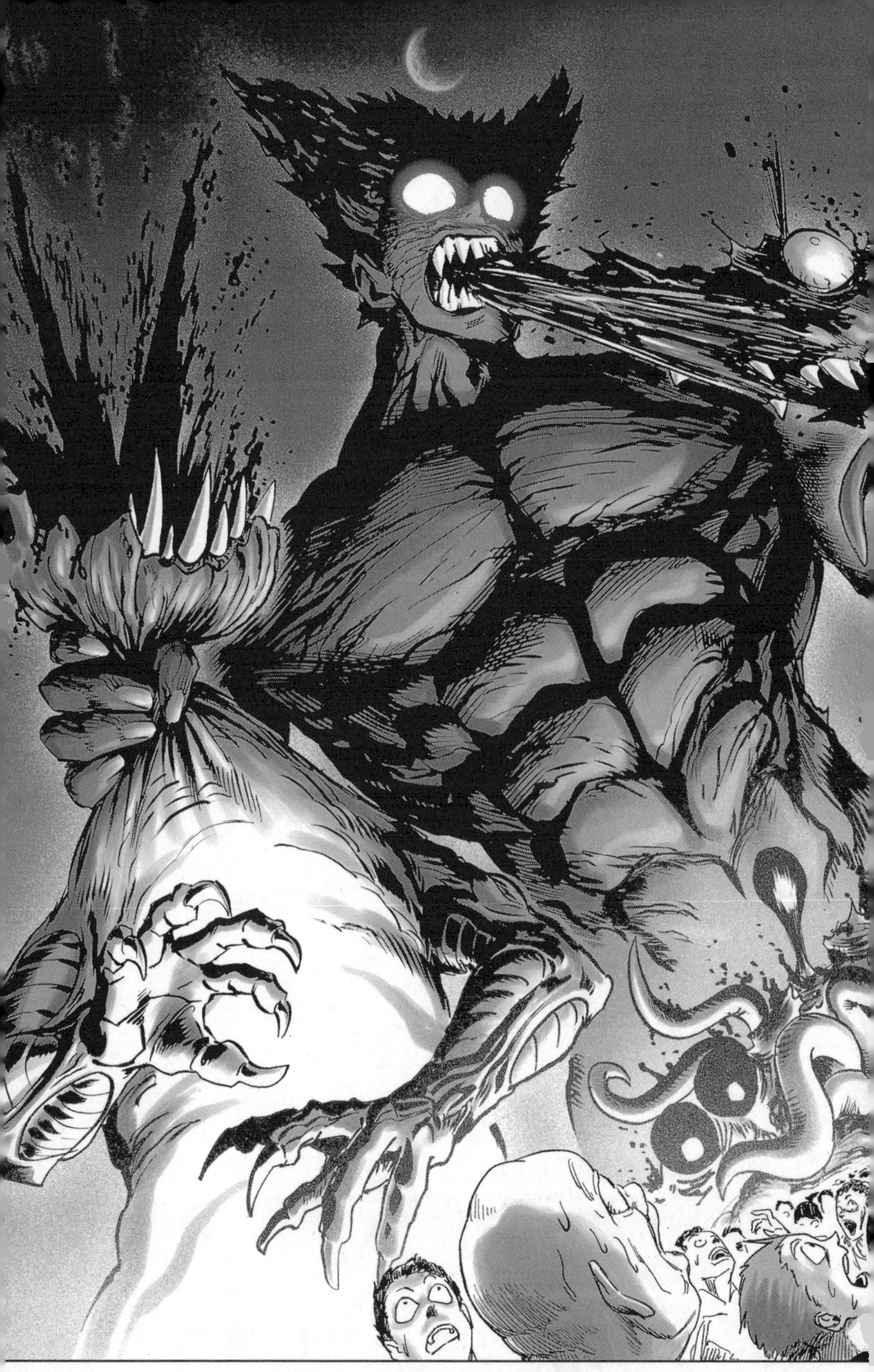

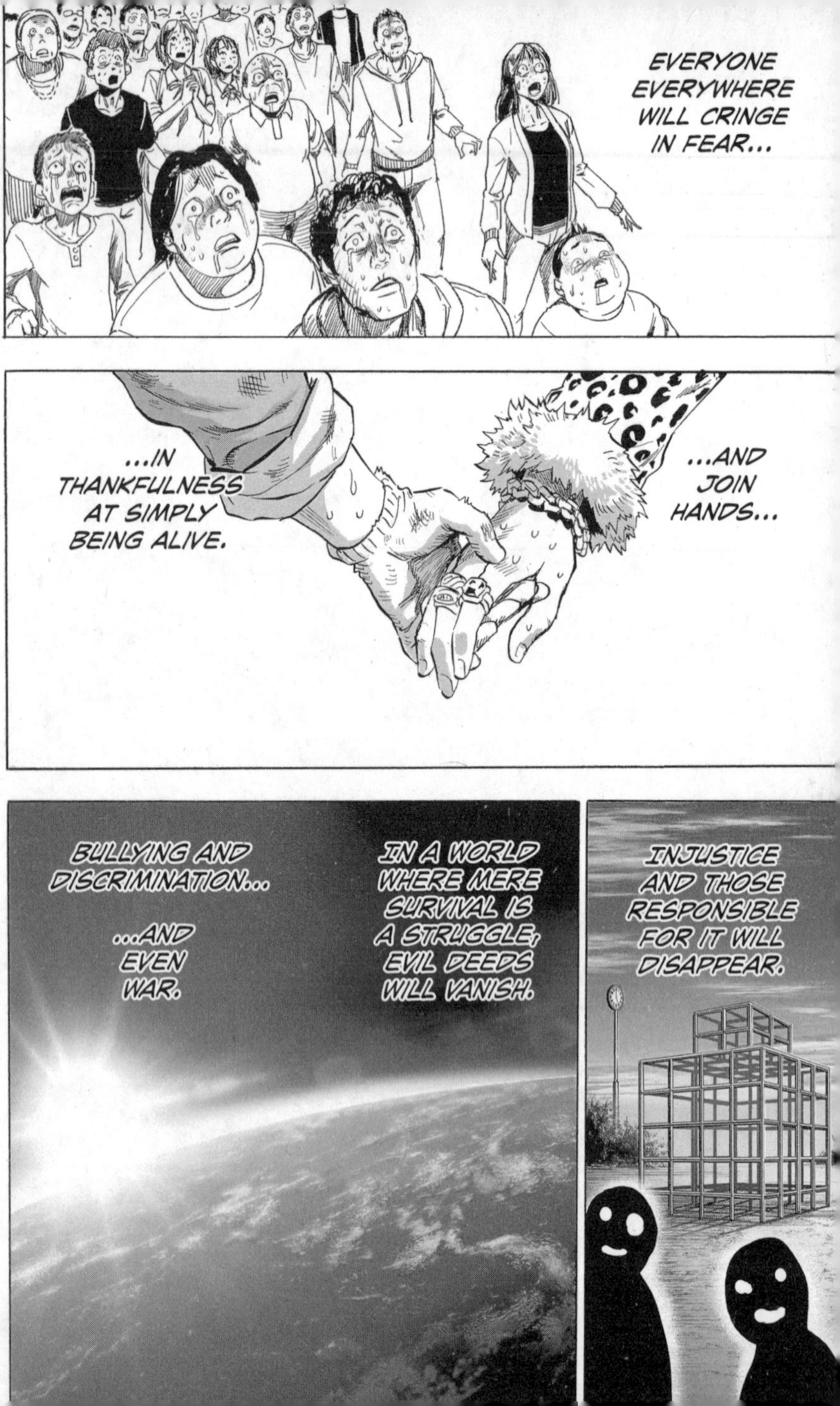
EVERYONE EVERYWHERE WILL CRINGE IN FEAR...
...AND JOIN HANDS...
...IN THANKFULNESS AT SIMPLY BEING ALIVE.
INJUSTICE AND THOSE RESPONSIBLE FOR IT WILL DISAPPEAR.
IN A WORLD WHERE MERE SURVIVAL IS A STRUGGLE, EVIL DEEDS WILL VANISH.
BULLYING AND DISCRIMINATION...
...AND EVEN WAR.

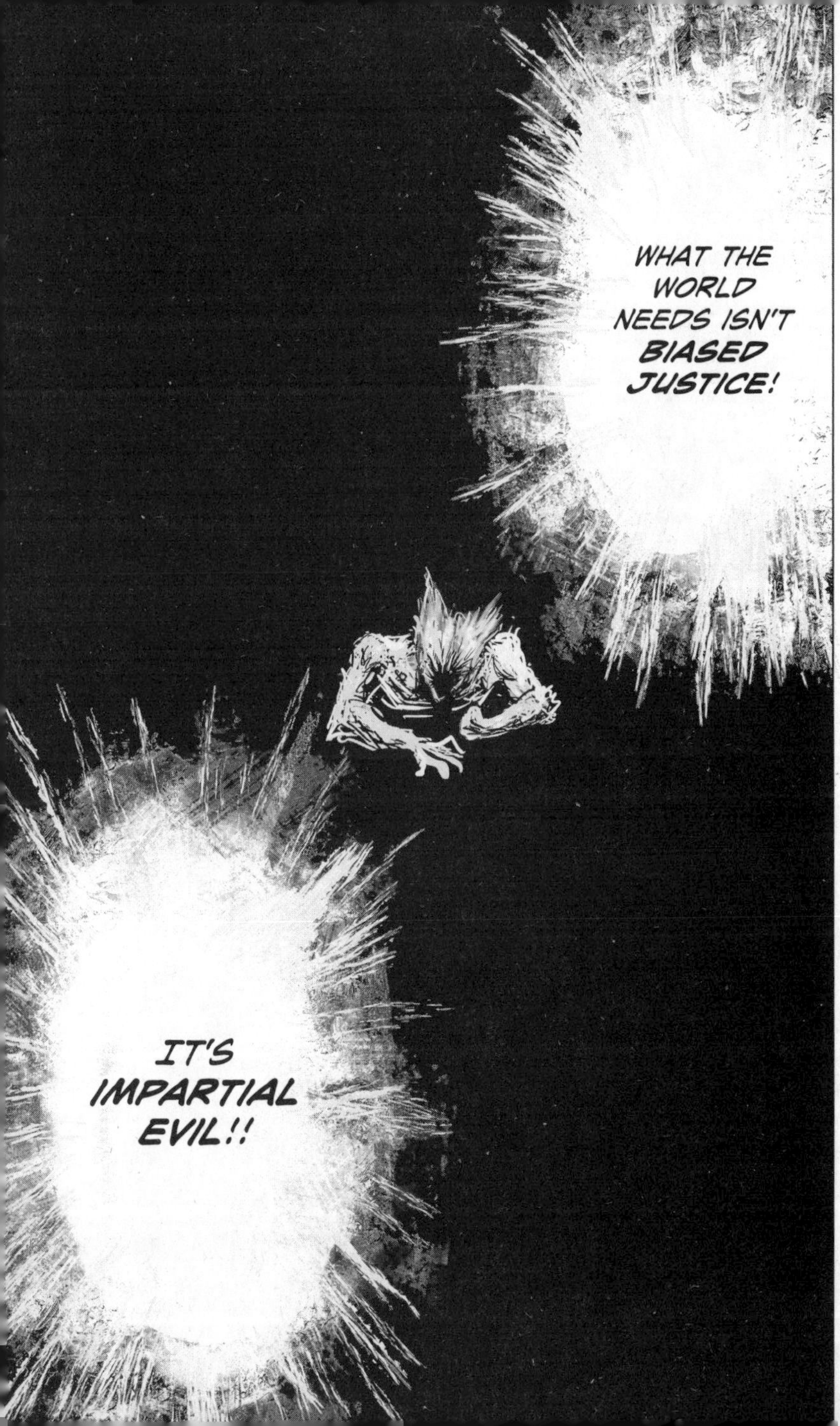
WHAT THE WORLD NEEDS ISN'T BIASED JUSTICE!
IT'S IMPARTIAL EVIL!!

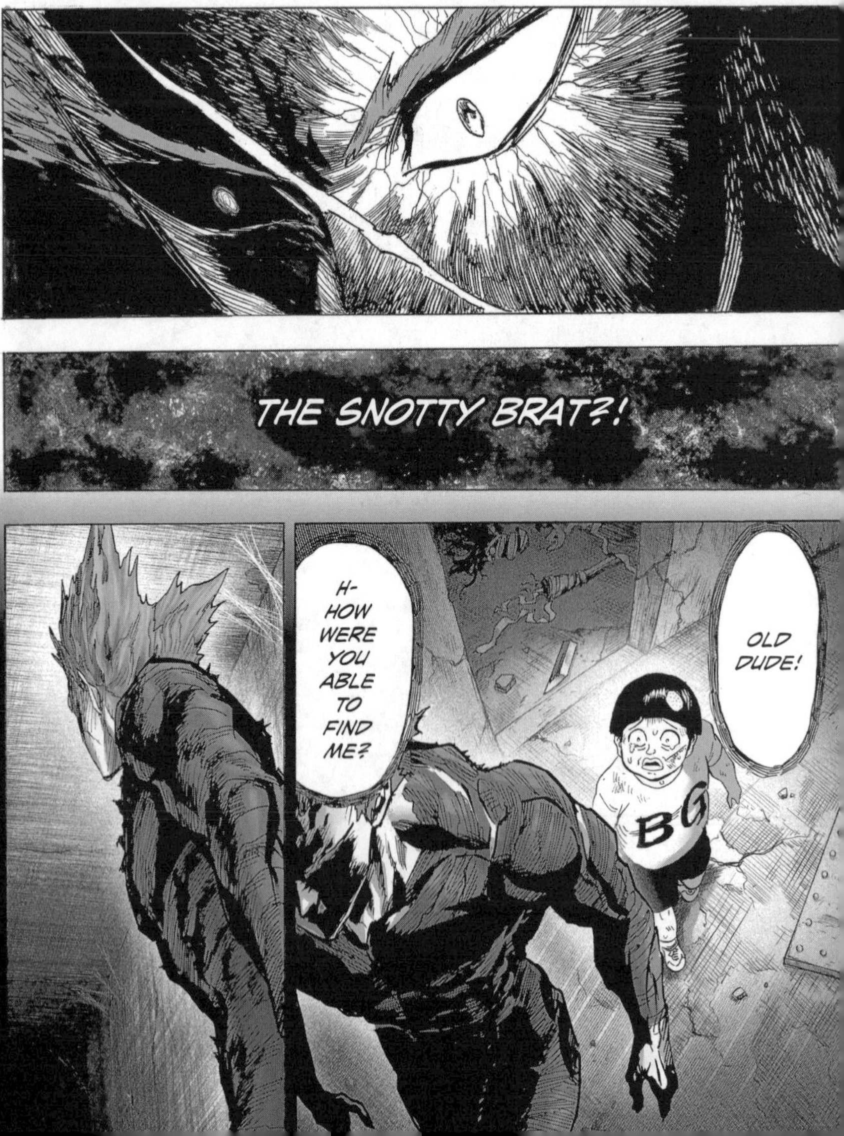
THE SNOTTY BRAT?!
OLD DUDE!
H-HOW WERE YOU ABLE TO FIND ME?

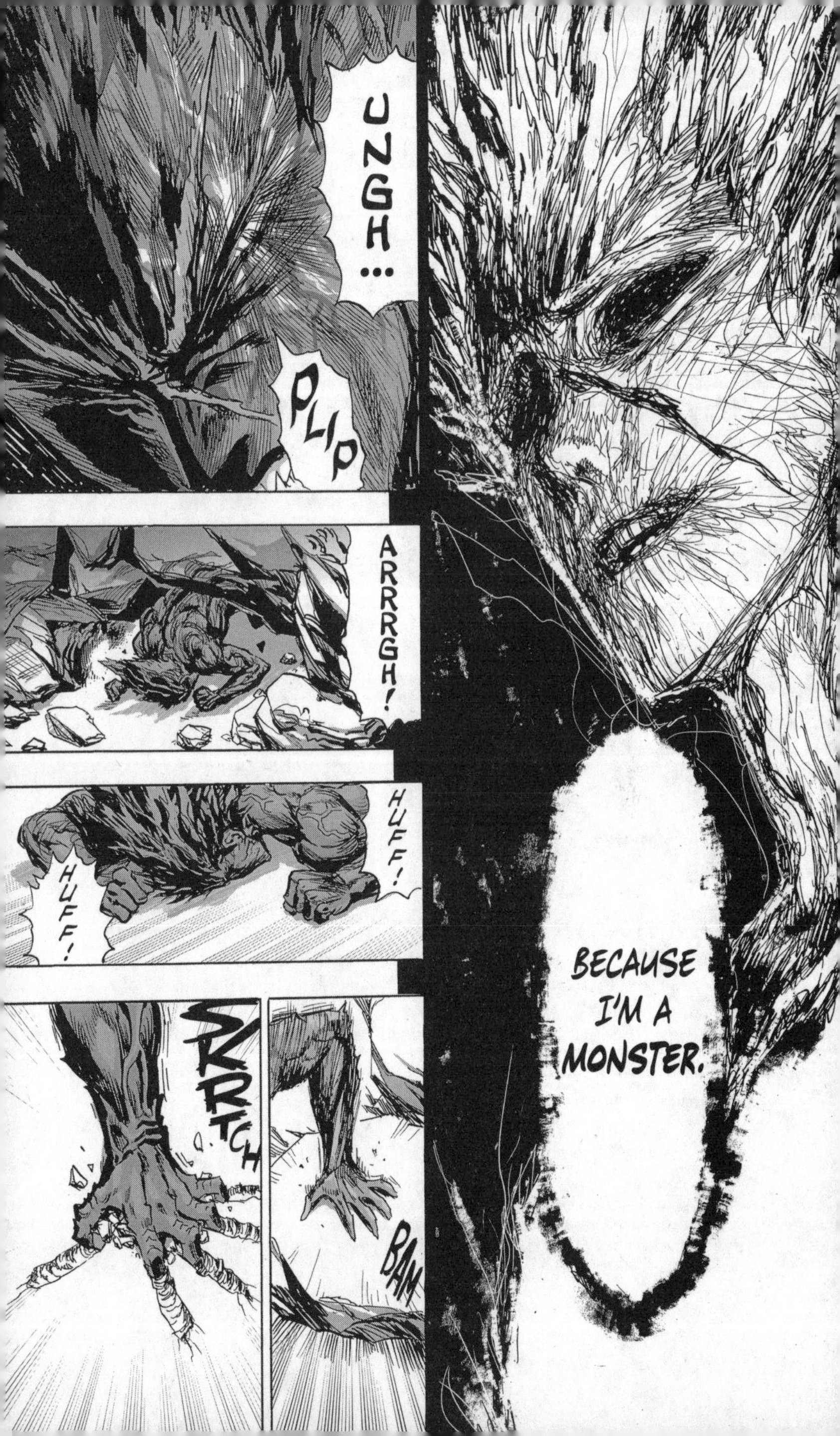
BECAUSE I'M A MONSTER.
UNGH...
PLIP
ARRRGH!
HUFF!
HUFF!
BAM
SKRTCH

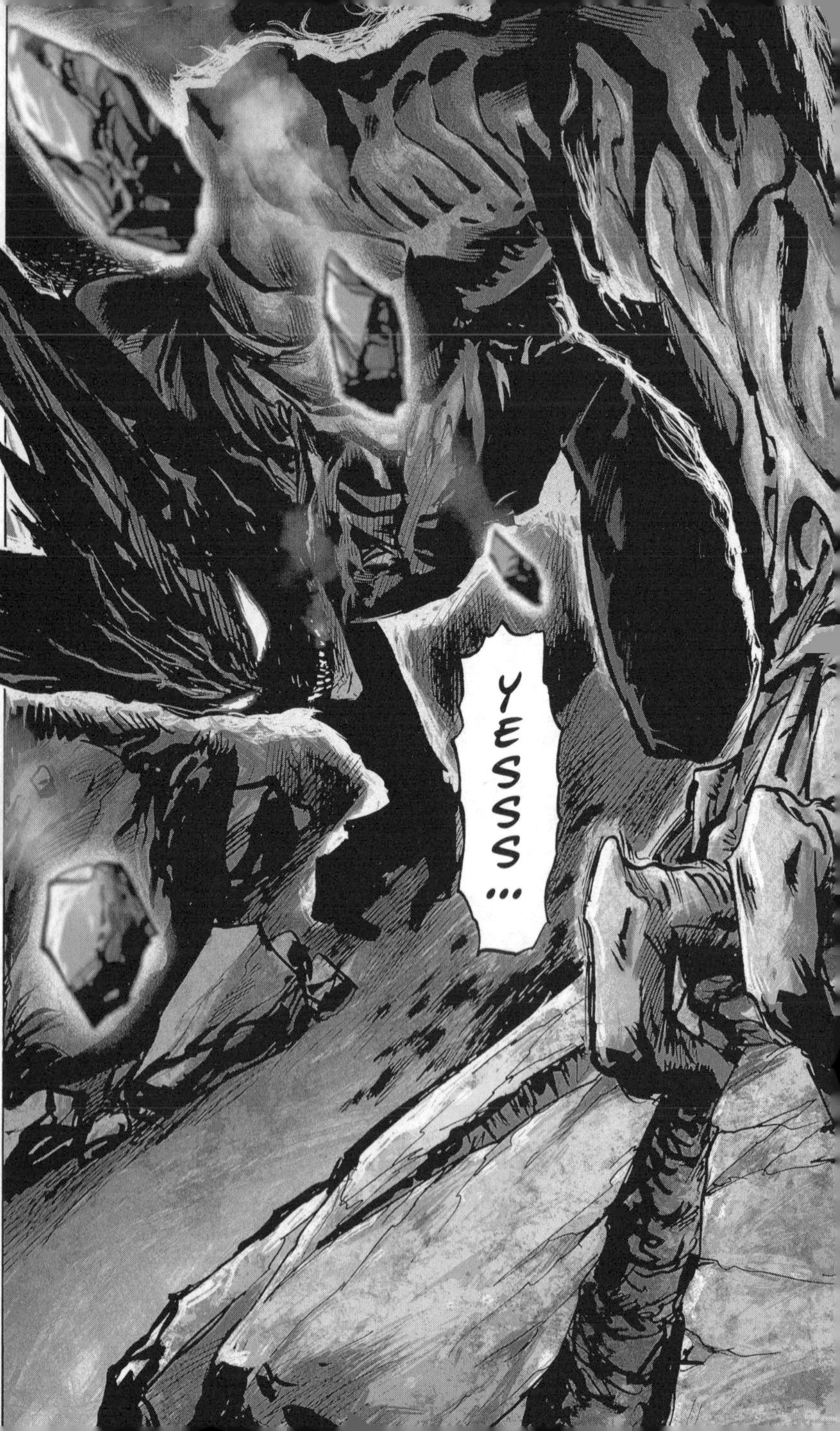
YESSS...

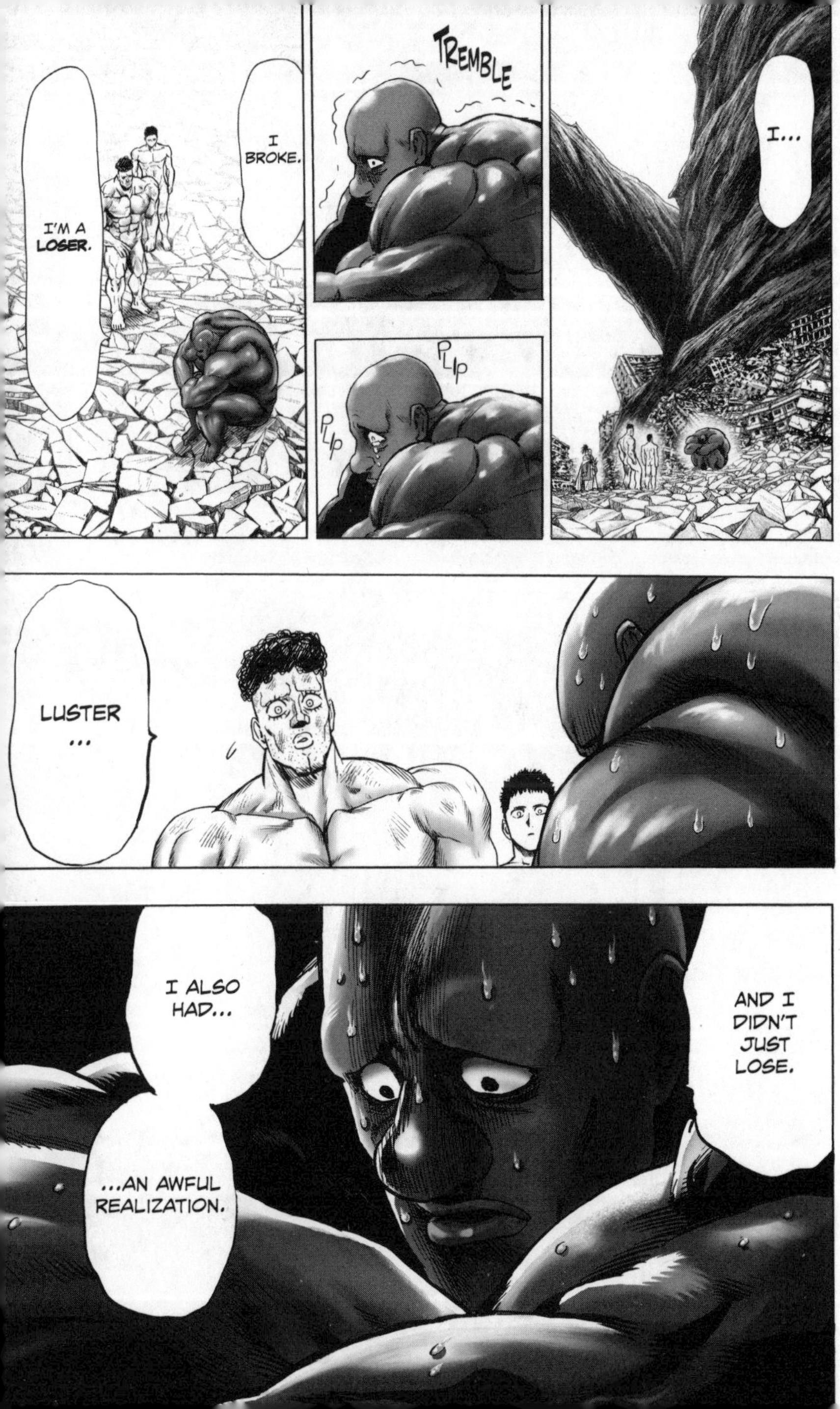
I...
TREMBLE
PLIP
PLIP
I BROKE.
I'M A LOSER.
LUSTER ...
AND I DIDN'T JUST LOSE.
I ALSO HAD...
...AN AWFUL REALIZATION.

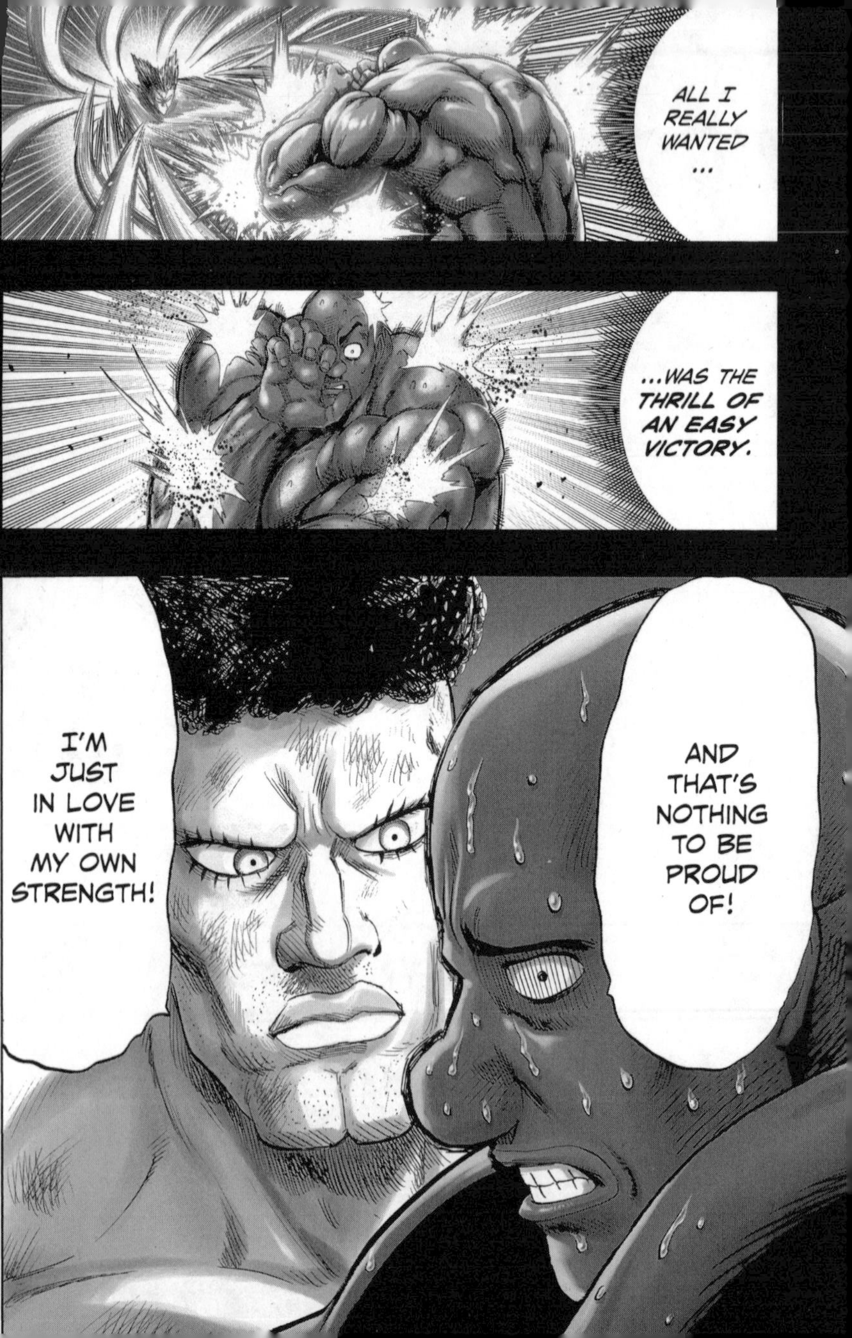
ALL I REALLY WANTED ...
...WAS THE THRILL OF AN EASY VICTORY.
AND THAT'S NOTHING TO BE PROUD OF!
I'M JUST IN LOVE WITH MY OWN STRENGTH!

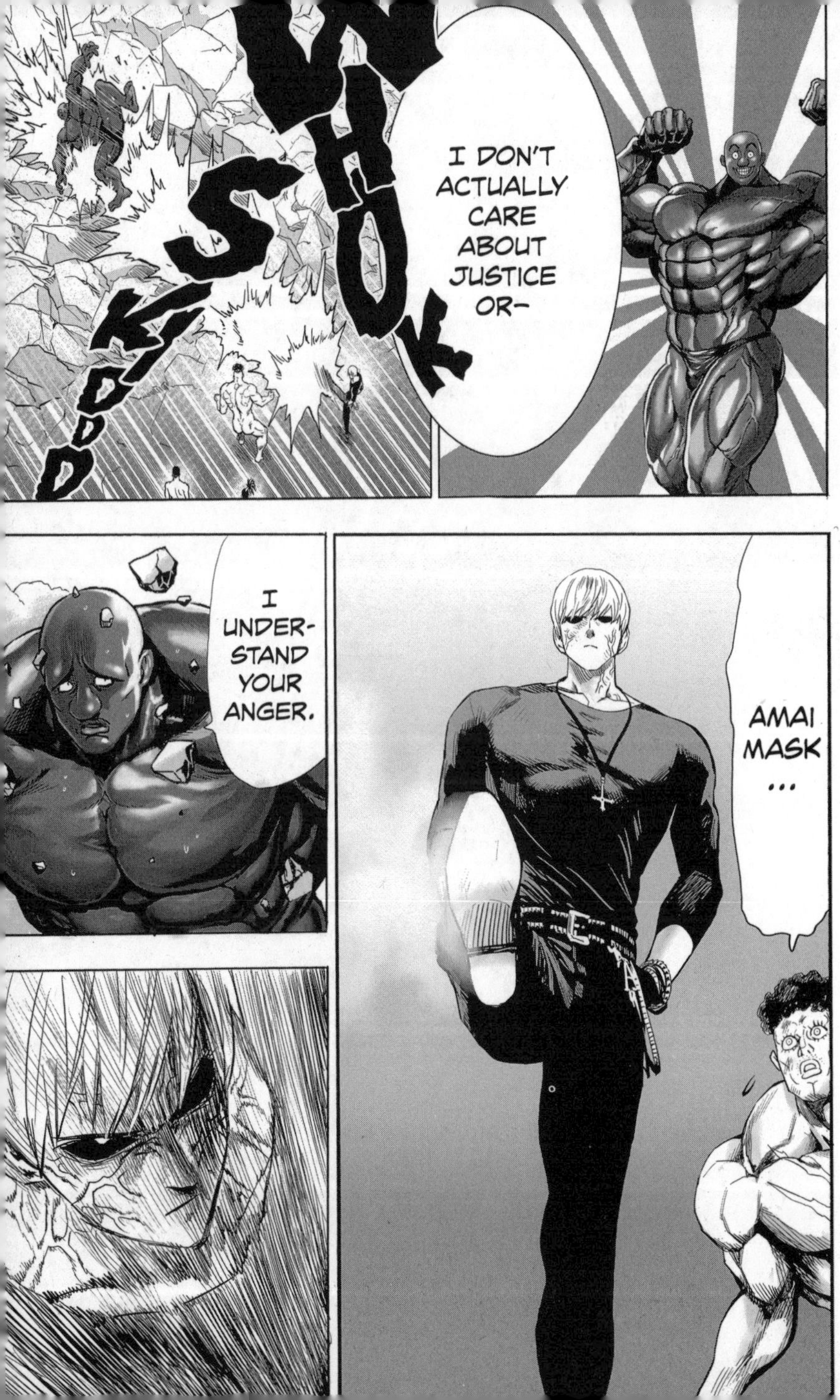
I DON'T ACTUALLY CARE ABOUT JUSTICE OR—
WHOK
SKYDDD
AMAI MASK ...
I UNDER-STAND YOUR ANGER.

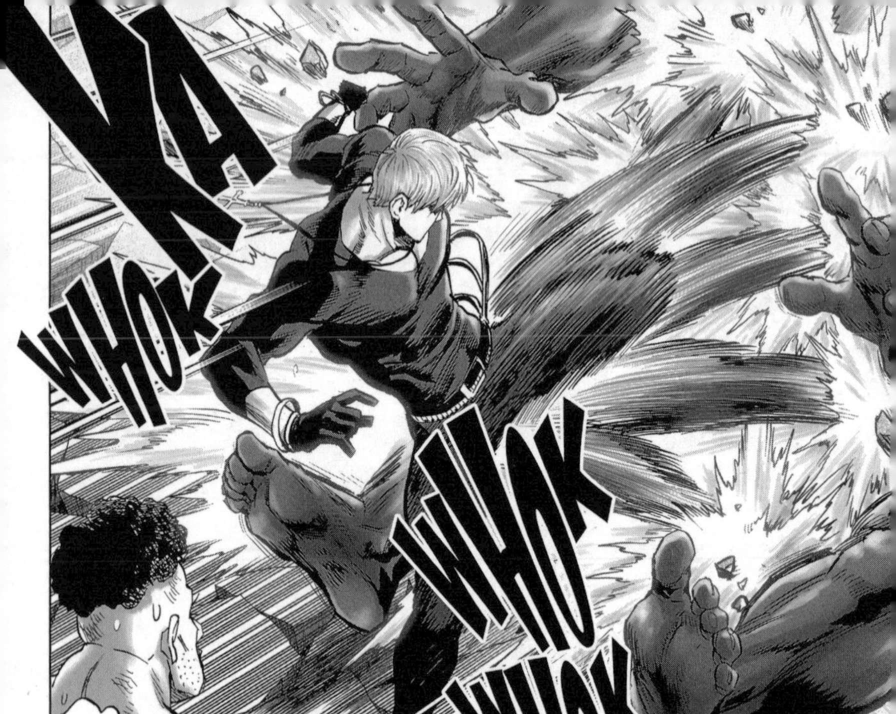
YA!
WHOK
WHOK
WHOK
HEY!
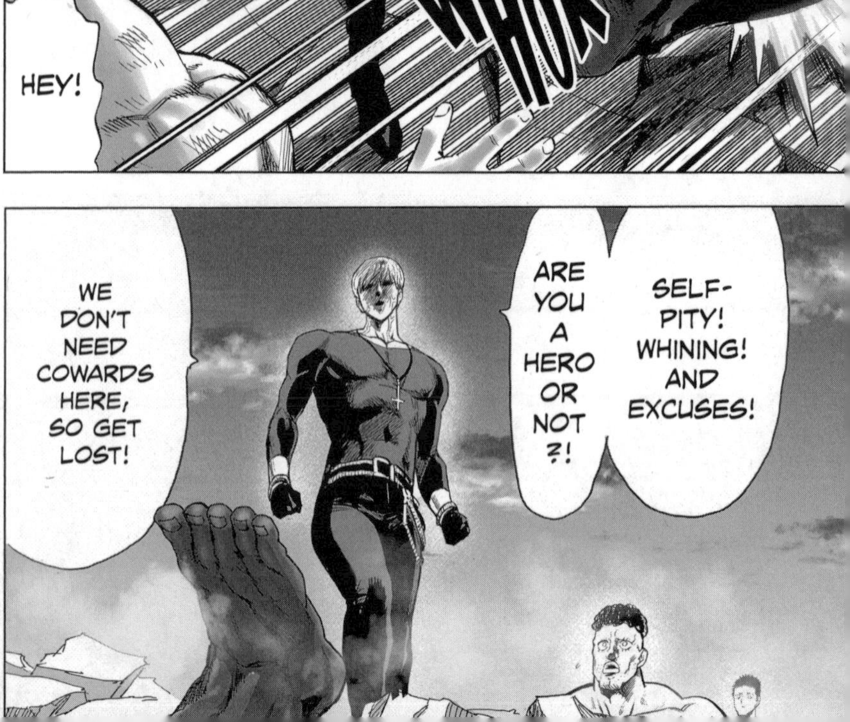
SELF-PITY! WHINING! AND EXCUSES!
ARE YOU A HERO OR NOT?!
WE DON'T NEED COWARDS HERE, SO GET LOST!

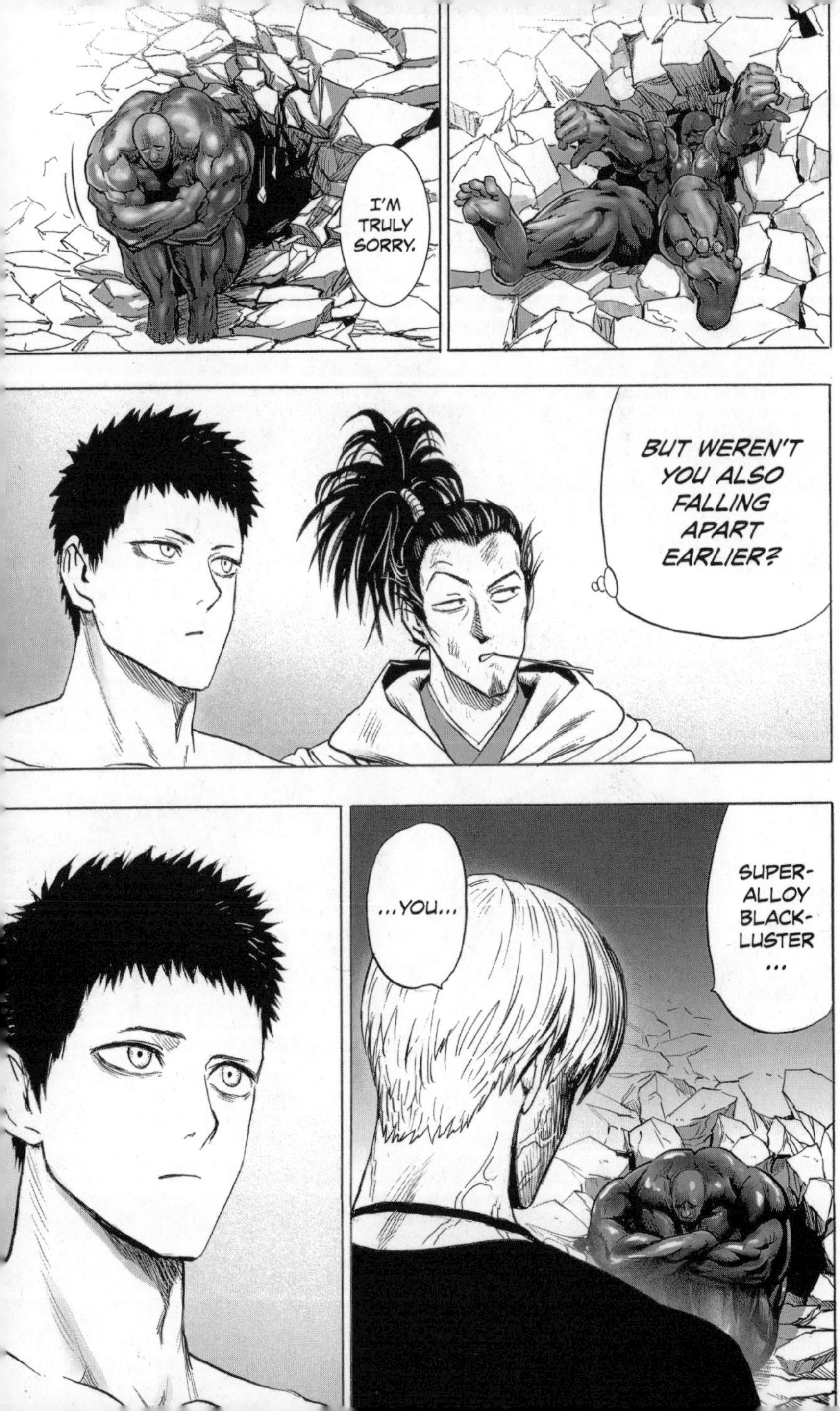
I'M TRULY SORRY.
BUT WEREN'T YOU ALSO FALLING APART EARLIER?
SUPER-ALLOY BLACK-LUSTER ...
...YOU...

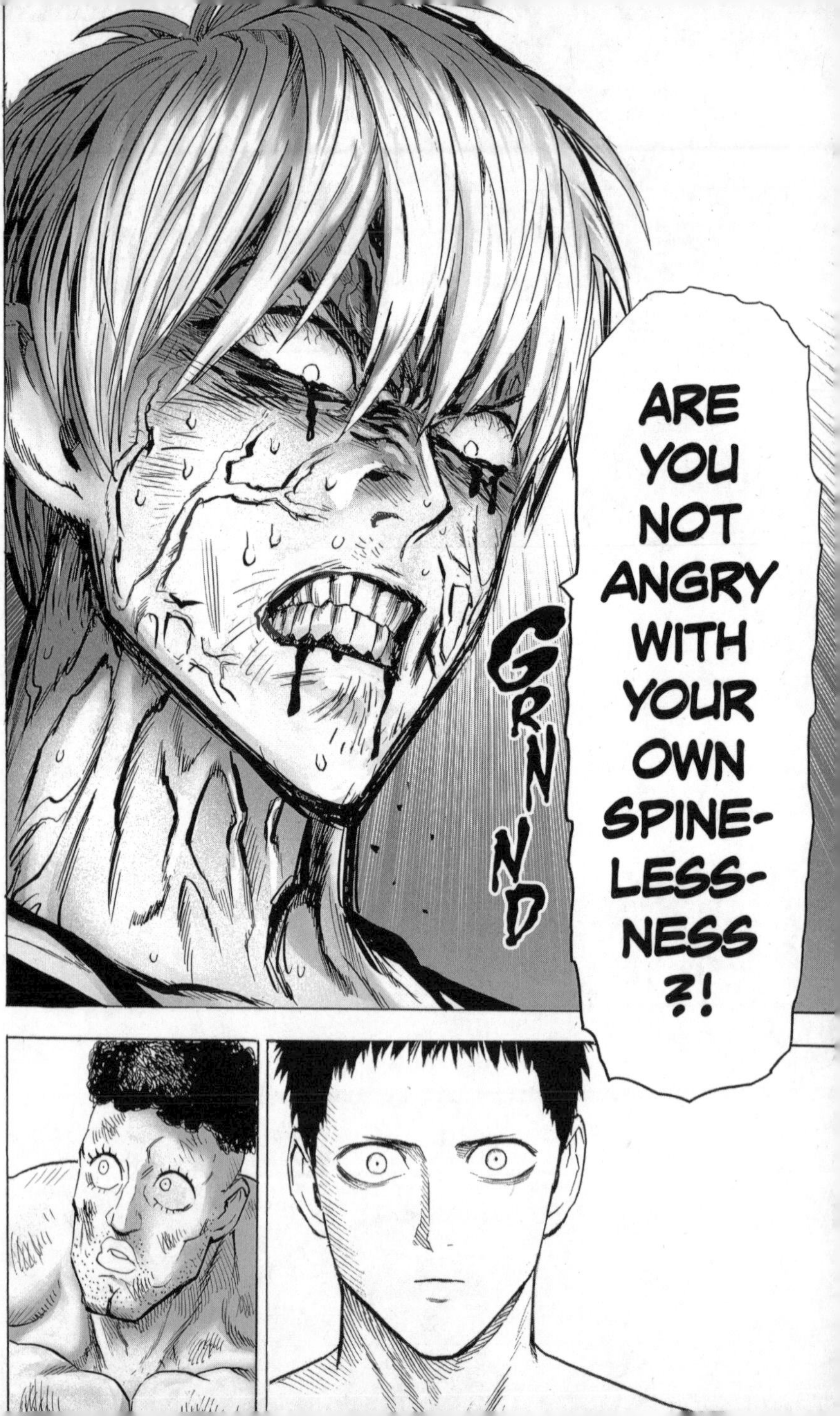
ARE YOU NOT ANGRY WITH YOUR OWN SPINE-LESS-NESS?!
GRNND

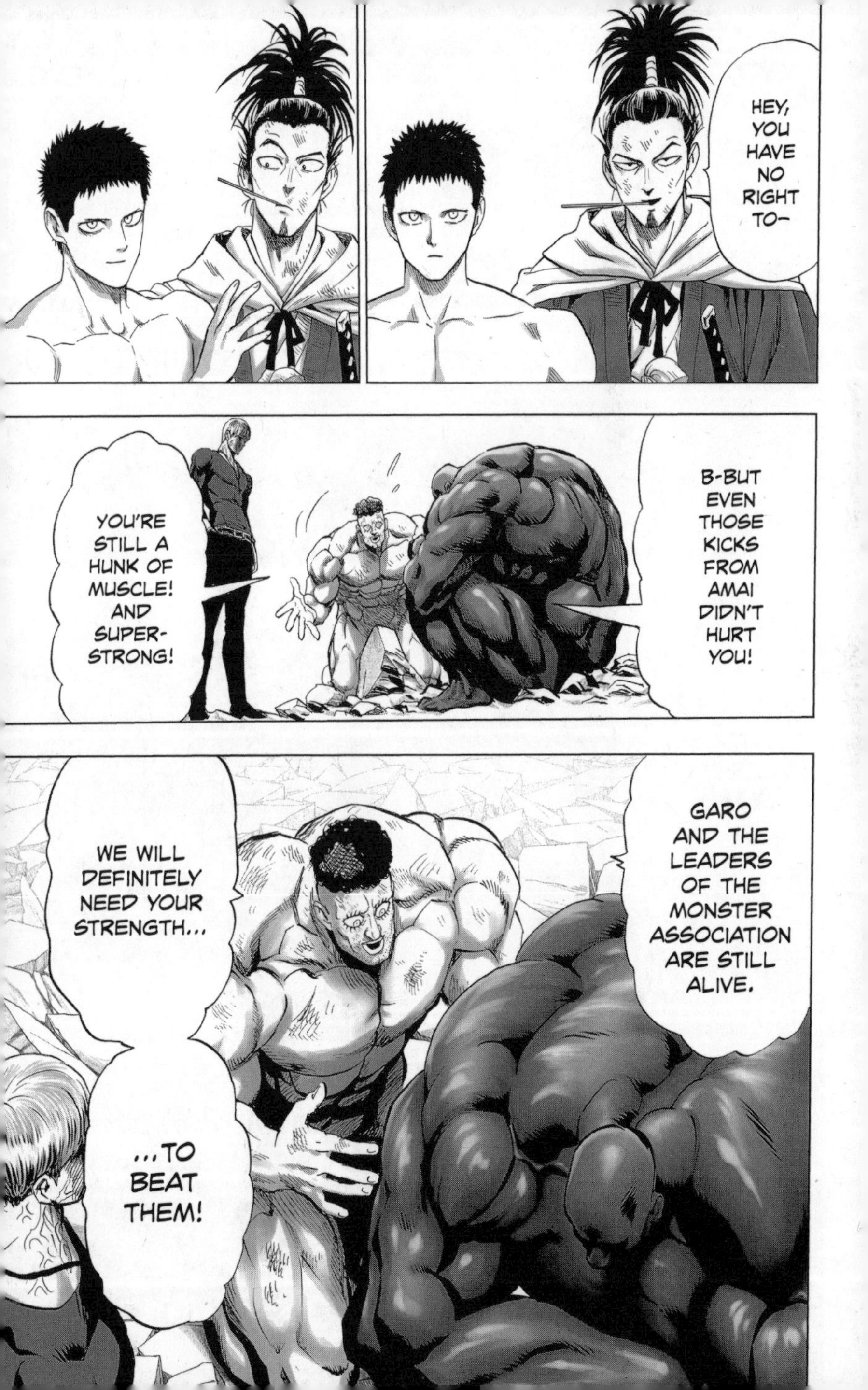
HEY, YOU HAVE NO RIGHT TO–
B-BUT EVEN THOSE KICKS FROM AMAI DIDN'T HURT YOU!
YOU'RE STILL A HUNK OF MUSCLE! AND SUPER-STRONG!
GARO AND THE LEADERS OF THE MONSTER ASSOCIATION ARE STILL ALIVE.
WE WILL DEFINITELY NEED YOUR STRENGTH...
...TO BEAT THEM!

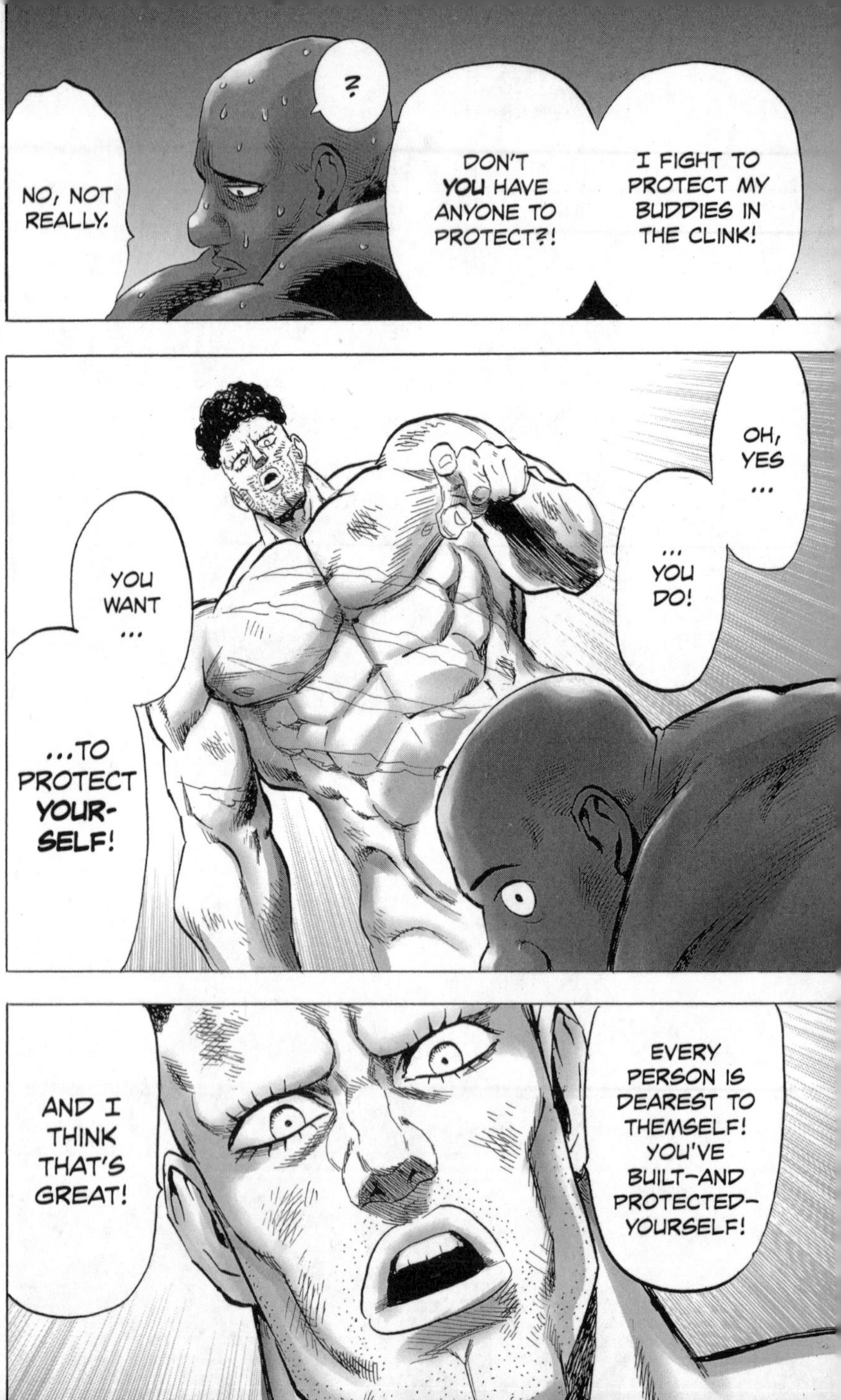
I FIGHT TO PROTECT MY BUDDIES IN THE CLINK!
DON'T **YOU** HAVE ANYONE TO PROTECT?!
?
NO, NOT REALLY.
OH, YES ...
... YOU DO!
YOU WANT ...
...TO PROTECT **YOURSELF**!
EVERY PERSON IS DEAREST TO THEMSELF! YOU'VE BUILT—AND PROTECTED—YOURSELF!
AND I THINK THAT'S GREAT!

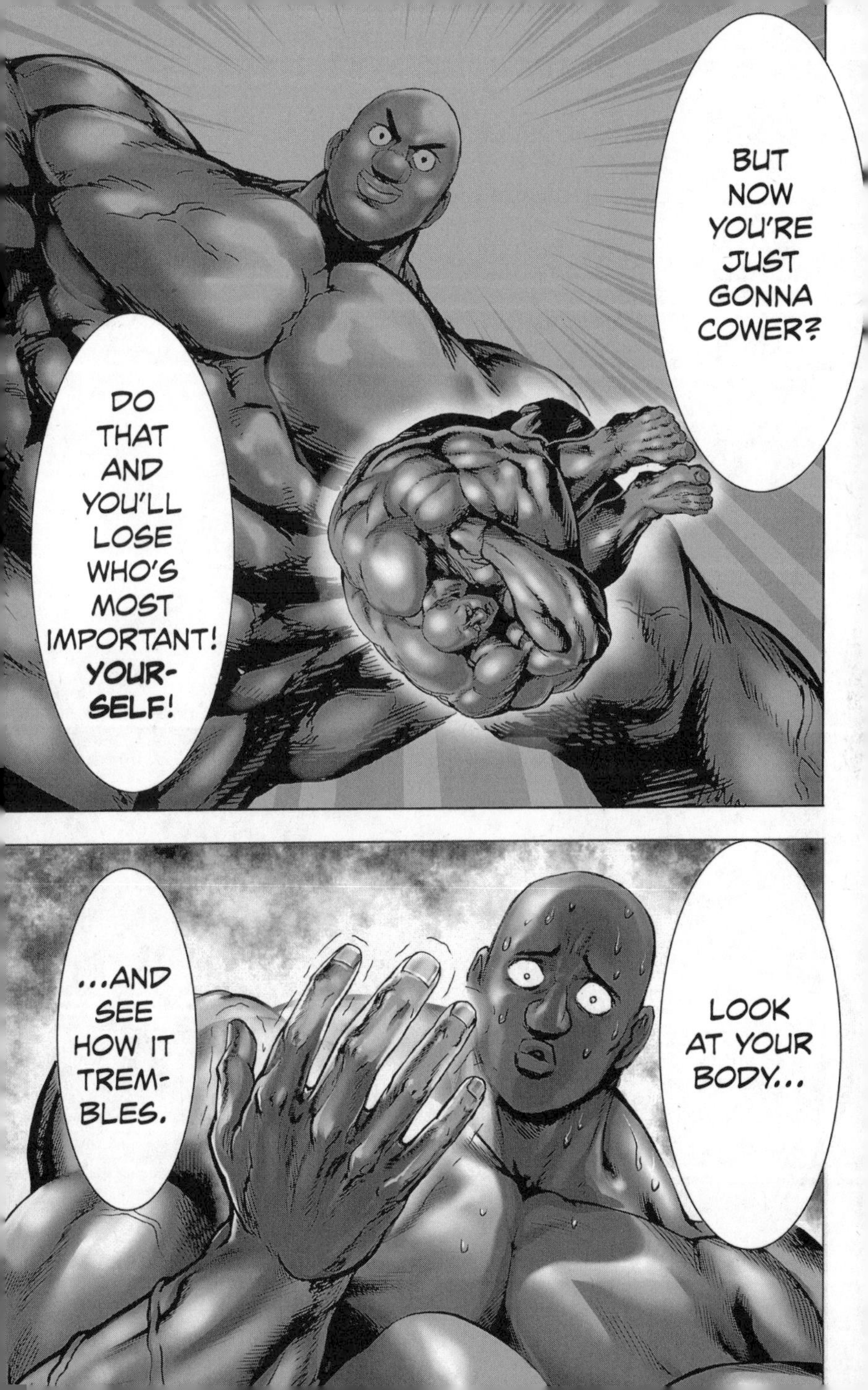
BUT NOW YOU'RE JUST GONNA COWER?
DO THAT AND YOU'LL LOSE WHO'S MOST IMPORTANT! **YOURSELF!**
LOOK AT YOUR BODY...
...AND SEE HOW IT TREMBLES.

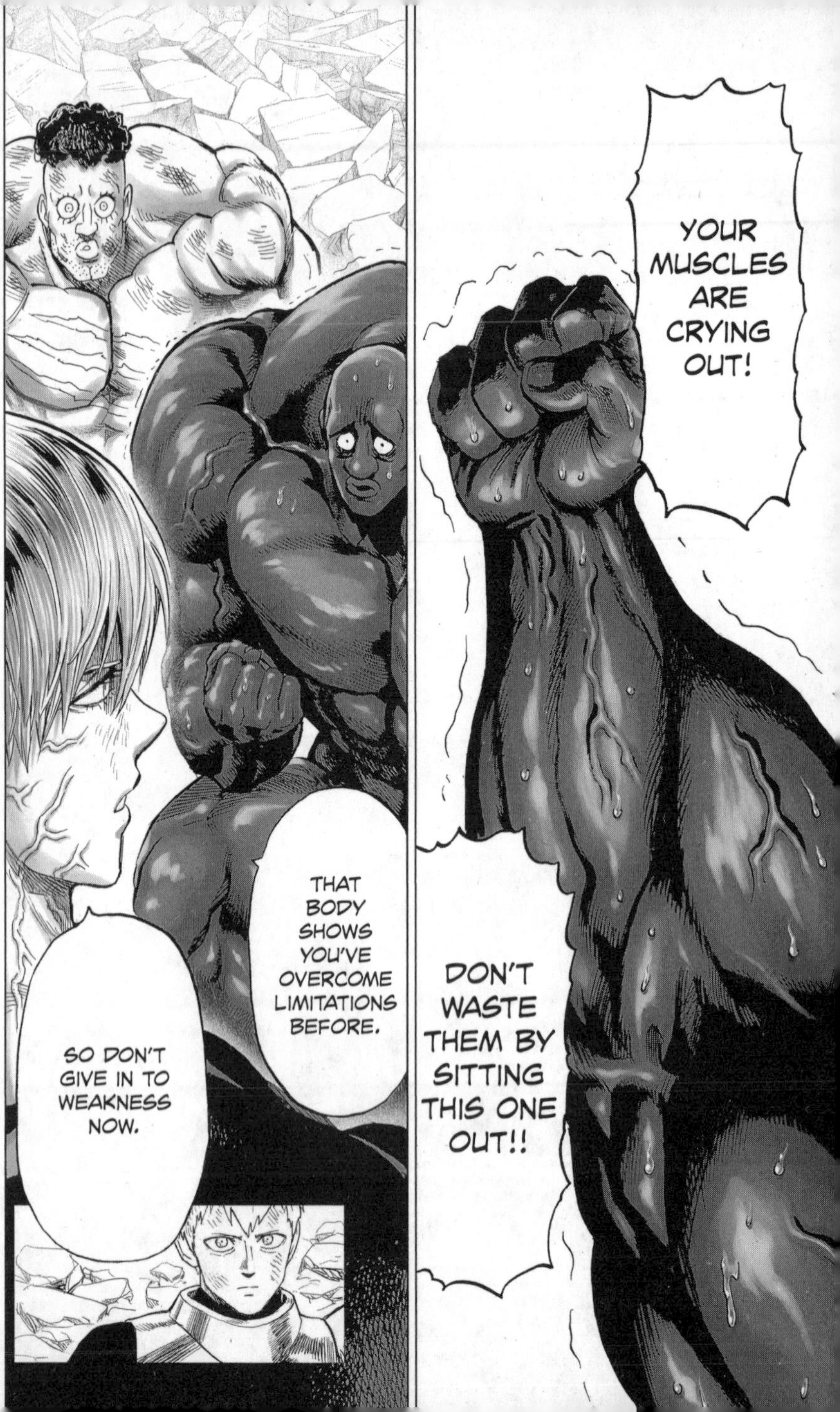
YOUR MUSCLES ARE CRYING OUT!
DON'T WASTE THEM BY SITTING THIS ONE OUT!!
THAT BODY SHOWS YOU'VE OVERCOME LIMITATIONS BEFORE.
SO DON'T GIVE IN TO WEAKNESS NOW.

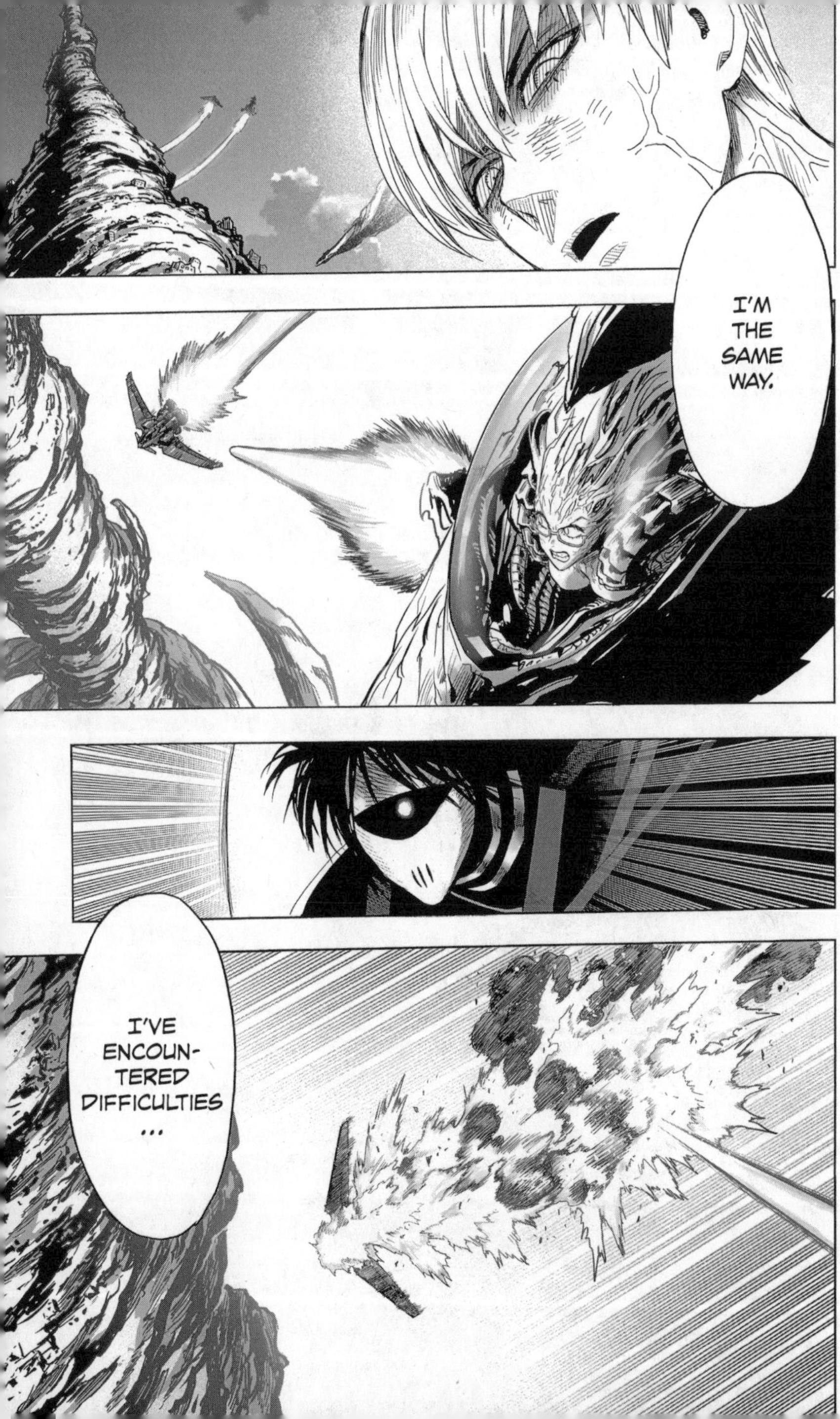
I'M THE SAME WAY.
I'VE ENCOUNTERED DIFFICULTIES...

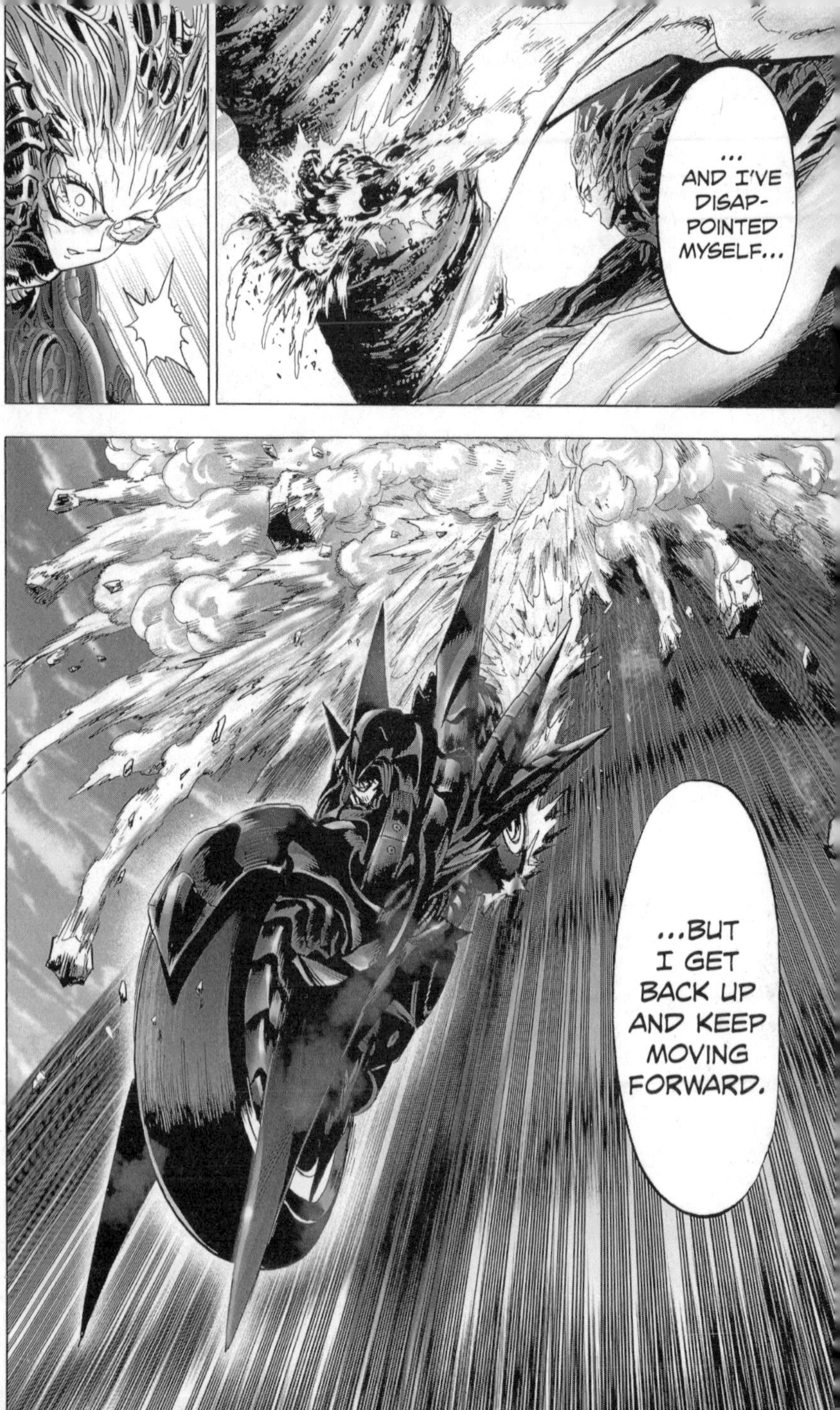
... AND I'VE DISAP- POINTED MYSELF...
...BUT I GET BACK UP AND KEEP MOVING FORWARD.

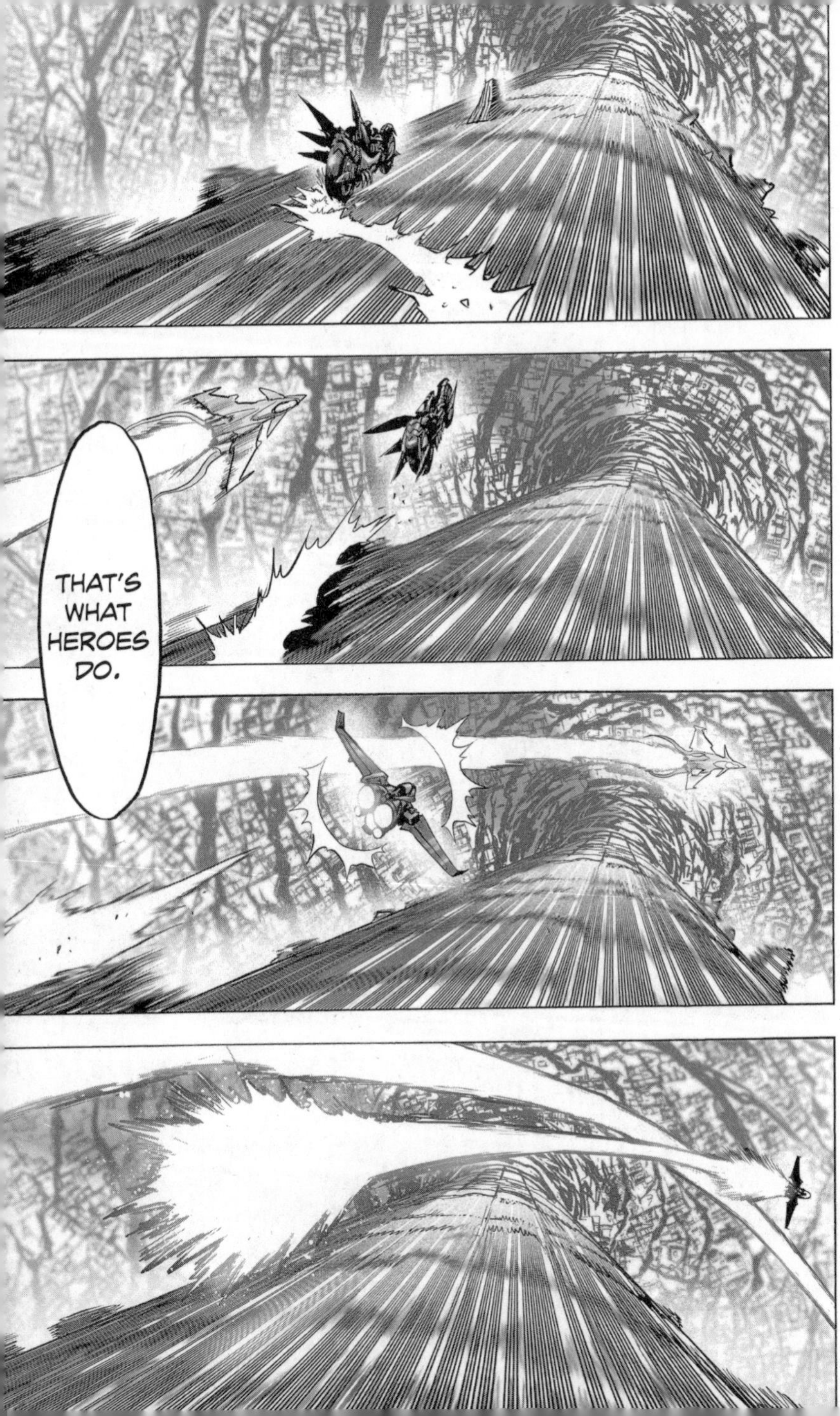
THAT'S WHAT HEROES DO.

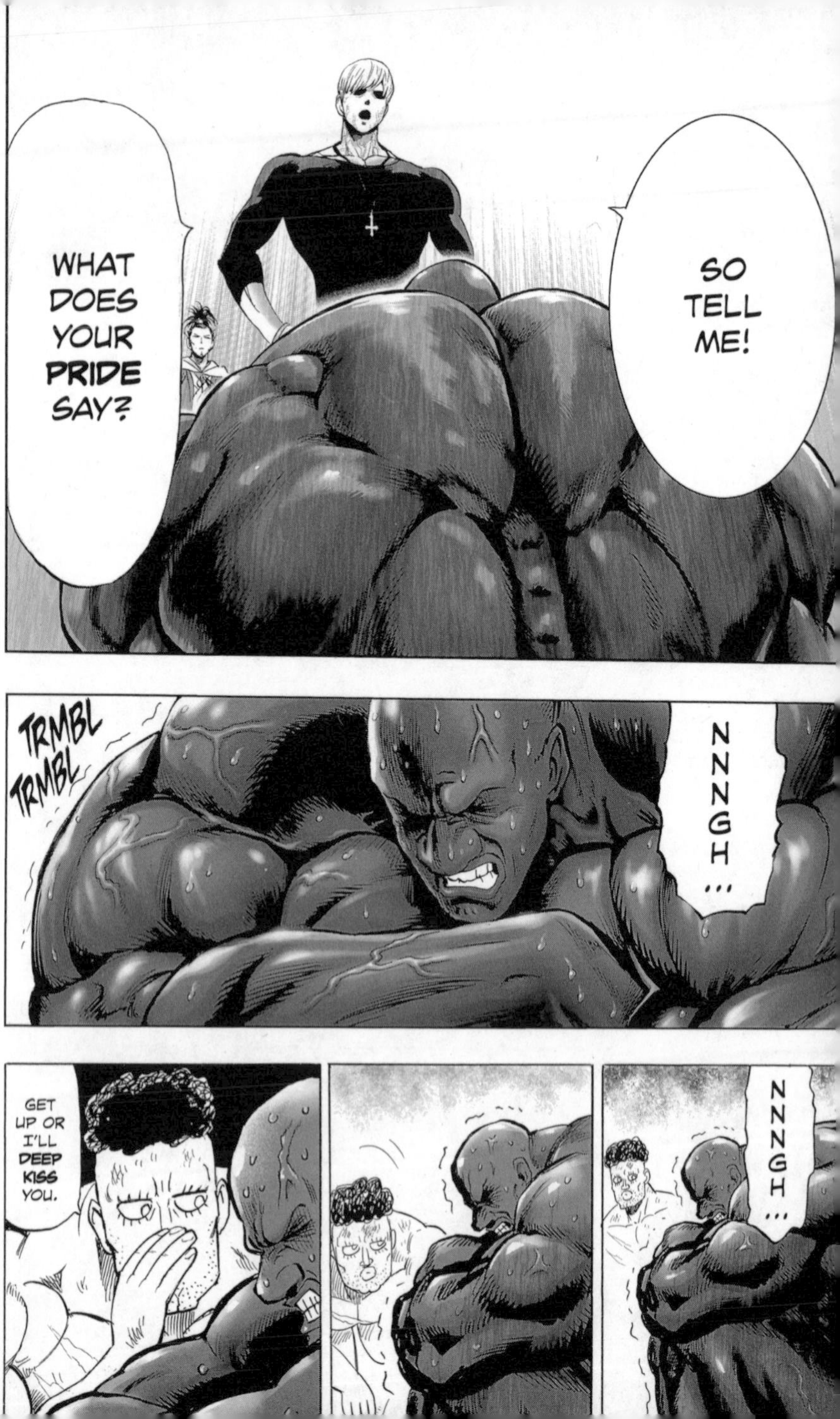
SO TELL ME!
WHAT DOES YOUR PRIDE SAY?
NNNGH...
TRMBL TRMBL
NNNGH...
GET UP OR I'LL DEEP KISS YOU.

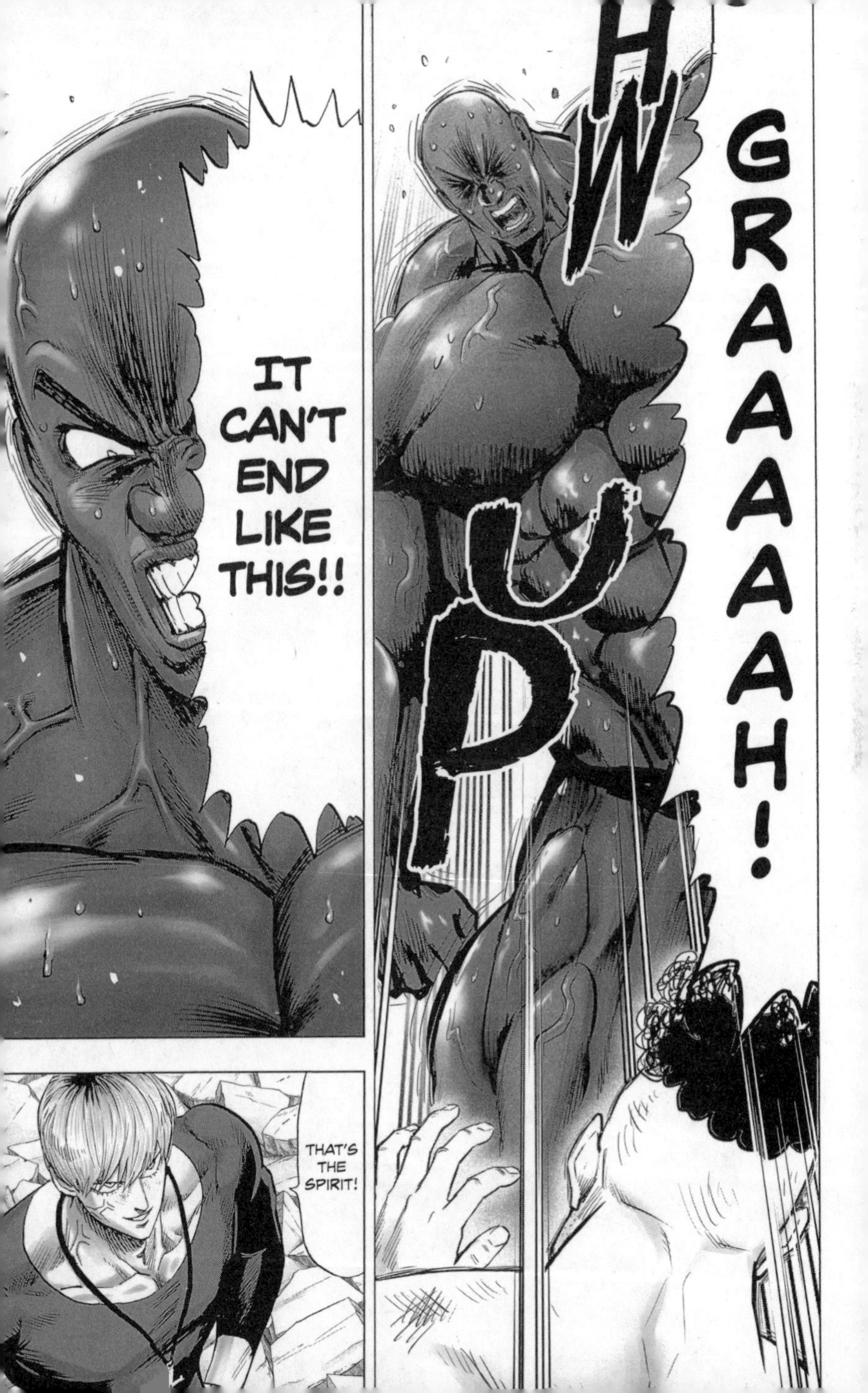
GRAAAAAH!
HWUP
IT CAN'T END LIKE THIS!!
THAT'S THE SPIRIT!

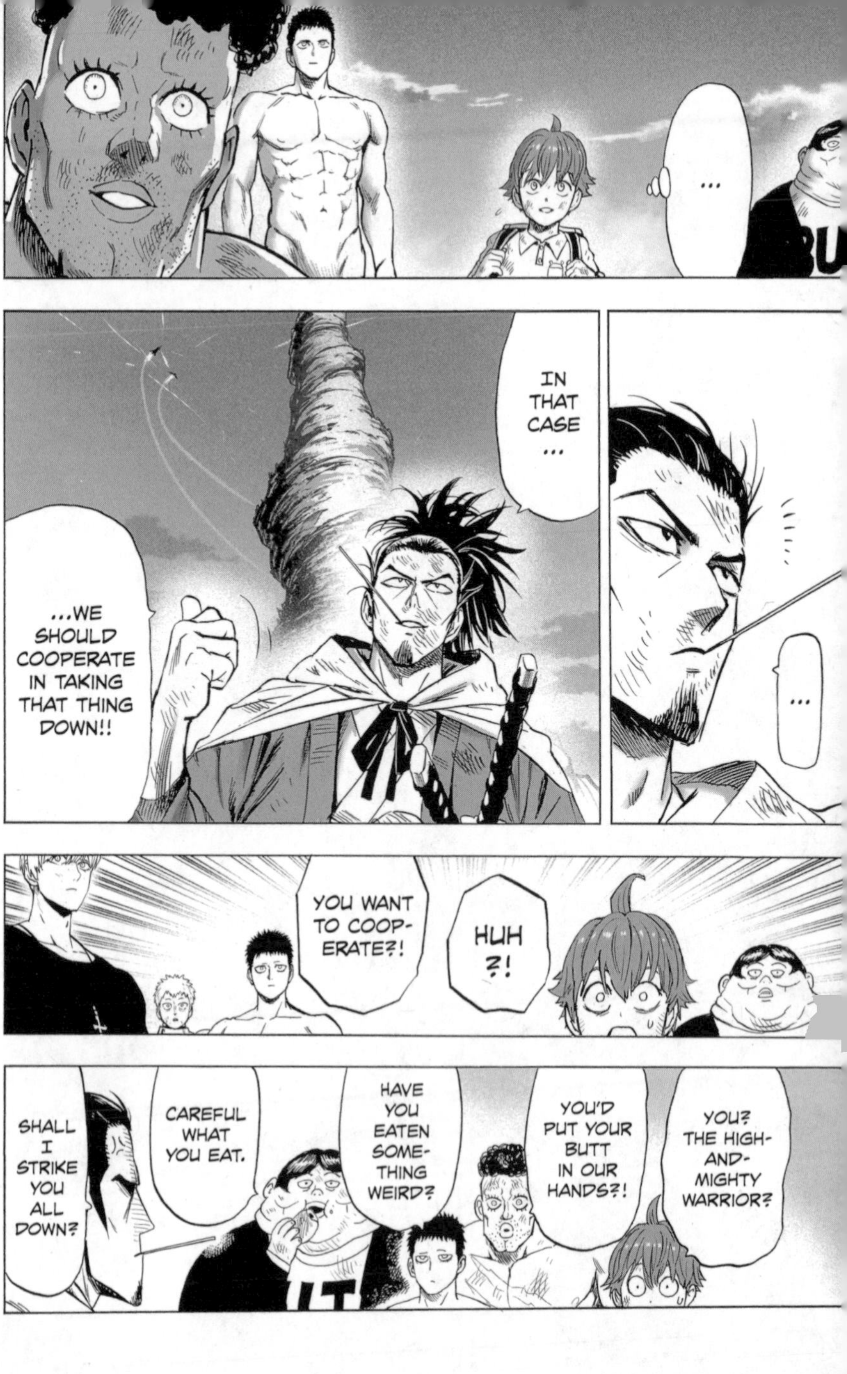
...
...
IN THAT CASE ...
...WE SHOULD COOPERATE IN TAKING THAT THING DOWN!!
HUH?!
YOU WANT TO COOP-ERATE?!
YOU? THE HIGH-AND-MIGHTY WARRIOR?
YOU'D PUT YOUR BUTT IN OUR HANDS?!
HAVE YOU EATEN SOME-THING WEIRD?
CAREFUL WHAT YOU EAT.
SHALL I STRIKE YOU ALL DOWN?

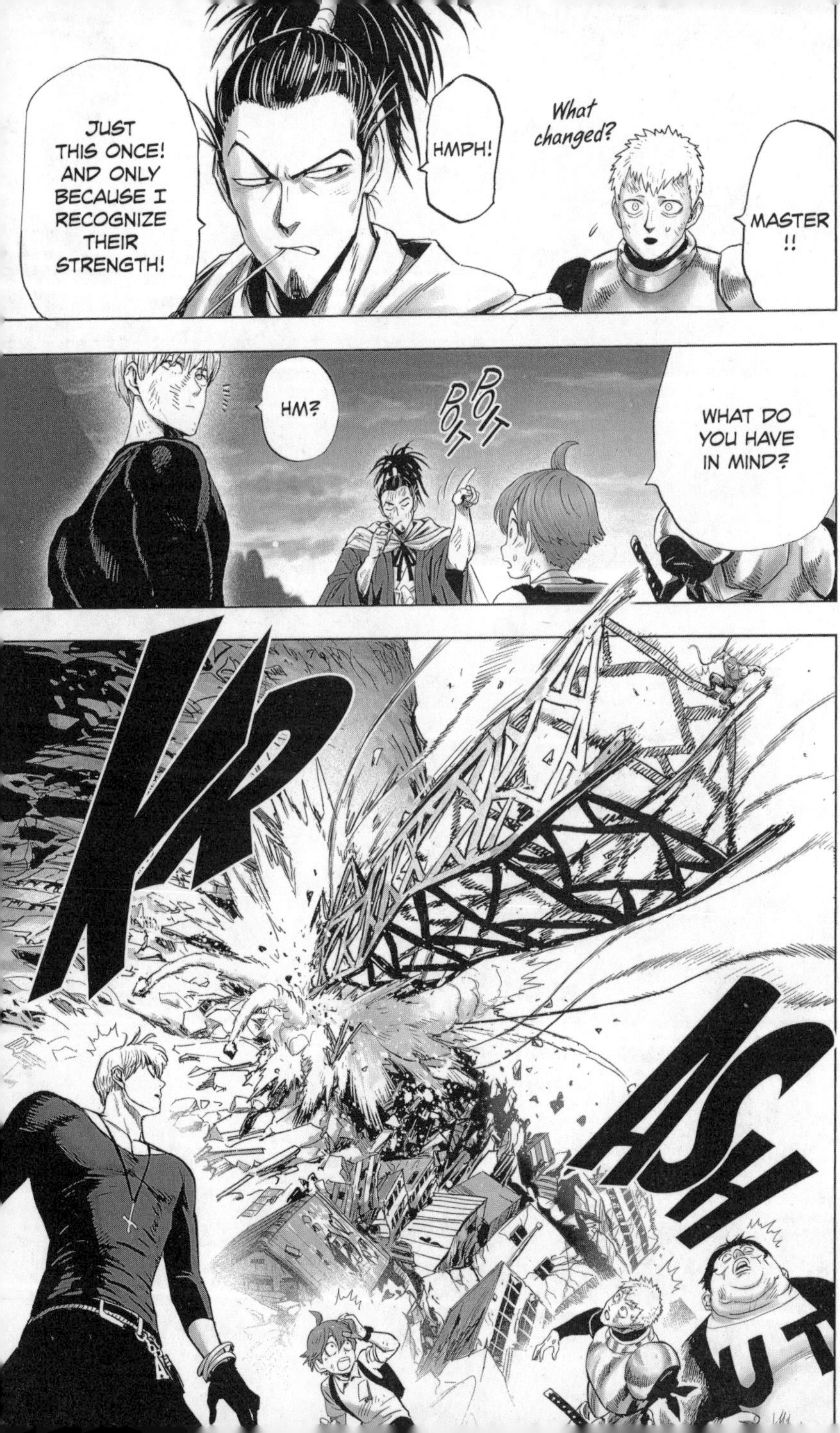
MASTER !!
What changed?
HMPH!
JUST THIS ONCE! AND ONLY BECAUSE I RECOGNIZE THEIR STRENGTH!
WHAT DO YOU HAVE IN MIND?
POIT POIT
HM?
KRASH

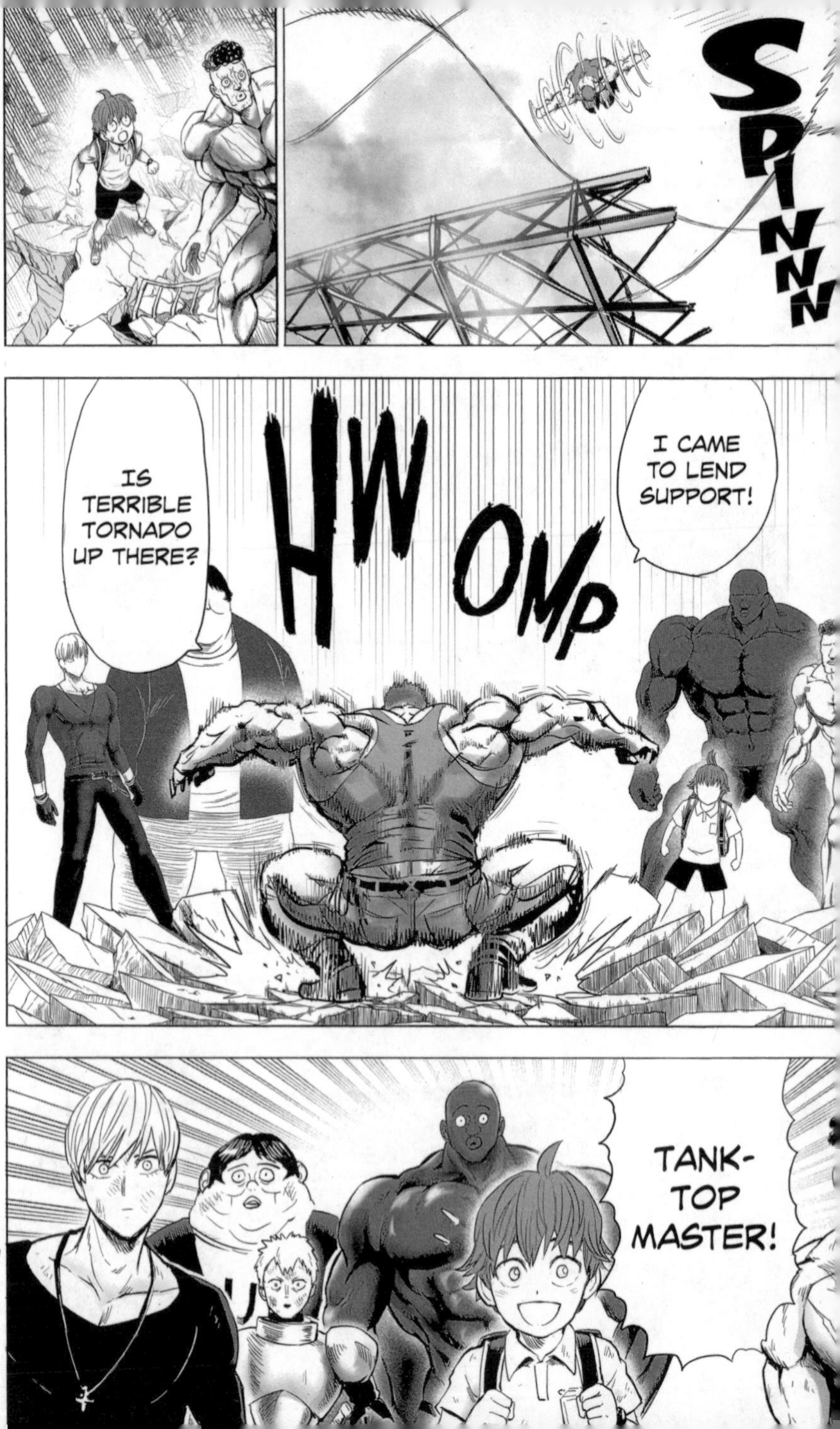
SPINNN
HWOMP
I CAME TO LEND SUPPORT!
IS TERRIBLE TORNADO UP THERE?
TANK-TOP MASTER!

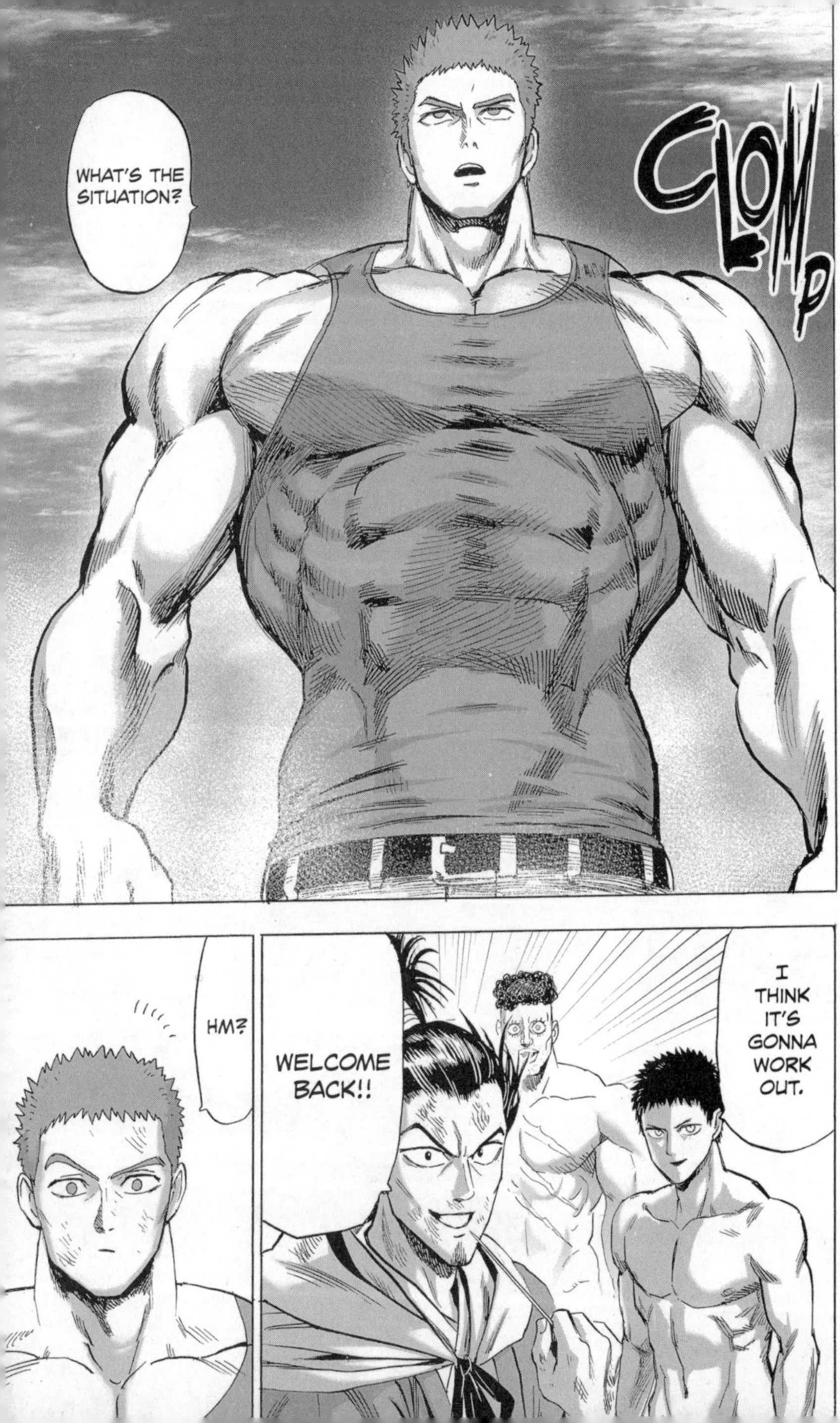
CLOMP
WHAT'S THE SITUATION?
I THINK IT'S GONNA WORK OUT.
WELCOME BACK!!
HM?

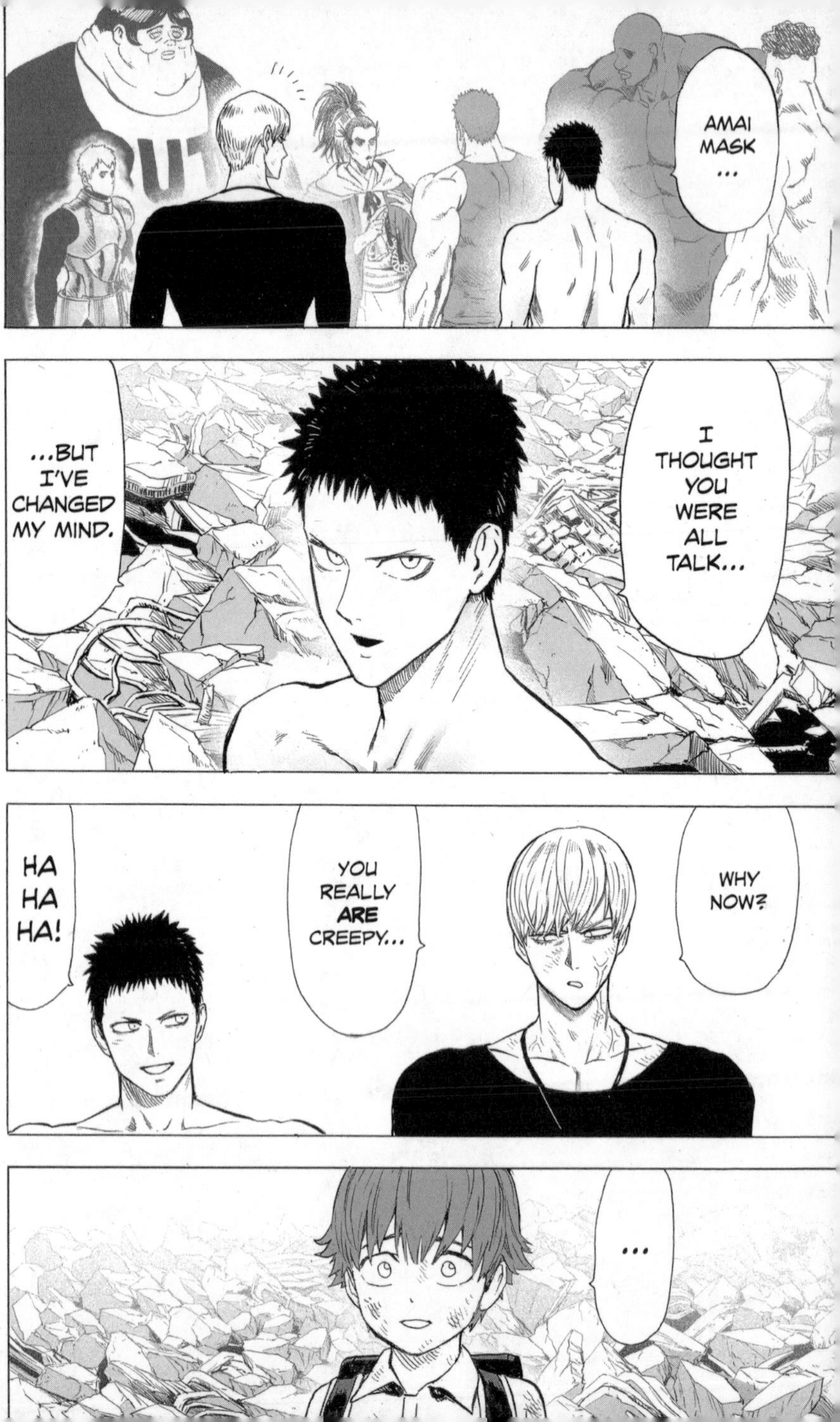
AMAI MASK ...
I THOUGHT YOU WERE ALL TALK...
...BUT I'VE CHANGED MY MIND.
WHY NOW?
YOU REALLY **ARE** CREEPY...
HA HA HA!
...

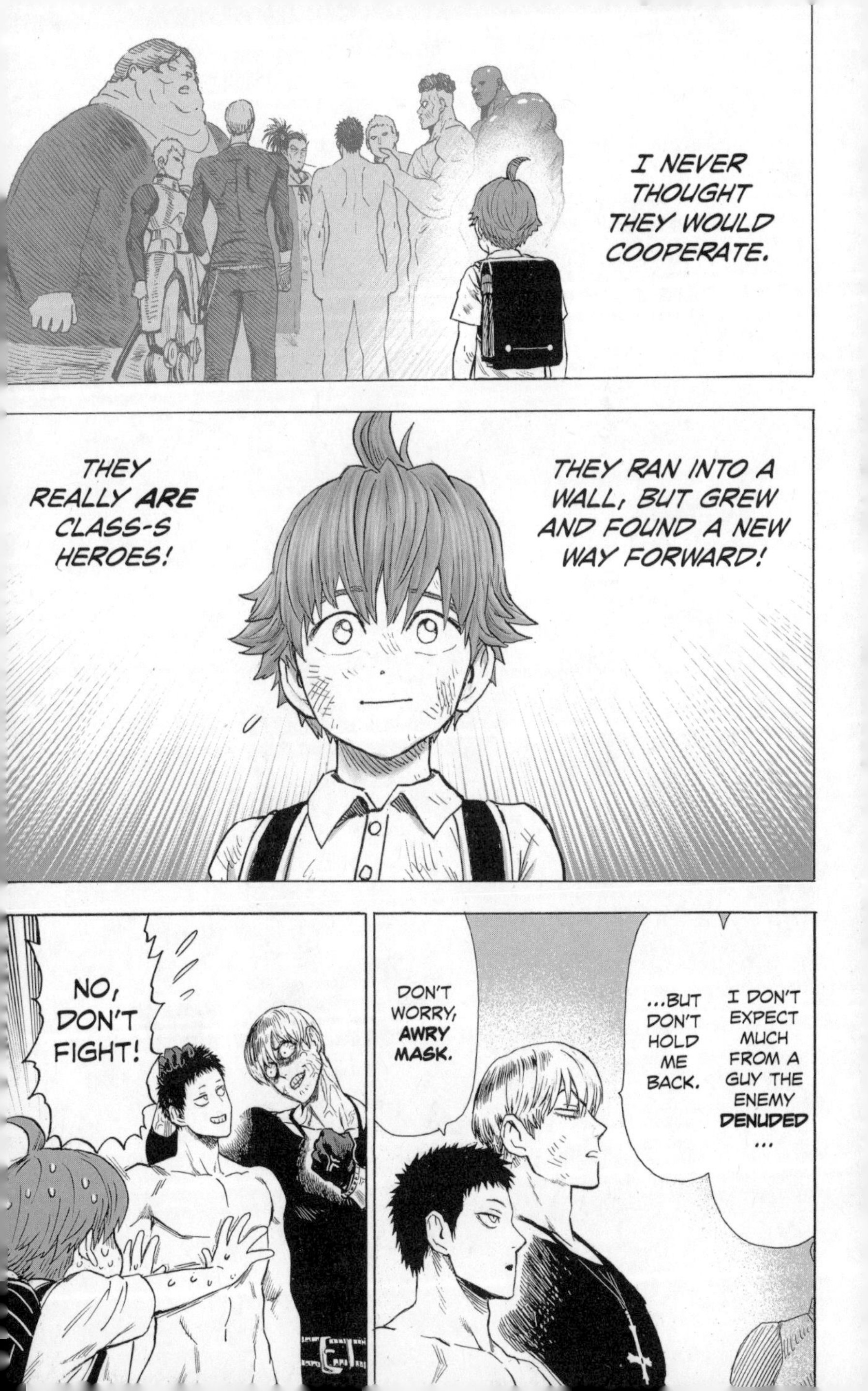
I NEVER THOUGHT THEY WOULD COOPERATE.
THEY RAN INTO A WALL, BUT GREW AND FOUND A NEW WAY FORWARD!
THEY REALLY **ARE** CLASS-S HEROES!
I DON'T EXPECT MUCH FROM A GUY THE ENEMY **DENUDED**...
...BUT DON'T HOLD ME BACK.
DON'T WORRY, **AWRY MASK.**
NO, DON'T FIGHT!

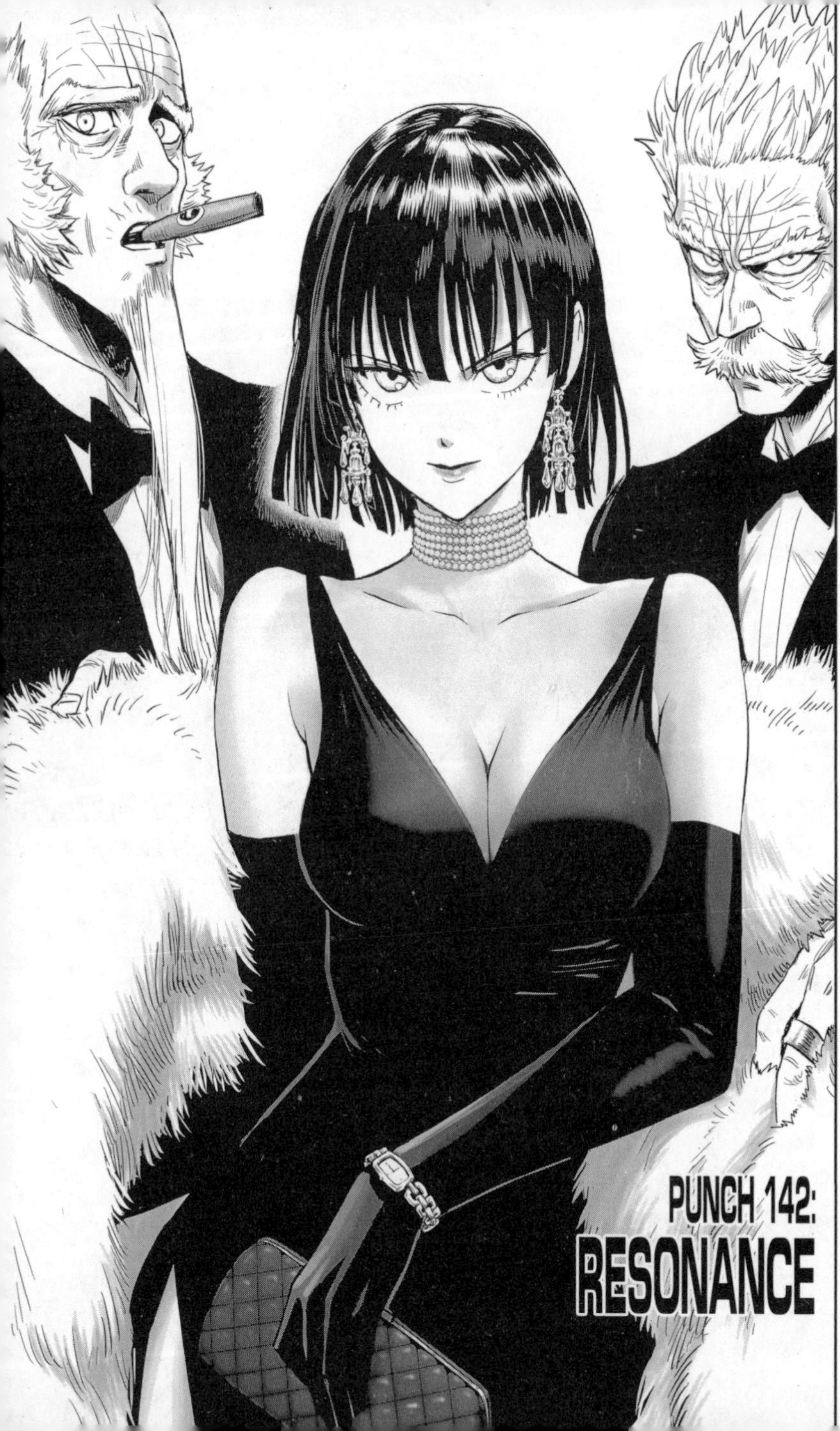
PUNCH 142:
RESONANCE

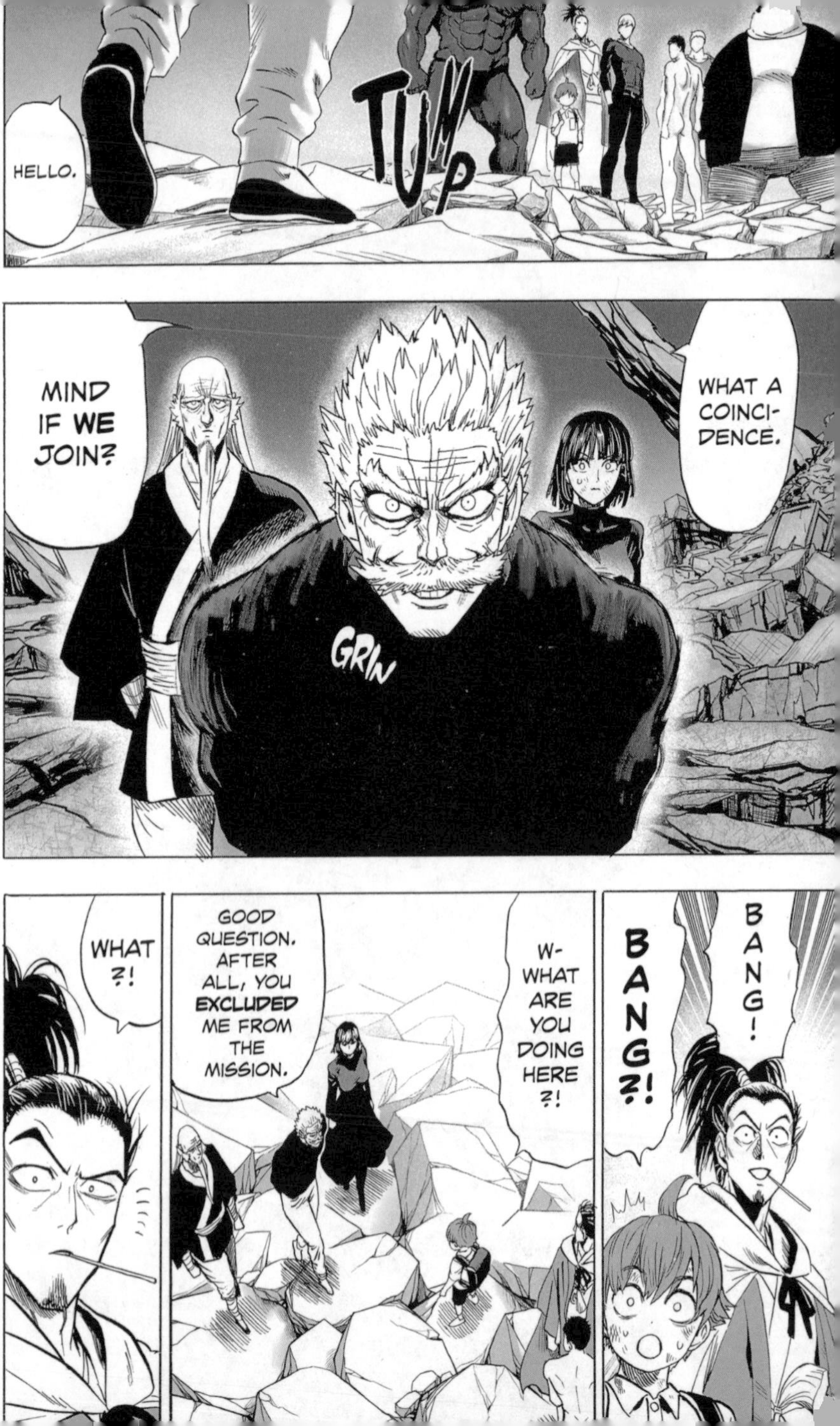
TUMP
HELLO.
WHAT A COINCIDENCE.
MIND IF WE JOIN?
GRIN
BANG!
BANG?!
W-WHAT ARE YOU DOING HERE?!
GOOD QUESTION. AFTER ALL, YOU EXCLUDED ME FROM THE MISSION.
WHAT?!

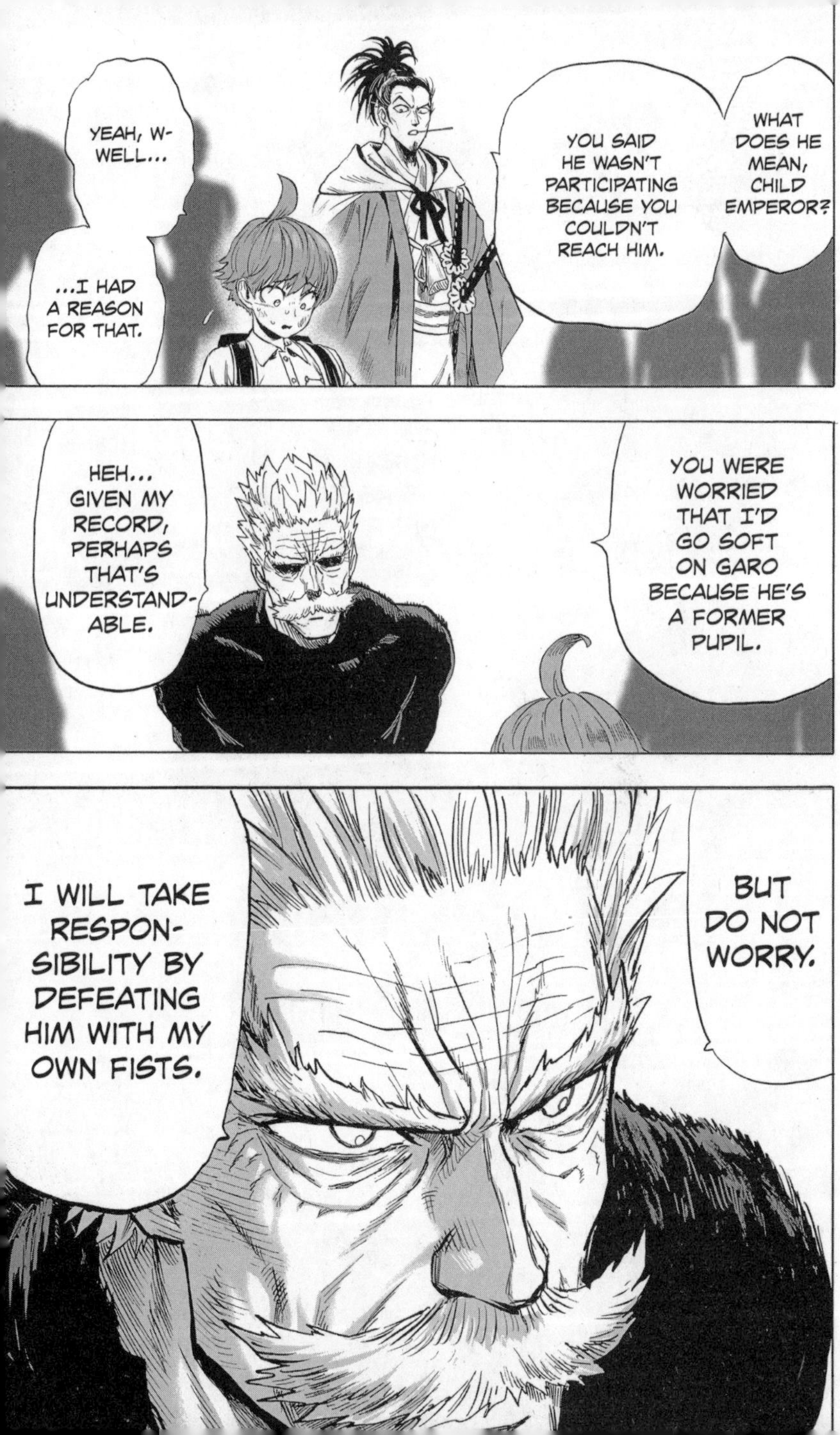
WHAT DOES HE MEAN, CHILD EMPEROR?
YOU SAID HE WASN'T PARTICIPATING BECAUSE YOU COULDN'T REACH HIM.
YEAH, W-WELL...
...I HAD A REASON FOR THAT.
YOU WERE WORRIED THAT I'D GO SOFT ON GARO BECAUSE HE'S A FORMER PUPIL.
HEH... GIVEN MY RECORD, PERHAPS THAT'S UNDERSTAND-ABLE.
BUT DO NOT WORRY.
I WILL TAKE RESPON-SIBILITY BY DEFEATING HIM WITH MY OWN FISTS.

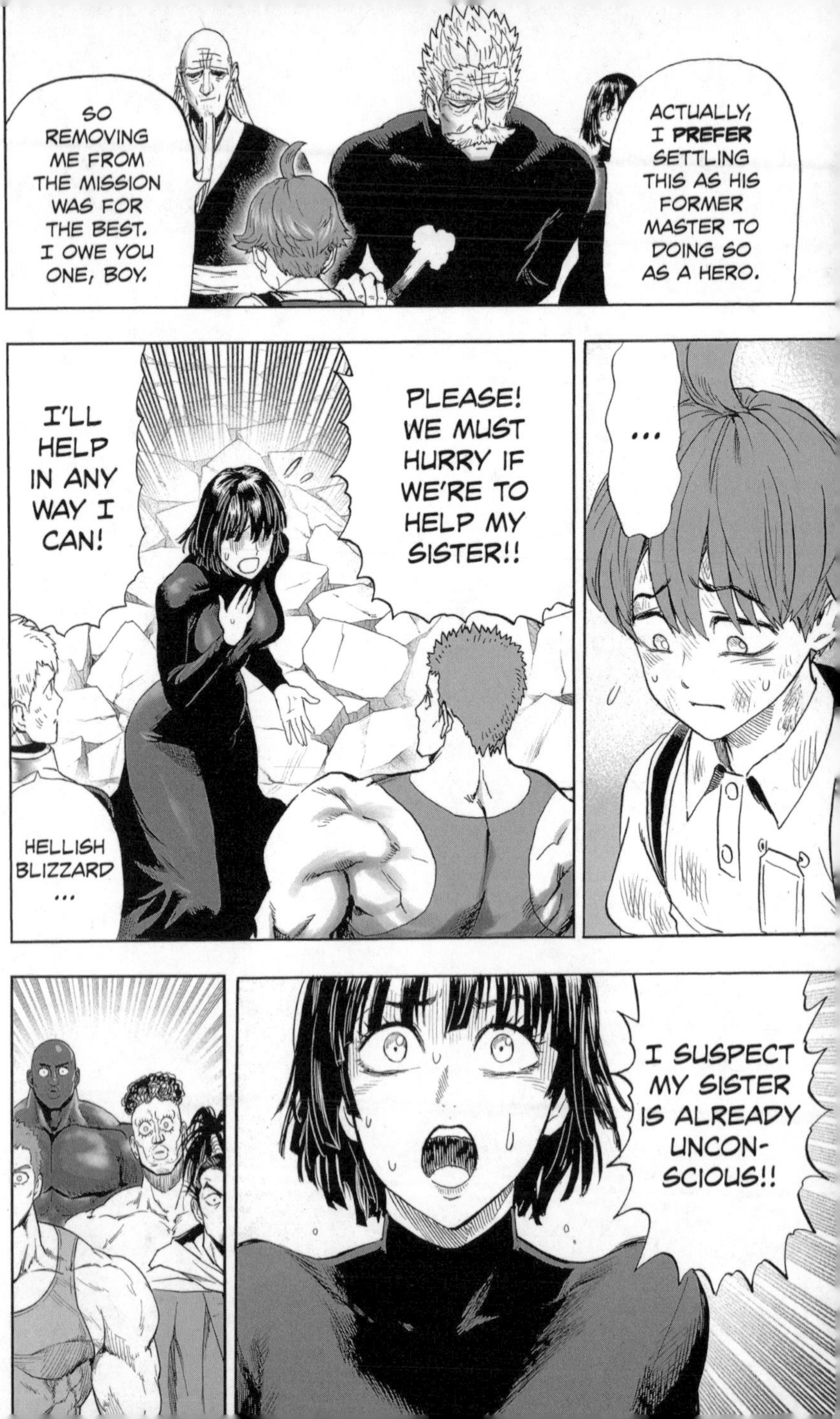
ACTUALLY, I **PREFER** SETTLING THIS AS HIS FORMER MASTER TO DOING SO AS A HERO.
SO REMOVING ME FROM THE MISSION WAS FOR THE BEST. I OWE YOU ONE, BOY.
...
PLEASE! WE MUST HURRY IF WE'RE TO HELP MY SISTER!!
I'LL HELP IN ANY WAY I CAN!
HELLISH BLIZZARD ...
I SUSPECT MY SISTER IS ALREADY UNCON- SCIOUS!!

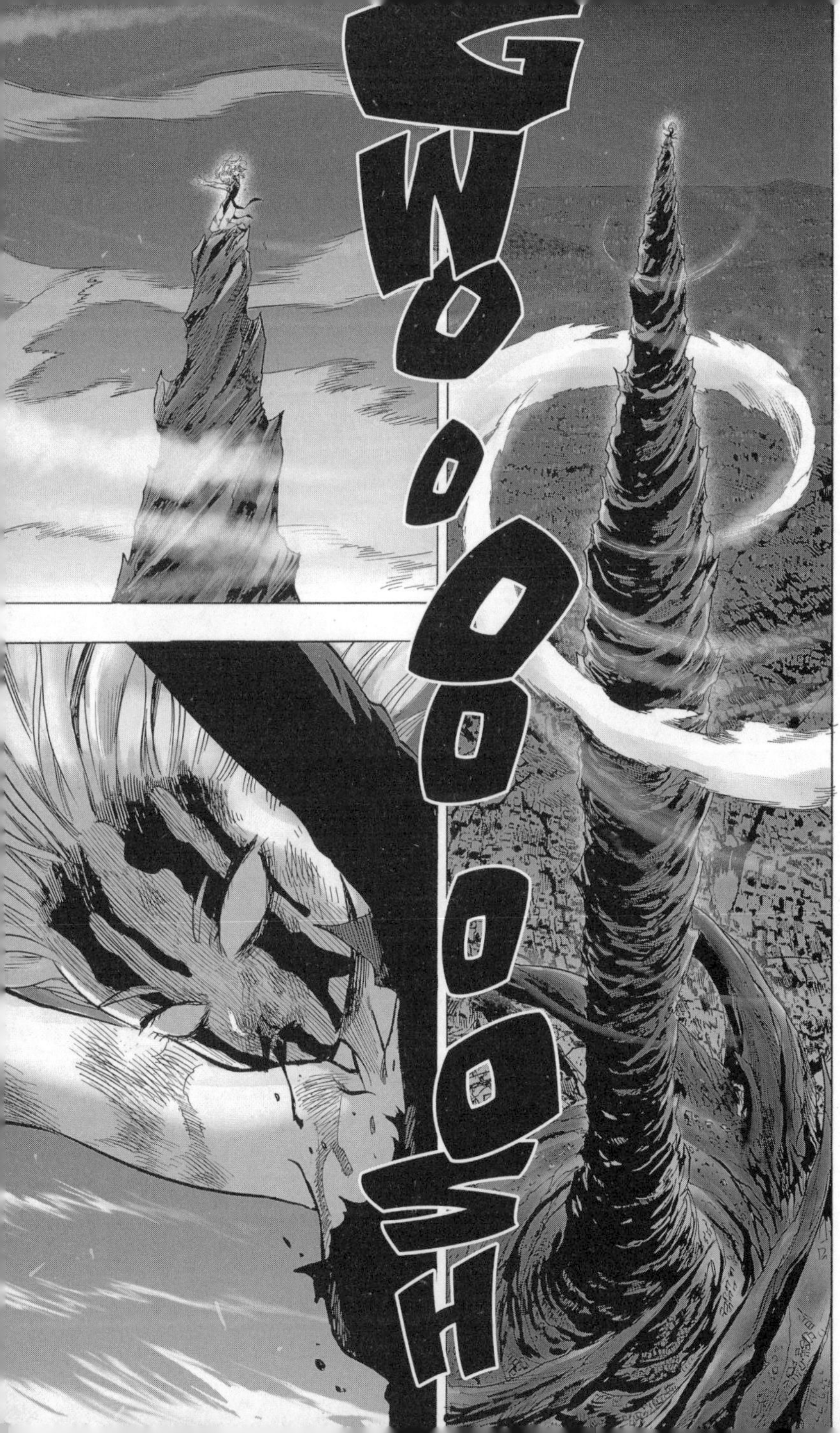
GWOOOOOOSH

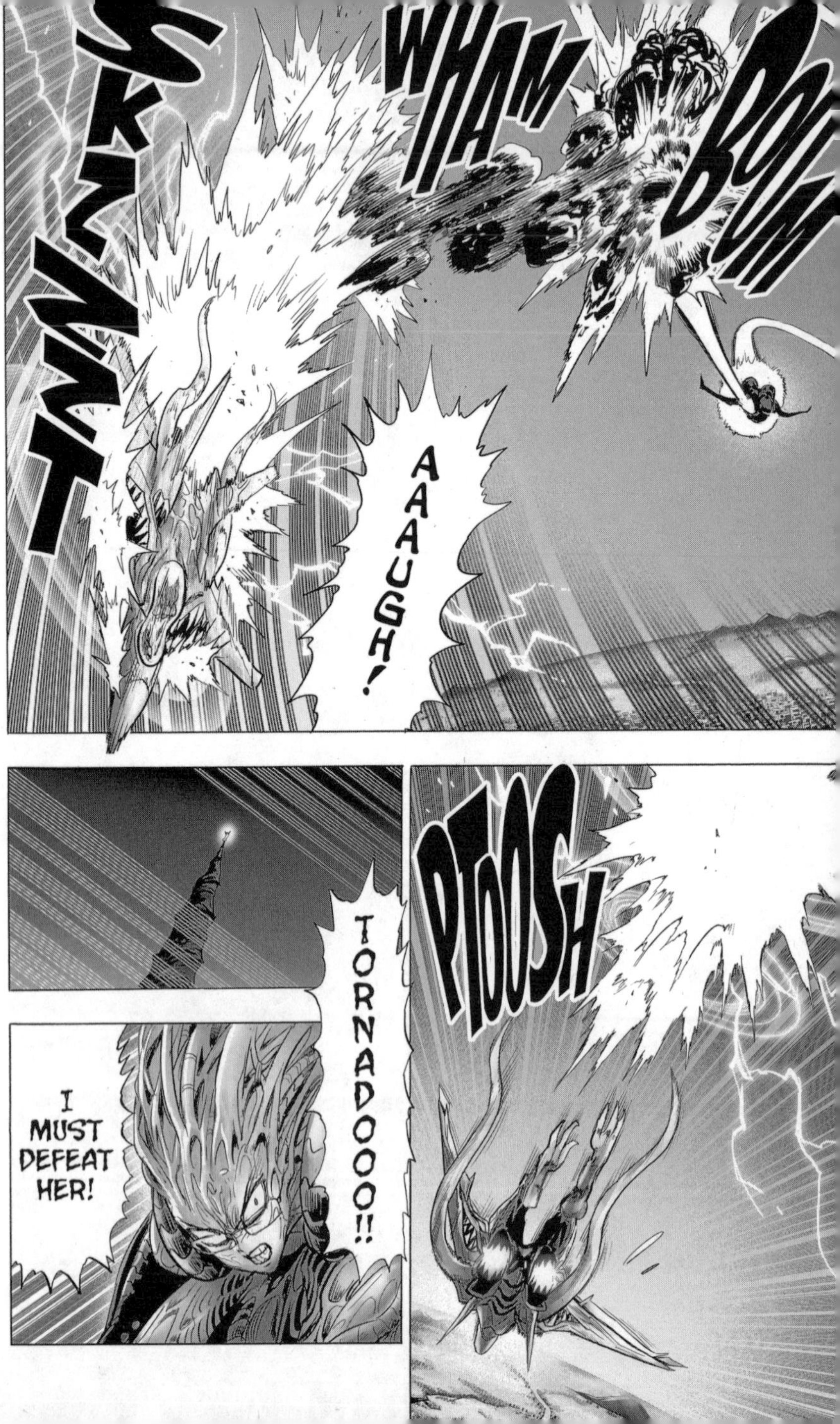
WHAM
AAAUGH!
PTOOSH
TORNADOOOO!!
I MUST DEFEAT HER!

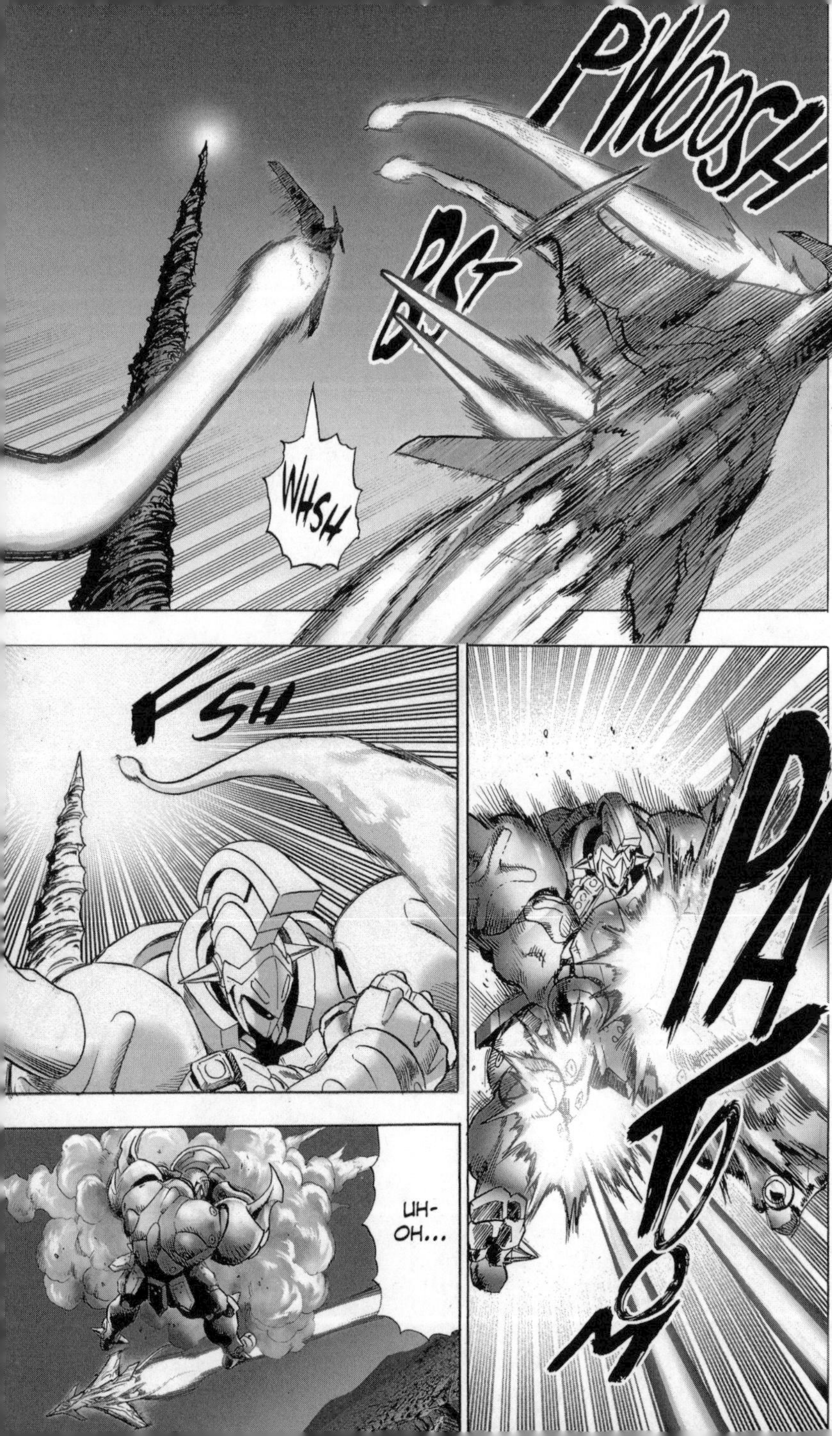
PWOOSH
WHSH
PATOOM
FSH
UH-
OH...

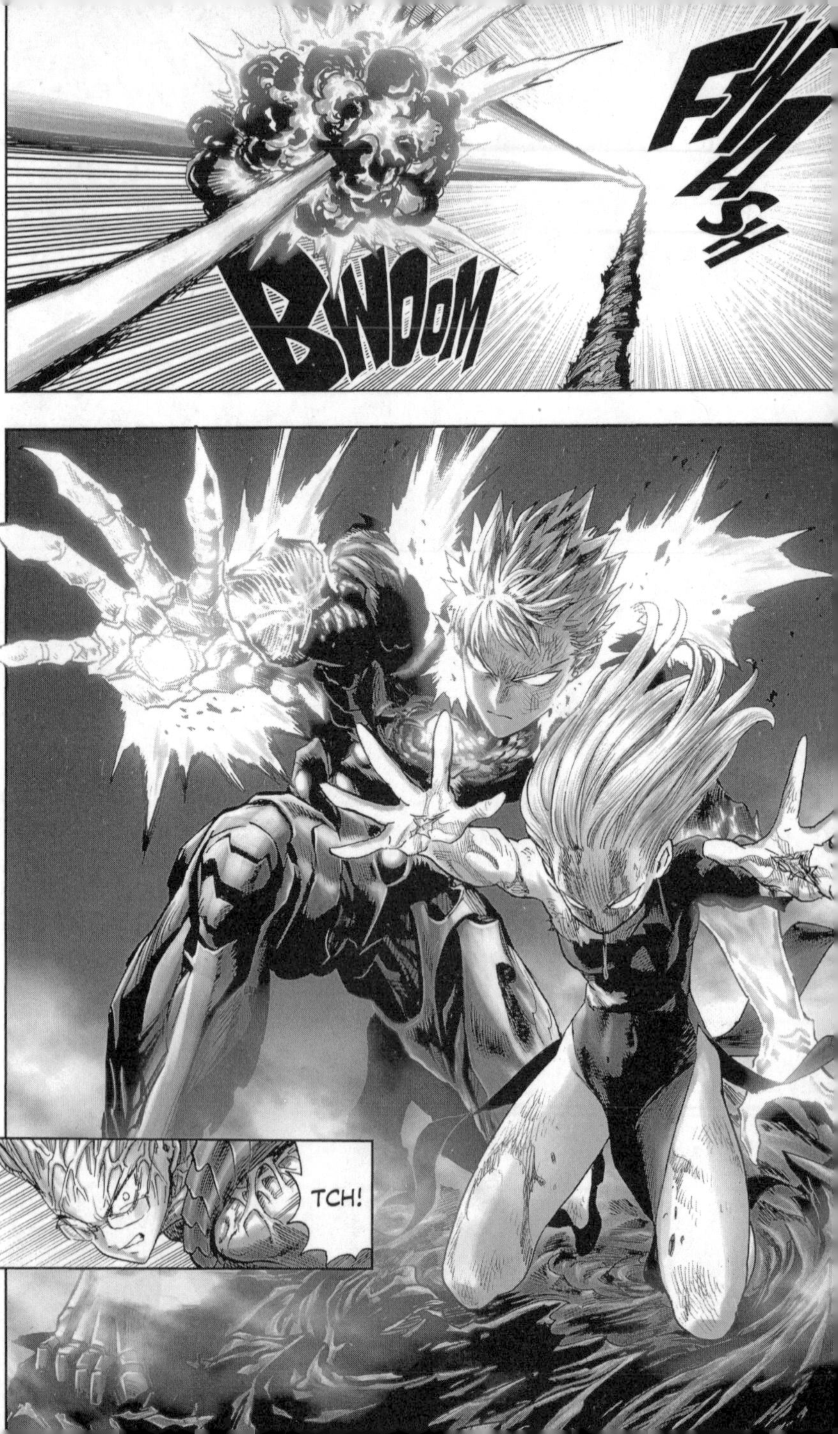
FWASH
BWOOM
TCH!

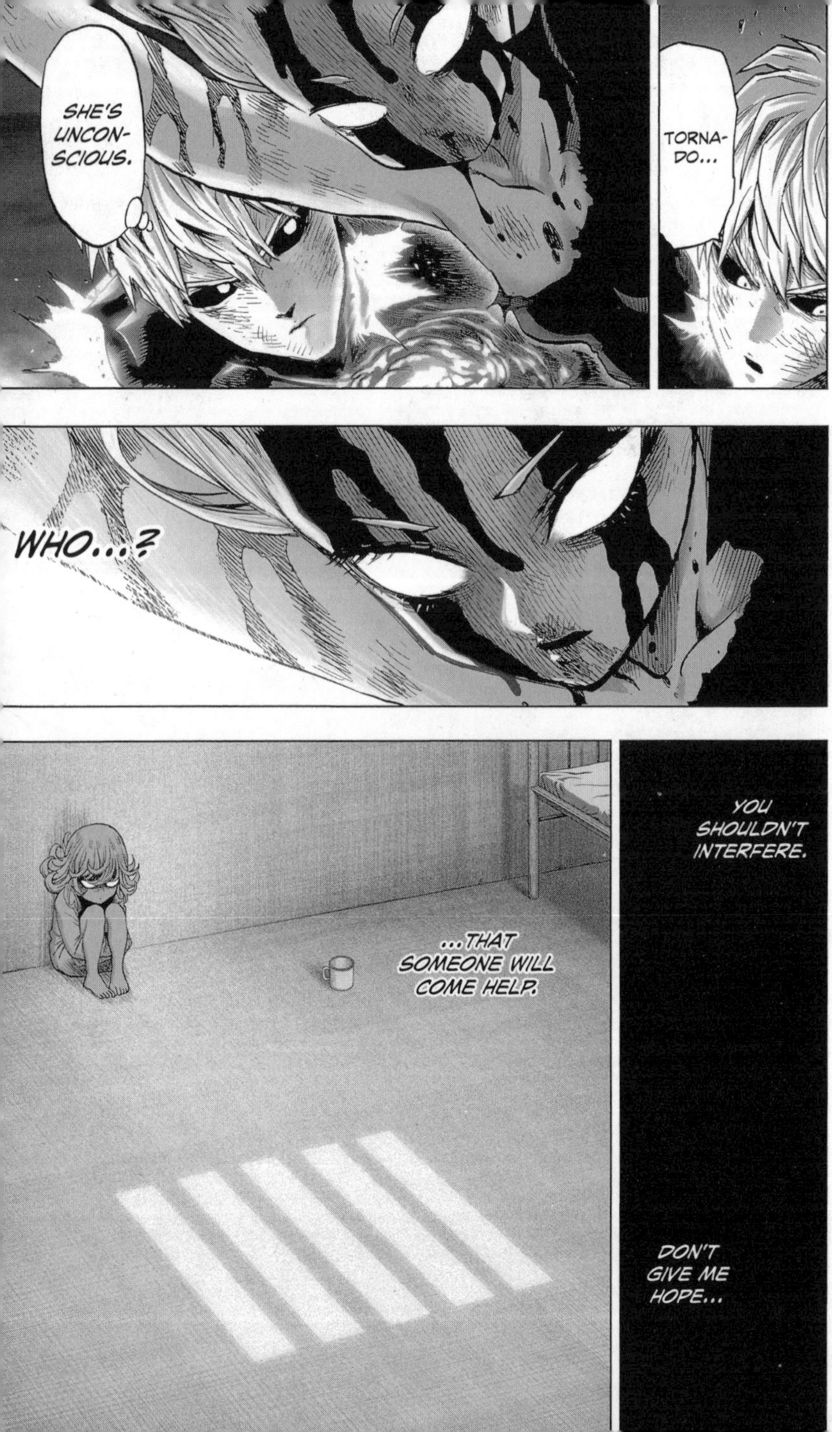
TORNA-DO...
SHE'S UNCON-SCIOUS.
WHO...?
YOU SHOULDN'T INTERFERE.
DON'T GIVE ME HOPE...
...THAT SOMEONE WILL COME HELP.

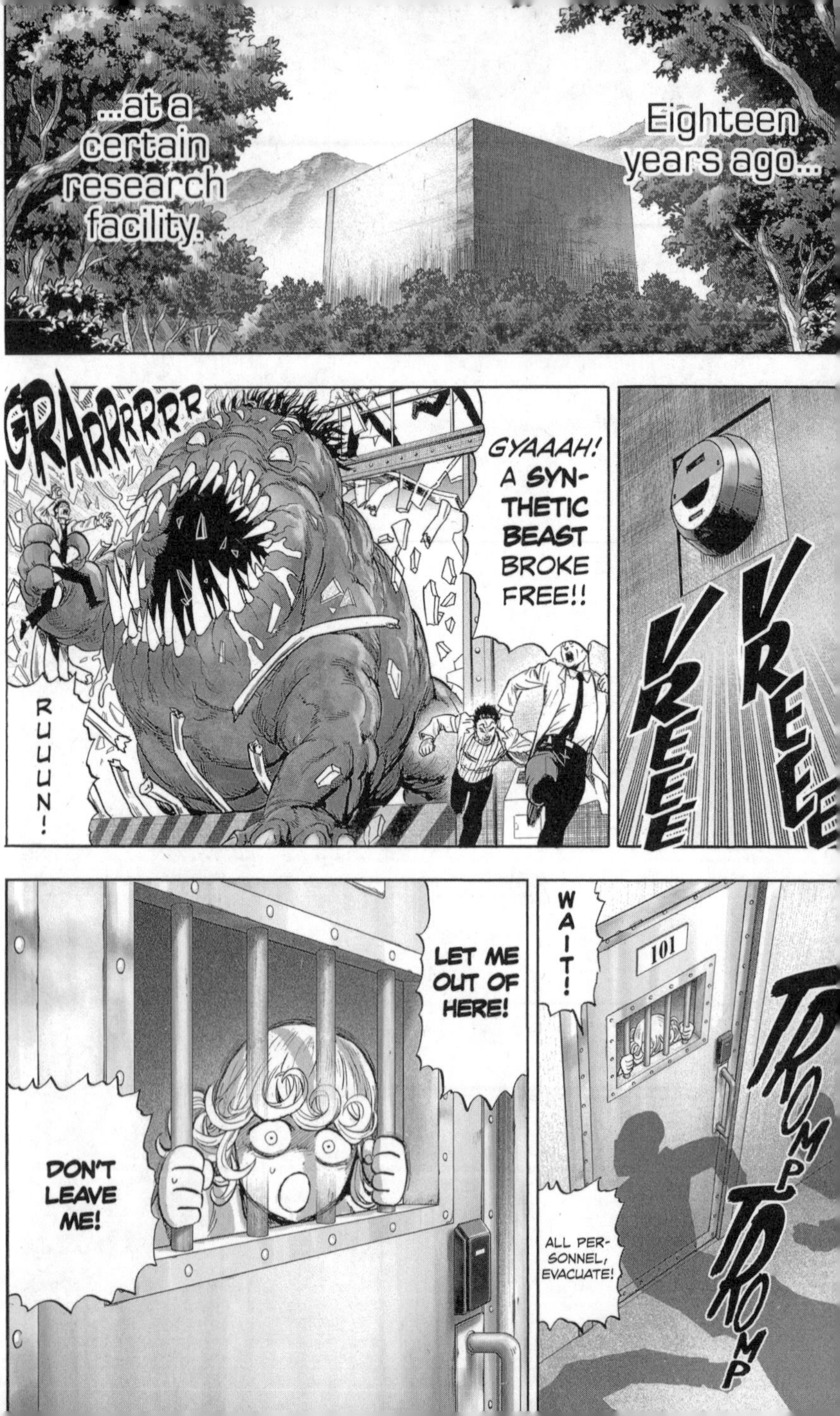
Eighteen years ago...
...at a certain research facility.
VREEEE
VREEEE
GYAAAH! A SYNTHETIC BEAST BROKE FREE!!
GRARRRRR
RUUUN!
WAIT!
TROMP TROMP TROMP
ALL PERSONNEL, EVACUATE!
LET ME OUT OF HERE!
DON'T LEAVE ME!

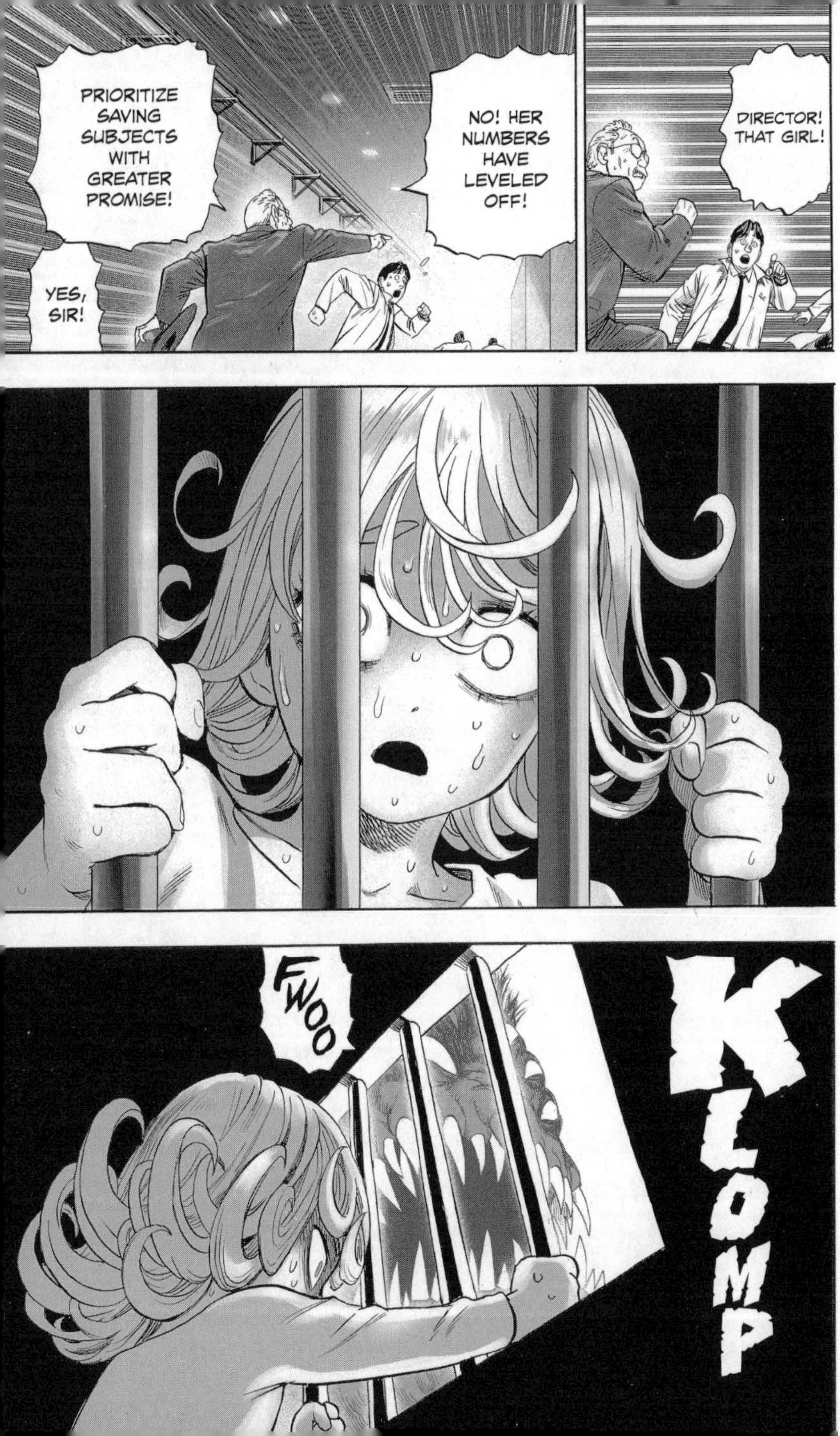
DIRECTOR! THAT GIRL!
NO! HER NUMBERS HAVE LEVELED OFF!
PRIORITIZE SAVING SUBJECTS WITH GREATER PROMISE!
YES, SIR!
KLOMP
FWOO

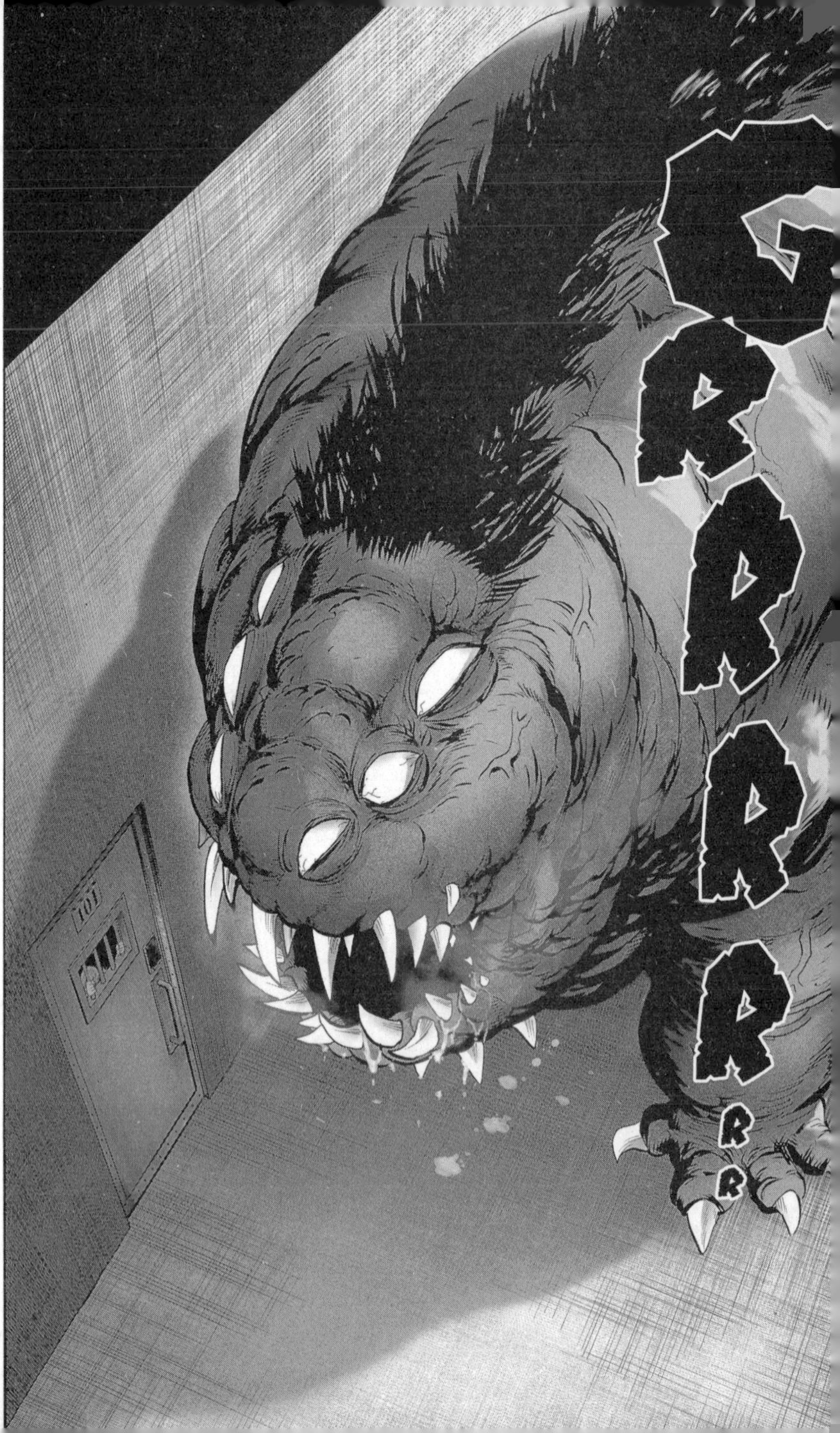
101
GRRRR
RR

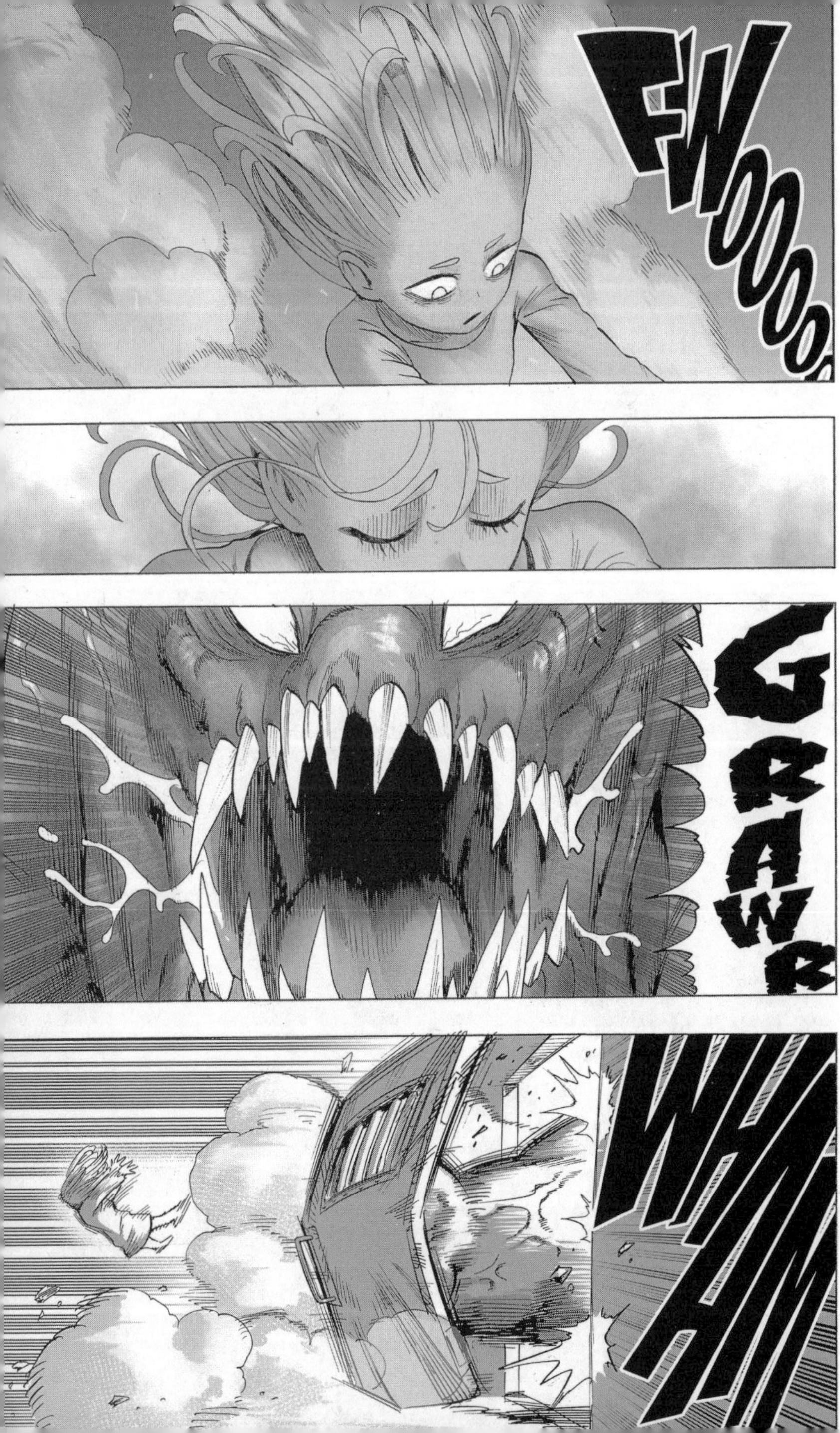
FWOOOO
GRAWR

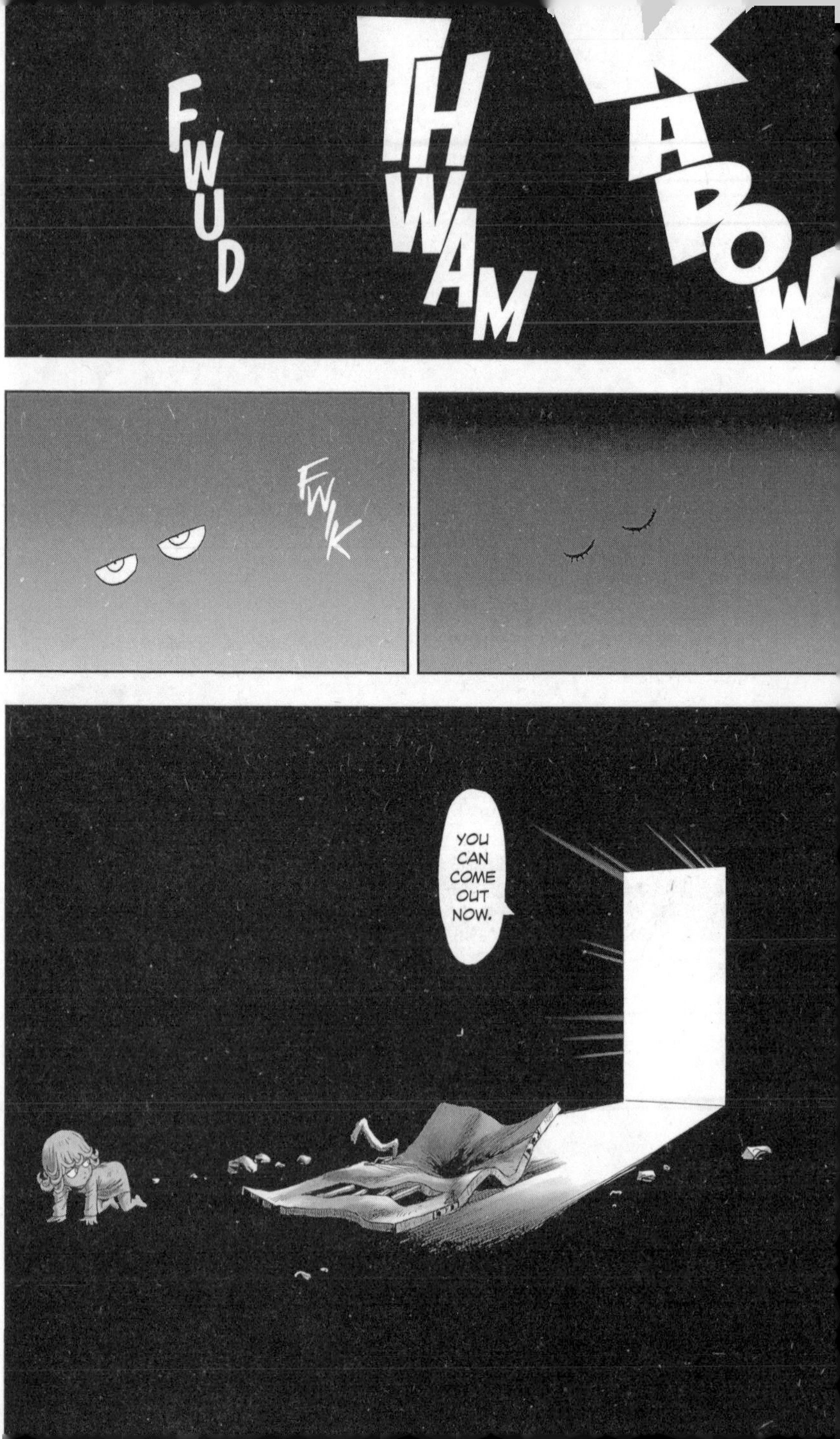
KAPOW
THWAM
FWUD
FWIK
YOU CAN COME OUT NOW.

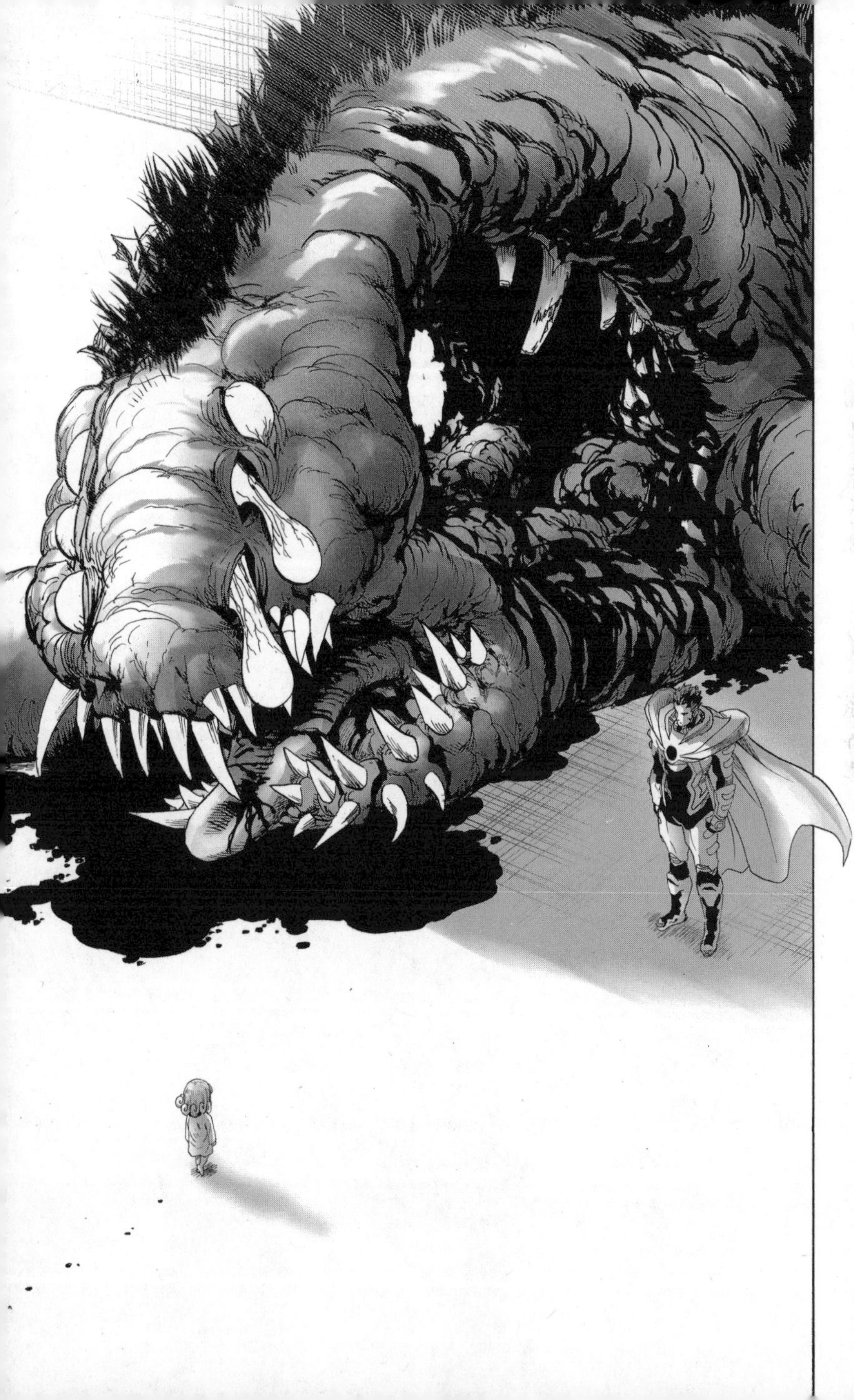

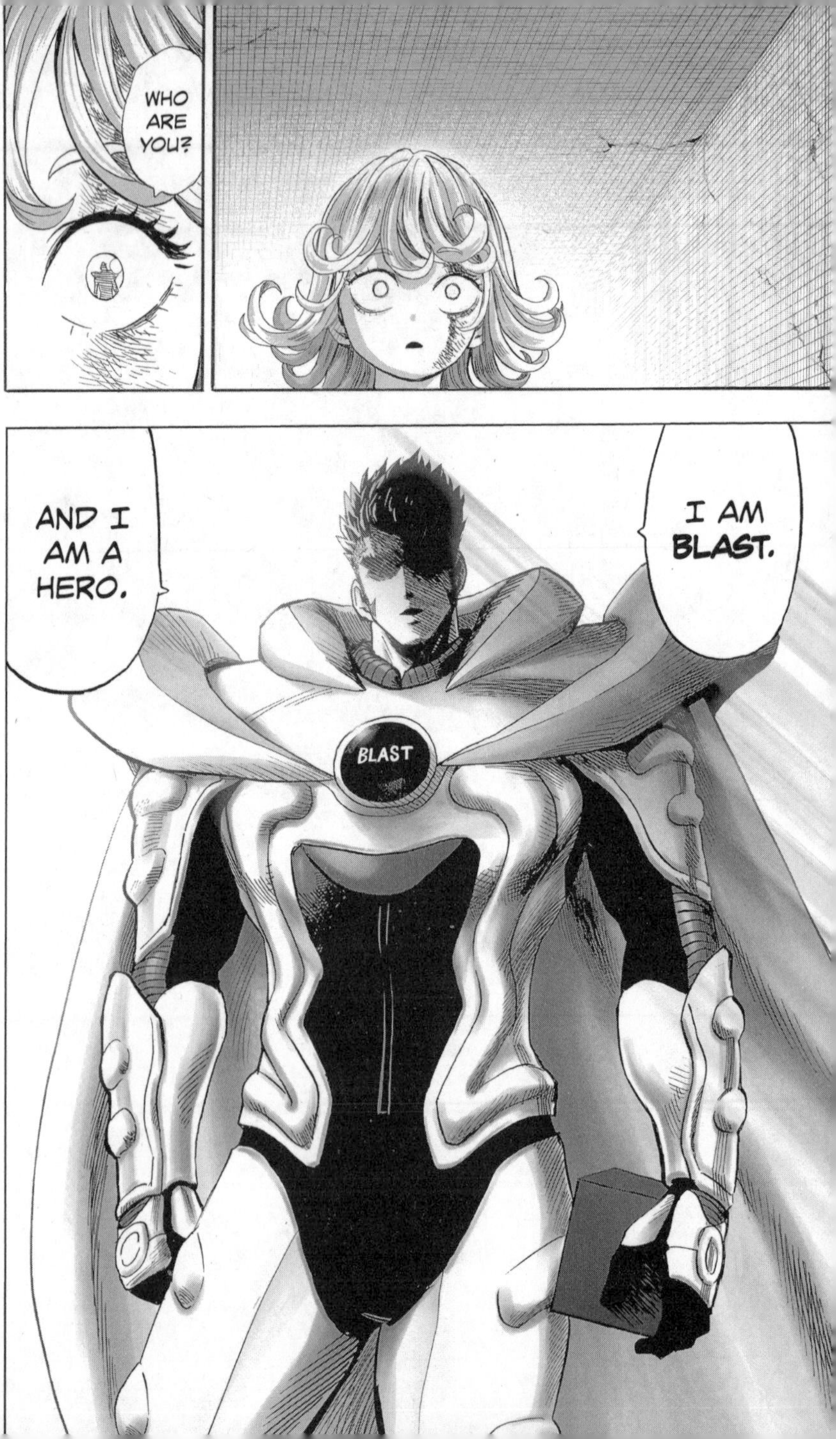
WHO ARE YOU?
I AM BLAST.
AND I AM A HERO.
BLAST

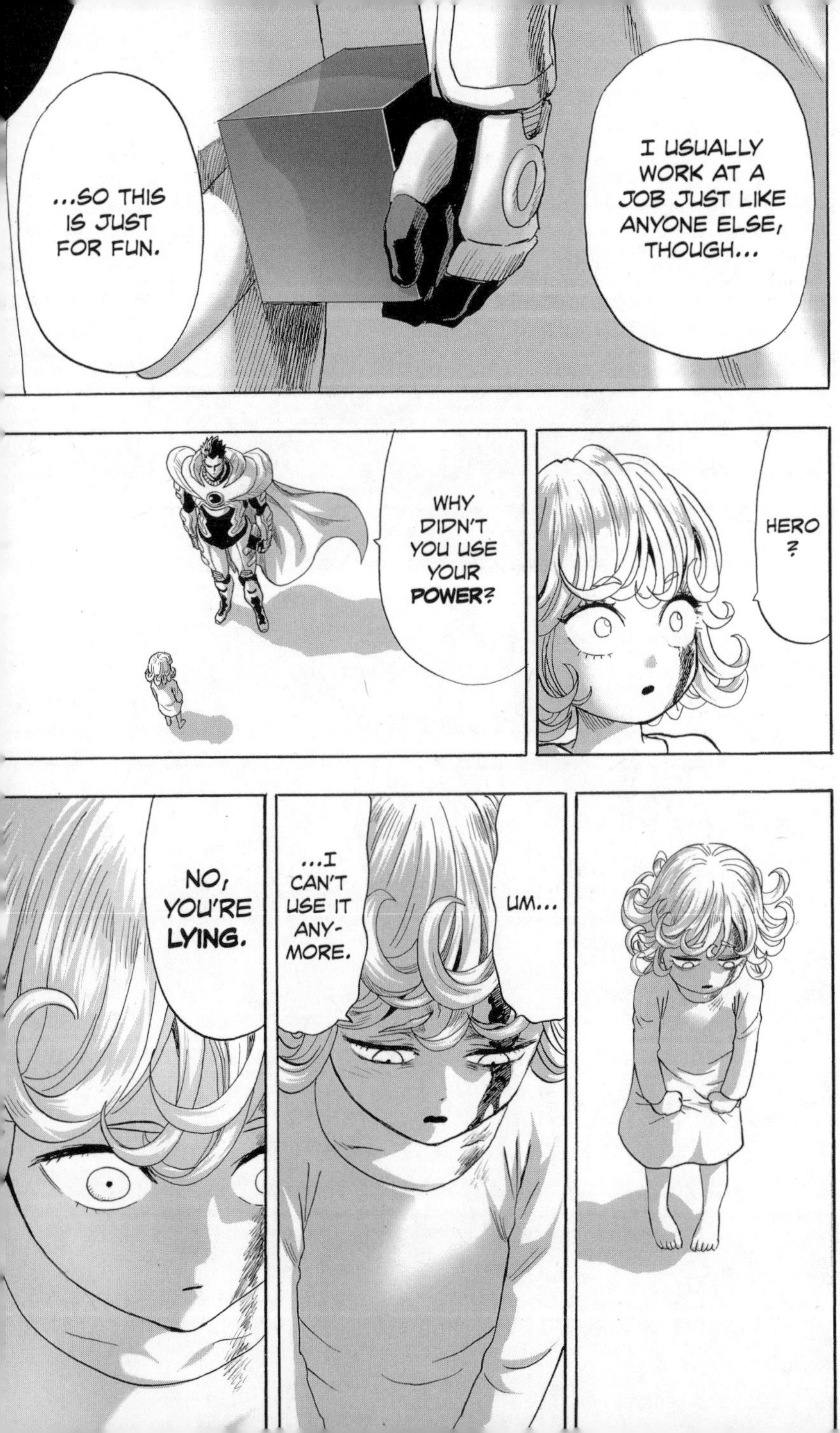
I USUALLY WORK AT A JOB JUST LIKE ANYONE ELSE, THOUGH...
...SO THIS IS JUST FOR FUN.
HERO?
WHY DIDN'T YOU USE YOUR POWER?
UM...
...I CAN'T USE IT ANY-MORE.
NO, YOU'RE LYING.

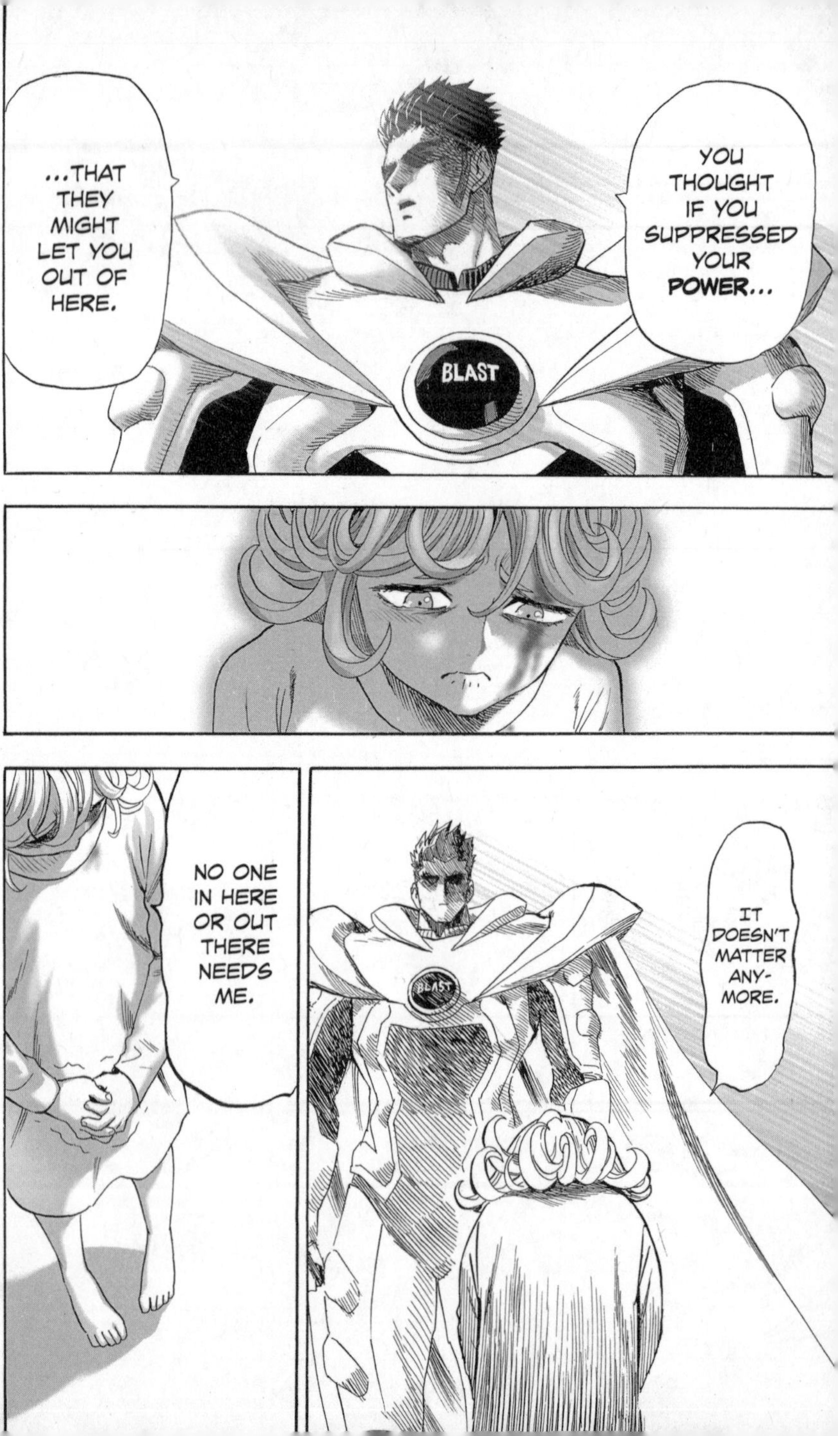
YOU THOUGHT IF YOU SUPPRESSED YOUR **POWER...**
...THAT THEY MIGHT LET YOU OUT OF HERE.
IT DOESN'T MATTER ANY-MORE.
NO ONE IN HERE OR OUT THERE NEEDS ME.

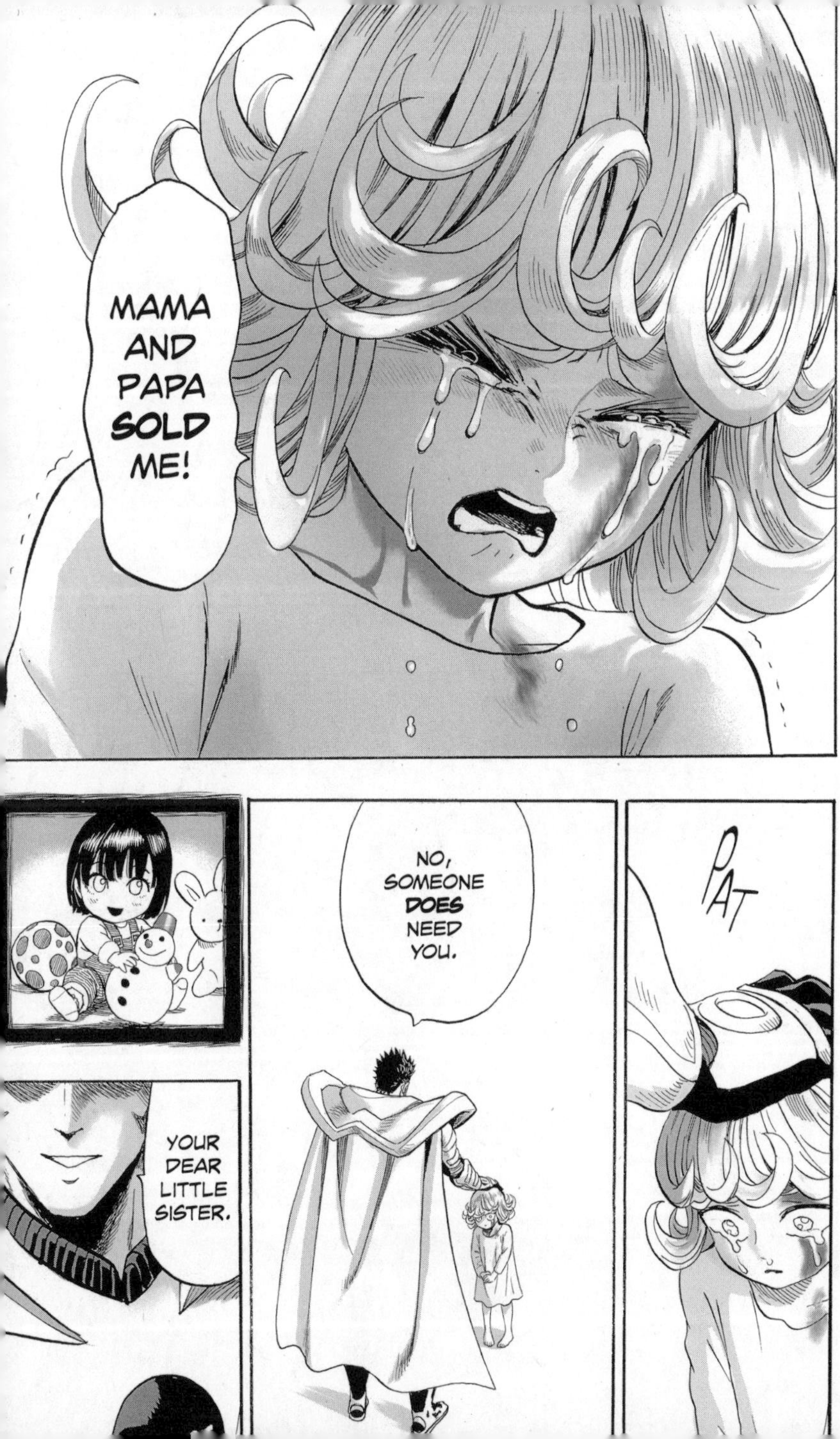
MAMA AND PAPA SOLD ME!
PAT
NO, SOMEONE DOES NEED YOU.
YOUR DEAR LITTLE SISTER.

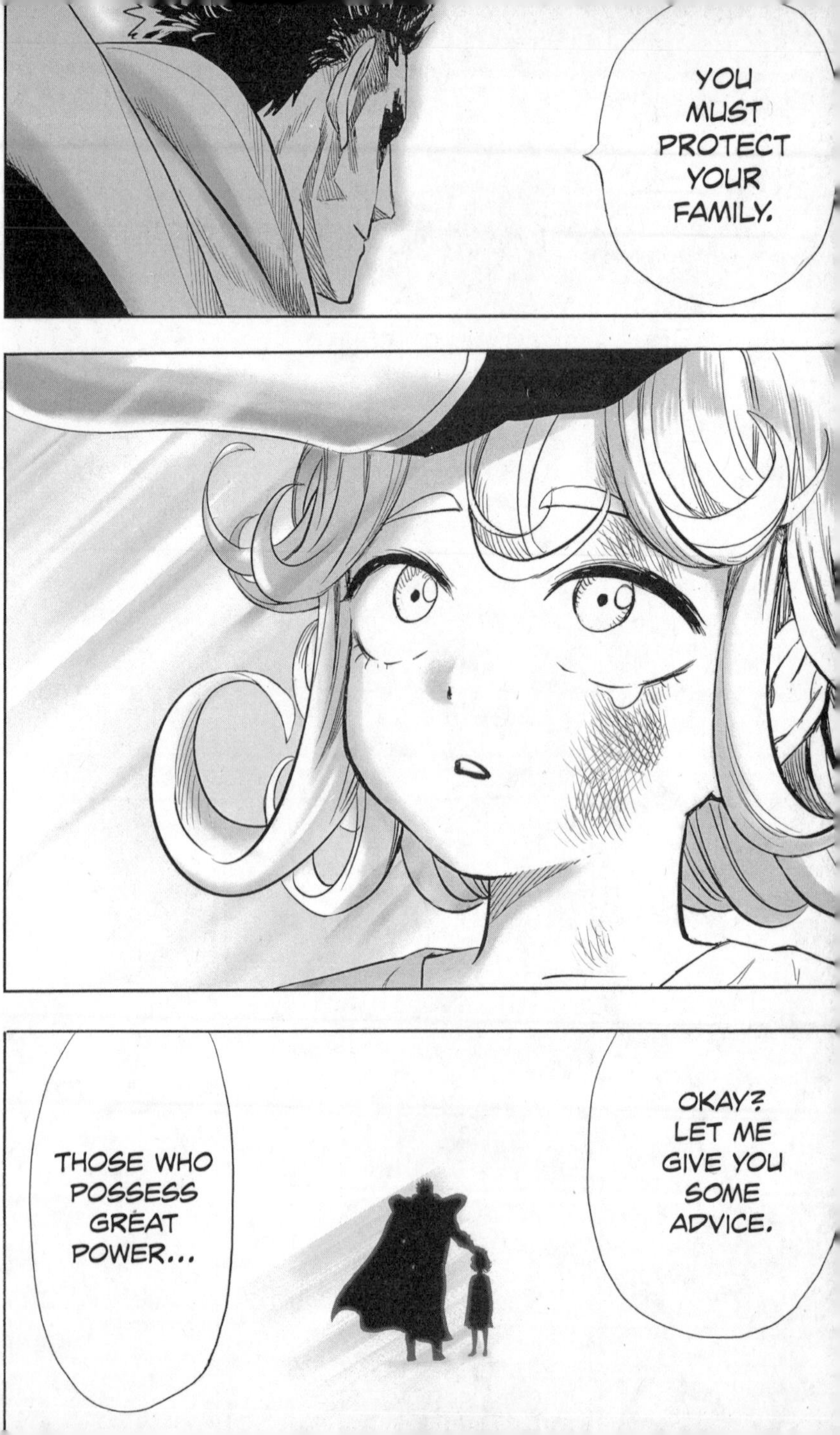
YOU MUST PROTECT YOUR FAMILY.
OKAY? LET ME GIVE YOU SOME ADVICE.
THOSE WHO POSSESS GREAT POWER...

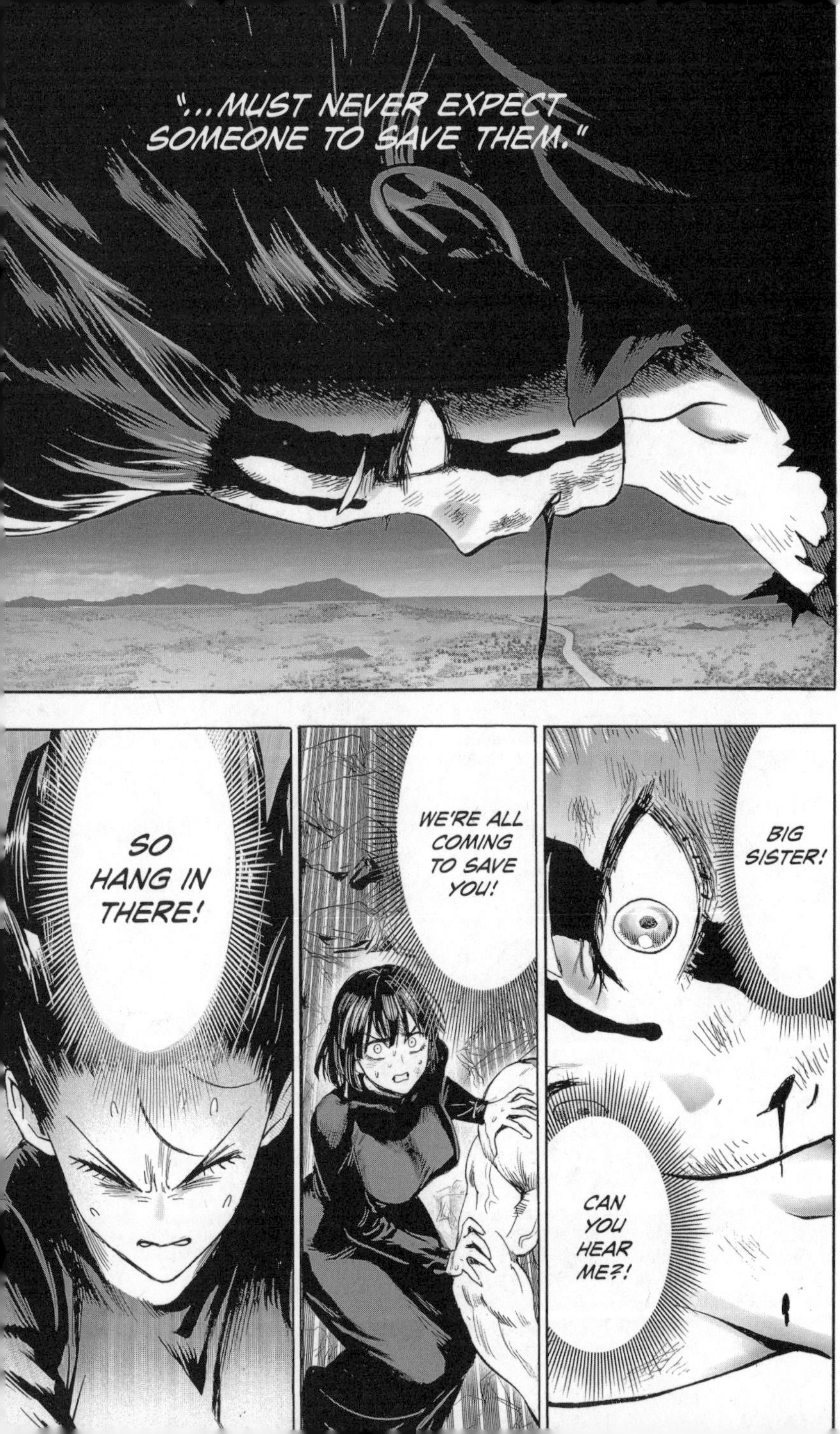
"...MUST NEVER EXPECT SOMEONE TO SAVE THEM."
BIG SISTER!
CAN YOU HEAR ME?!
WE'RE ALL COMING TO SAVE YOU!
SO HANG IN THERE!

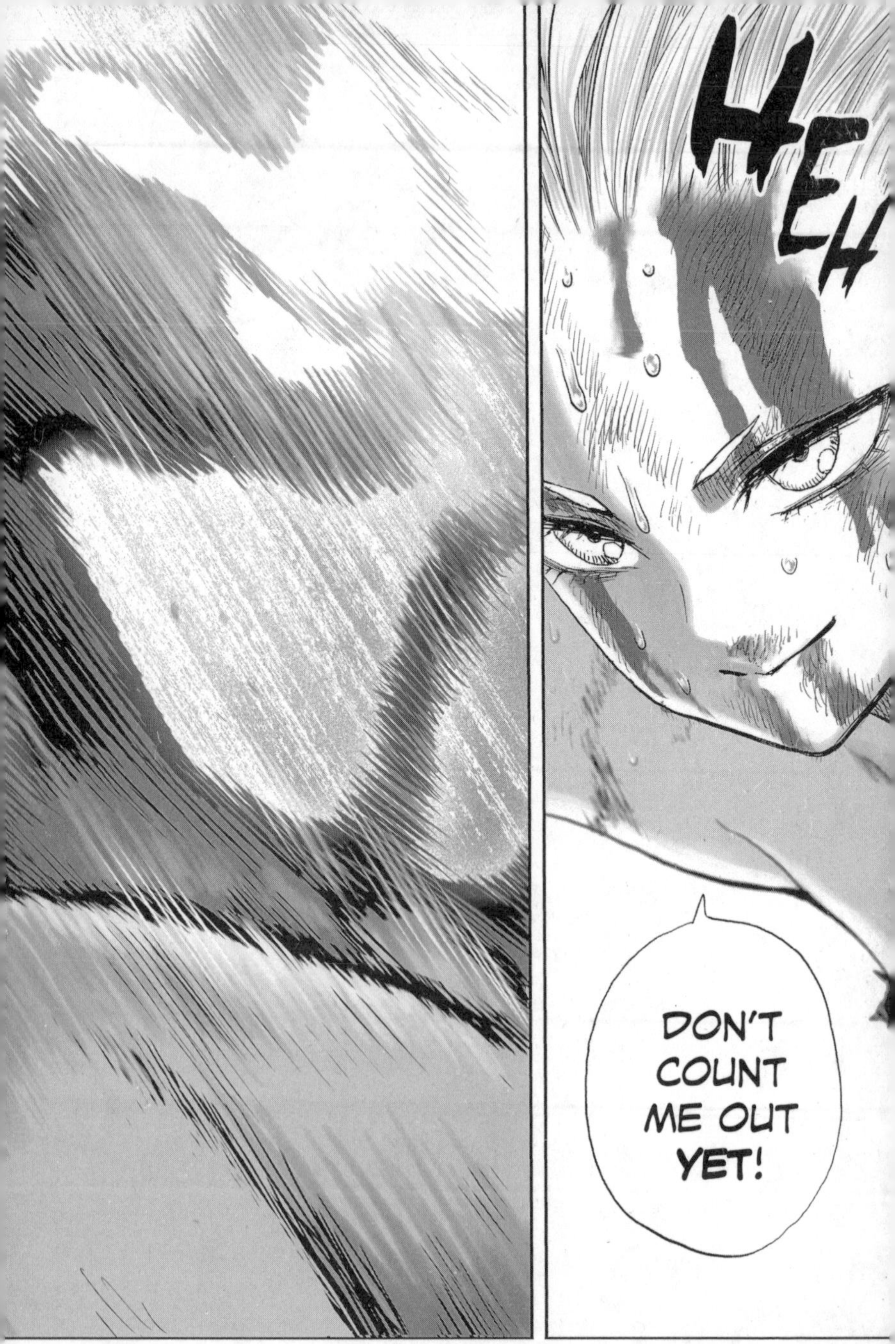
HEH
DON'T COUNT ME OUT YET!

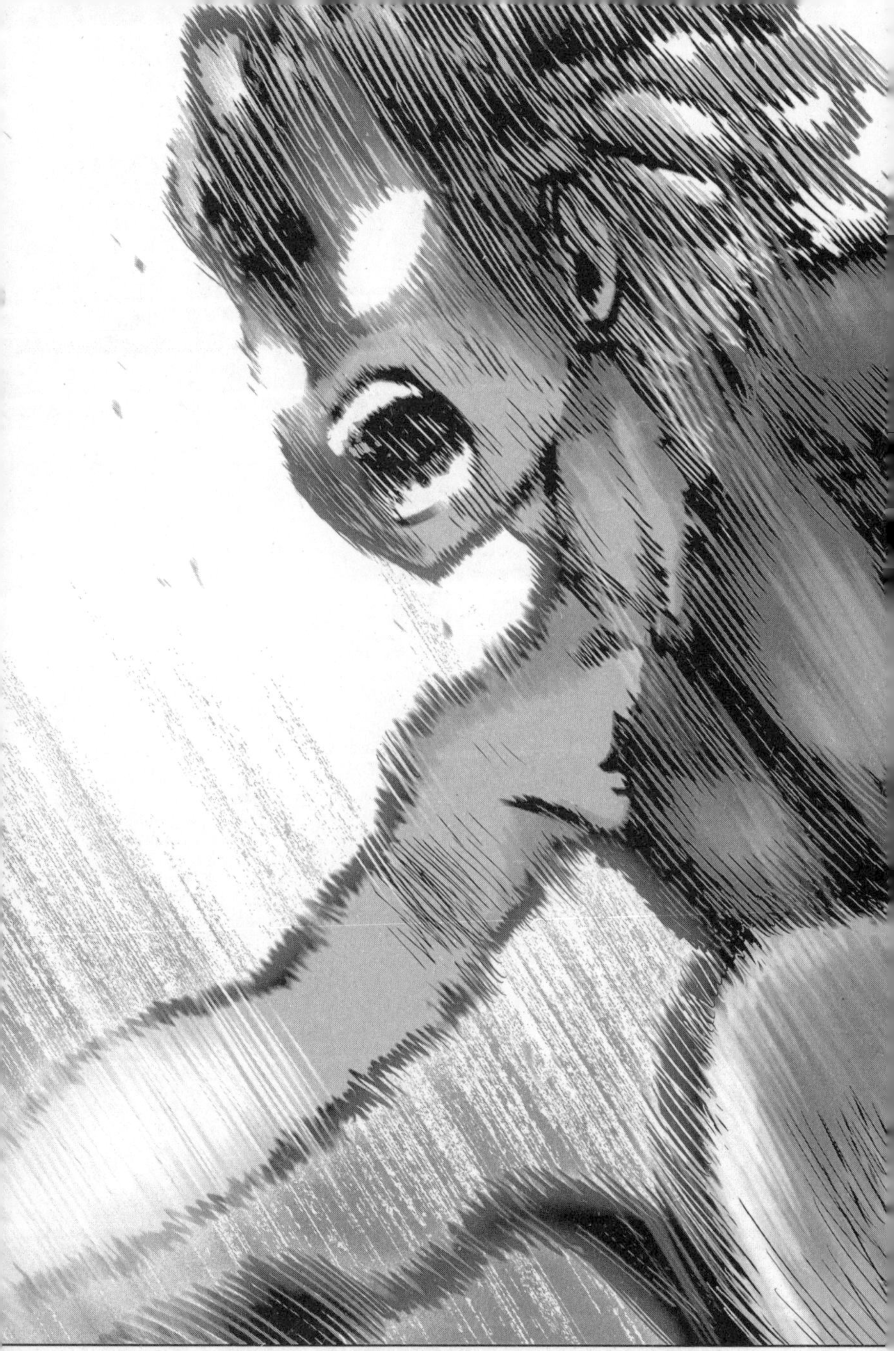

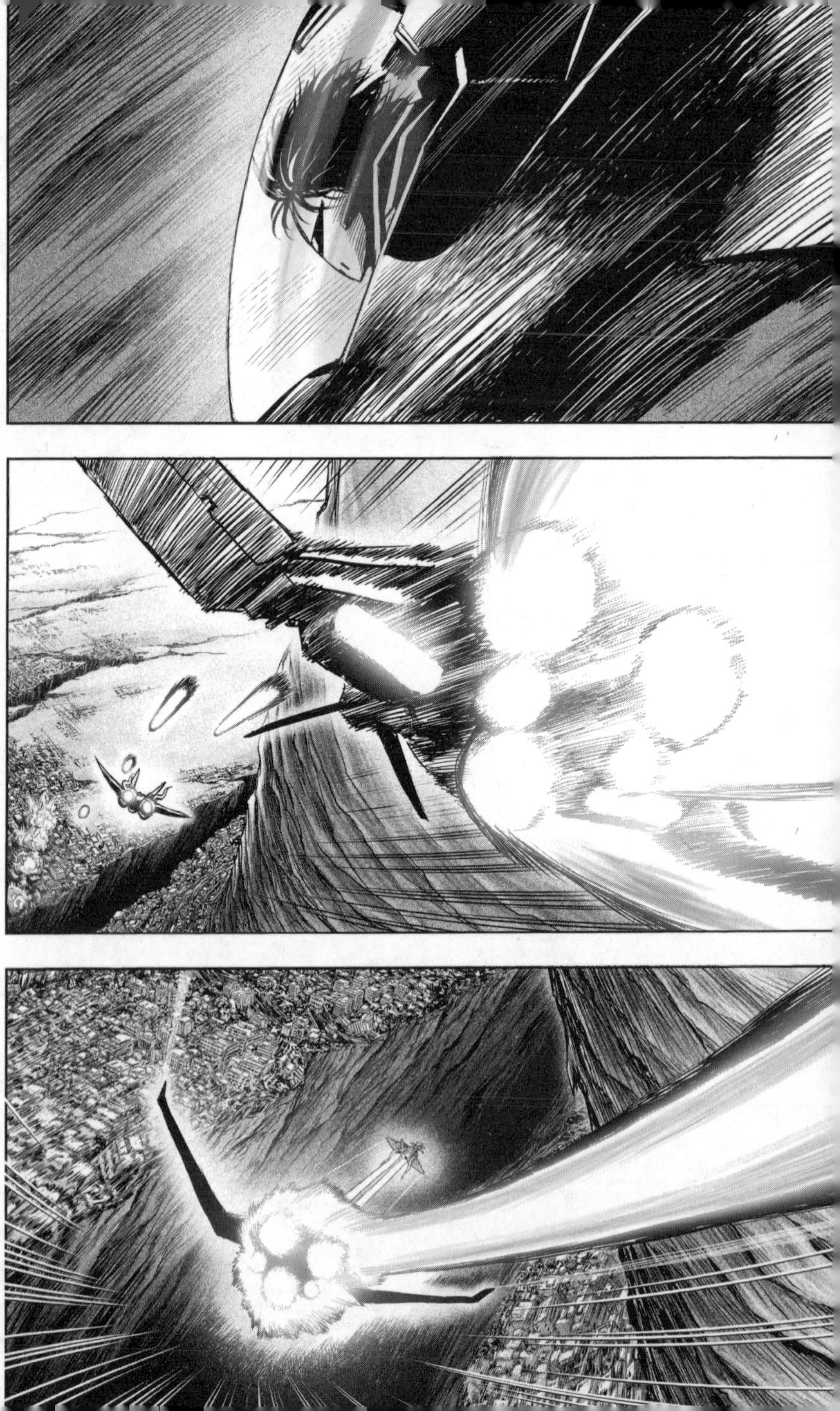

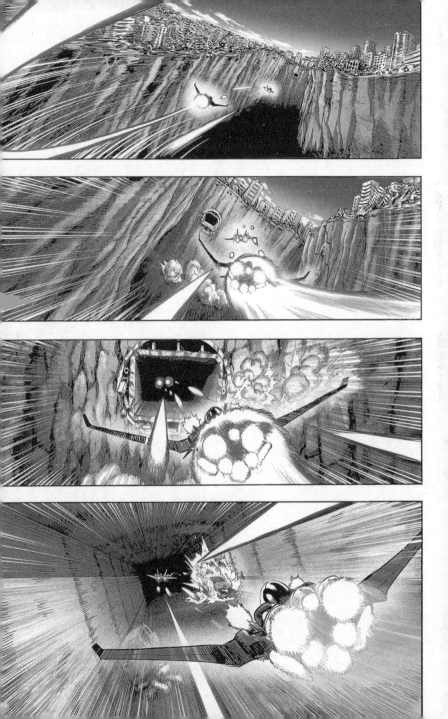

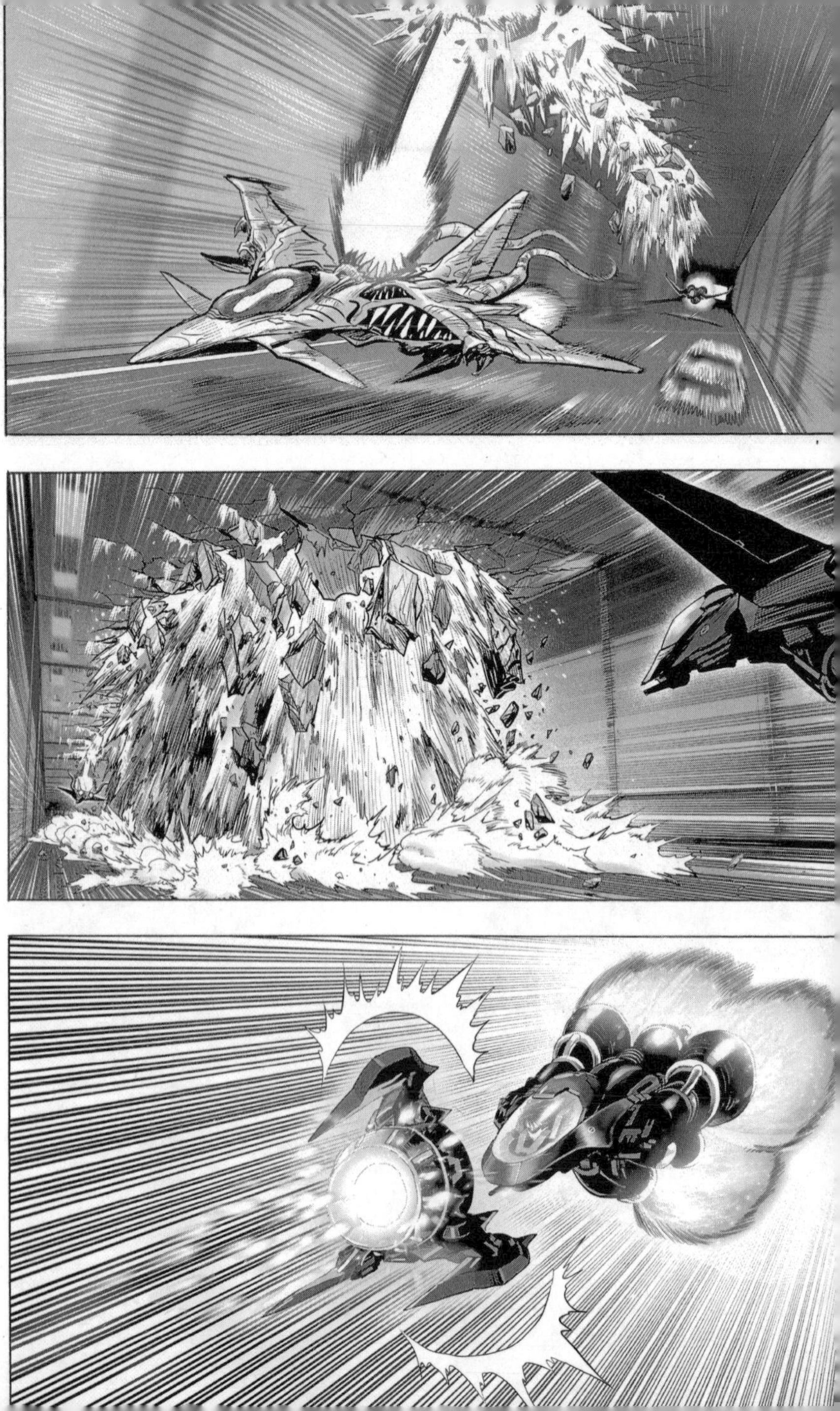

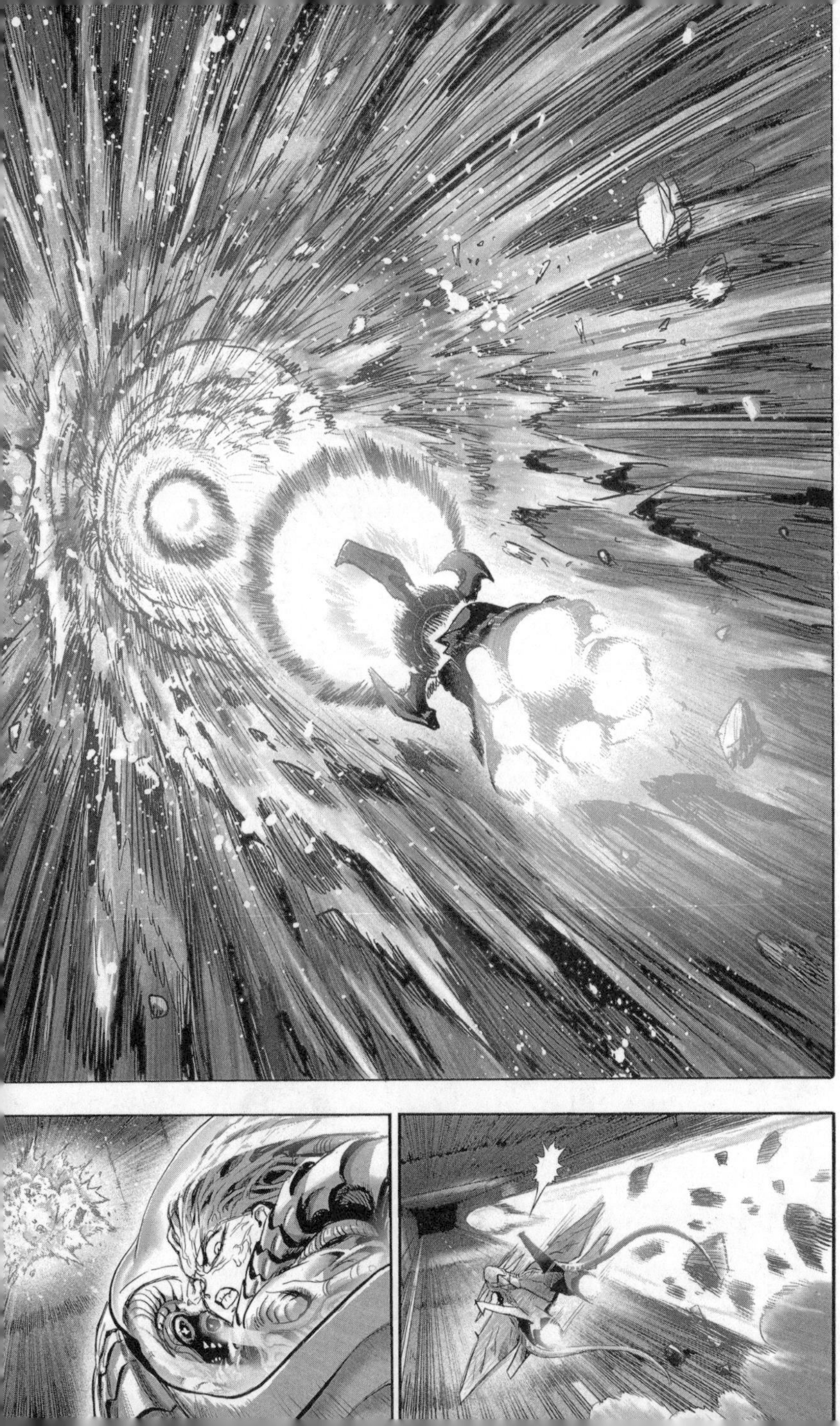

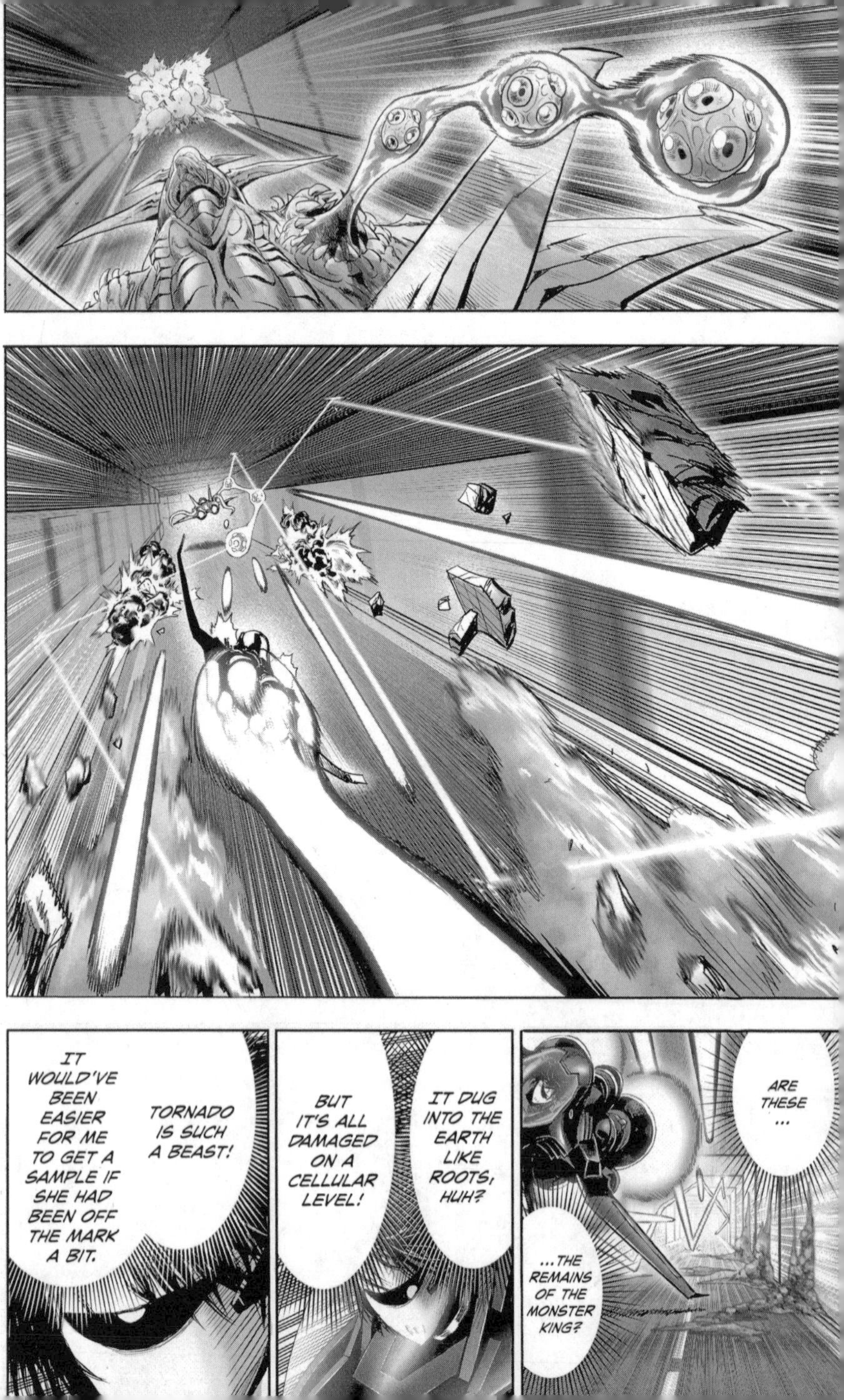
ARE THESE ...
...THE REMAINS OF THE MONSTER KING?
IT DUG INTO THE EARTH LIKE ROOTS, HUH?
BUT IT'S ALL DAMAGED ON A CELLULAR LEVEL!
TORNADO IS SUCH A BEAST!
IT WOULD'VE BEEN EASIER FOR ME TO GET A SAMPLE IF SHE HAD BEEN OFF THE MARK A BIT.

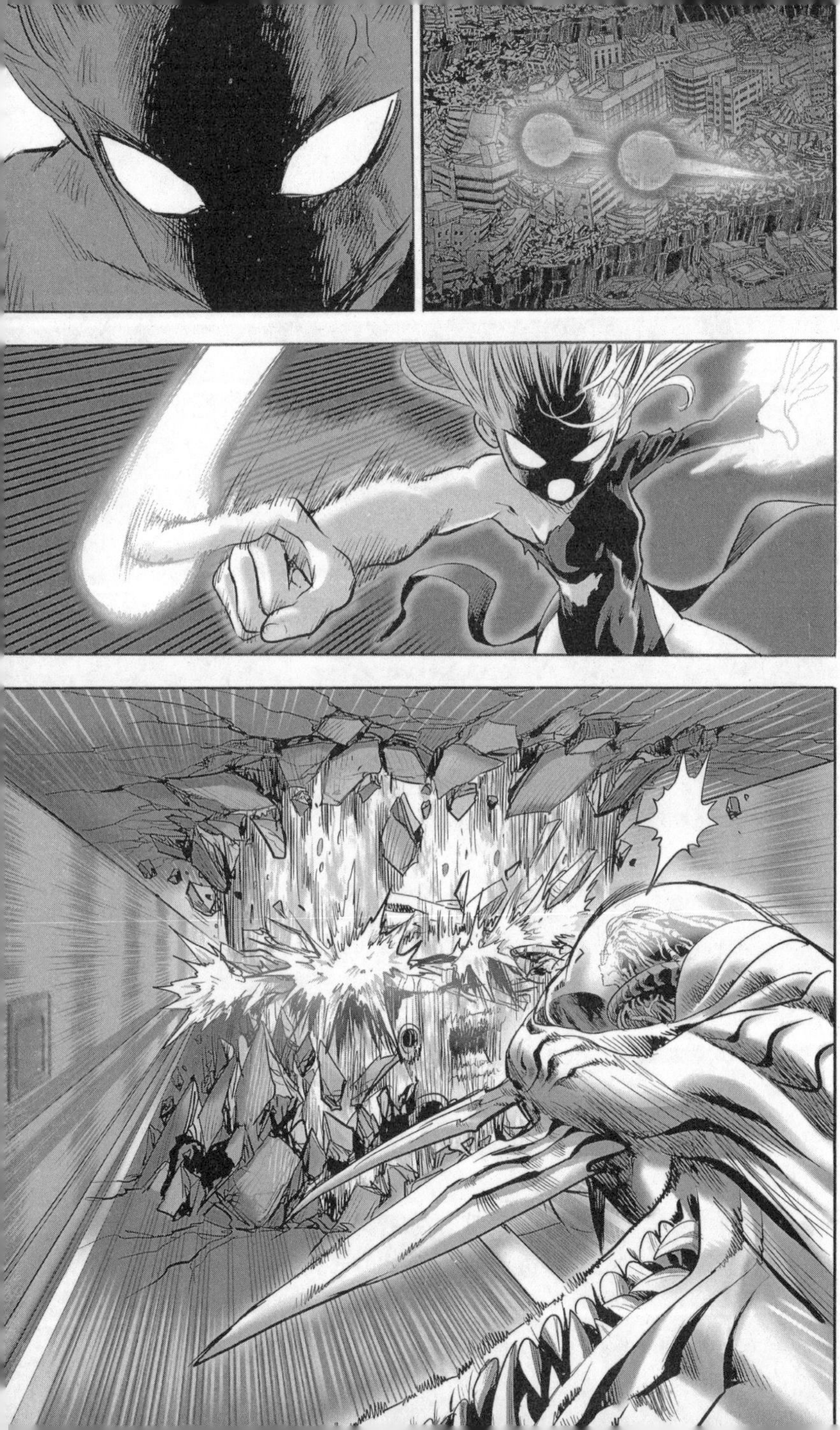

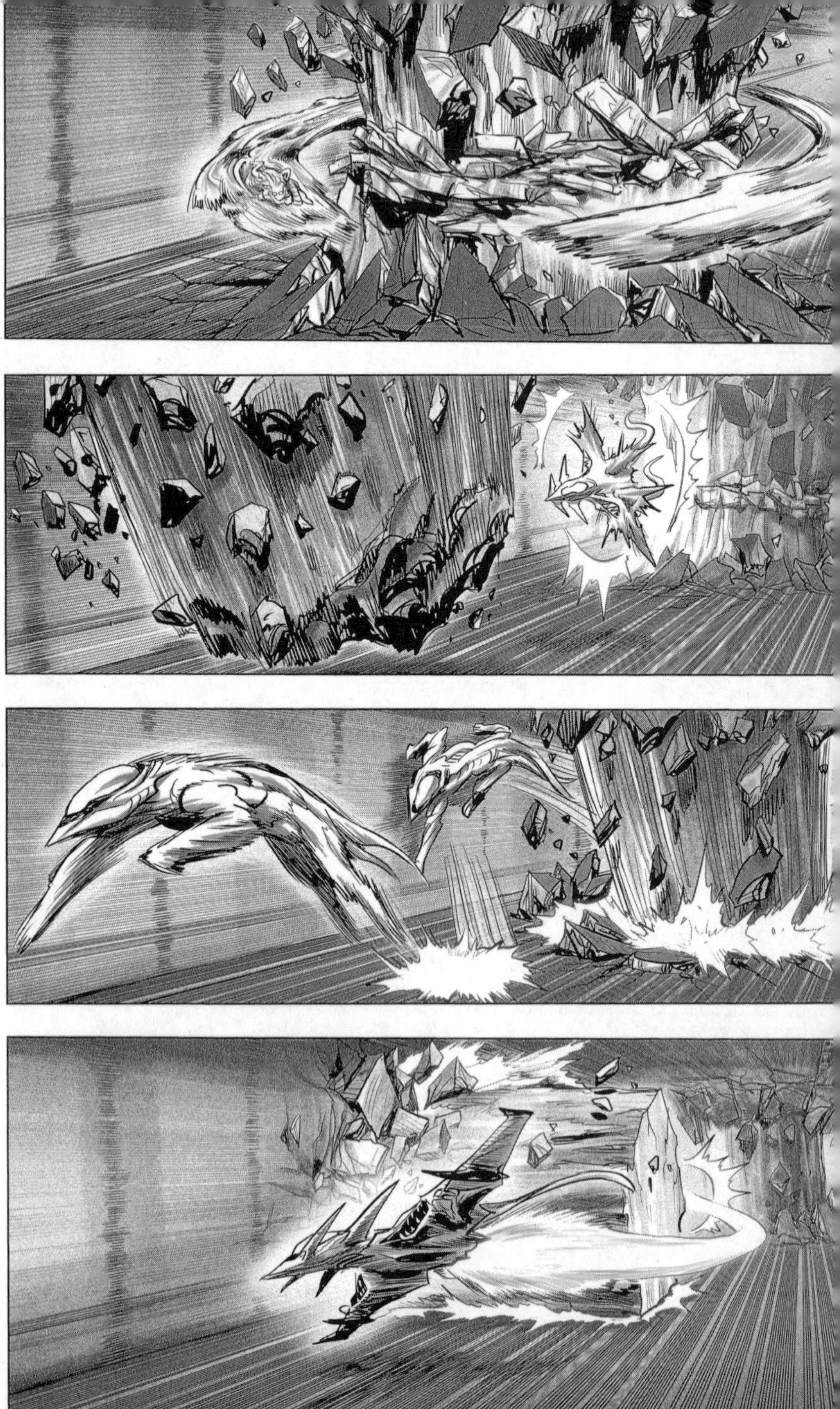

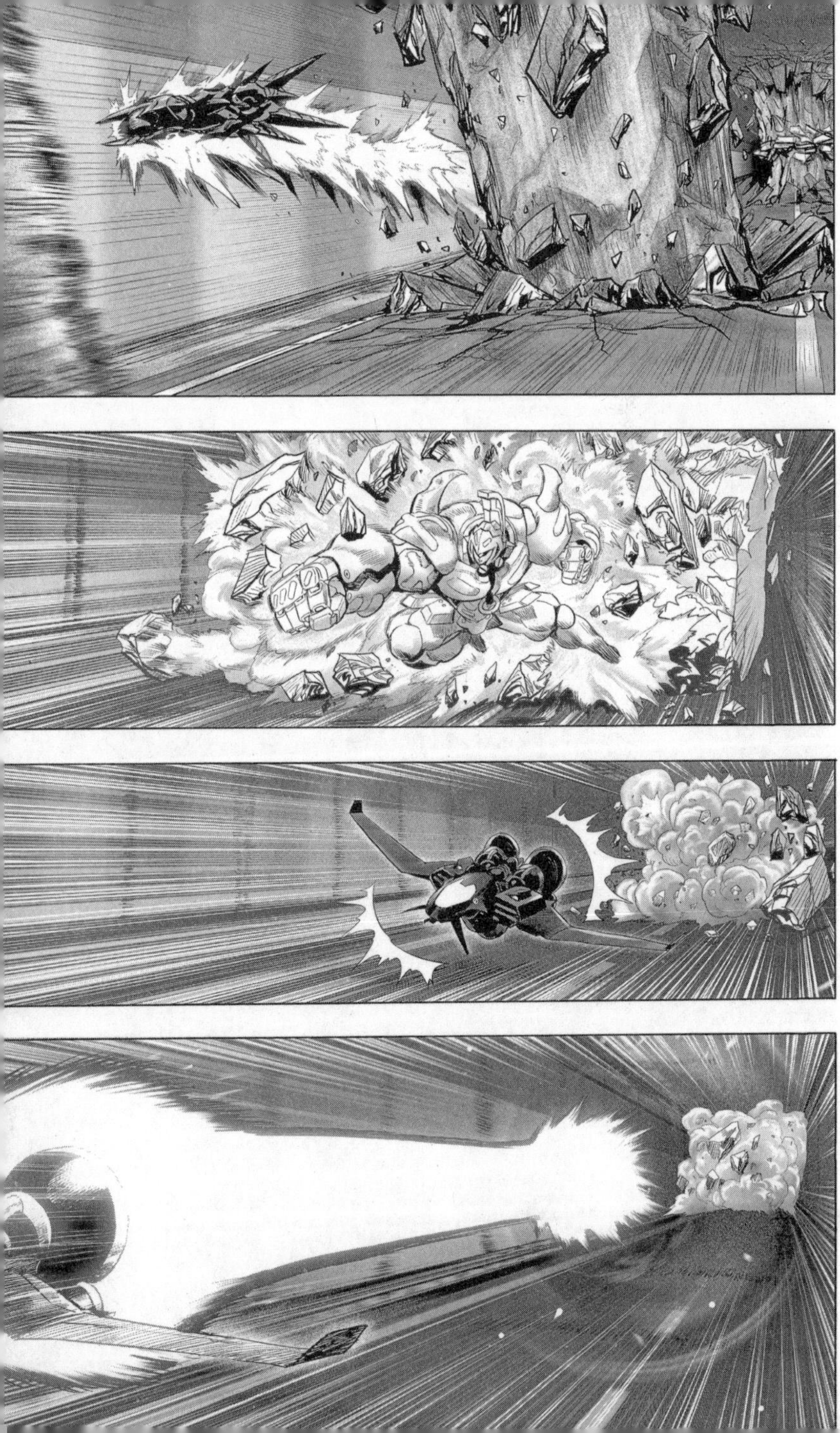

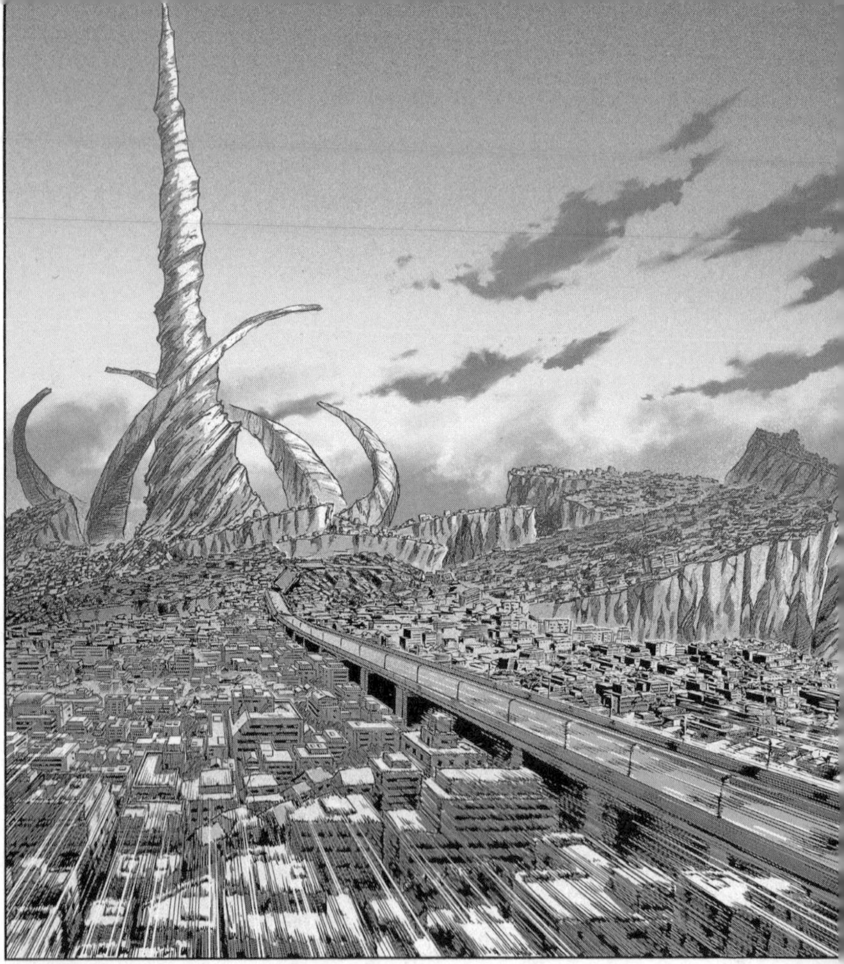
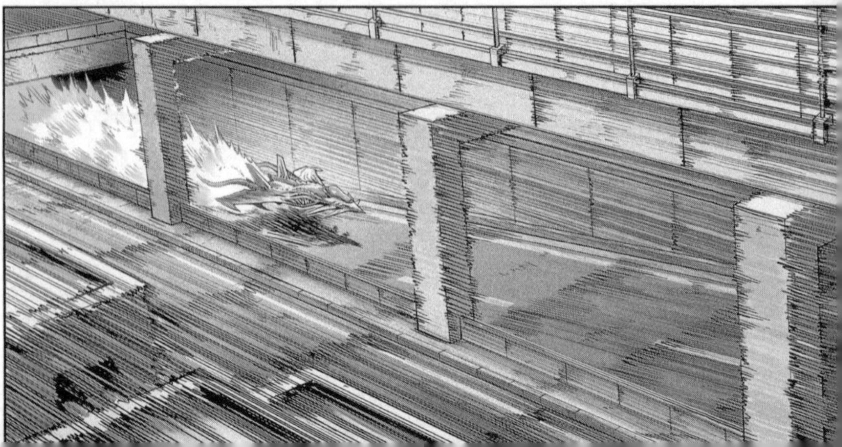

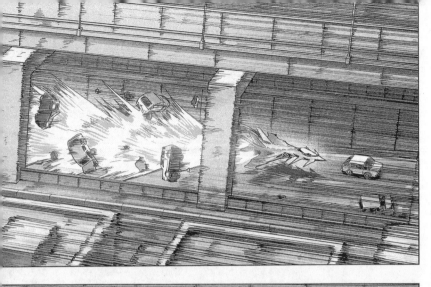

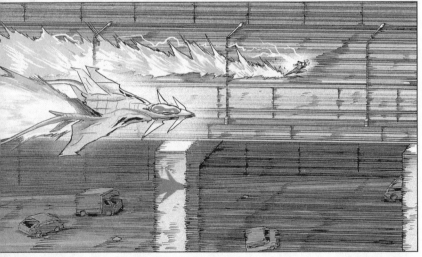

HWUP

DEMON CYBORG!

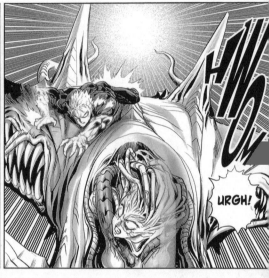

HWOM

URGH!

EXCEL-LENT!

KLANK

GWOOSH

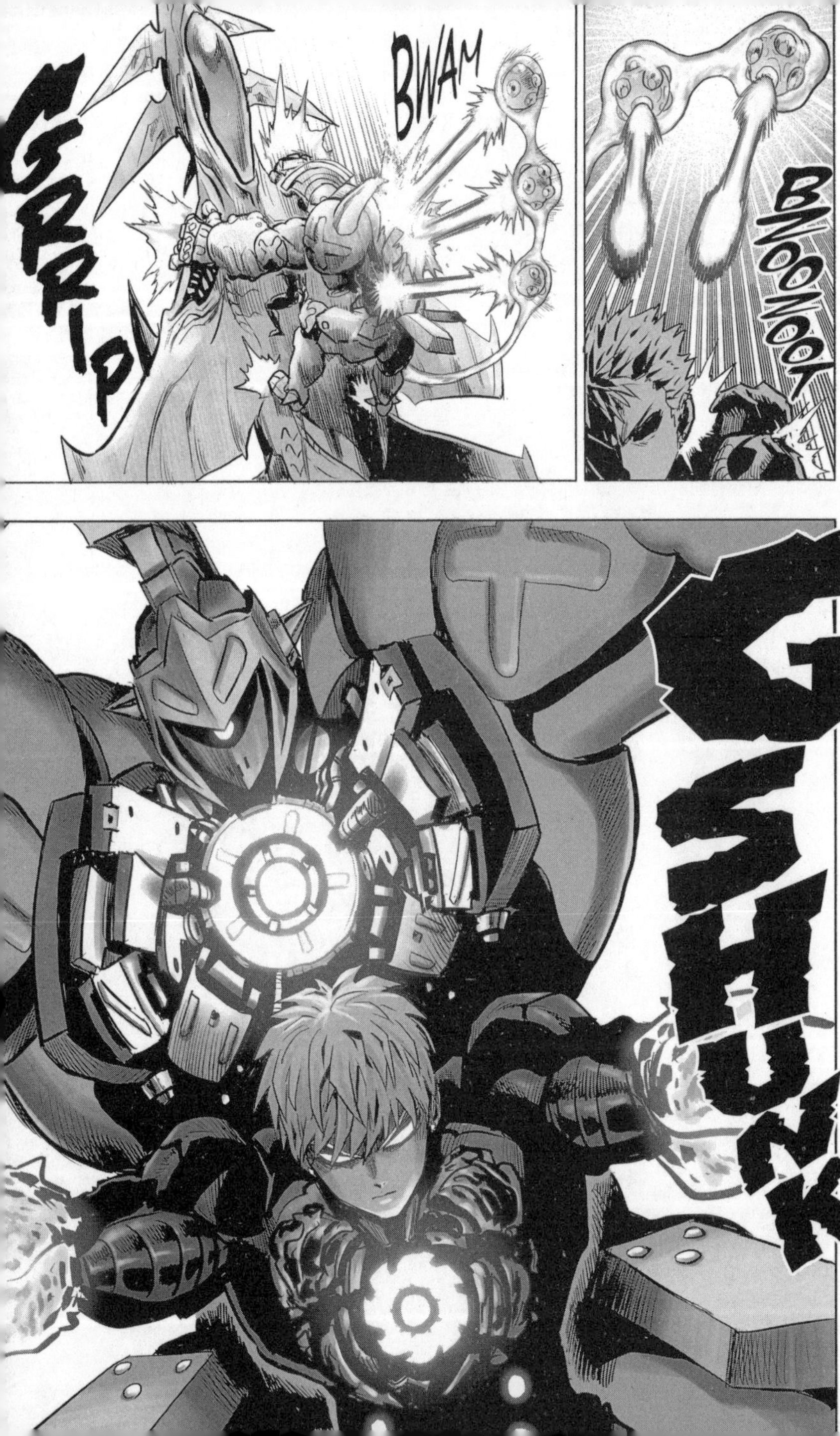
BZOOZOOK
BWAM
GRRIP!
GSHUNK

PUNCH 143: INTO THE ABYSS

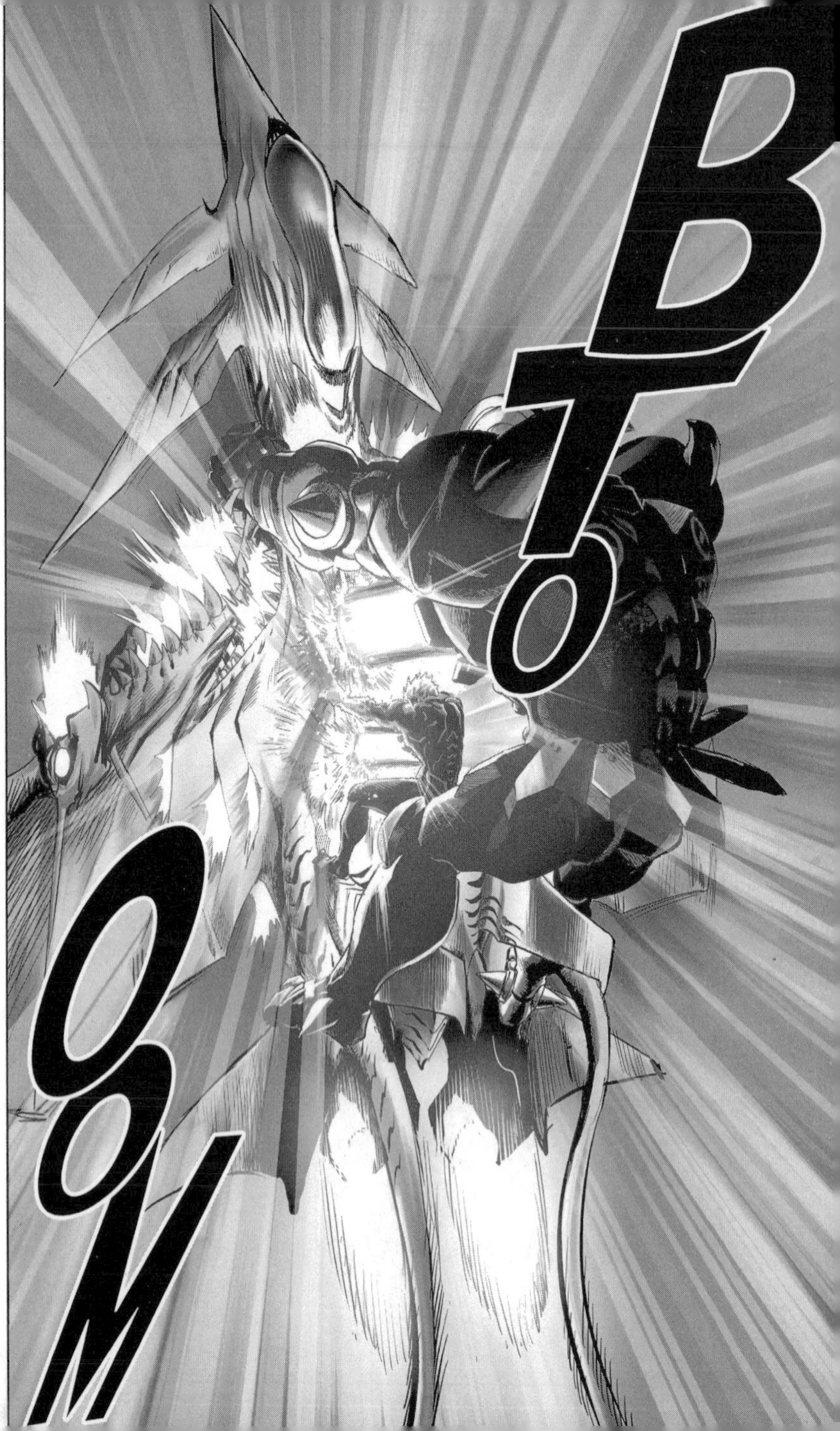
BTO
OOM

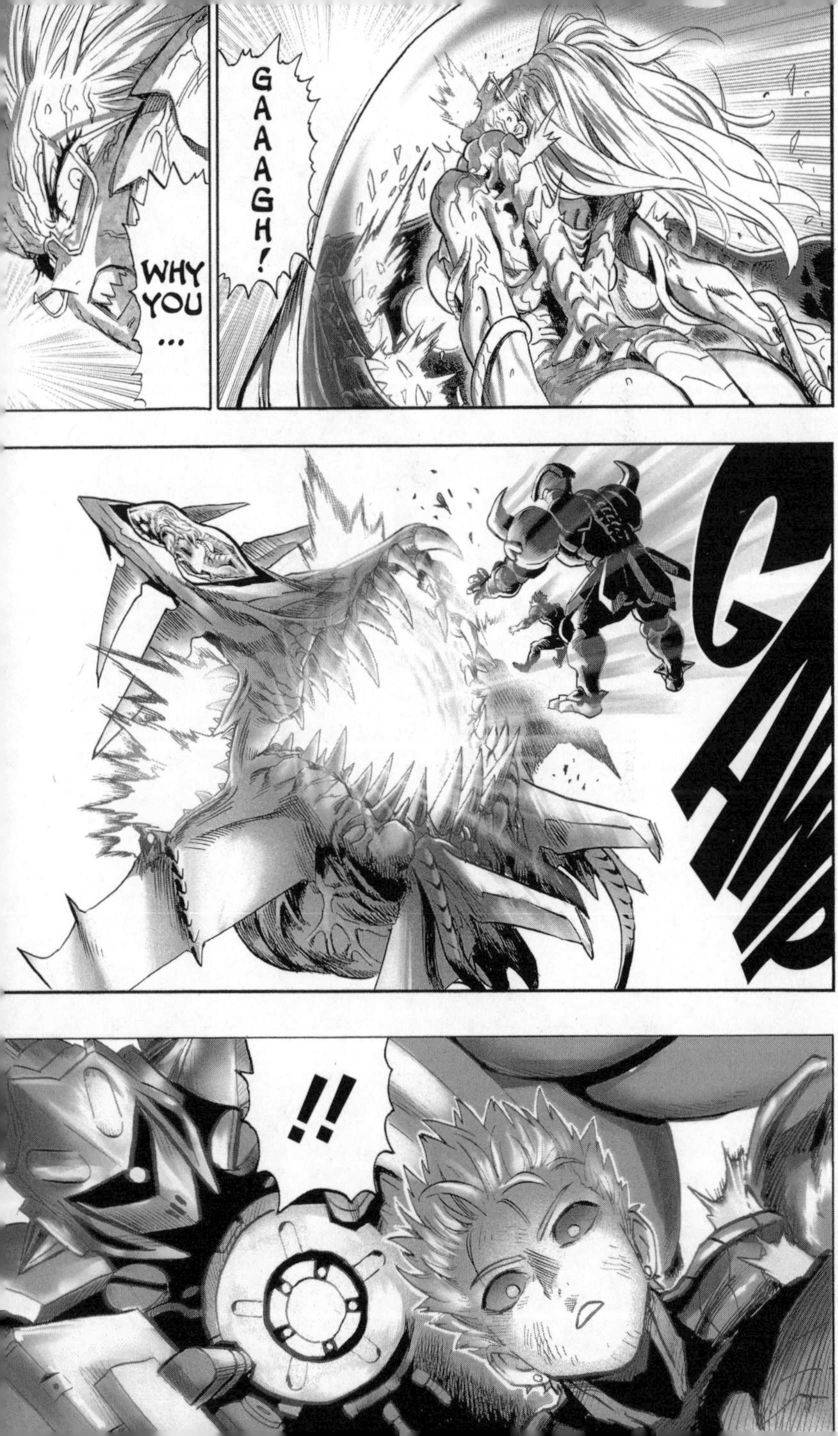
GAAAAGH!
WHY YOU ...
!!

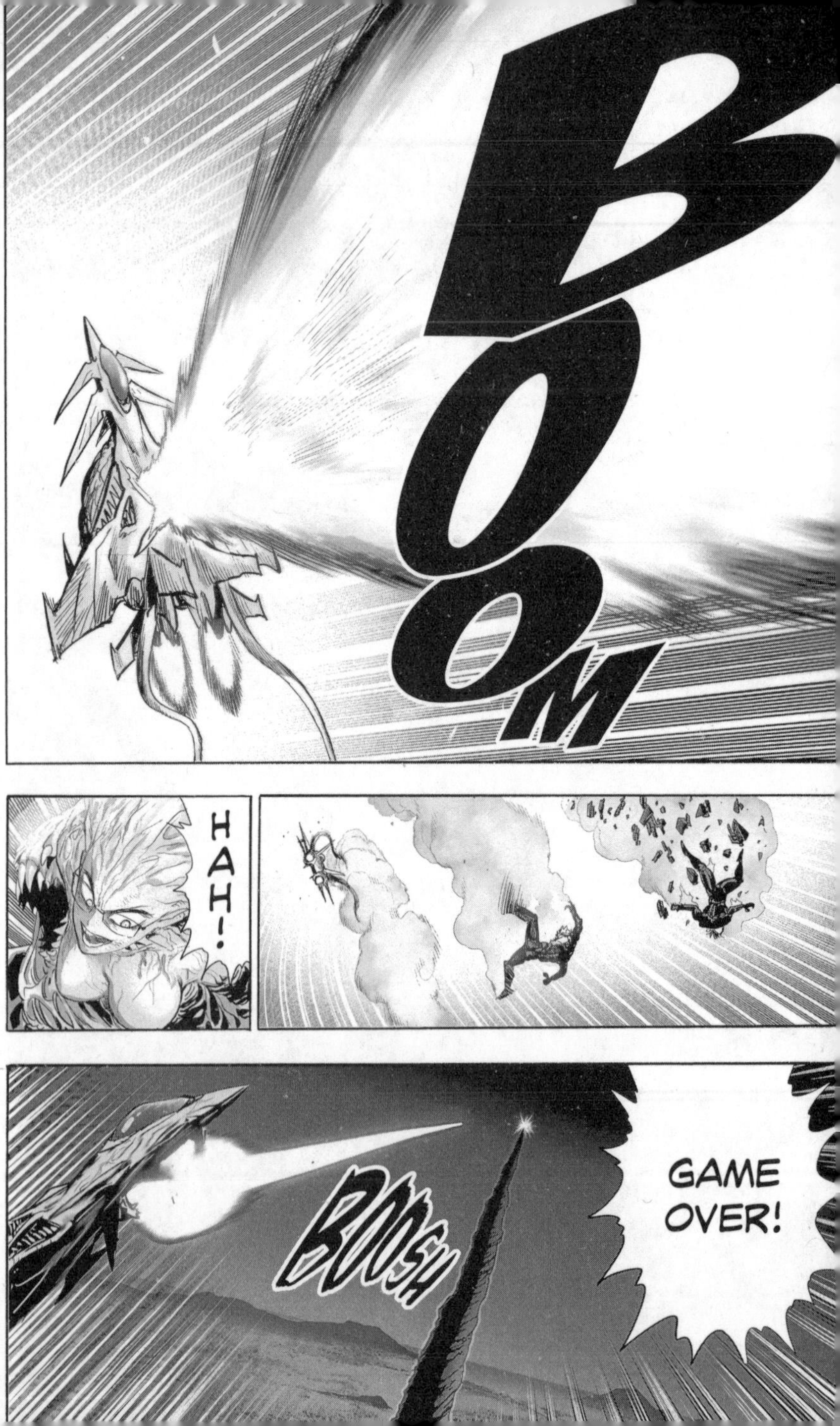
BOOM
HAH!
GAME OVER!
BOOSH

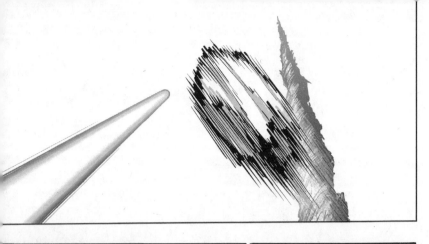

?!

BOOM

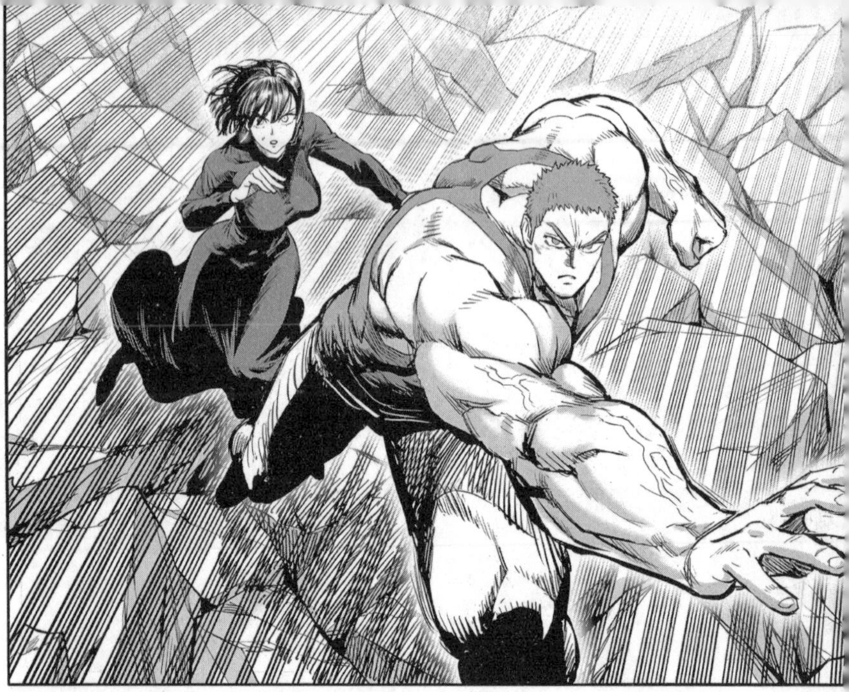

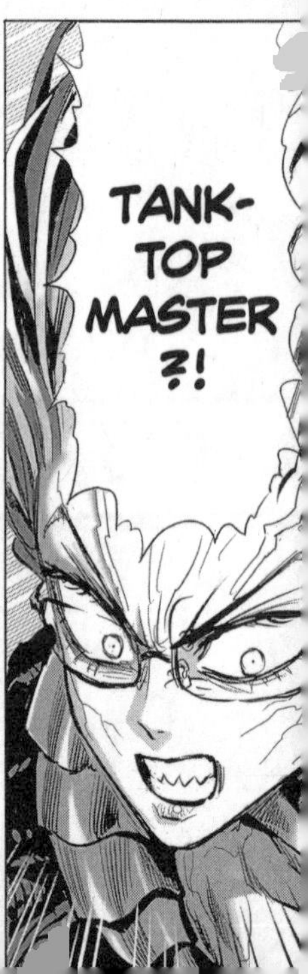
TANK-
TOP
MASTER
?!

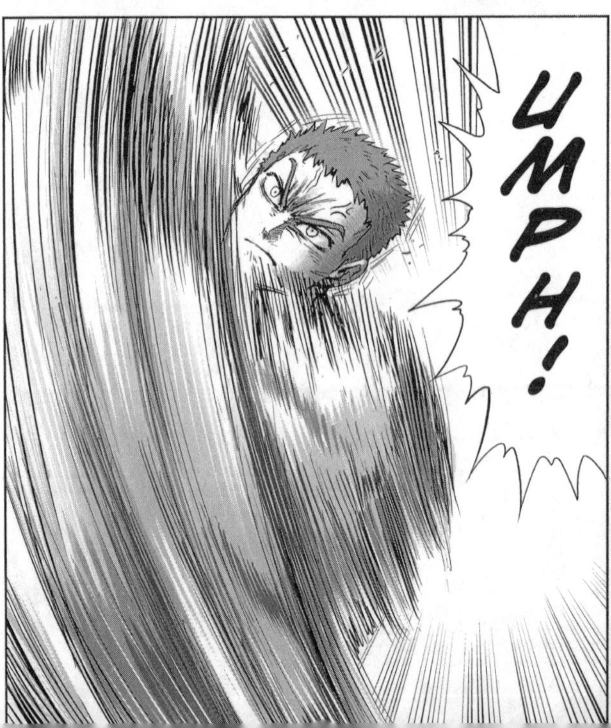
UMPH!

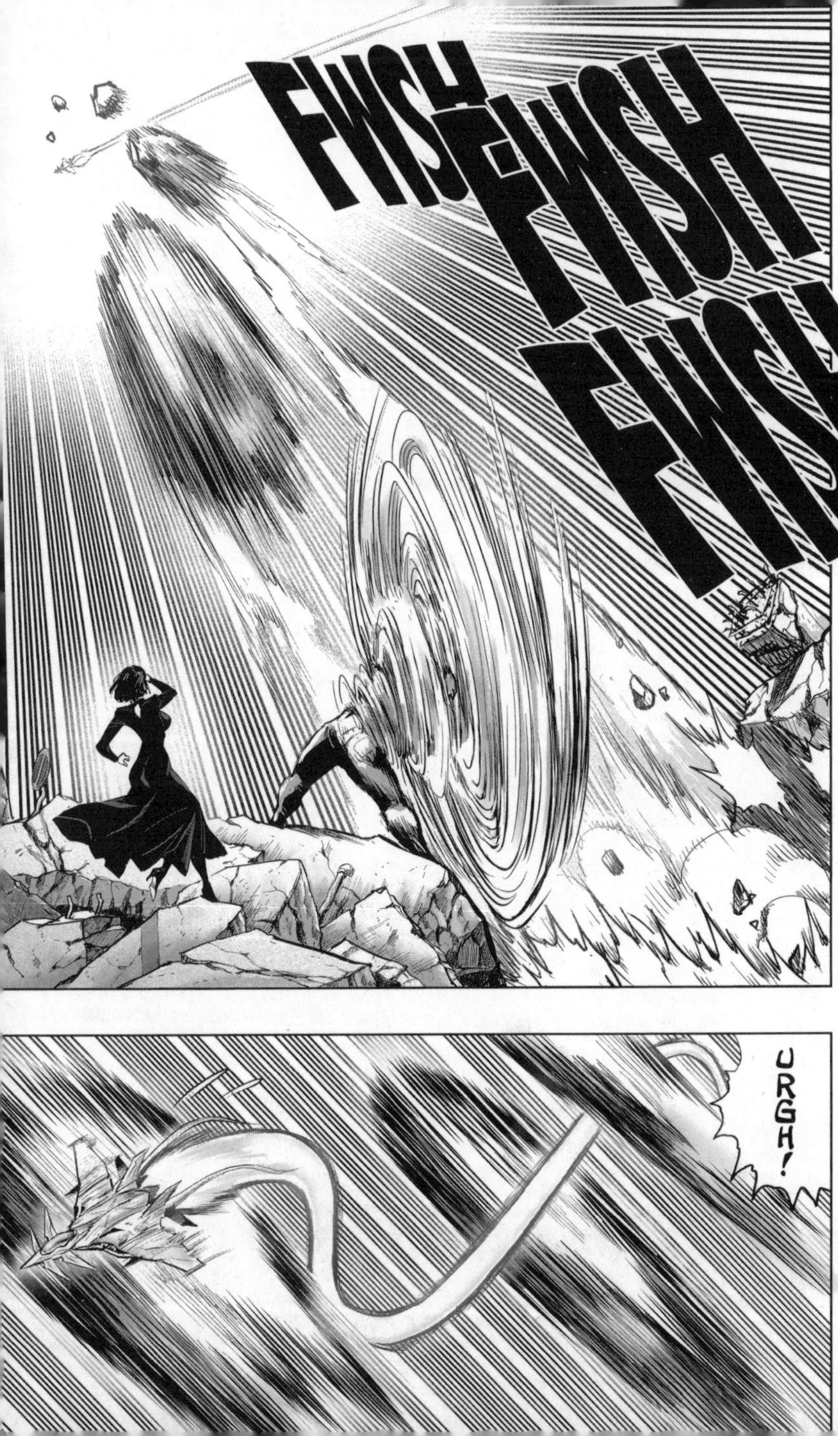
FWSH
FWSH
FWSH
FWSH
URGH!

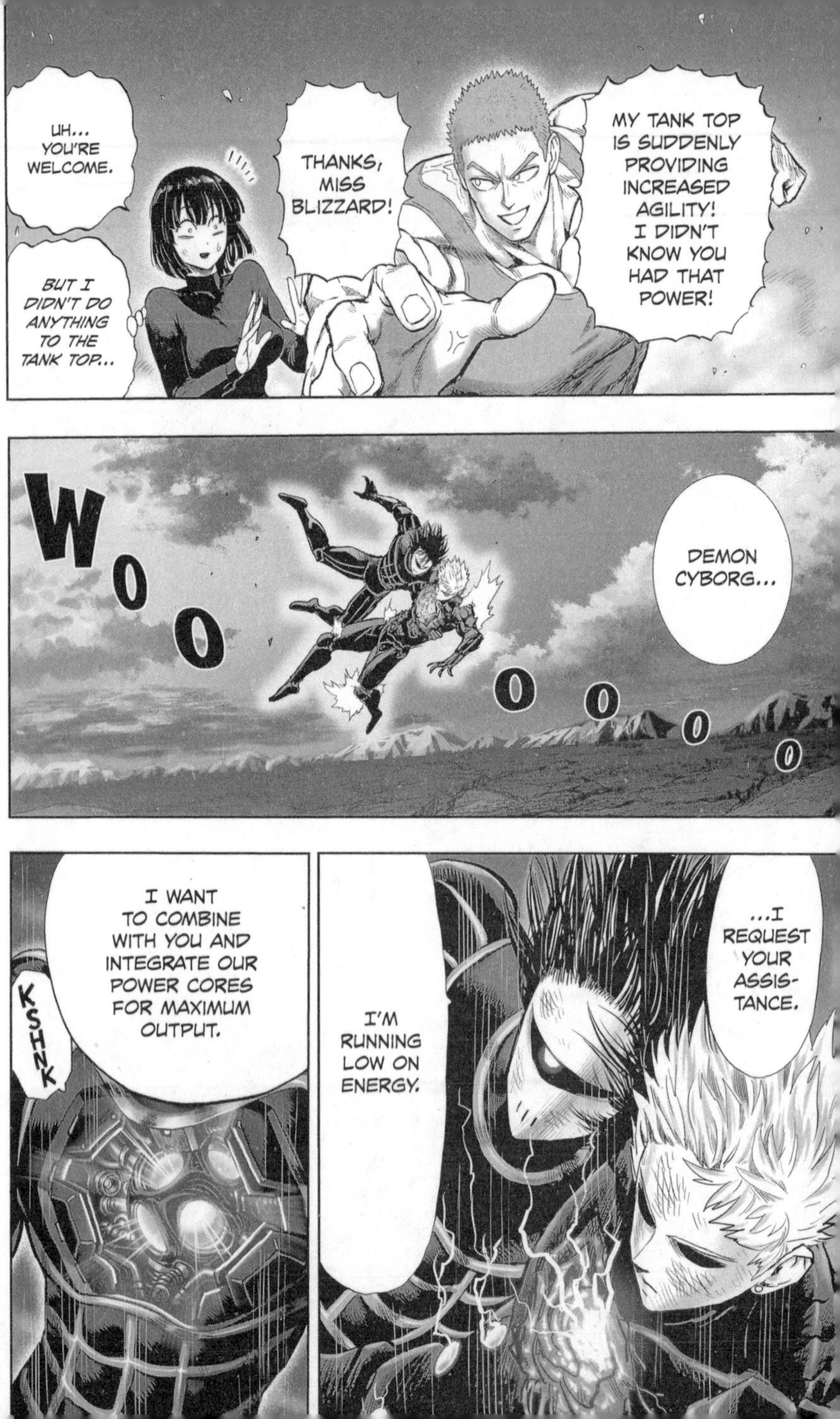
MY TANK TOP IS SUDDENLY PROVIDING INCREASED AGILITY! I DIDN'T KNOW YOU HAD THAT POWER!
THANKS, MISS BLIZZARD!
UH... YOU'RE WELCOME.
BUT I DIDN'T DO ANYTHING TO THE TANK TOP...
DEMON CYBORG...
WOOOOOO
...I REQUEST YOUR ASSIS-TANCE.
I'M RUNNING LOW ON ENERGY.
I WANT TO COMBINE WITH YOU AND INTEGRATE OUR POWER CORES FOR MAXIMUM OUTPUT.
KSHNK

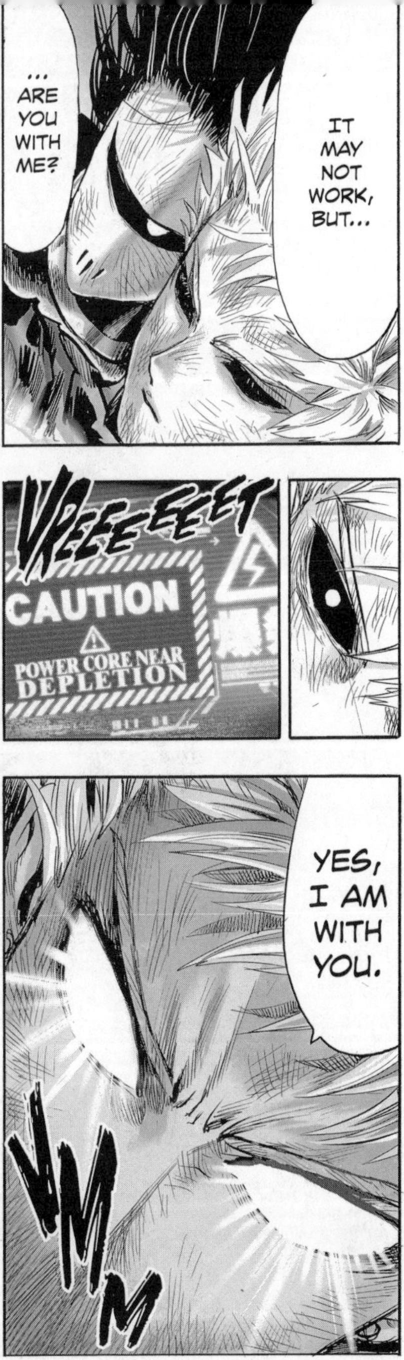
IT MAY NOT WORK, BUT...
...ARE YOU WITH ME?
VREEEEEEET
CAUTION
POWER CORE NEAR DEPLETION
YES, I AM WITH YOU.
VMMM
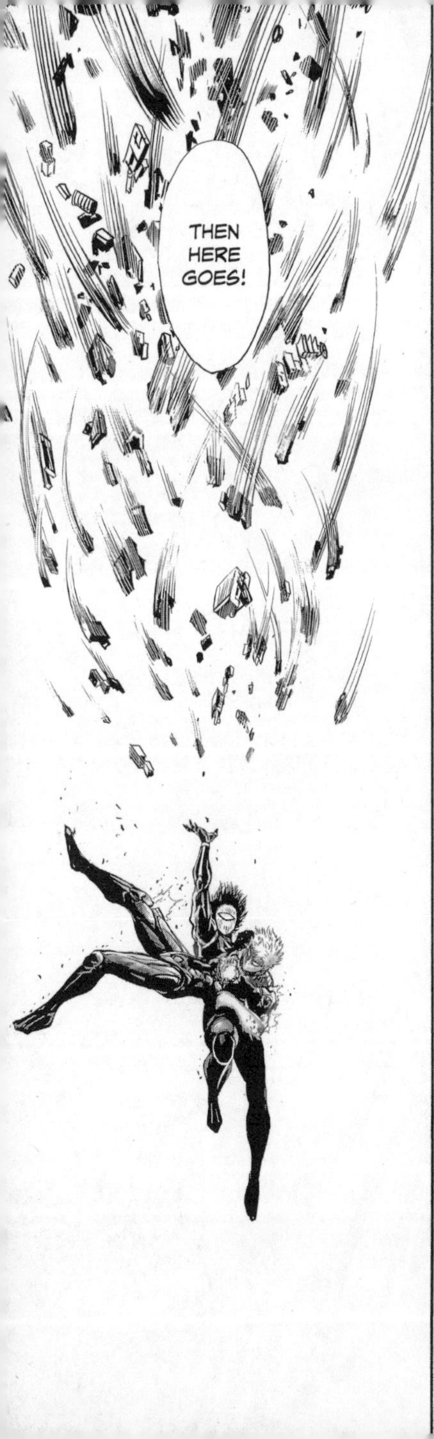
THEN HERE GOES!

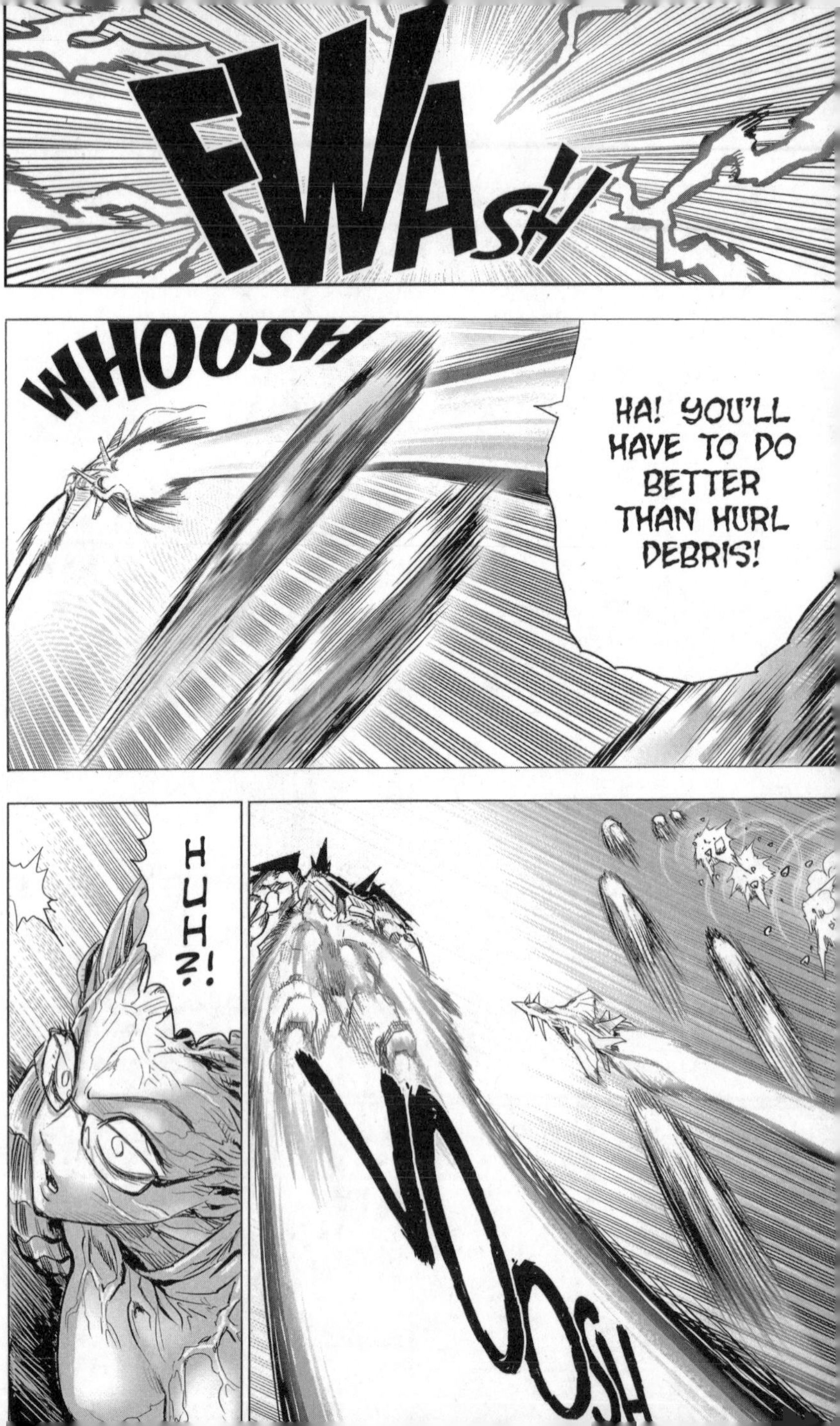
FWASH
HA! YOU'LL HAVE TO DO BETTER THAN HURL DEBRIS!
WHOOSH
VOOSH
HUH?!

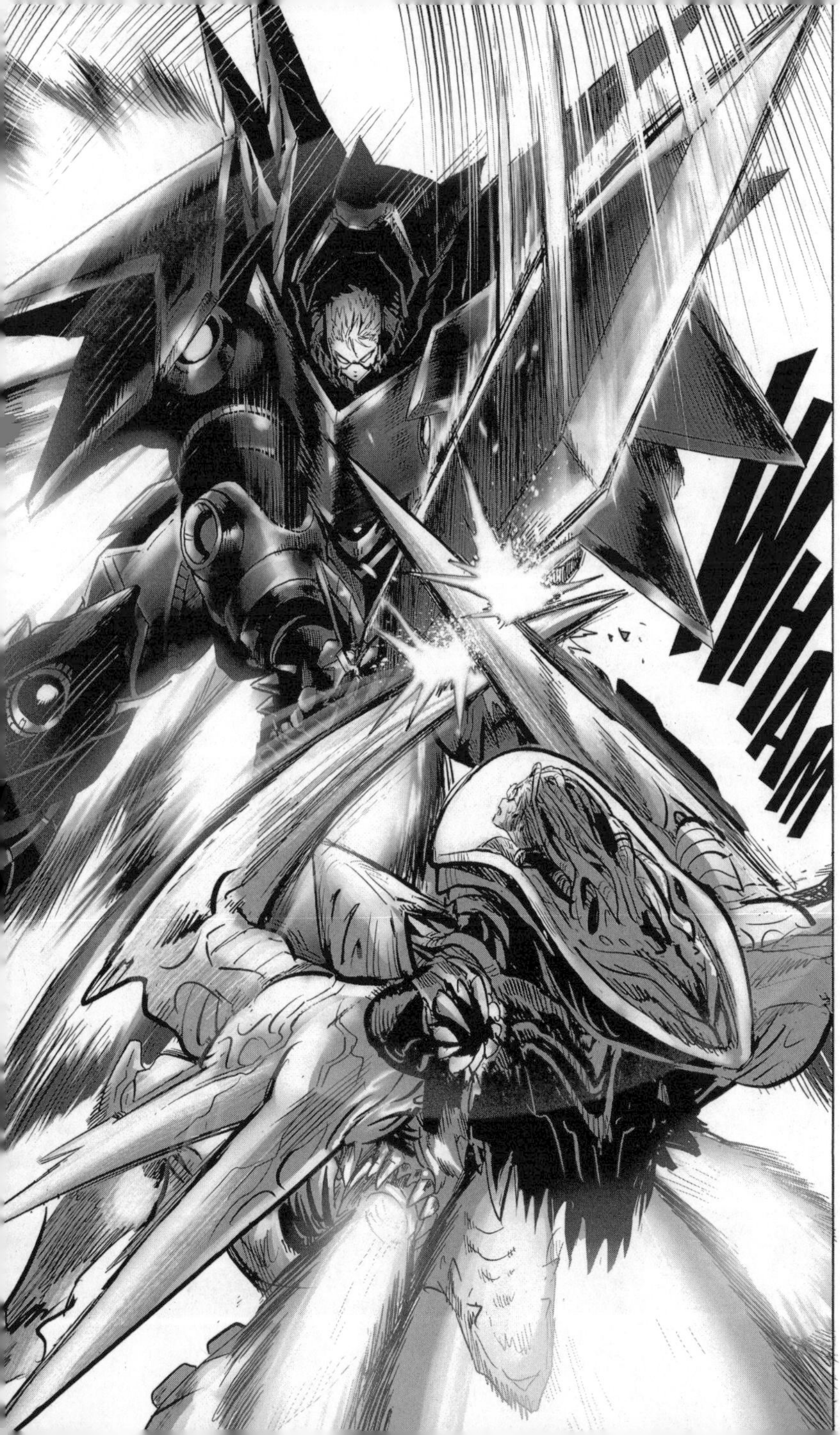
WHAM

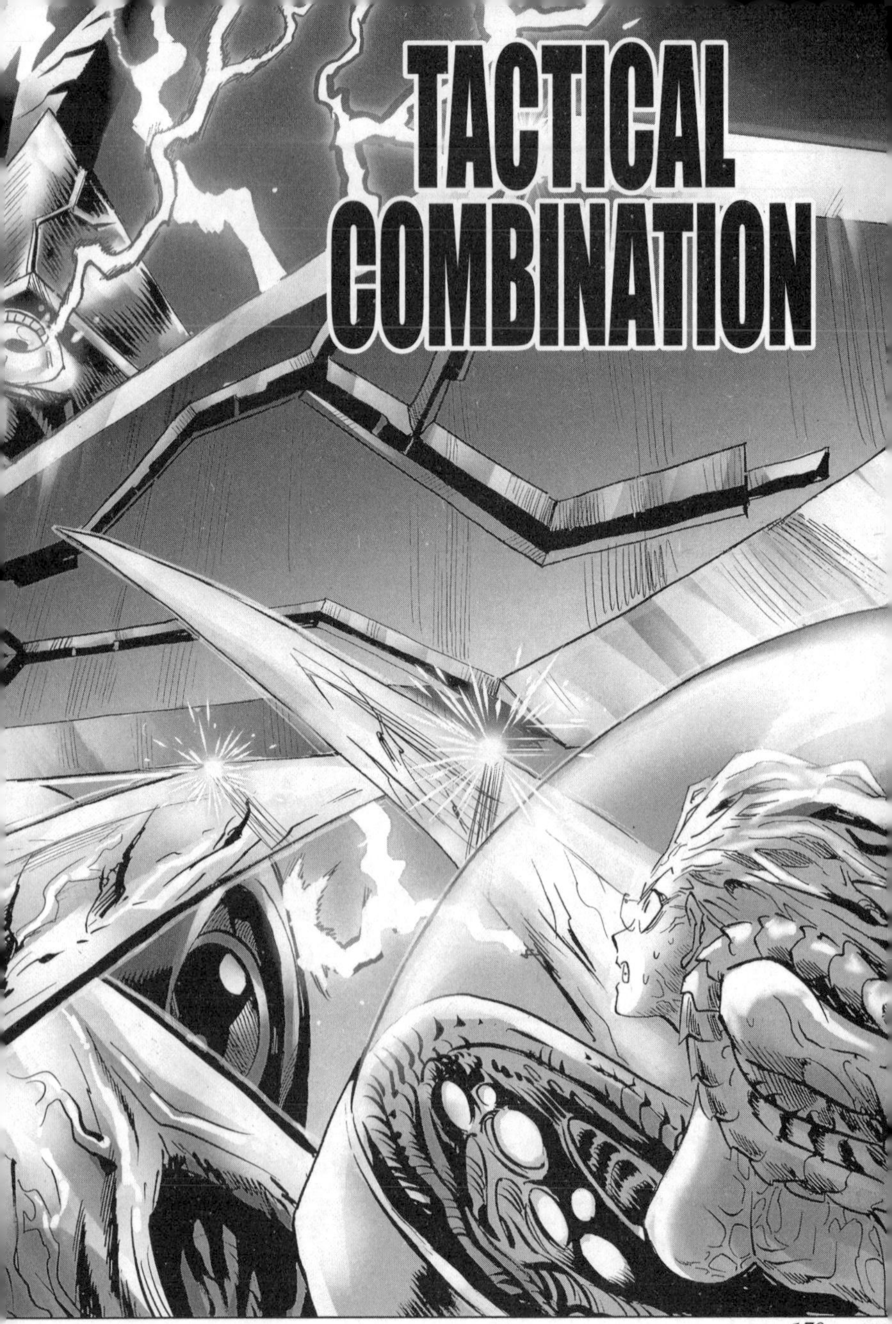
TACTICAL
COMBINATION

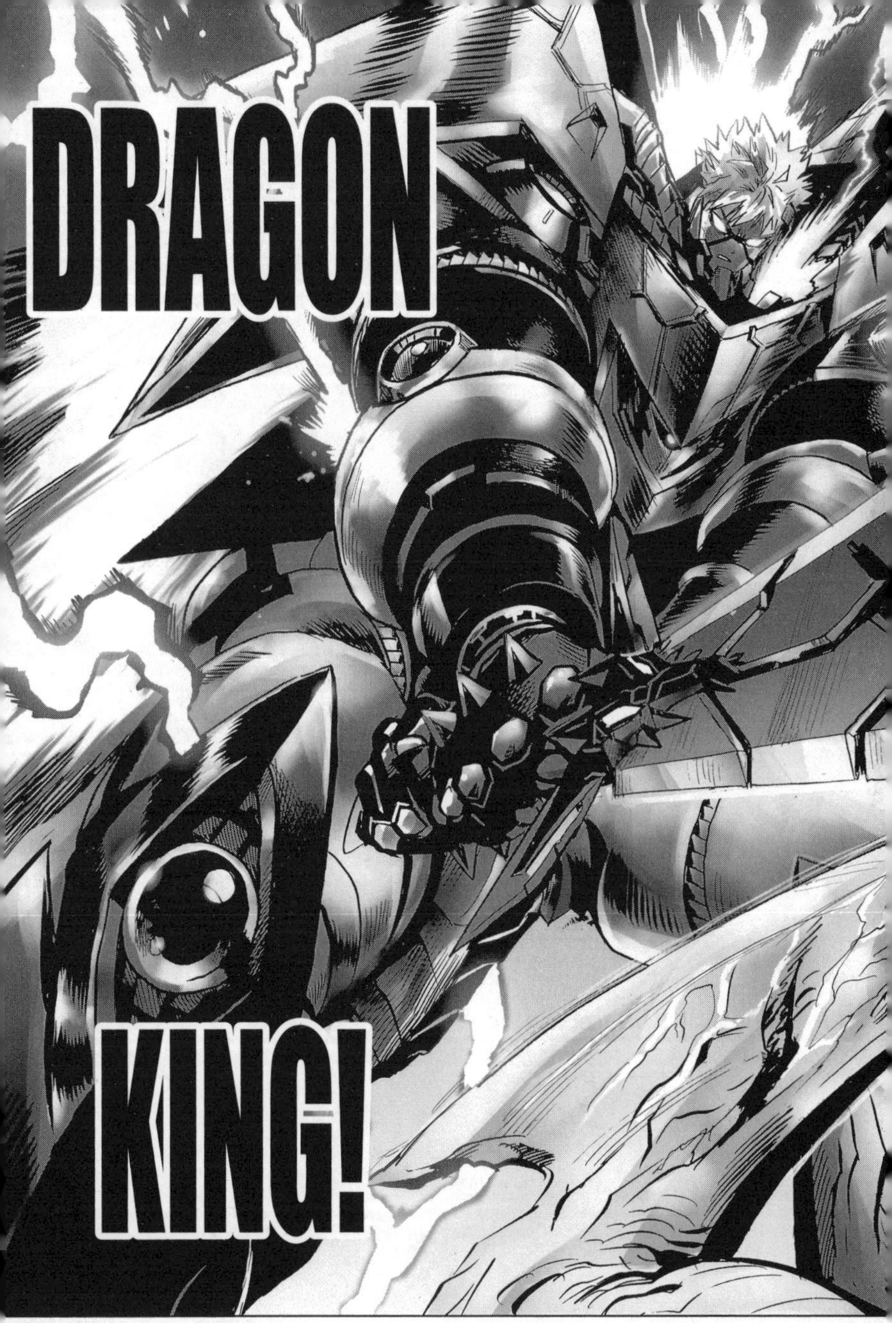
DRAGON
KING!

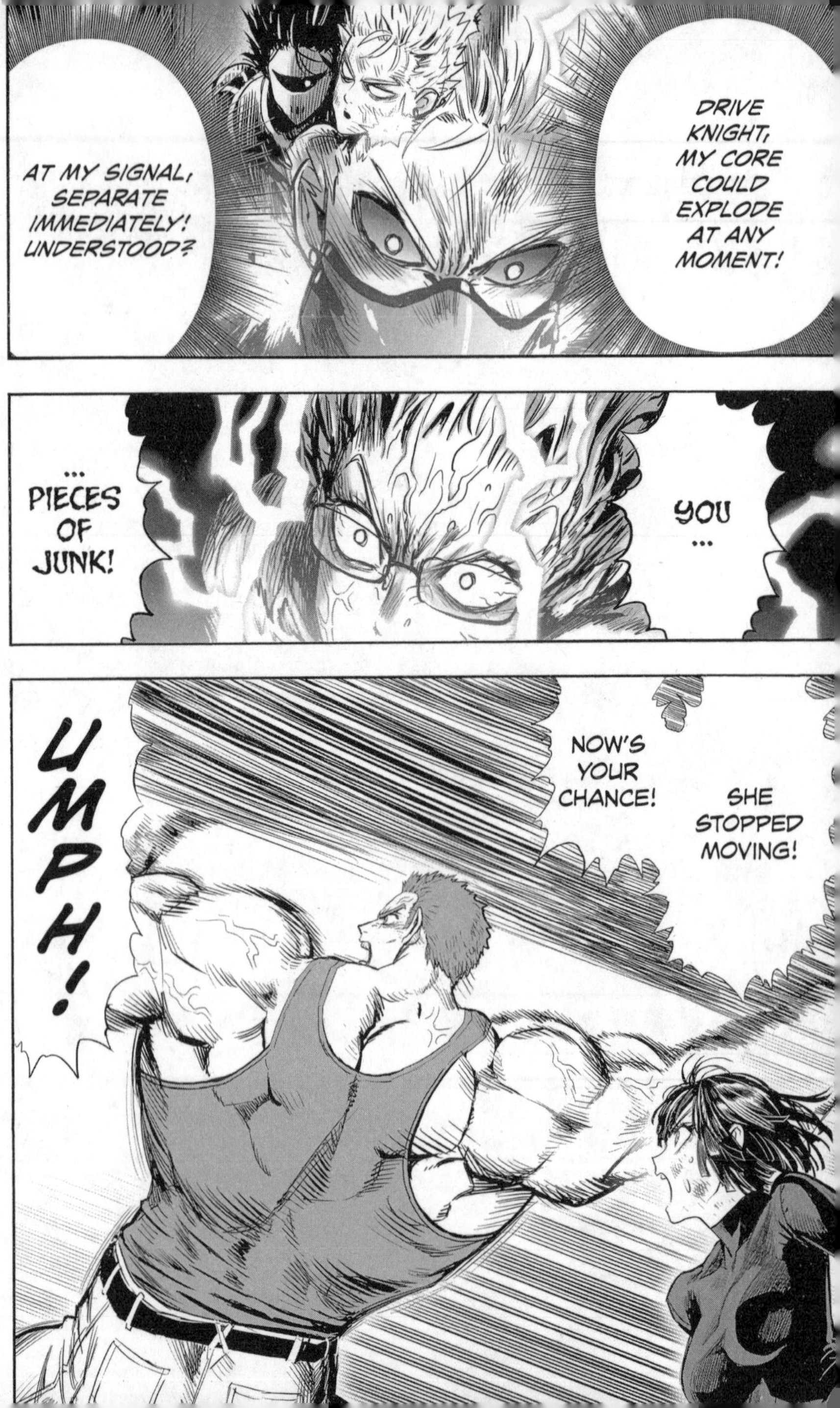
DRIVE KNIGHT, MY CORE COULD EXPLODE AT ANY MOMENT!
AT MY SIGNAL, SEPARATE IMMEDIATELY! UNDERSTOOD?
YOU ...
... PIECES OF JUNK!
SHE STOPPED MOVING!
NOW'S YOUR CHANCE!
UMPH!

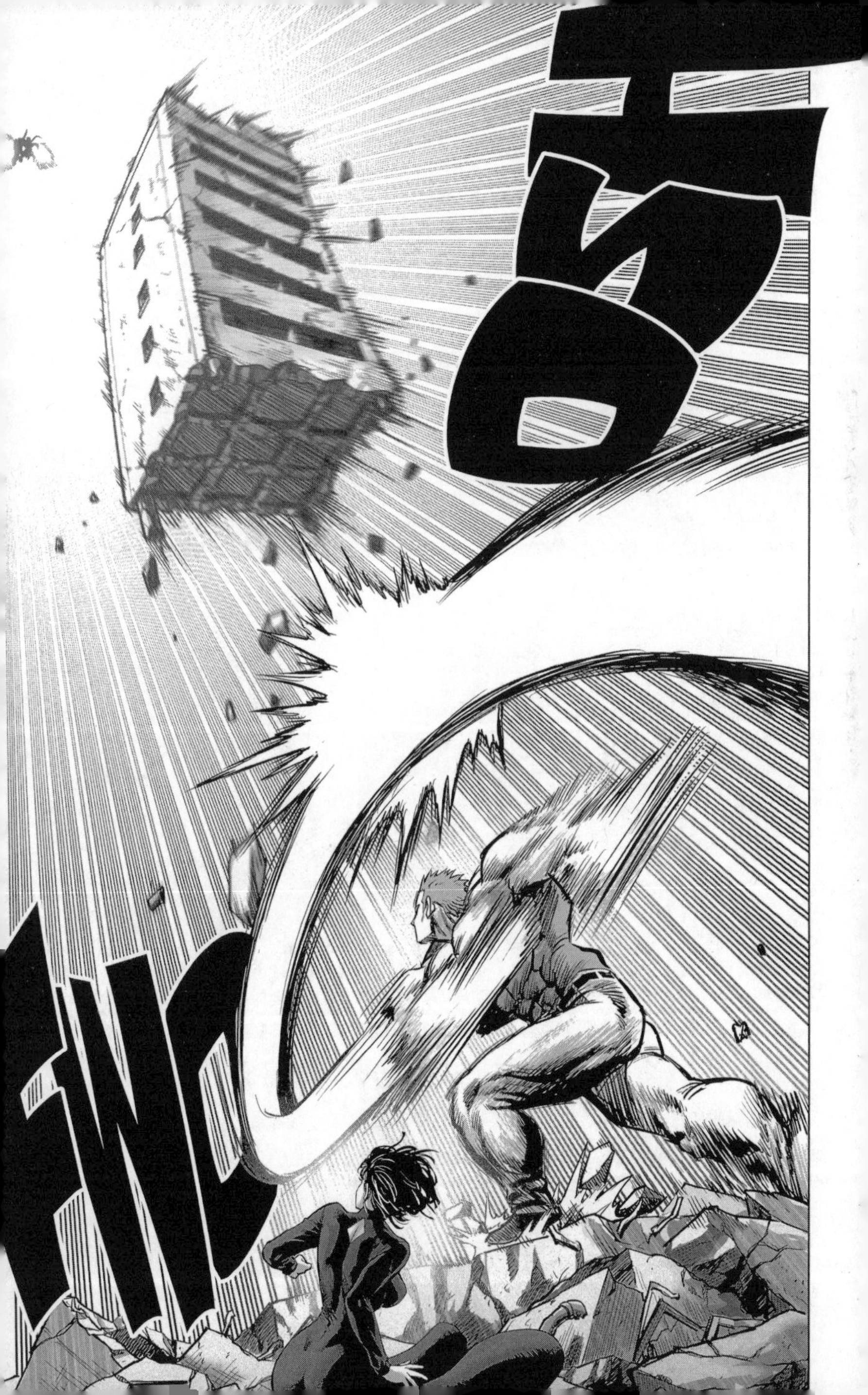

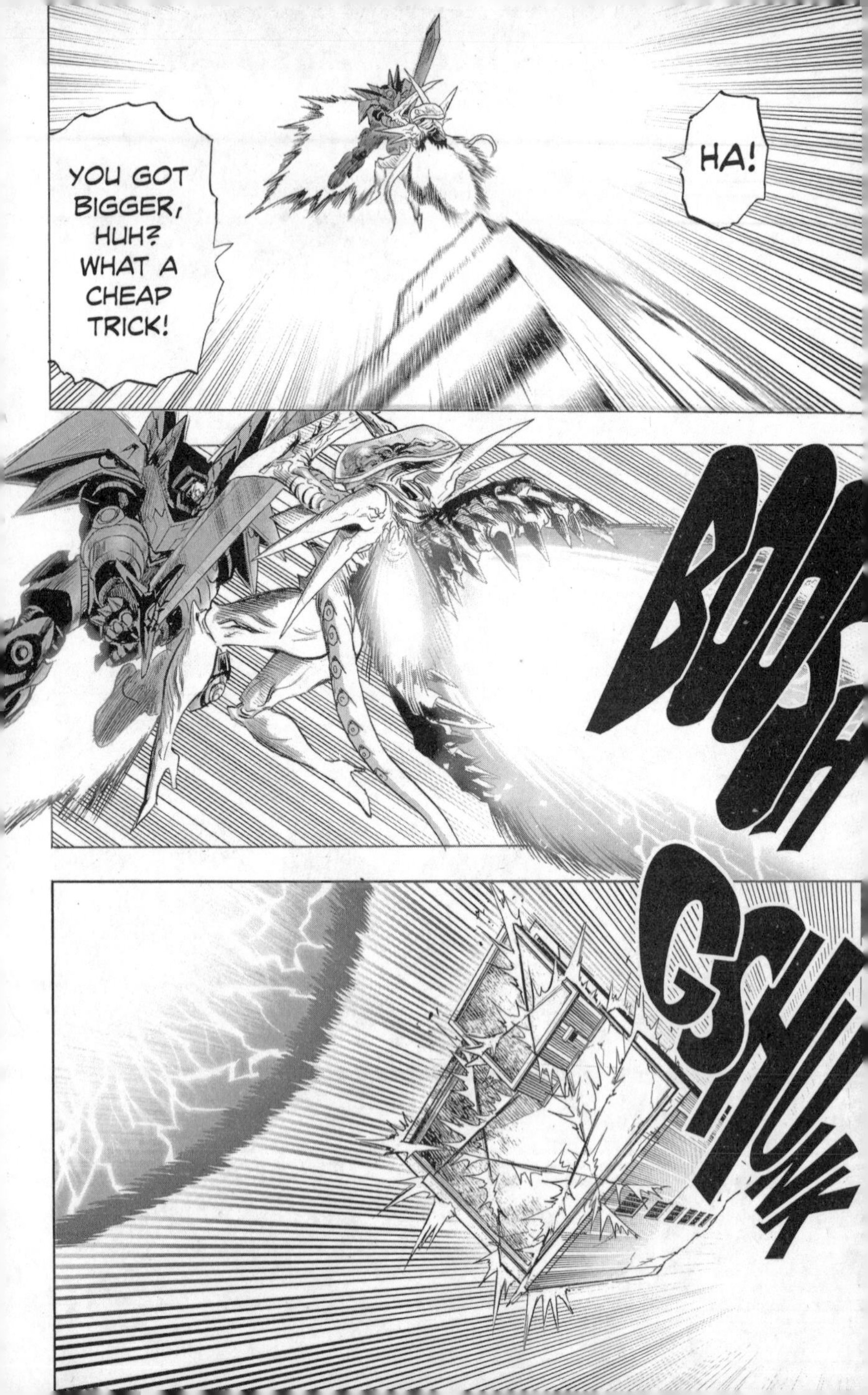
HA!
YOU GOT BIGGER, HUH? WHAT A CHEAP TRICK!
GSHUNK

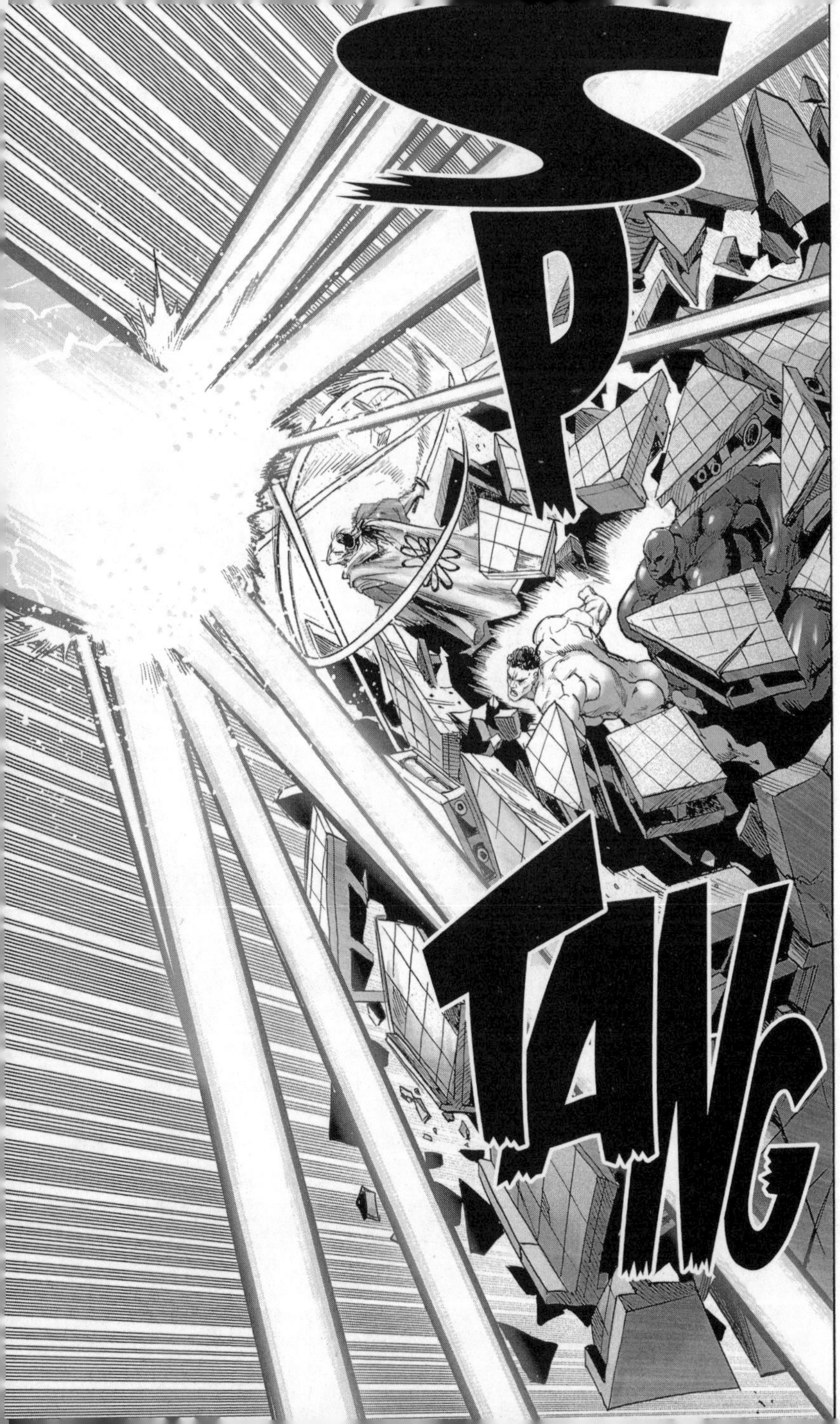
SPTANG

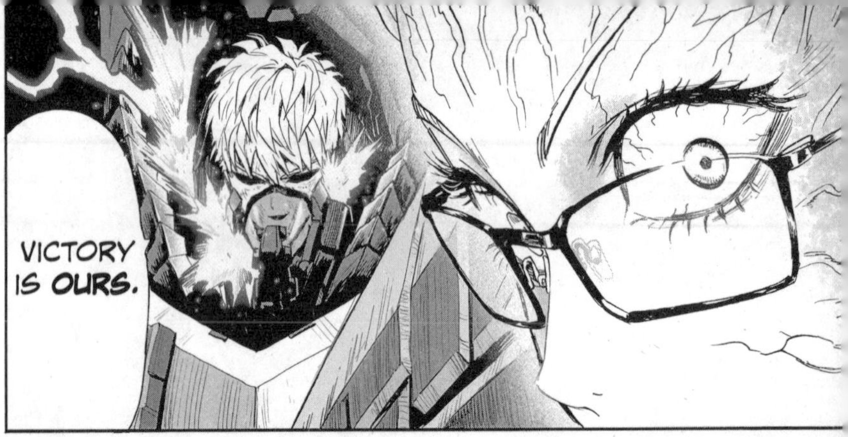
VICTORY IS OURS.

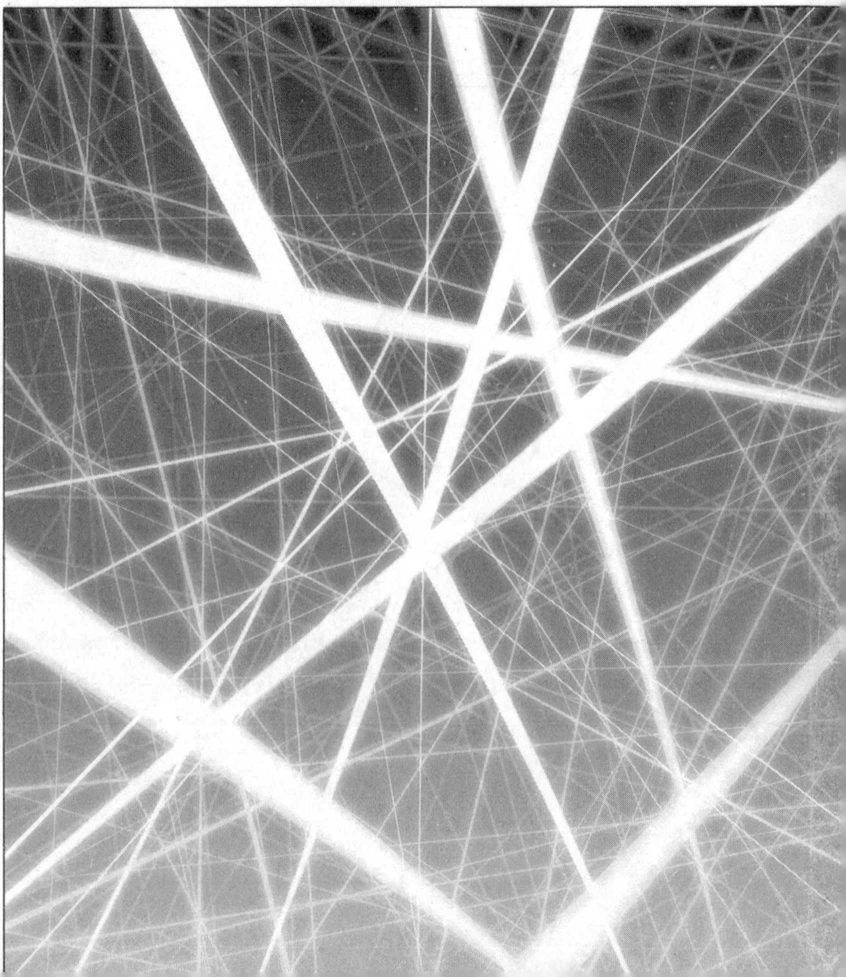

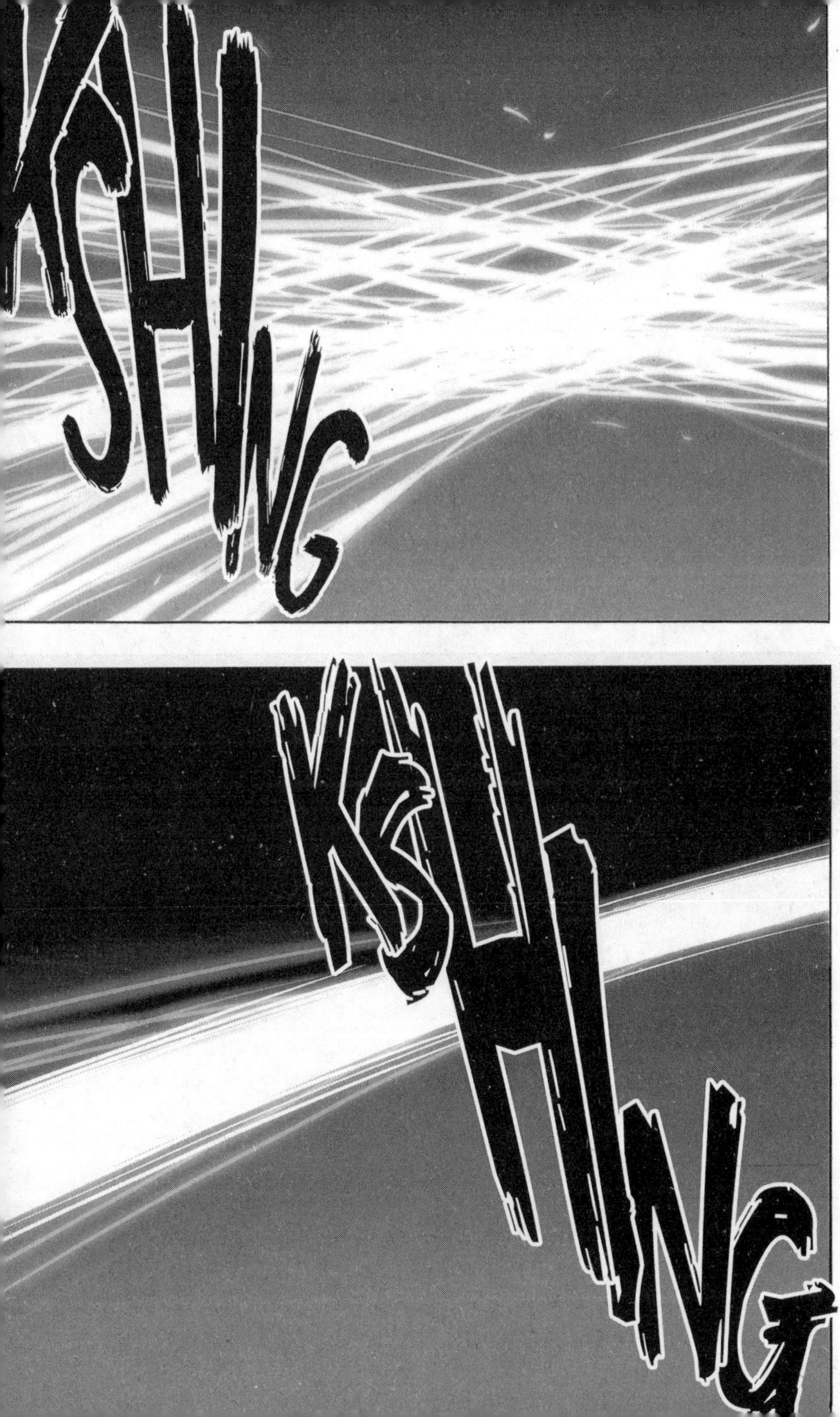
KSHING
KSHING

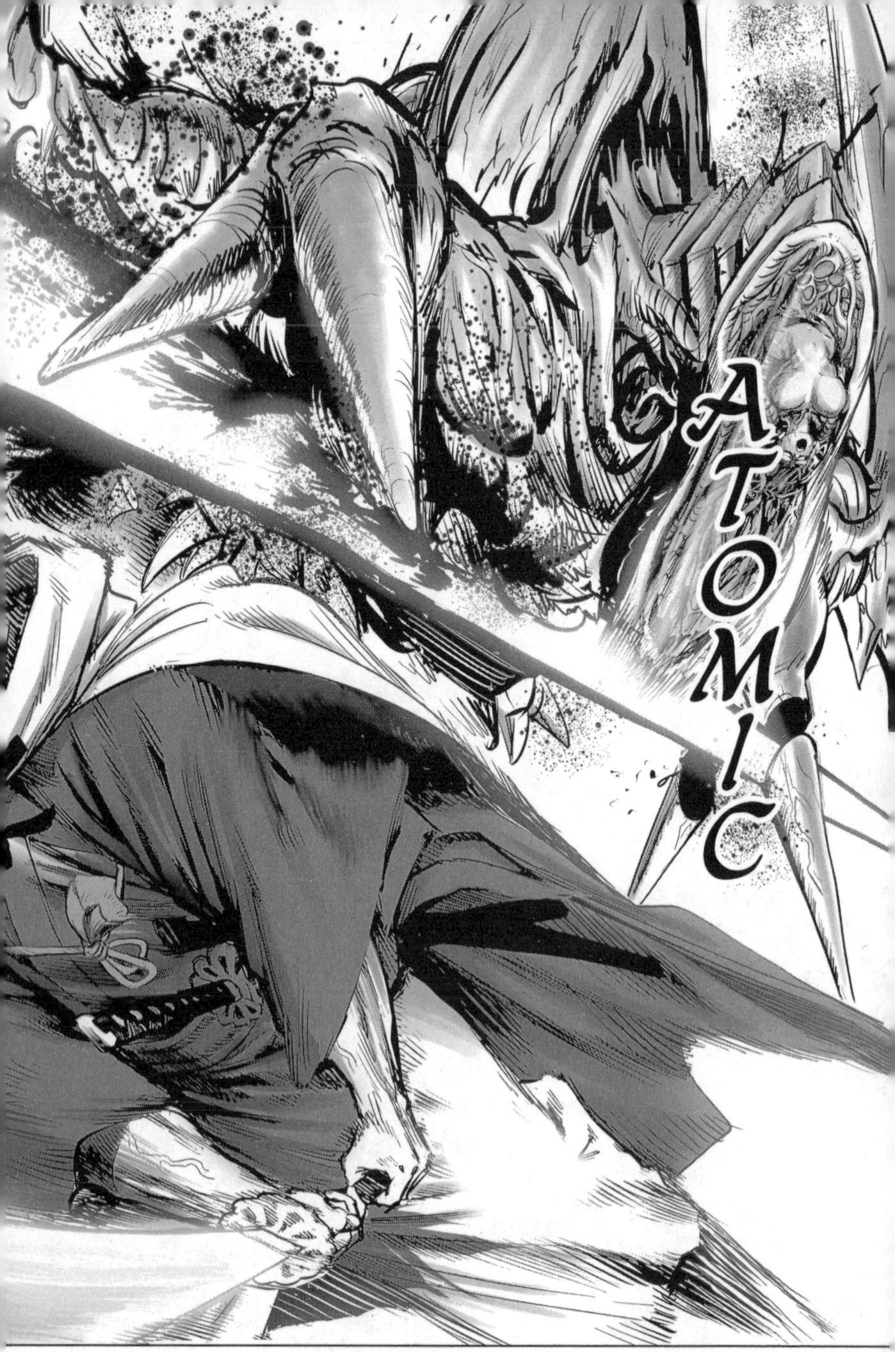
ATOMIC

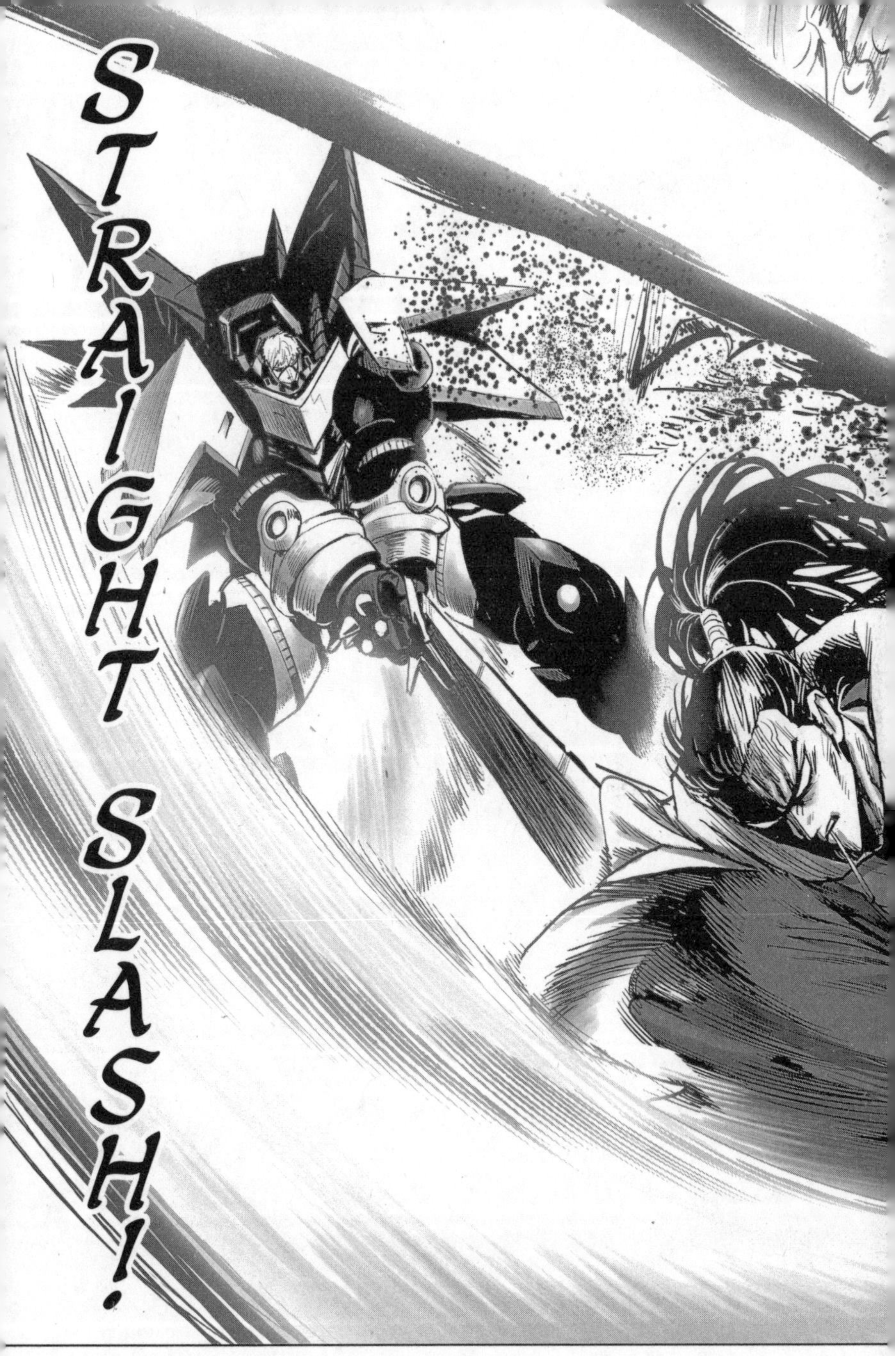
STRAIGHT SLASH!

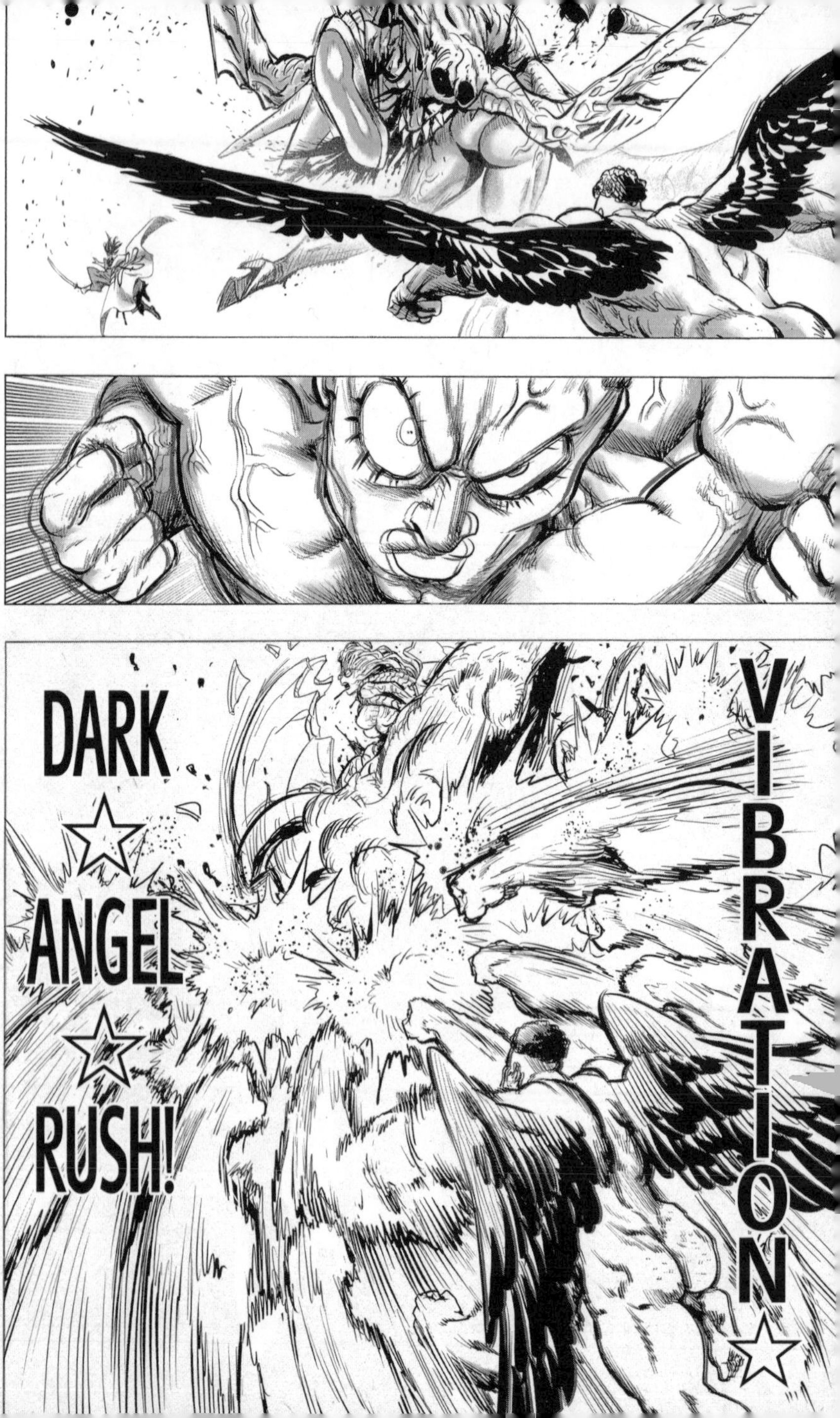
VIBRATION☆
DARK☆ANGEL☆RUSH!

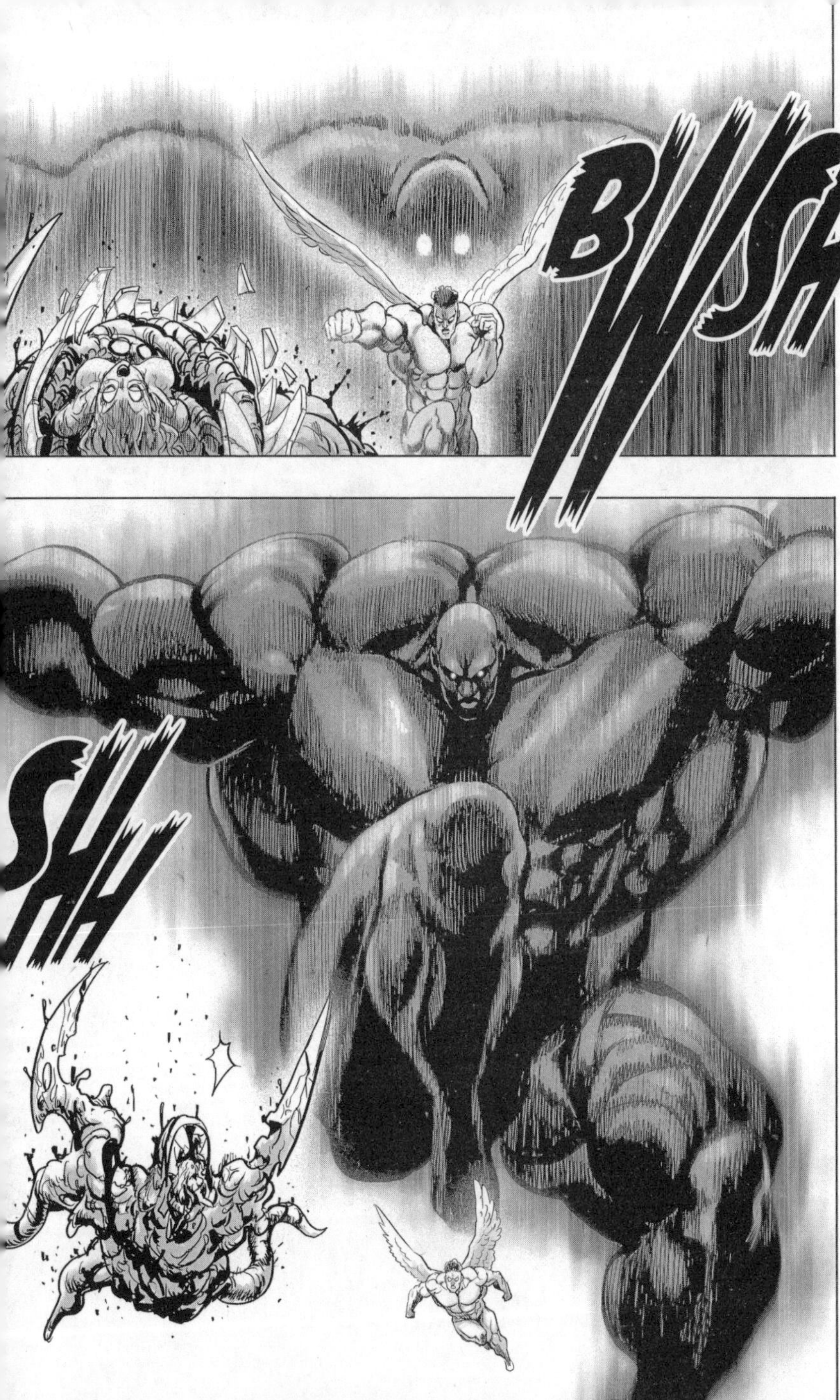
BWSH
SHH

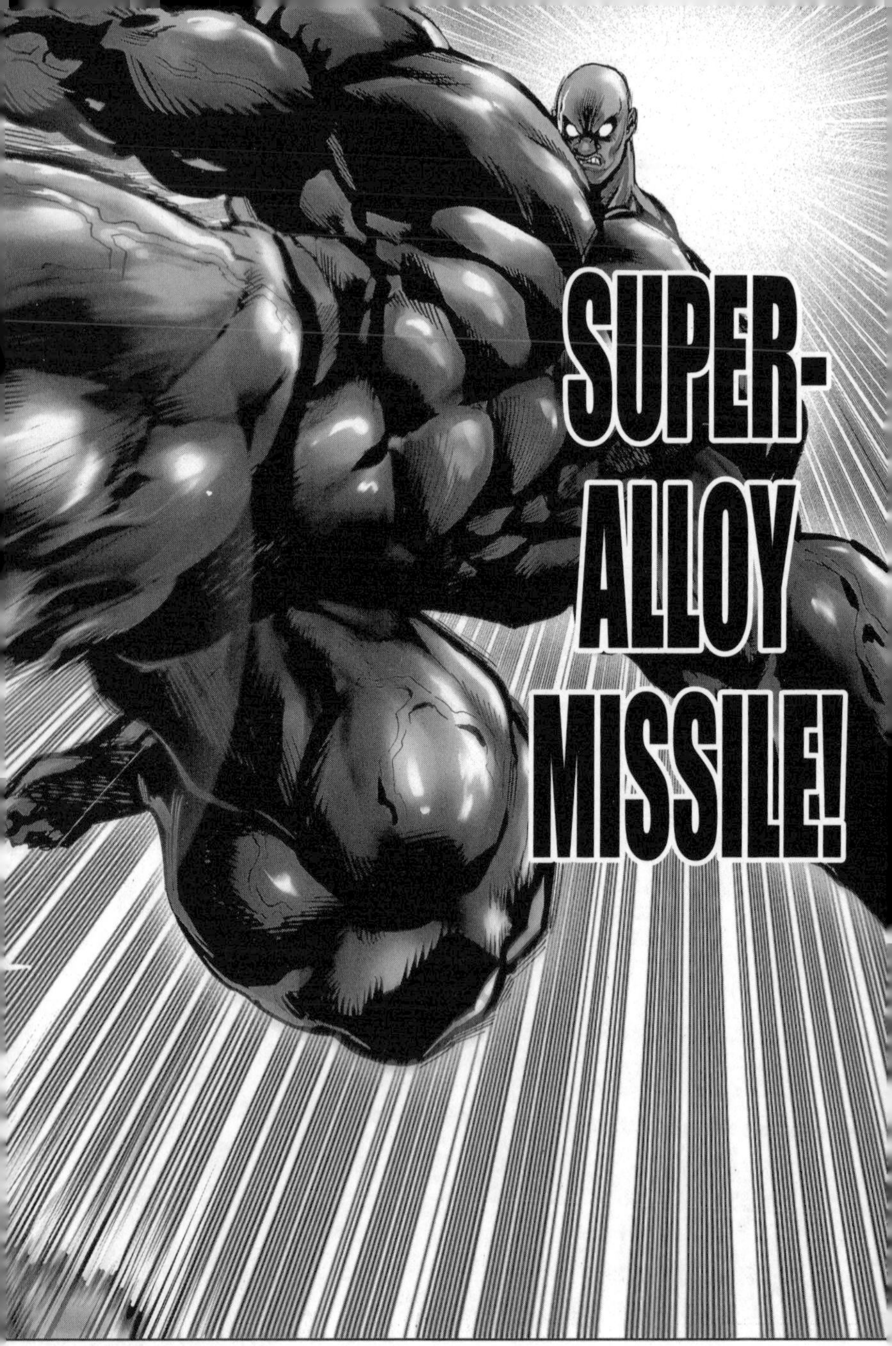
SUPER-
ALLOY
MISSILE!

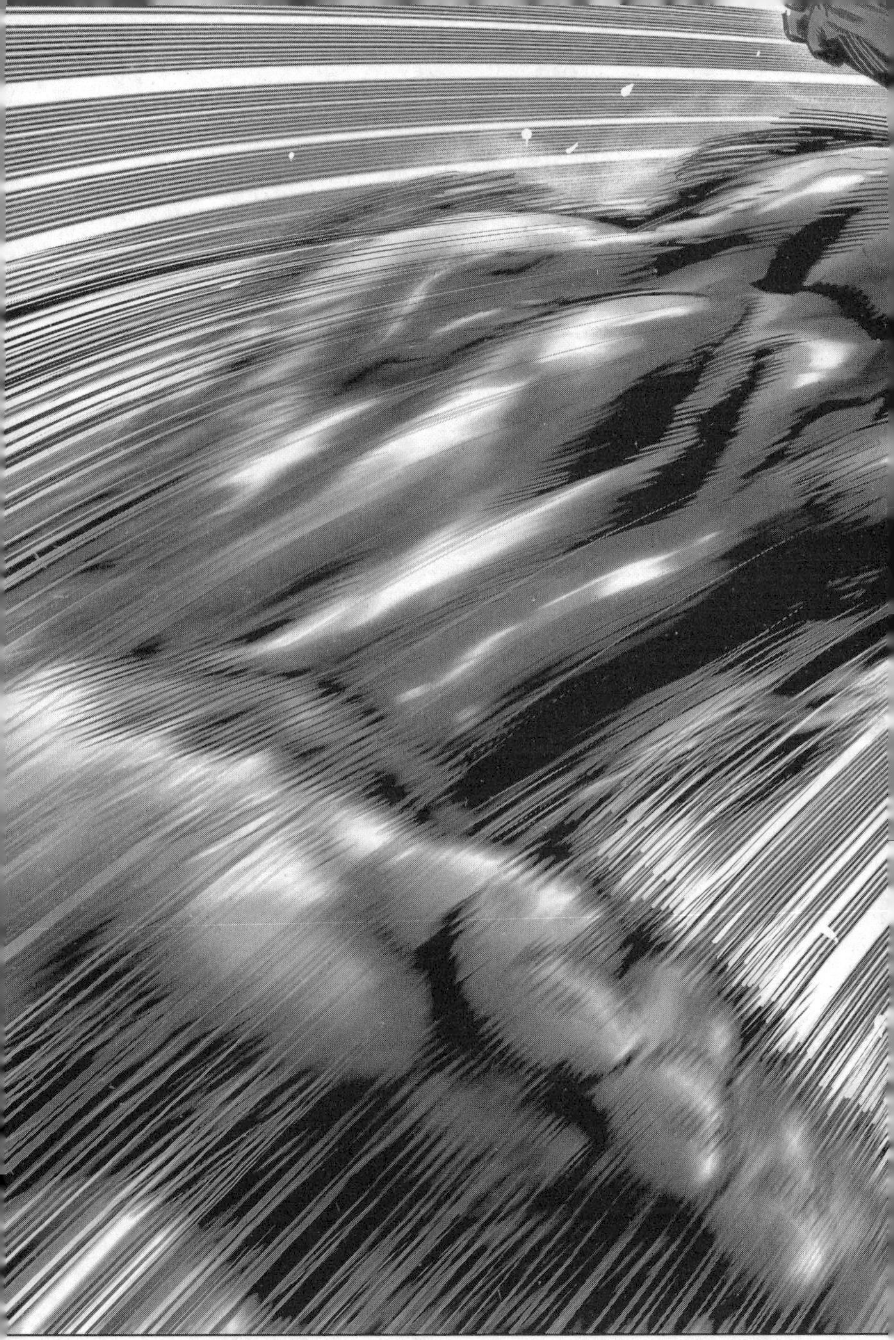

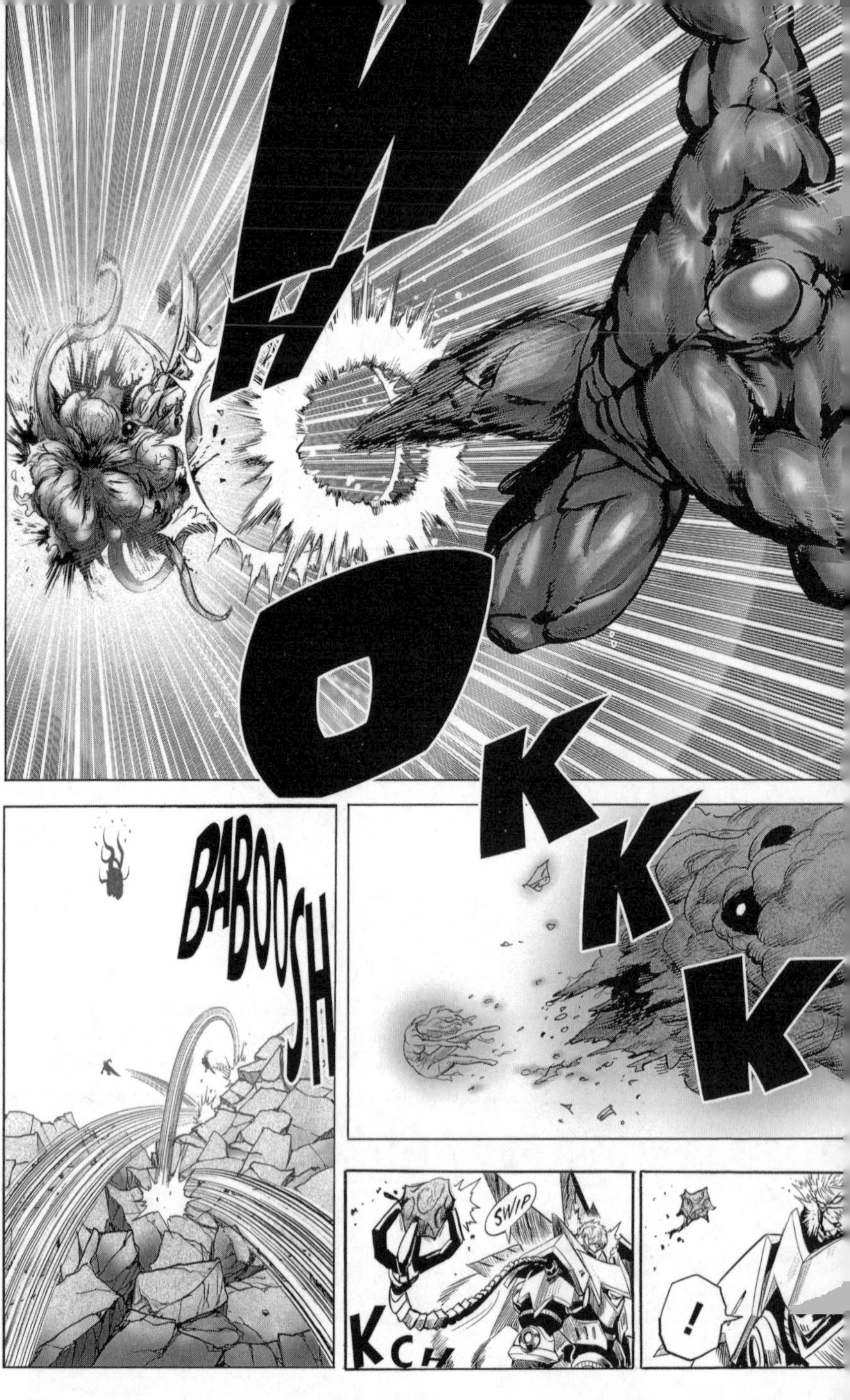
WHOKKK
BABOOSH
SWIP
KCH
!

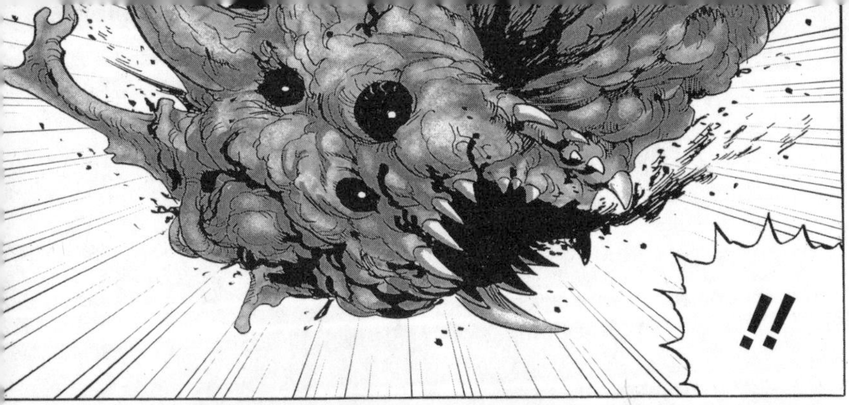
!!
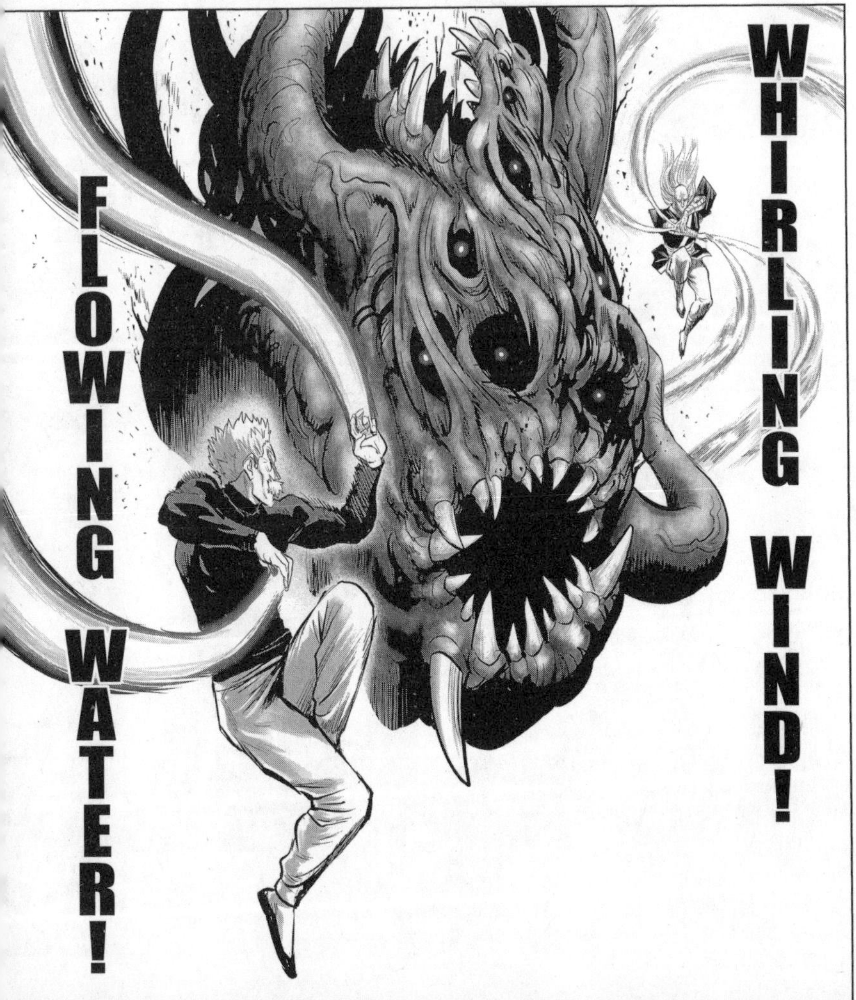
WHIRLING WIND!
FLOWING WATER!

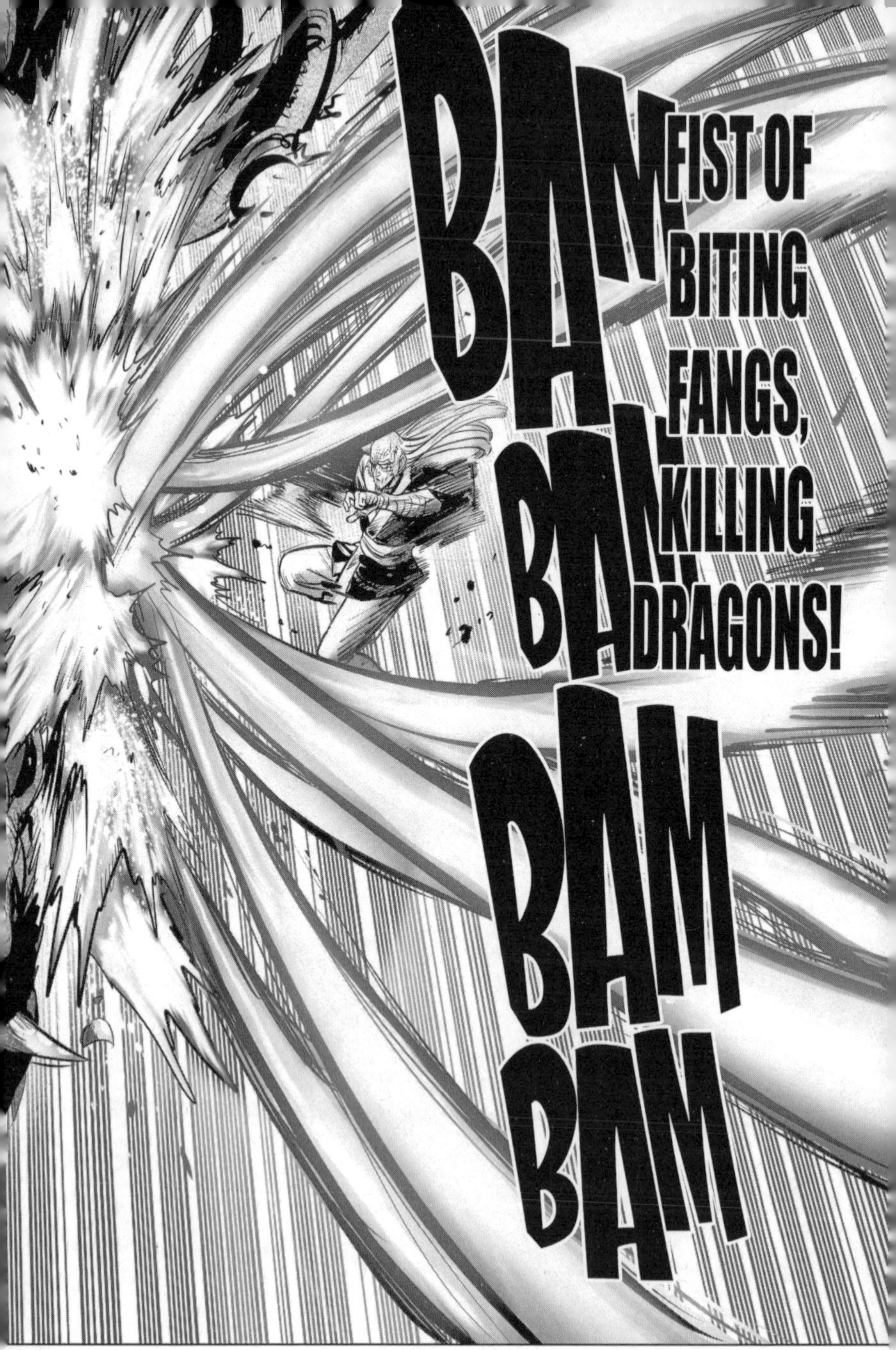
FIST OF BITING FANGS, KILLING DRAGONS!
BAM
BAM
BAM
BAM

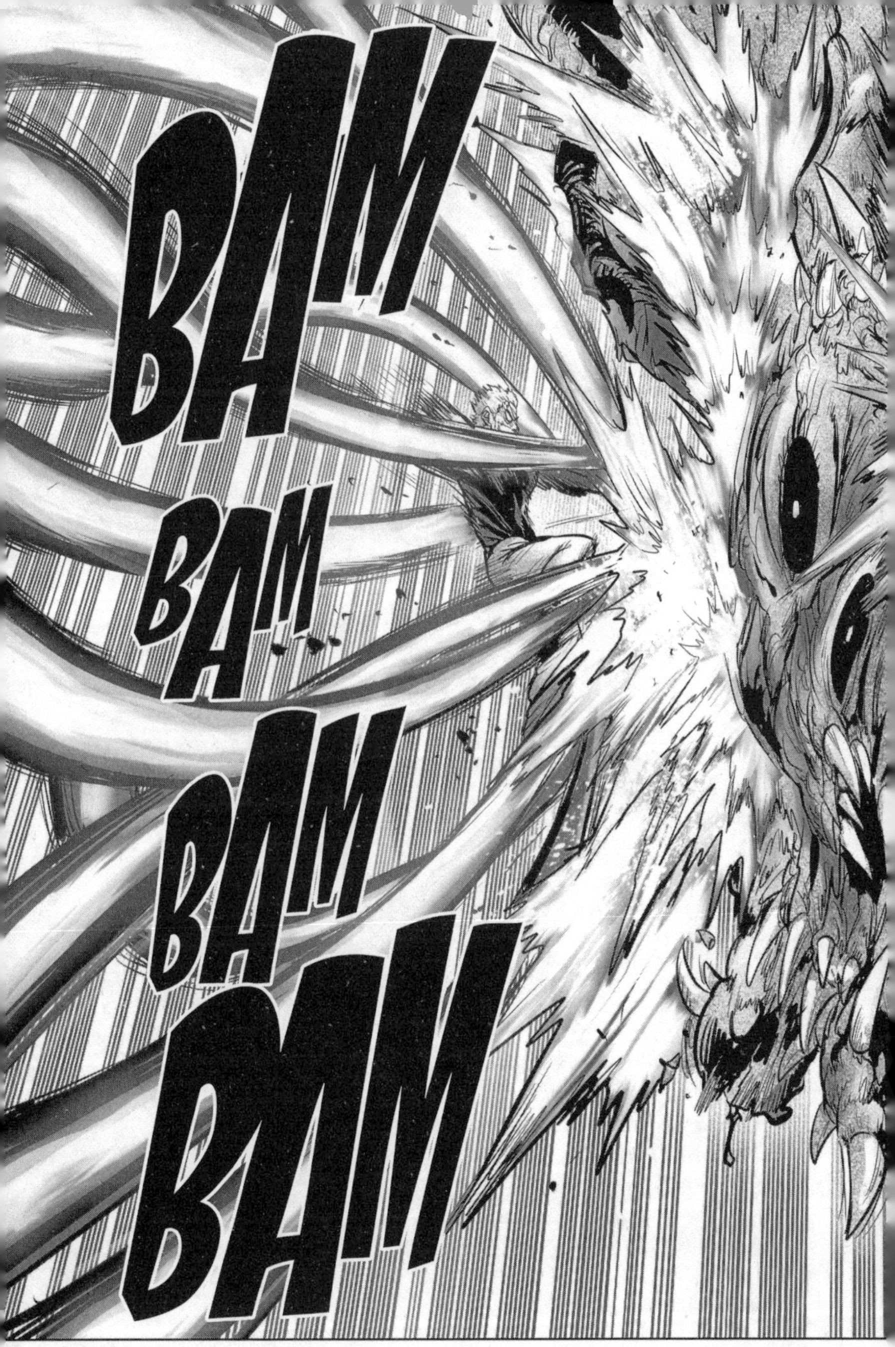
BAM
BAM
BAM
BAM

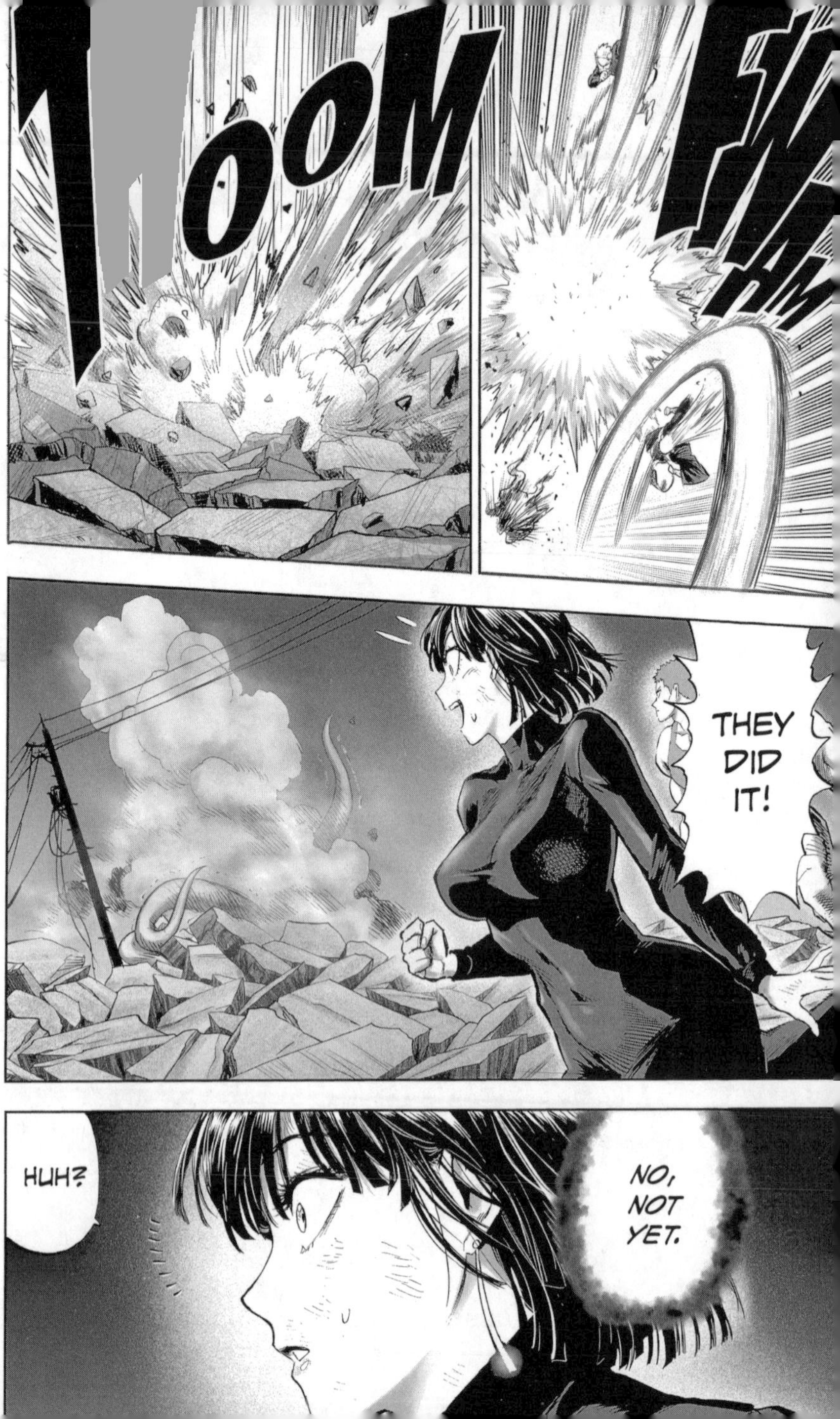
THEY DID IT!
NO, NOT YET.
HUH?

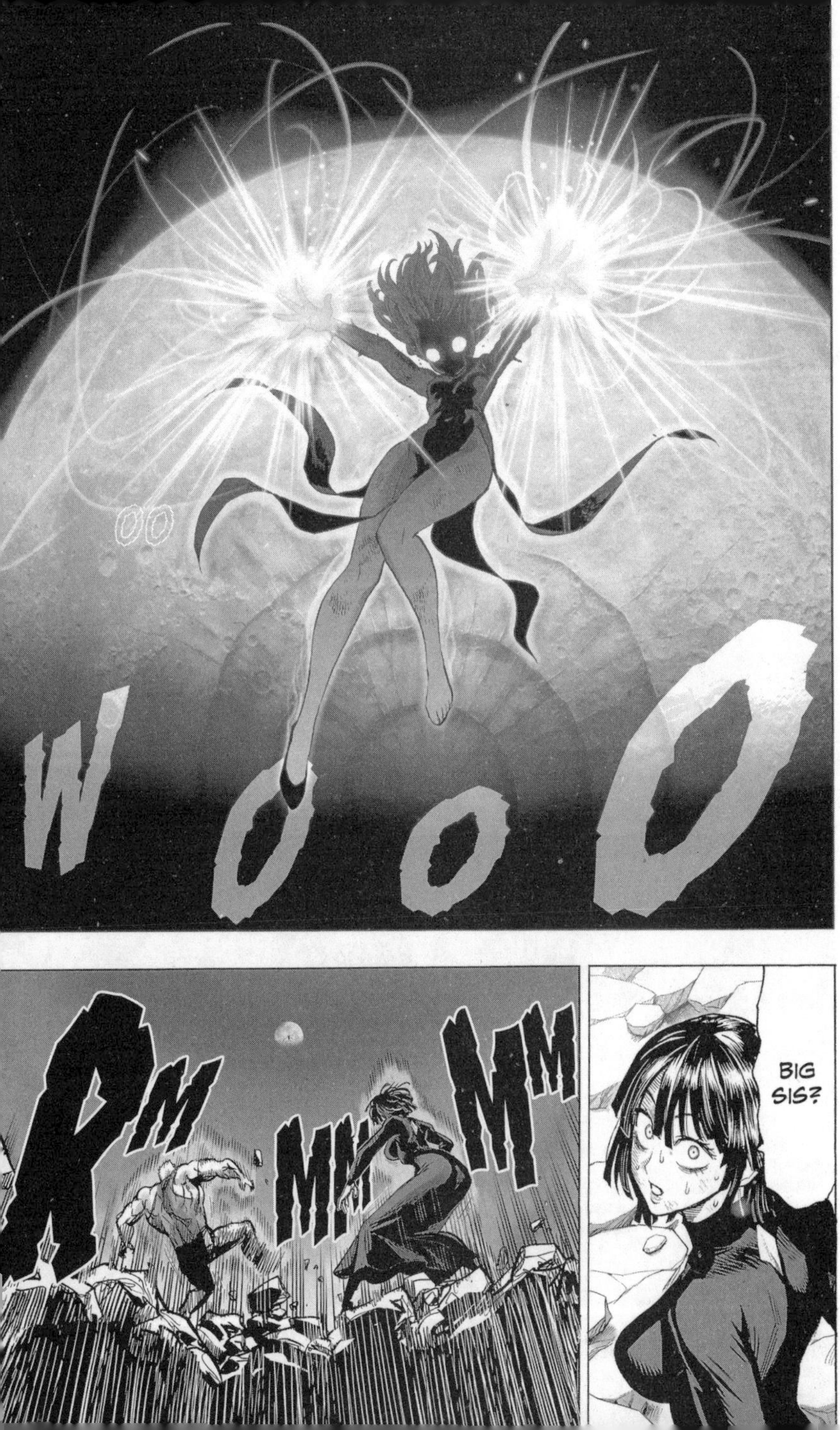
OO
WOOOO
BIG SIS?
RMMMMMM

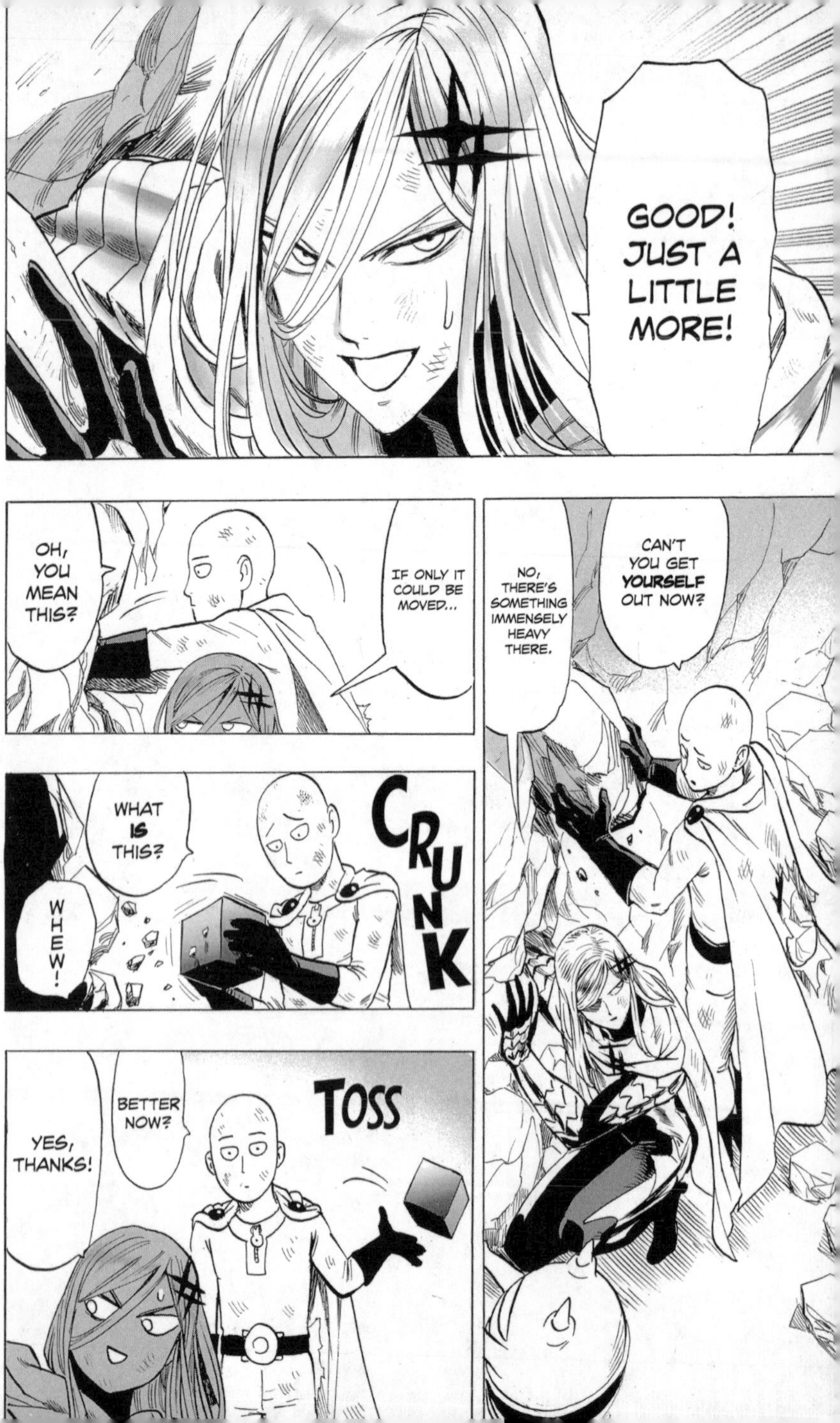
GOOD! JUST A LITTLE MORE!
CAN'T YOU GET YOURSELF OUT NOW?
NO, THERE'S SOMETHING IMMENSELY HEAVY THERE.
IF ONLY IT COULD BE MOVED...
OH, YOU MEAN THIS?
CRUNK
WHAT IS THIS?
WHEW!
TOSS
BETTER NOW?
YES, THANKS!

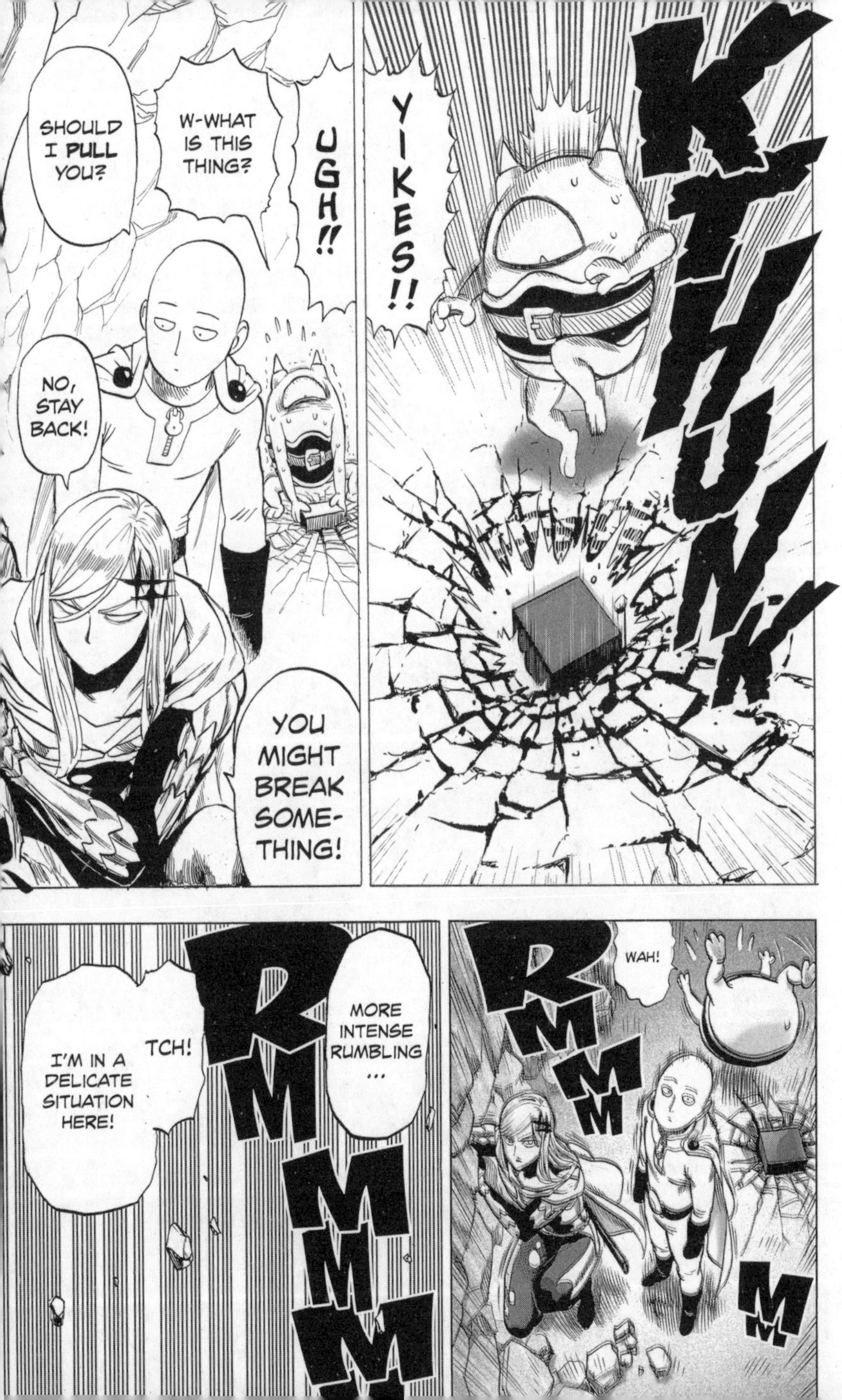
KTHUNK
YIKES!!
UGH!!
W-WHAT IS THIS THING?
SHOULD I PULL YOU?
NO, STAY BACK!
YOU MIGHT BREAK SOME-THING!
WAH!
RMMMM
MM
RMMMMM
MORE INTENSE RUMBLING...
TCH!
I'M IN A DELICATE SITUATION HERE!

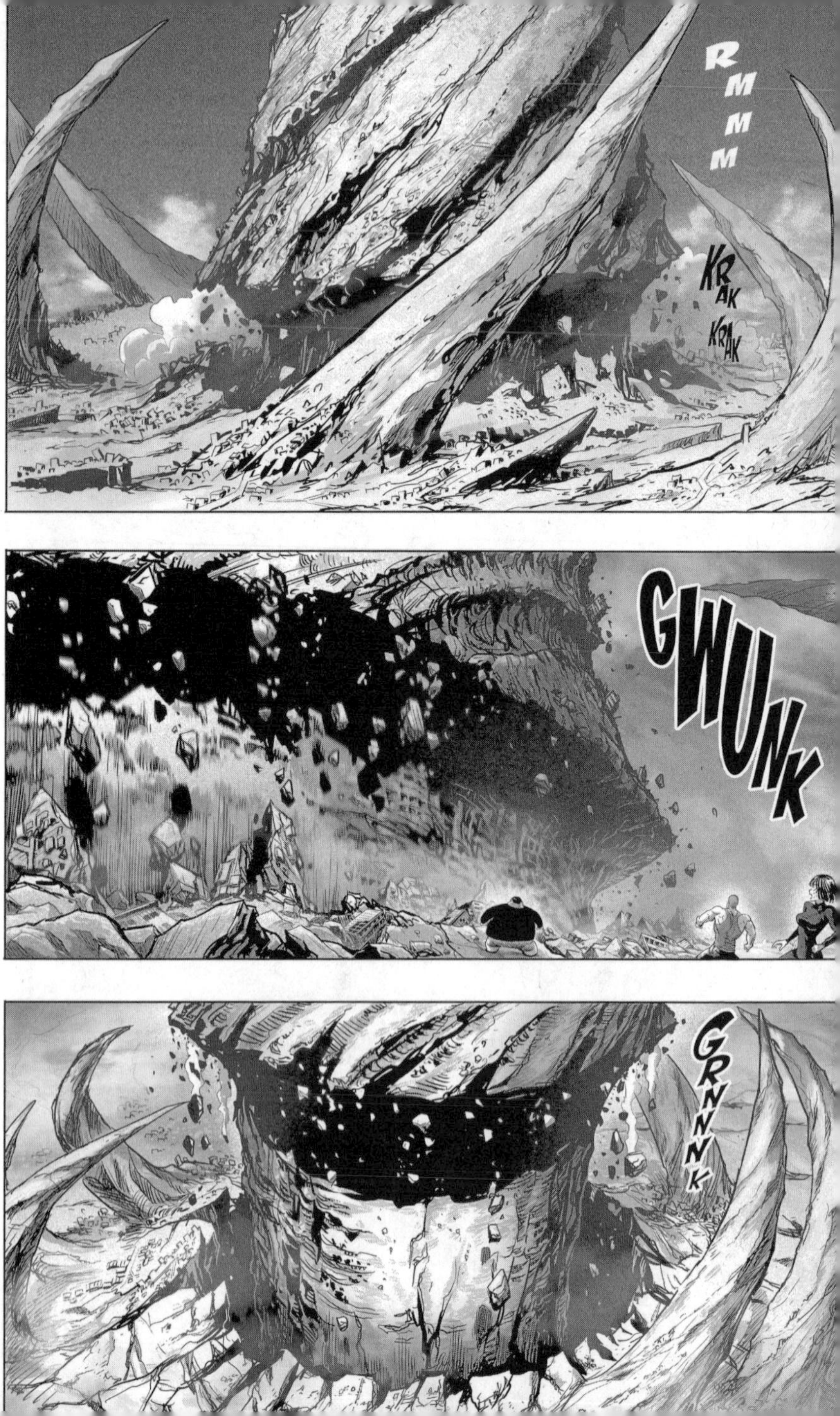
RMMM
KRAK KRAK
GWUNK
GRNNNK

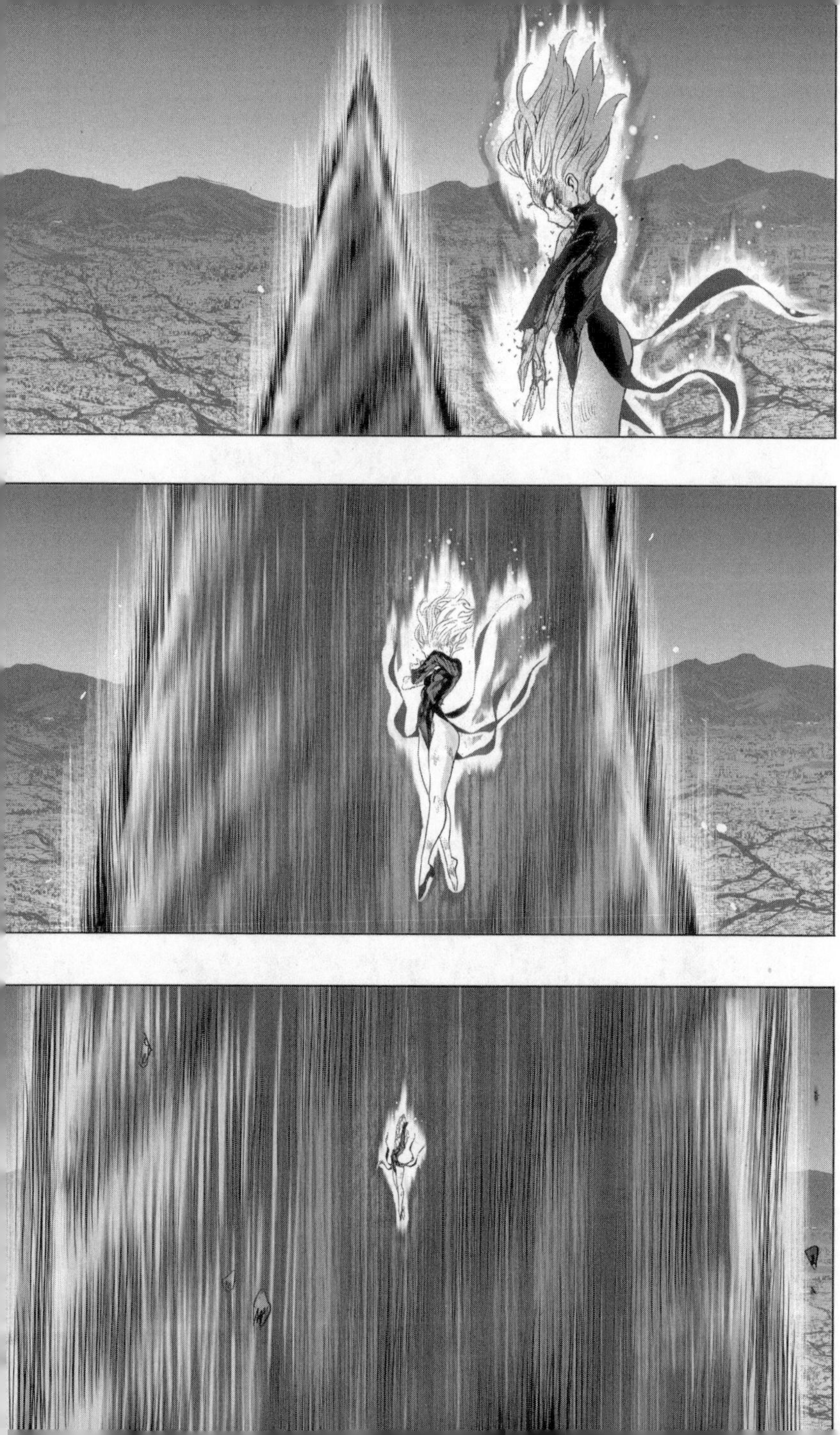

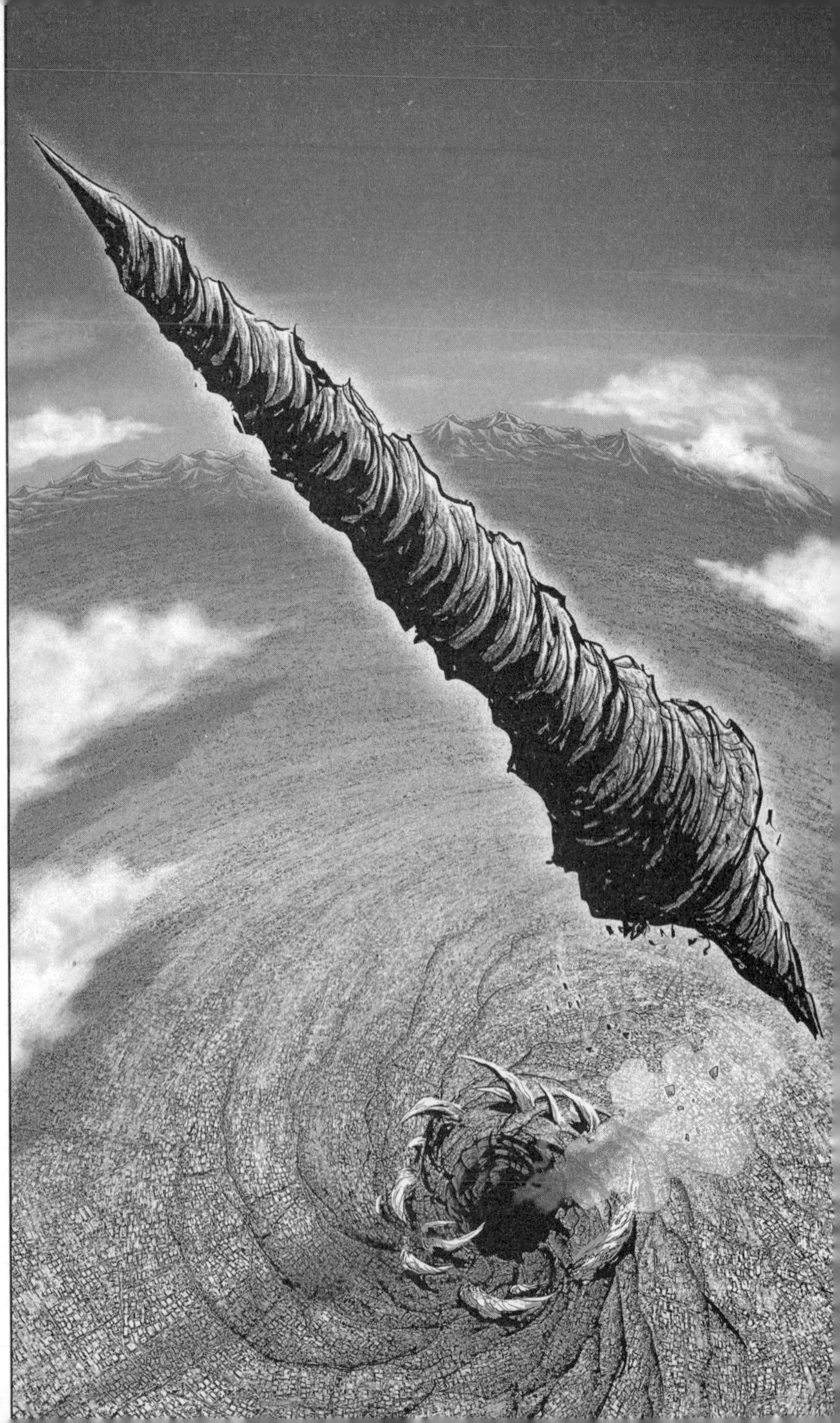

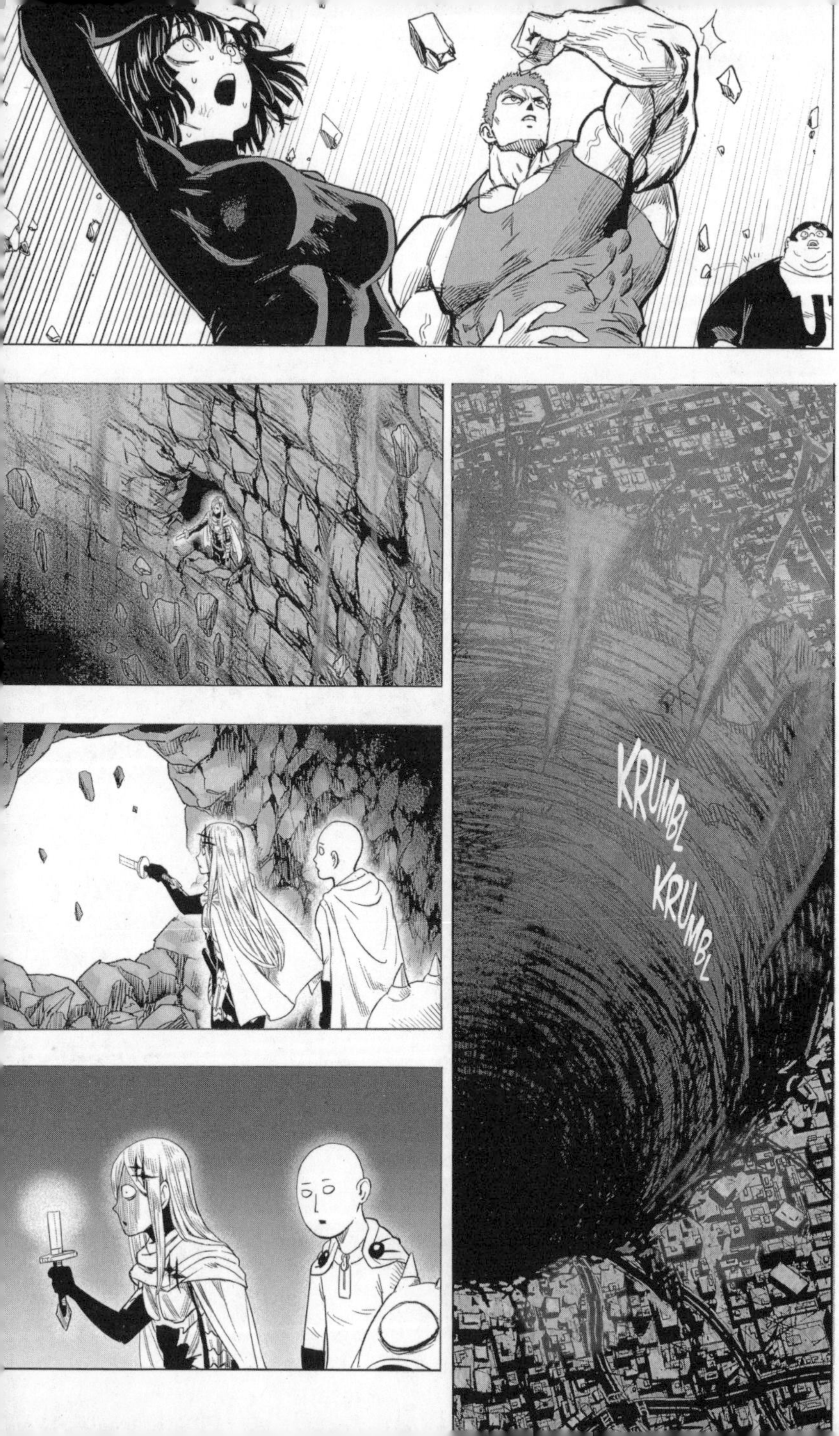
KRUMBL
KRUMBL

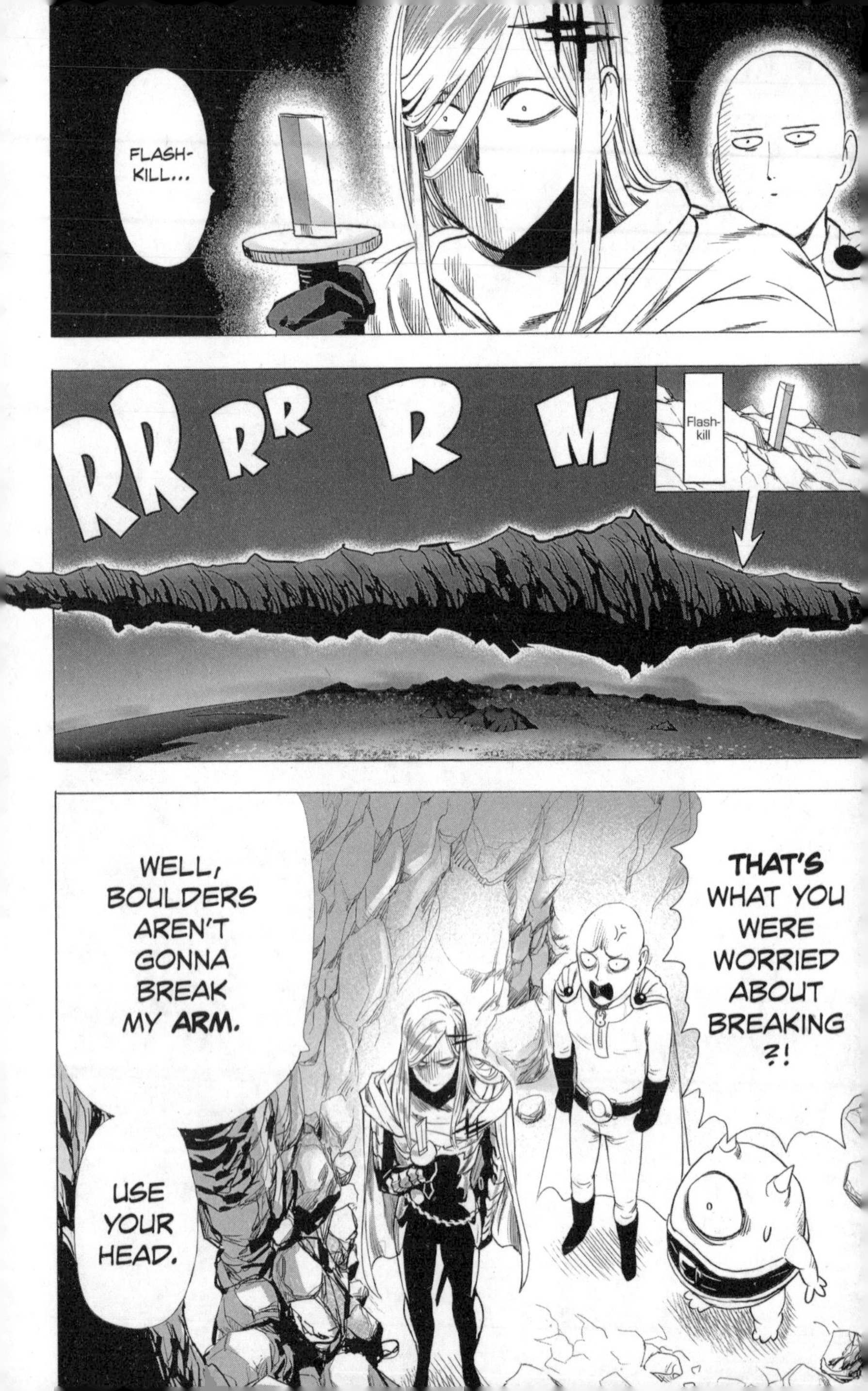
FLASH-KILL...
Flash-kill
RRRRRRM
THAT'S WHAT YOU WERE WORRIED ABOUT BREAKING?!
WELL, BOULDERS AREN'T GONNA BREAK MY ARM.
USE YOUR HEAD.

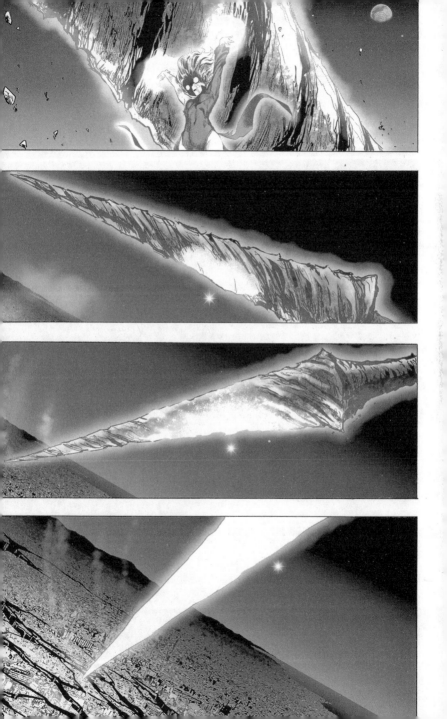

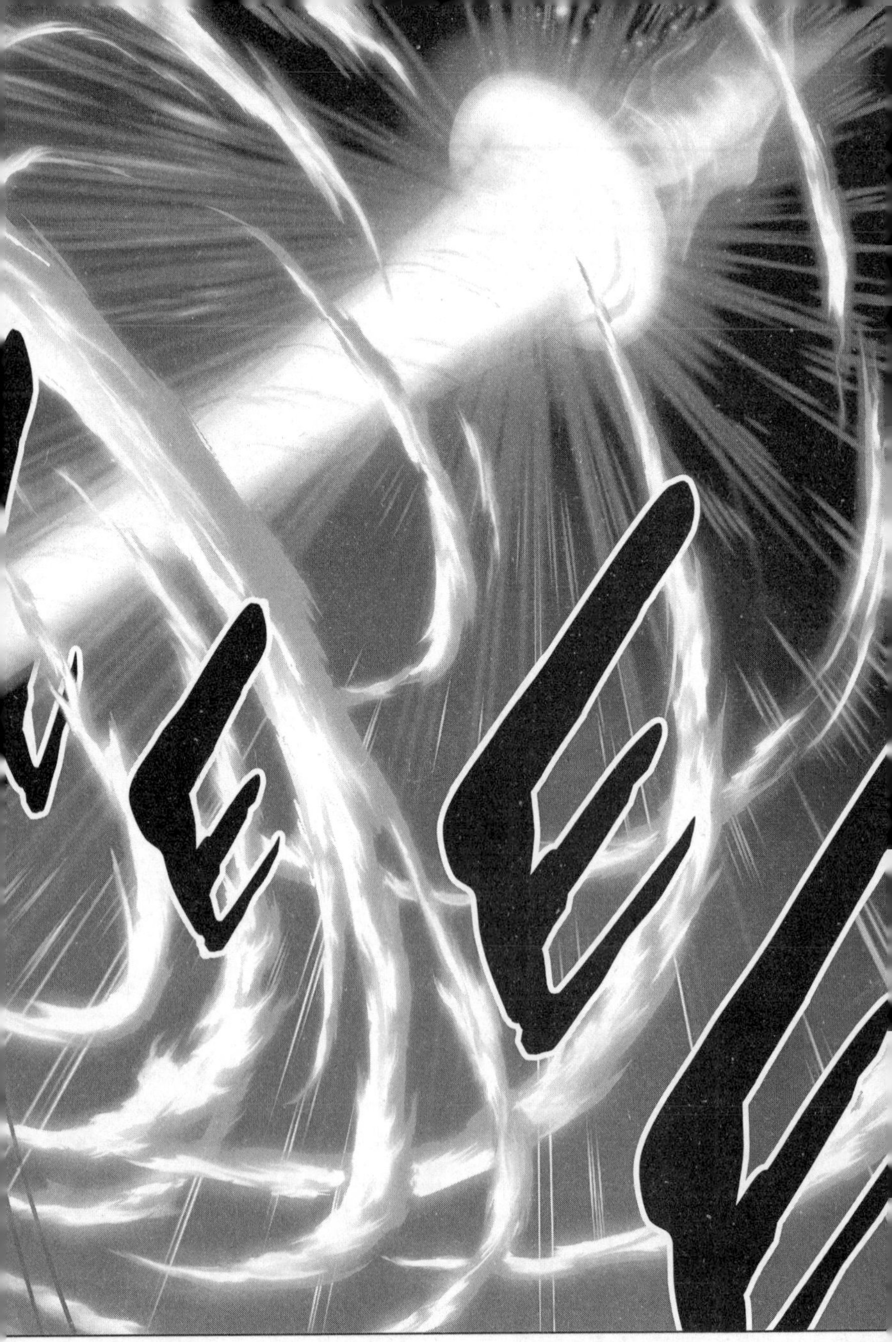
EE

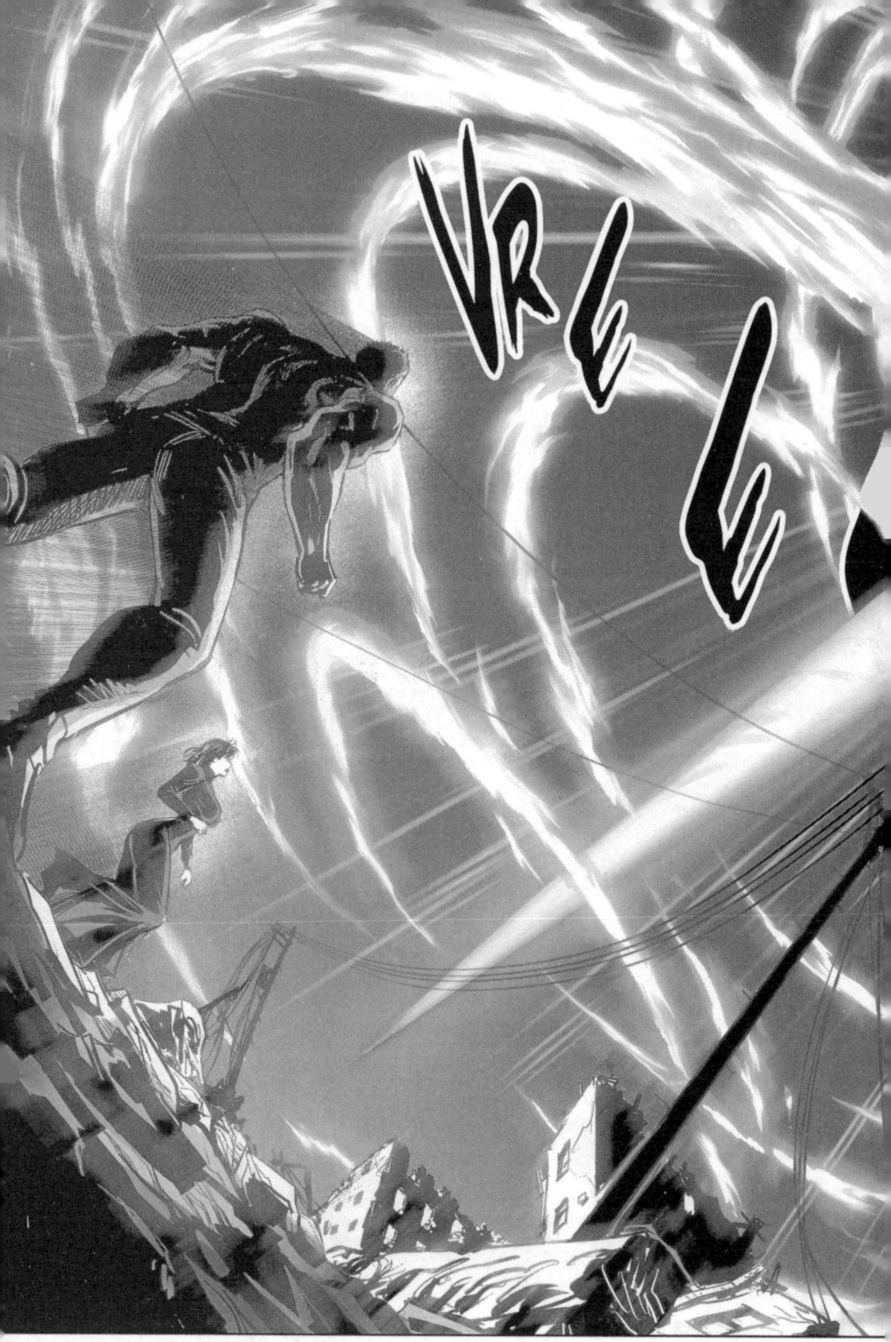
VREE

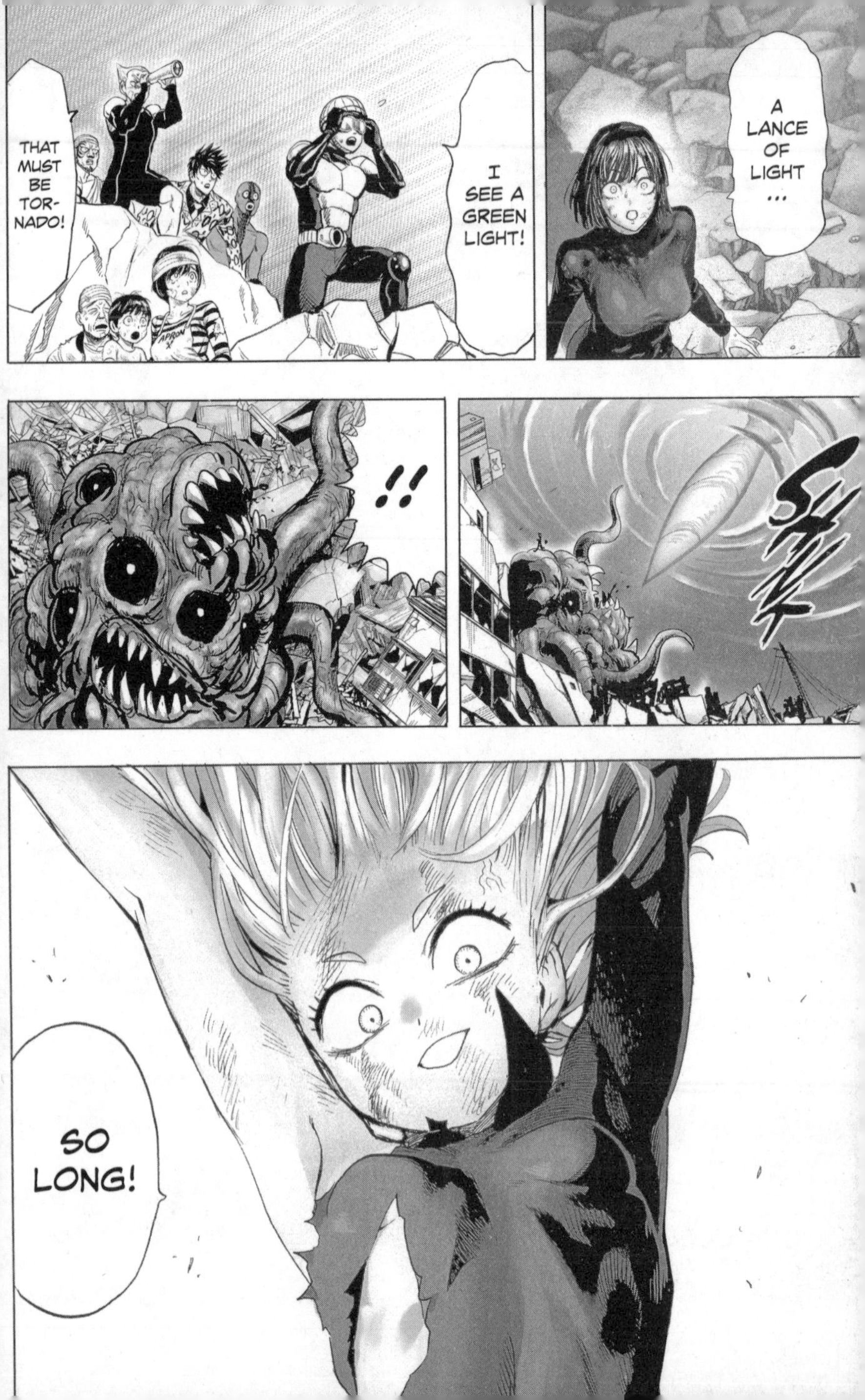
A LANCE OF LIGHT ...
I SEE A GREEN LIGHT!
THAT MUST BE TOR-NADO!
SHNK
!!
SO LONG!

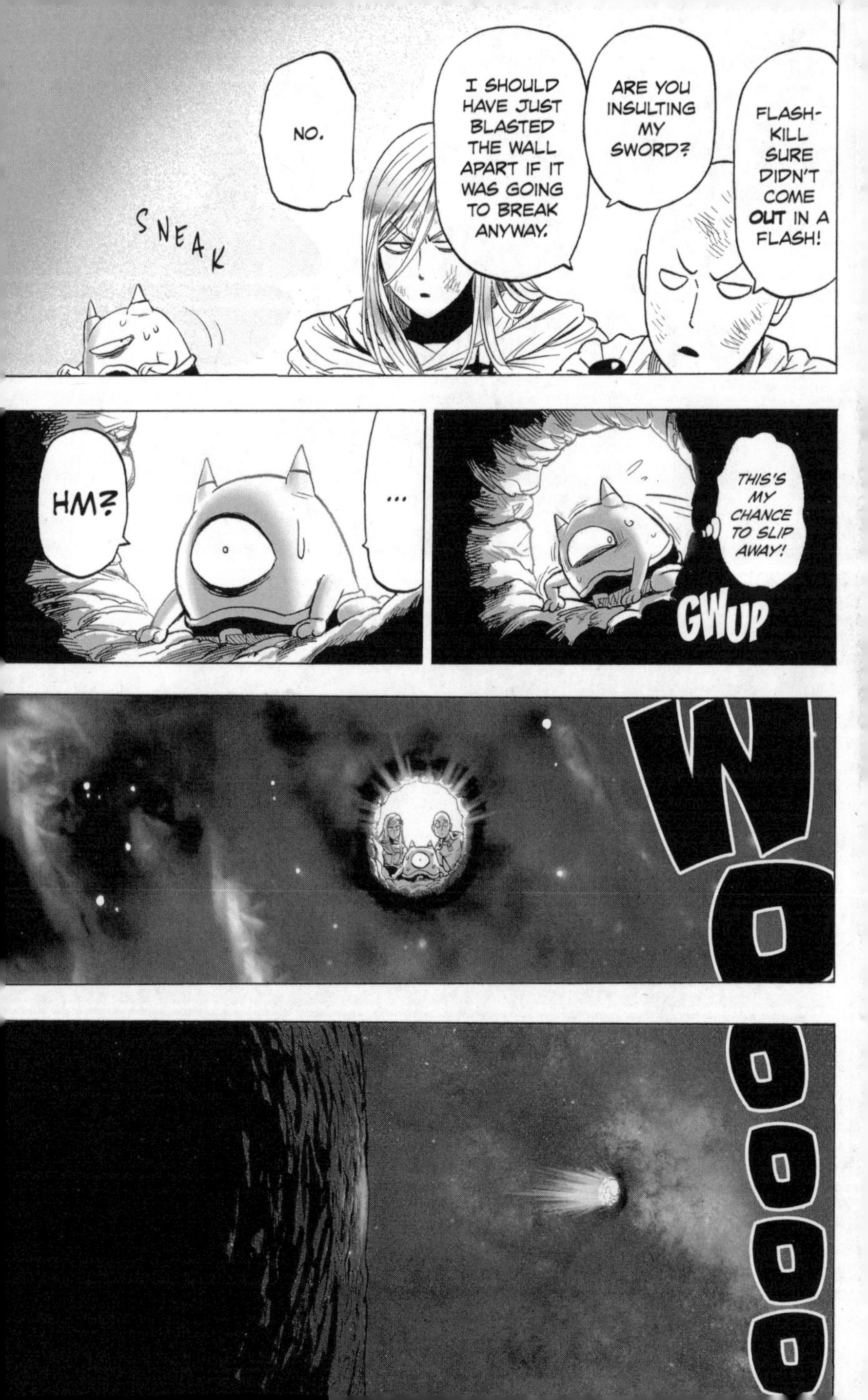
FLASH-KILL SURE DIDN'T COME OUT IN A FLASH!
ARE YOU INSULTING MY SWORD?
I SHOULD HAVE JUST BLASTED THE WALL APART IF IT WAS GOING TO BREAK ANYWAY.
NO.
SNEAK
THIS'S MY CHANCE TO SLIP AWAY!
GWUP
...
HM?
WOOOOOOOO

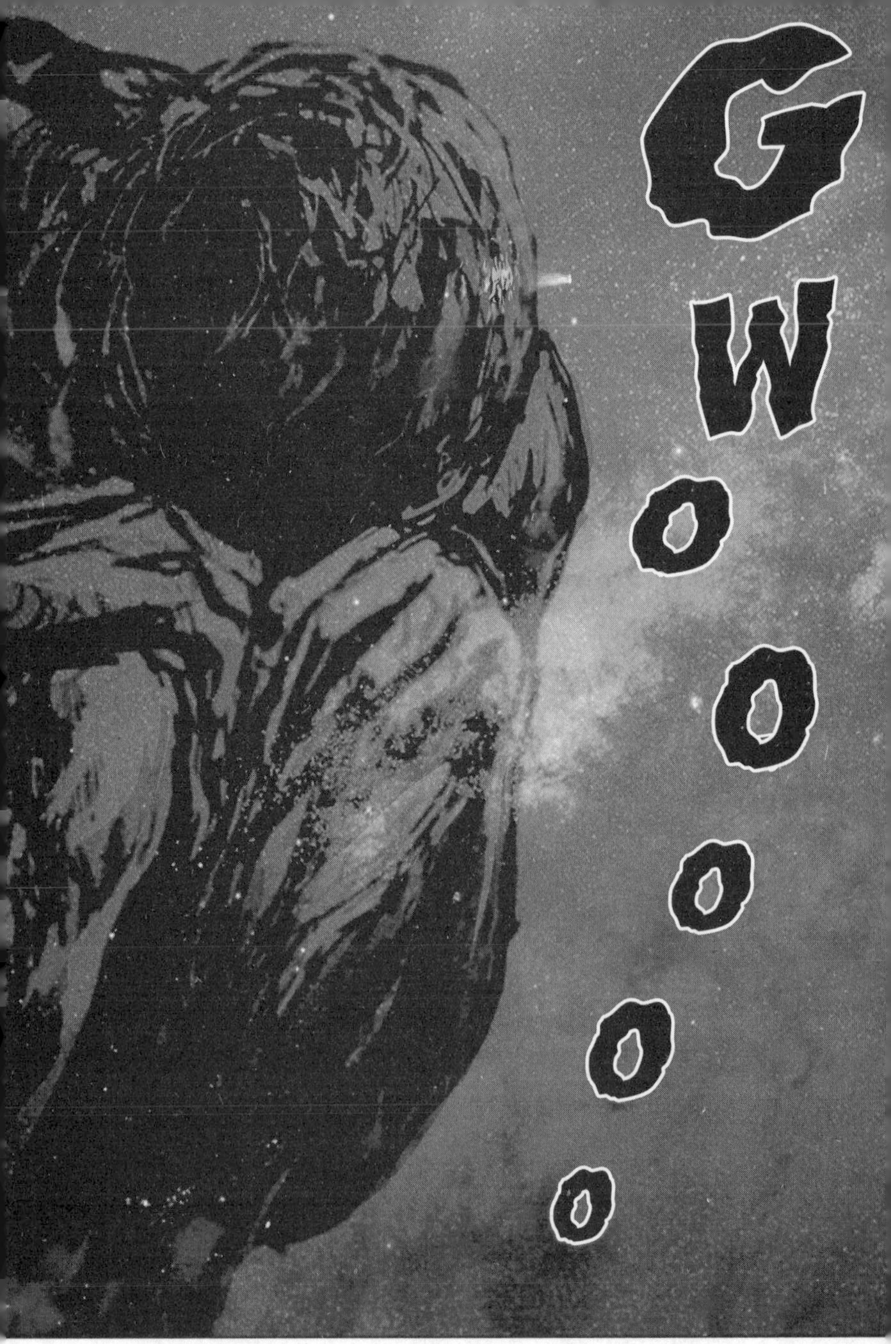
GWOOOOO

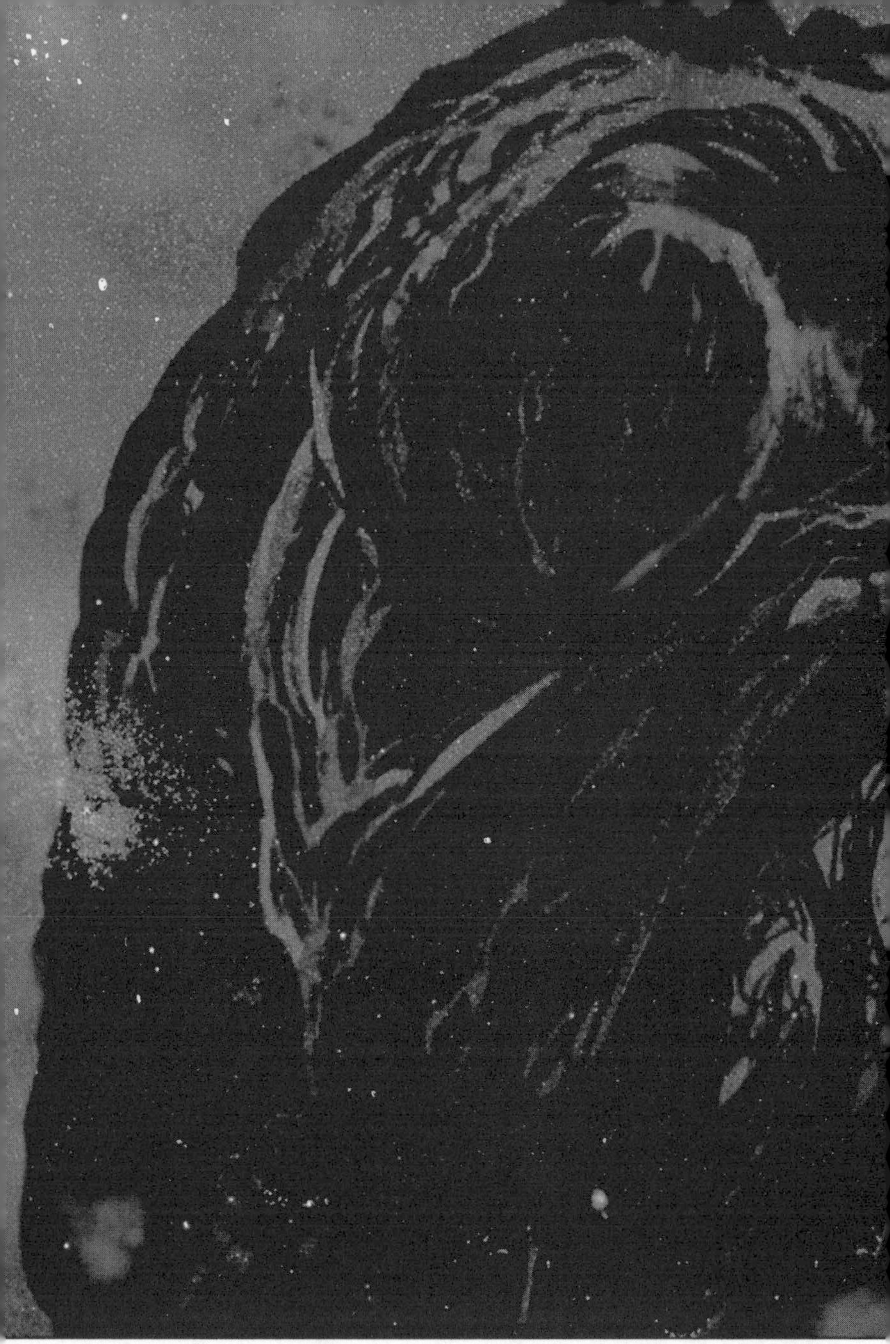

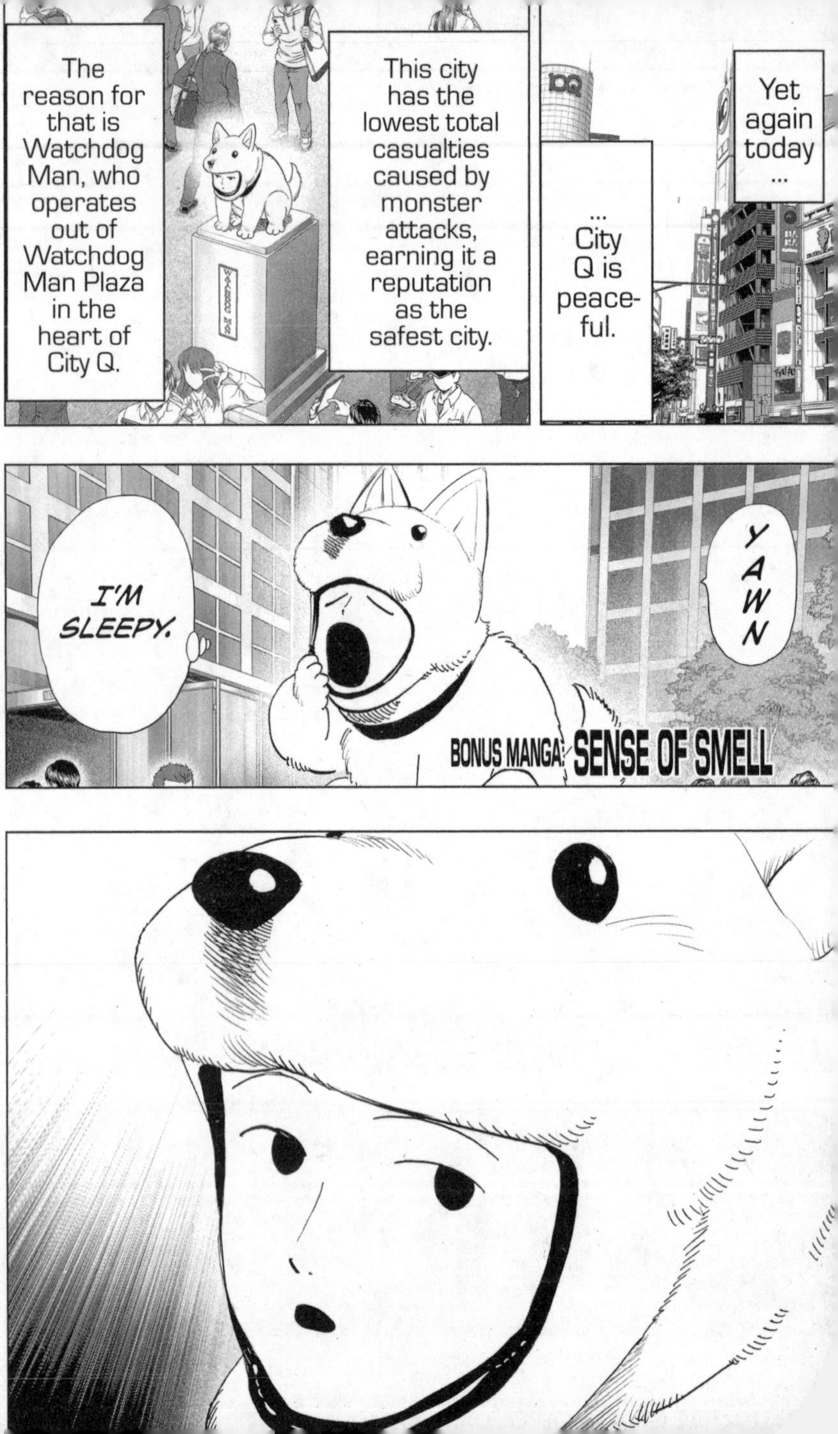
Yet again today ...
... City Q is peace-ful.
This city has the lowest total casualties caused by monster attacks, earning it a reputation as the safest city.
The reason for that is Watchdog Man, who operates out of Watchdog Man Plaza in the heart of City Q.
YAWN
I'M SLEEPY.
BONUS MANGA: SENSE OF SMELL

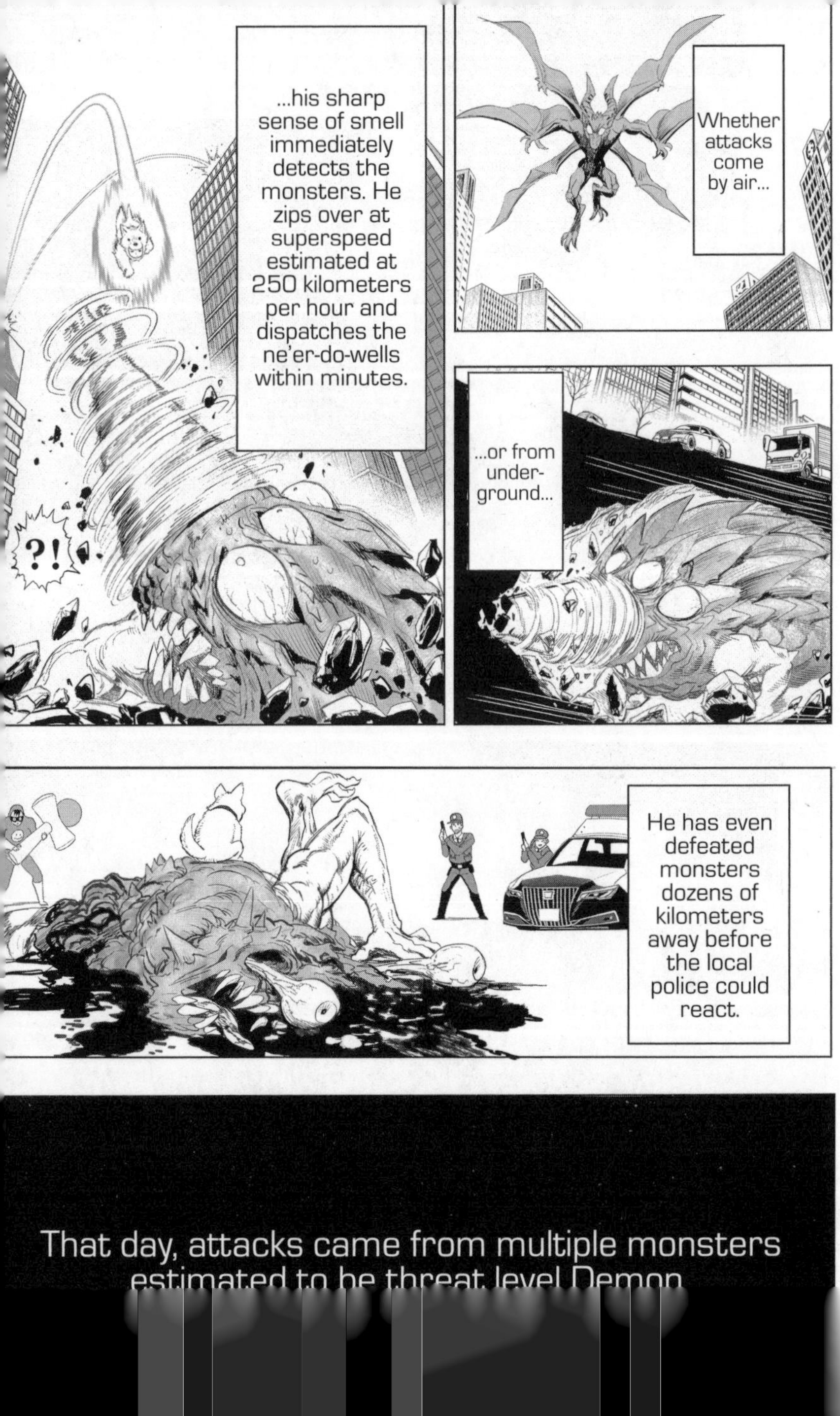

Whether attacks come by air...
...or from underground...
...his sharp sense of smell immediately detects the monsters. He zips over at superspeed estimated at 250 kilometers per hour and dispatches the ne'er-do-wells within minutes.
?!
He has even defeated monsters dozens of kilometers away before the local police could react.
That day, attacks came from multiple monsters estimated to be threat level Demon

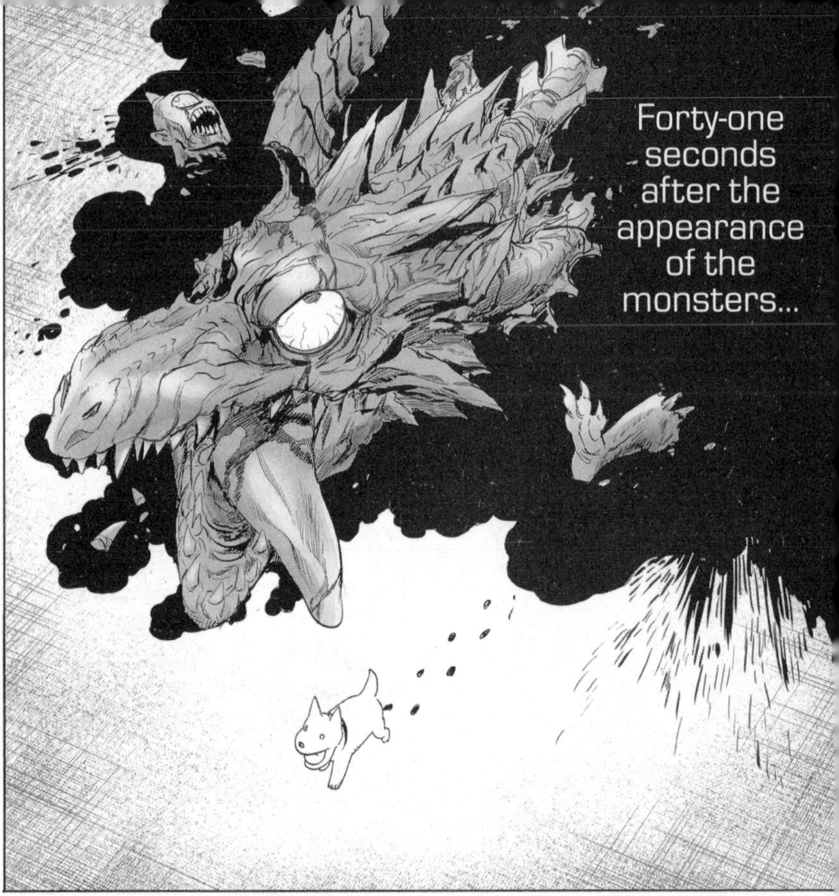
Forty-one seconds after the appearance of the monsters...

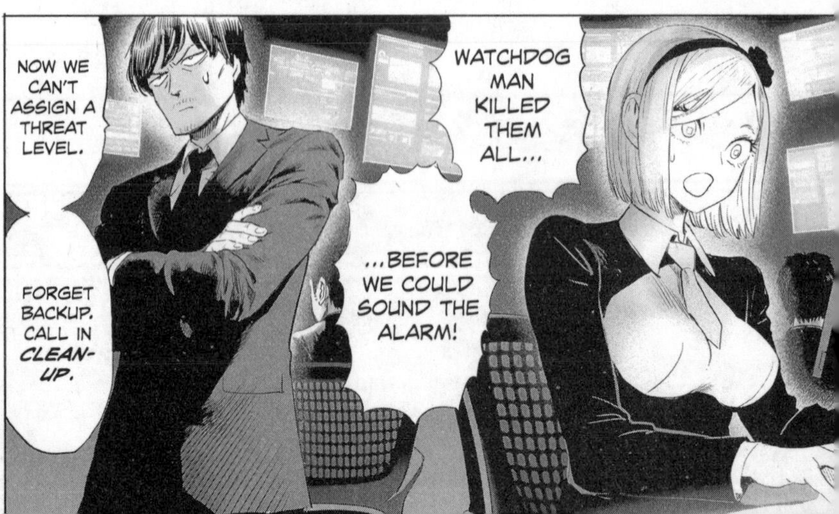
WATCHDOG MAN KILLED THEM ALL...
...BEFORE WE COULD SOUND THE ALARM!
NOW WE CAN'T ASSIGN A THREAT LEVEL.
FORGET BACKUP. CALL IN *CLEAN-UP*.

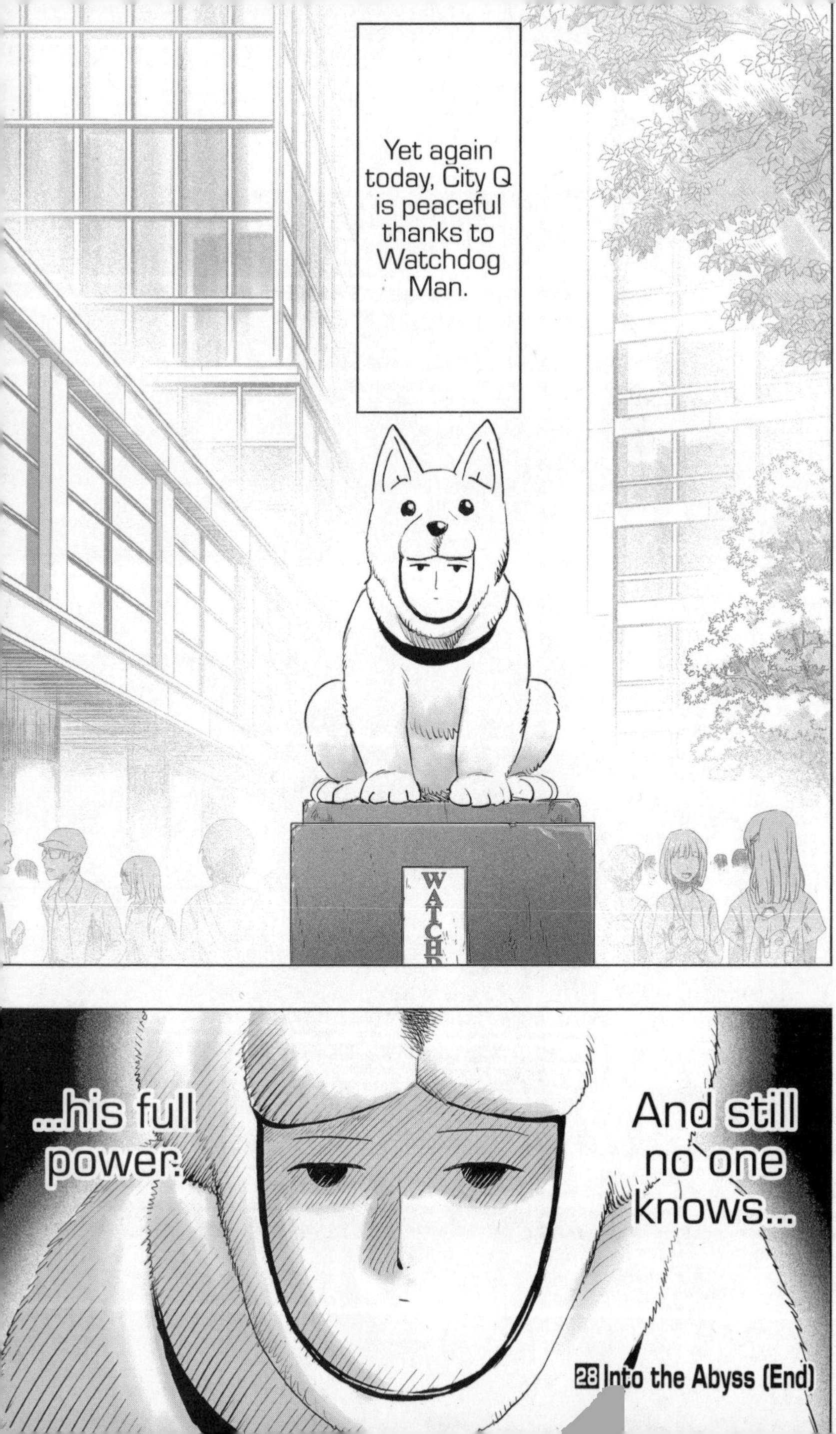
Yet again today, City Q is peaceful thanks to Watchdog Man.
And still no one knows...
...his full power.

28 Into the Abyss (End)

ONE-PUNCH MAN
VOLUME 28
SHONEN JUMP EDITION

STORY BY | ONE
ART BY | YUSUKE MURATA

TRANSLATION | JOHN WERRY
TOUCH-UP ART AND LETTERING | JAMES GAUBATZ
DESIGN | PAUL PADURARIU
EDITOR | JOHN BAE

ONE-PUNCH MAN © 2012 by ONE, Yusuke Murata
All rights reserved.
First published in Japan in 2012 by SHUEISHA Inc., Tokyo
English translation rights arranged by SHUEISHA Inc.

The stories, characters, and incidents mentioned in this
publication are entirely fictional.

Printed in the U.S.A.

Published by VIZ Media, LLC
P.O. Box 77010
San Francisco, CA 94107

10 9 8 7 6 5 4 3 2 1
First printing, May 2024

VIZ MEDIA
viz.com

SHONEN JUMP

PARENTAL ADVISORY
ONE-PUNCH MAN is rated T for Teen and
is recommended for ages 13 and up. This
volume contains realistic and fantasy violence.
ratings.viz.com